THE FICTIONAL REPUBLIC

The Fictional Republic

HORATIO ALGER AND AMERICAN POLITICAL DISCOURSE

Carol Nackenoff

New York   Oxford
OXFORD UNIVERSITY PRESS
1994

Oxford University Press

Oxford   New York   Toronto
Delhi   Bombay   Calcutta   Madras   Karachi
Kuala Lumpur   Singapore   Hong Kong   Tokyo
Nairobi   Dar es Salaam   Cape Town
Melbourne   Auckland   Madrid

and associated companies in
Berlin   Ibadan

Copyright © 1994 by Oxford University Press, Inc.

Published by Oxford University Press, Inc.
200 Madison Avenue, New York, New York 10016

Oxford is a registered trademark of Oxford University Press

Library of Congress Cataloging-in-Publication Data
Nackenoff, Carol.
The fictional republic : Horatio Alger and
American political discourse / Carol Nackenoff.
p. cm.   Includes bibliographical references and index.
ISBN 0-19-507923-X
1. Alger, Horatio, 1832–1899 — Political and social views.
2. Politics and literature — United States — History — 19th century.
3. Political fiction, American — History and criticism.   I. Title.
PS1029.A3Z73   1994
813'.4 — dc20   93-18732

1 3 5 7 9 8 6 4 2

Printed in the United States of America
on acid-free paper

For Jim Greer and Alexander Nackenoff,
who nurtured me through
this process of production

Contents

Preface

I began collecting and reading Horatio Alger novels years ago as I became engrossed in a challenge offered by Louis Hartz's *The Liberal Tradition in America*. Hartz argued that all America had been captured by the Horatio Alger, liberal Lockean dream; political thought became impervious to transformations of the economic and social order. With this wedding of Alger and Locke, "a new social outlook took shape, dynamic, restless, competitive . . . its impact ultimately became enormous."[1] Like everyone else, I had heard the name "Alger"; it is part of the common vocabulary. But I wanted to become better acquainted with the author's formula. From this encounter developed a passion to write about Alger.

Hartz argued that American political ideology had been forged around 1840 and remained static ever since, much to the impoverishment of political thought, since self-evident truths generate little debate. The ideology combined fear of the state with limitations on state power; a desire to protect minorities against a potential mob who would attack property; blindness to sources of social and economic power apart from the state; and a "harnessing" or channeling of the masses' ambitions into the race for acquisition of property with the notion that by playing by the rules of the capitalist game, they too could aspire to reap comparable rewards. The rules included self-help and individualism. This ideology legitimated unequal outcomes and made the farmer and the laborer believe all were of the same estate.

In this consensus view of American politics, homogeneity of opinion reigns—or is enforced. Hartz believed that ideologies were the product of the relationship between social classes. In the absence of a feudal aristocracy against which the bourgeoisie could define itself, no self-conscious proletariat was likely to emerge. No class was likely to forge a socialist ideology to challenge the dominant liberal ideology. This claim was *American Exceptionalism* par excellence.

There were many defects in the Hartzian account and much fuel for scholarly debate. Claims of near-homogeneity of thought were unsatisfactory. There was no adequate explanation for the endurance of liberal Lockeanism in the twentieth century, to say nothing of the problem of explaining the Civil War. And even Hartz's understanding of Alger appears to have been shaped by a notorious hoax biography. The Scottish Enlightenment eclipsed Locke, and the Atlantic Republicanism thesis—at least until recently—eclipsed Hartz.

Nonetheless, Hartz had posed an important challenge to materialist understandings of ideology—to the view that ideology somehow arises from conditions of material life and makes sense of the experiences in which classes live out their existence, even if it "masks" the nature of these material relations.

The challenge, as I saw it, was to explain how a political formulation about self-help and individualism manages to survive or transform itself. How does one understand the durability of ideological formulations that make little "sense" of this world? Why could Ronald Reagan adopt Calvin Coolidge as his hero and employ the language and rhetoric of a very different era? What kind of relationship exists between changes in the structure of economy and society and American political discourse?

The more immersed I became in the Alger stories and formula, the more convinced I became that they provided an important clue about the *kind* of sense "ideologies" make of the world. As I followed this nineteenth century author into the realm of popular culture, I had occasion to reconsider the relationship between narratives and lived experience. And as I learned, I turned to a different language—of political discourse, narratives, and grammar.

I owe enormous and abiding debts to several scholars. The late J. David Greenstone prompted me to ask the questions that would come to constitute the center of my academic career. He also read and provided comments on earlier drafts of this manuscript, offered assistance, encouragement, and inspiration. Ira Katznelson has also helped shape this discourse, has read and commented on this work at various stages, and has offered enthusiasm and assistance. And Joseph Cropsey, with whom I read texts many years ago, has helped and supported me even as I changed focus, direction, and method.

Many scholars' labors helped me to see. To Gary Scharnhorst, who, with Jack Bales produced several vital works on Alger, including biography, background, and a guide to sources, comment, and criticism, I owe an enormous debt. Robert Darnton's *Great Cat Massacre*, especially "Peasants Tell Tales," argues for the historical and contextual rooting of popular narratives. His recasting of these tales, as vehicles through which peasants recognized the deprivations of their world and generated limited fantasies, has been particularly helpful in directing me to Alger's hard times story.

New literary historians helped shape my perspective that Alger's work, like other cultural productions, is rooted in desires and fears, contradictions and tensions of the period. The recent work of Walter Benn Michaels stands out as a provocative attempt to reread part of the late-nineteenth century canon.

Janice Radway and other American literary scholars have been seeking to demonstrate that "reading is not like eating," and that readers appropriate and constitute the texts they read as their own. She, along with Jane Tompkins, Annette Kolodny, Roland Barthes, and many other literary scholars probing the noncanon, and the relationship between readers and reading, have helped me reformulate my understanding of the narratives of political discourse.

Michael Denning's *Mechanic Accents* provoked me to consider the relationship between Alger's fiction and nineteenth century working-class literature and cultural vehicles. Studies by Karen Halttunen, Daniel Walker Howe, Dee Garrison, and David Reynolds have been extremely influential in allowing me to locate Alger in various nineteenth century moral and cultural debates. My notes acknowledge many additional debts.

Although I own a large collection of Alger's novels, I have travelled to examine collections of letters, stories, novels, and other primary materials. In this connection, I would like to thank the staff of the American Antiquarian Society in Worcester, Massachusetts; the Huntington Library in San Marino, California; Harvard University Archives, with special thanks to Michael Raines; the staff of the Houghton Library, Harvard University; Andover-Harvard Theological Seminary, with thanks to Alan Seaburg; the rare books and manuscripts section of the Boston Public Library; the staffs of the manuscript and rare book collections at the Library of Congress; Columbia University Rare Books and Manuscripts—Seligman Collection; the University of Chicago Library and special collections; and the New York Public Library, including rare books and manuscripts (the Arendt and Berg Collections). Mr. John Y. Cole, Director, Center for the Book, Library of Congress, Washington, D.C. provided important assistance. The University of Virginia Library; the Beinecke Rare Book and Manuscript Library, Yale University; and the Clements Library of the University of Michigan kindly provided me material from their collections by mail.

I would like to thank the Swarthmore College Research Support Committee for assistance in preparing this manuscript for publication. The Library Company of Philadelphia provided a 1992-93 McLean Contribution Fellowship, which allowed me to initiate a new project and put final touches on the current manuscript. Receipt of an Asher Edelman Release Time Fellowship and junior faculty sabbatical from Bard College permitted me to travel to research collections. The material assistance of my parents, J. L. and Catherine Nackenoff, greatly facilitated this enterprise.

I would like to thank the following people for their comments on various drafts of this manuscript: Myra Young Armstead, Sanjib Baruah, Mario Bick, Bruce Chilton, Rayna Coller, John Fout, Dee Garrison, James Green of the Library Company of Philadelphia, Olympia Gonzalez, Louise Haberman, Rosemary Jann, Jack Jacobsen, Andrew Molloy, David Pierce, Gordon Schochet, Alice Stroup, and Ellen Sullins. Discussions with Barbara Callaway, Susan Crane, Susan Gal, Judith Gerson, James Kurth, Phil Lapsansky, and John Patten have also been very helpful, as have recent conversations with Robert Kasper, President of the Horatio Alger Society. Gary Scharnhorst kindly responded to my questions by telephone, read the manuscript, and identified several errors. Martin Ostwald, William Turpin, Chris Callanan, Lisa Anderson Cox, and Stephen Epstein provided Greek and Latin assistance. My editor, David Roll, at Oxford University Press, has been tremendously helpful and supportive; I am also indebted to Melinda Wirkus and other members of the editorial staff, and to Valerie Aubry, formerly editor at Oxford, for her interest in this project.

Finally, I thank James L. Greer, who helped me think about my arguments, and who read more draft material and listened to more about Alger than any human could reasonably be asked to do. Although I ultimately lay claim to the result, the above debts must remind one that, isolating though the process of production sometimes feels, a text is, in many ways, a social product.

Swarthmore, Pa.   C. J. N.
October 1993

THE FICTIONAL REPUBLIC

"Aspirations." (William Makepeace Thayer, *Success and Its Achievers*. Boston: A. M. Thayer, Publishers, 1891 [the subscription version of the book, with which Alger was familiar].)

1

Allegory of the Republic:
On Interpretation and Method

More than a century after Horatio Alger, Jr. achieved his greatest fame with *Ragged Dick*, the author's name stands as a symbol that has become associated with central values in the American political creed.[1] Alger, author of over a hundred juvenile novels and stories (plus a few adult romances), which appeared from the late 1850s until roughly the turn of the new century, has become a household name unlike almost any other. It is not because his works are still widely read or known, but because the name itself is a stand-in for ideas supposedly derived from his fiction that "Horatio Alger" has entered the language and discourse of daily life.

Alger is the literary figure most closely associated with the ahistorical self-help formulas of popular culture. He has been called one of the two most influential writers in America. To Alger has been attributed an influence on American culture probably broader than any other author except Mark Twain.[2] "To call Horatio Alger, Jr., America's most influential writer may seem like an overstatement...but...only Benjamin Franklin meant as much to the formation of the American popular mind."[3] The Grolier Club in New York listed *Ragged Dick* among the One Hundred Influential American Books Printed before 1900.[4] The name is invoked to capture something thought to be true about America.

The way in which the Alger story is formulated and the nature of its promises seem to have captured the imagination. Alger heroes are part of our language of discourse about social mobility and economic opportunity, about determination, self-reliance, and success. They are symbols for individual initiative, permeability of economic and social hierarchies, opportunities, and honest dealing. "Horatio Alger" is shorthand for someone who has risen through the ranks—the self-made man, against the odds. The prevailing *form* of this discourse in the United States concerns strong-willed, courageous individuals who struggle against the odds and triumph rather than engage in collective struggle or collective action. They reap rewards for doing what they ought to do. Alger's name is also frequently associated with defense of capitalism and conservative values. (Horatio Alger awards are given annually to prominent Americans associated with the gospel of free enterprise and laissez-faire.) "Self-made" entrepreneurs are held up as examples of the Horatio Alger rags-to-riches story.

The author died on the eve of the new century (1899); his works continued to be read in great number for another two decades.[5] But the routes and methods of the Alger heroes are held up as prescriptions available for late twentieth century individuals, although the social and economic world in which the Alger characters moved has long since vanished.

The stories of this minor American novelist and story writer have been debunked, maligned, and lampooned. Something nevertheless endures. What makes this symbol so compelling and accessible in a much-changed economic environment? Why are its formulations articulated as obvious and natural truths so frequently? In what way did this author of juvenile fiction unwittingly put a finger on a form of expression that could define "the rules of the game" of the economic and social order and enter the political discourse about the meaning of America?

That Alger has been appropriated for use in American political culture is clear; yet the reasons these symbols are so pervasive and the thoughts the narrative can be used to invoke are not as obvious as we have supposed.

The appropriation of Alger is a tale about American political culture, discourse, and imagination. It invites reflection upon the relationship between the language of politics and conditions of material life. It demands attention to the relationship between fact and fiction, texts and readers, audiences and meanings.

This book poses a question that stands at the intersection of politics and culture. The object of investigation is a narrative—and a grammar of American politics. As such, it draws upon the contributions of contemporary literary theory, which is generating new ways of seeing the production of and struggle over culture. The primary data are texts, especially novels and stories, but also the author's extant letters, reliable biographical material, and other texts of the period that help situate the narrative. In choosing the narrative as a chief object of investigation, I accept the view that it is "a 'form of reasoning' about experience and society . . . of equal dignity to the various types of conceptual thought in service in daily life."[6]

In searching for the narrative, more than the author's meanings and putative intentions are under investigation. This book offers a "rereading" of Alger's plot, characters, foils, and meanings by relocating them in the historical, economic, and political context in which they were produced. This rereading offers the author in a new light, provides a different answer to the question, What kind of a formula is this?, and suggests what kind of sense he made of a range of Gilded Age experiences. I seek to understand not only whether such texts had any power in the world but also for whom the texts appeared to work out problems.[7]

But rereading a Gilded Age author is not the endpoint of the investigation. The compelling question for me concerns the durability—the persistence— of the formula. Inaccurate as a description of the world even when written, why does an outmoded formulation about our experience survive? When the political economy of the late twentieth century would seem to lay such beliefs to rest, they appear to flourish. In what way is this formula and set of symbols available to be appropriated and patterned into American political discourse?

What kind of sense do political grammars need to make of conditions of material life in order to be "successful"? As we rethink the kind of correspondence established between beliefs and conditions of material life at the point of production of Alger stories in the Gilded Age, we will be better able to approach this important issue.

READING ALGER

Horatio Alger, Jr. has been portrayed alternately as an unabashed booster of capitalism and materialism, a romanticizer of a dying era, a genteel moralist, and a hack writer of cheap, sensational fiction whose moral influence on the young was highly questionable.[8] This literature has tended to treat Alger as a very poor "reader" of the Gilded Age. The pro- or anticapitalist tenor of the vast majority of these portraits is ultimately not very helpful in locating the author, his texts, or their appeal.

The *prevailing* image of Alger's stories is that they celebrate the rise of capitalism and the proliferation of economic opportunities and riches.[9]

Typical is the claim that "Horatio Alger can be held largely responsible for instilling into American boys of a former generation purely materialistic ideals."[10] Or, "Alger's fictional heroes started poor and finished rich."[11] Critics see Alger as universalizing a myth of success that at best pertained to only a few. Adventure stories for boys and large pots of gold at the end of the adventure were mere fantasies. This "Alger" universalized aspirations that few could reasonably hope to attain; he is an apologist for the emerging capitalist order.

Some late nineteenth century critics determined that Alger was a vulgar sensationalist in his own day. However, his reputation as capitalist apologist grew in the 1900s, partly through the efforts of his 1928 biographer, upon whose "hoax" work many subsequent interpretations were based.[12] The Herbert Mayes hoax stood virtually uncontested for half a century. It was the vehicle through which many would come to understand Alger heroes in rags-to-riches terms. Alger's fine recent biographer Gary Scharnhorst (with Jack Bales) has contributed a great deal to the understanding of the transformation of Alger's identity and meanings by his biographers and critics.

Another version of "Alger" posits an author who may have wanted to write recipes for success in the new order, but gave antiquated and inappropriate advice or who retreated from change. He was a romanticizer of the dying era who yearned to roll back time. He engaged in deliberate anachronism.[13] Most Alger heroes achieve middle class rewards.[14] The virtues encouraged—punctuality, loyalty, honesty, bookkeeping skills, penmanship, thrift—are more appropriate to middle-level employees than to achieving success in the changing world of the Gilded Age.[15] Alger's world is filled with small shopkeepers, mercantile establishments, and white-collar workers. Rarely do the boys attain extraordinary wealth.[16] Rather than the celebrator of capitalism, we are presented with the "nostalgic spokesman of a dying order."[17] Alger's vision of success "is, in effect, a reassertion of the values of a bygone era in an age of dramatic change and expansion."[18] This Alger was impotent in the new order.

These approaches are more correct in portraying Alger as someone who rejected many of the economic tenets of capitalism and who waged war upon unrestrained accumulation.[19] The best insight to date has come from his biographer, Gary Scharnhorst, who realizes that the "historical Horatio Alger was a Harvard-educated patrician whose moderately popular nineteenth-century morality tracts for boys expressed his genteel abhorrence of the mercenary Gilded Age."[20] At best, we get a portrait of an author who was ambivalent about many of the changes associated with the rise of industrialism. But Alger's stance as a moralist is still seen as largely reactive—and outside capitalism.

One of the most astute readers of Alger, Daniel Rodgers, clearly saw that Alger struggled with the dislocating changes of his era. Rodgers found tension riddling the works of Alger and his patron, Oliver Optic (William T. Adams). Both attempted to capture the child's imagination while engaging in moral instruction. For Rodgers, the synthesis was not successful. These authors, seeking to advise and entertain the young, delivered "split and uncertain," even "schizophrenic," counsel. They claimed their stories illustrated the virtues of self-discipline and hard work, but "the announced story and the one actually told were rarely quite the same; the preface and the tale itself were often disconcertingly out of joint." "If Alger admired the fluidity of his age, he was profoundly distrustful of industrialization itself."

> Absorbing both the extravagant confidences of an expansive economy and its nervous fears, he [Alger] wrote his tales in the teeth of these difficulties, preaching his sober, cautionary lessons and weaving the heady romances that undercut them.[21]

The conclusion is that these stories are seen to have their greatest affinity to the conventions of the classic fairy tales.[22]

Was this, then, a literature of utopian longing? Were Alger—and, by implication, his readers—into "la mode retro," thriving on nostalgia and reviving the good old days when life was simpler, when the community was not coming apart at the seams, and when self-interested men did not triumph? Alger wrote formula stories, and Cawelti has suggested:

> We might loosely distinguish between formula stories and their "serious" counterparts on the ground that the latter tend toward some kind of encounter with our sense of the limitations of reality, while formulas embody moral fantasies of a world more exciting, more fulfilling, or more benevolent than the one we inhabit.[23]

It *is* true that Alger's world is more benevolent than the one we inhabit. But I hope to demonstrate that these are not merely fairy tales and that the Alger narratives endure not simply because of their affinity with some kind of fairy-tale type.[24] Nor will this be a tale about bread and circuses or mass manipulation. These stories struggled to maintain a correspondence with the emerging world that has gone unnoticed.

Alger's blend of fact and fiction affords a more complex response to industrialization than that with which he has been credited. It is not the case that these stories "reflect truth no more accurately than a Coney Island mirror."[25] The tales referred to a world with which the contemporary audience was becoming acquainted; they are rooted in tensions surrounding the Gilded Age transformation of the conditions of material life. Alger offered guidebooks to surviving the economic dislocations occasioned by the rise of capitalism. Figures that reappear constantly in Alger tales work out scripts on major political and economic controversies.

Power is central to this narrative as the author struggles to keep youth from being overpowered by some of the changes in their environment. The struggle for power concerns the power of manipulators and seducers over the morals of youth; the struggle to maintain power over oneself, one's character, and one's labor; illegitimate power and performance in politics and society; the power (or lack thereof) of the author of mass fiction in the literary marketplace, and the struggle to connect certain images of production with manliness. These issues are all addressed in the following chapters. So, too, is the power of fiction to guide the young, the central issue in Chapter 12. As tastes, habits, and culture diverged in class-specific ways, Alger did battle over literature, theater, and other entertainments. The battle for the Republic was a struggle to contain the meaning of diversity and class: we were all one estate. This struggle was over the power to define identity and shape political discourse.

Juxtapositions in Alger reveal a constant concern with true or natural value, representation, resemblance, and artifice; substance is distinguished from shadow. Natural value is juxtaposed to manipulated value and manipulators of value. Solid, plain virtues are opposed to fancy and artificial manners and social pretense. Genuine, honest, and sincere characters are contrasted with those who would appear to be so. Those who are human are juxtaposed to those without feeling, who are machinelike and who trample others in pursuit of their self-interest. Those who depend upon themselves, their characters, and efforts for their advancement are juxtaposed to those who depend upon luck and who try to create value out of thin air. As the author upholds traditional values and community, the new men of industry are frequently villains who need to be taught lessons in justice.

The author was part of a struggle over culture, language, habits, class, and meanings in a society in which differences and social distance were becoming ever more apparent. The struggle to maintain the notion that we are all of one estate took place in an era giving the lie to such a message. The identity of the Republic was at stake; its unity was entailed in its identity. Alger's battle against distinctions and class-specific entertainments could be seen as allied with elite and bourgeois attempts to master pleasures— pleasures which "are not only textualised but are also institutionalised and politicised."[26]

As he reacted against amusements, habits, and dispositions that were increasingly class-specific, Alger shared a language and agenda with nineteenth century writers of advice manuals, sermons, religious fiction, and moral reformers.

Alger's course for preserving the identity of the Republic and upholding the virtue of its citizens was deeply indebted to his Harvard training in the texts and lessons of antiquity. He looked to Athens and saw classes sitting side by side in cultural productions, enjoying the same pleasures, engaging in the same discourse. He saw, on these shores, the Astor Place riots.

Religious themes of an ex-minister, trained by Harvard Unitarian moralists steeped in the Scottish Enlightenment, also deeply penetrated this literature. Emphasis on character was testimony to Alger's attachment to rules of success other than those suggested by the emergence of capitalism. Character was fundamentally based on tenets of scripture, but neither church nor other institutions could monopolize access to virtue. And if the young required persuasion that justice was in one's self-interest, Alger arranged a payoff in the currency of the day.

The voices of moral and cultural elites anxiously called out to influence the young, and one prevailing "voice" in Alger texts is that of these cultural guardians concerned for the virtue of the Republic where many new forces and influences threatened their moral leadership. *The Education of Henry Adams* may be a more self-conscious, poignant image of the lack of fit between the Bostonian of privilege and the new world than anything Alger ever wrote or thought, but the two Harvard men, only six years apart, nonetheless shared a great deal. Theirs was a class fraction with declining influence. Alger recognized that many of these genteel voices had lost their chance to be heard.

Alger did not merely replicate their messages. He probably could not have done so and, at the same time, made a living by his pen, which his own exclusion from the ministry and his family's economic position made mandatory. But it is no accident that these genteel voices did not have the impact on popular culture, public discourse, and political vision that Alger did. The particular combination of responses to industrial development, the nature of the literary output, and the vehicles of production themselves helped shape Alger's impact. As his fiction proliferated, it came under attack by those especially fearful for the Republic.

Alger was a participant in the transformation not only of economy and society but in the production of literary arts. He produced mass fiction, contributed to popular culture, and came to stand at the margins of respectable literature. The story papers and cheap magazines in which many of his tales appeared were viewed as working-class vehicles. Dependent upon the market, the author shaped a product that would be consumed. It was not easy to own one's own identity in the genres in which he worked.

Alger's own experience pointed out the struggle to define manliness and potency in relationship to production, consumption, and class.

At a time when reading publics were becoming increasingly class-differentiated, Alger's fiction enters and attempts to address the gap. There were pedagogical as well as economic justifications. We will discover how the texts spoke in overlapping class voices, and, through a brief exploration of the real and likely readership of Alger's fiction in Chapter 10, we will see why the different vehicles and means through which Alger fiction reached potential readers suggests that the same Alger story was very likely to have had different communities of readers.[28] There could hardly be one text in this class.

Alger did not write a formula for modern capitalism, but he fashioned one that could be used by diverse class audiences to make sense of, participate in, and even protest against and rectify abuses of modern capitalism. The narrative was not a straightjacket.

Readers and texts, like words and deeds, and historical subjects and agents of change constitute each other. This project presumes that readers make texts as members of communities.[29] It is important to grasp

> the pluralism of the play of styles, codes and languages which can now be seen to constitute the realm of the popular—the popular, that is, properly understood . . . in terms of a critical repertoire which could assess the significance of 'pleasure' and 'the popular' as at once democratic and socially managed, as contested and controlled, as a structured balance of forces rather than a con-trick.[30]

Locating the narratives and symbols of the Alger text in their historical context is a process of *de*familiarization, for "meanings and value have been variously constituted over time by changing audiences."[31] The author, literary critics, audiences, and later generations of users of the narrative all constructed Alger. This forces the conclusion that some things about responses to, and meanings of, these narratives remain unavoidably undiscoverable. Although we may not be able to determine why or how particular readers read and enjoyed these texts, this study argues that a great deal more *can* be said about Alger's contribution to the construction of a grammar of American politics.

This investigation asks how a particular vision and form of discourse became part of the common language. Voices competed in the battle for leading young audiences—for the privilege of defining the universe of discourse about the identity of the Republic and the meaning of American experience. The story of Alger is in part one about how one kind of political vision—articulated by one who was shaped by an intellectual elite with declining moral and economic power—became the dialect of mainstream political discourse, communicating with, while not simply reflecting, worldviews of subaltern classes.

Such an investigation improves our ability to understand how and why the Alger story lends itself to appropriation by different audiences and for different purposes. This investigation recasts the text as a political grammar and permits new reflection on the question of what made Alger as a symbol *available* to express beliefs about the way the American universe works. As we reconsider what *kind* of potential sense this is, we will discover one more piece to its appeal.

In Alger's formulas can be found an allegory. The adolescent of the Republic is the adolescent Republic. In this story, the young Republic faces dangers that threaten its moral fiber, strength, purpose, and identity. The real optimism of the Alger story lies in this story more than in that about wealth.

The Alger hero, whether a New York street boy or a boy from a small village in the hinterland, undertakes a journey that is a rite of passage. He not only promises to attain his manhood and his independence at the end, but his virtue is intact. The dangerous passage, in which the hero is torn from community and family and their moral influence to be thrown among strangers in the city, ends in triumph. The trials and struggle of the young hero standing on the verge of adolescence, when his identity and destiny will be forged, carry a great deal of cultural and political baggage. They are the struggles not merely of Ragged Dick and his acquaintances but of the nation undergoing transition. For this is an allegory of the Republic.

2

A Unitarian Project for
Moral Guidance

> He [Pericles] did not seek to control, but rather yielded to and
> regulated the irresistible current of the popular desire. No
> Athenian ever possessed so many qualities for obtaining great
> and lasting influence over the various classes of the citizens.
>
> Athenaicus (Horatio Alger, Jr.), "Athens in the Time of Socrates"[1]

Never has Alger been viewed as an author implementing a political project,
steeped in the classics and the religion of the Harvard Unitarian moralists.
Chapters 2 and 3 establish the linkage between Alger's work in the classics,
his religious training, and the agenda of his juvenile fiction. These connections
illuminate his project for moral guidance through fiction in a way that has
eluded supporters and critics alike—even those who recognize his role as
genteel moralist. The interests, values, and themes articulated in Alger's
prize-winning essays at Harvard pervade his literary career.[2]

The shaping of the young and molding of citizens were central political
questions for the ancient philosophers—and continued to be for the
antebellum Harvard neo-Platonists and Unitarian moralists.[3] Like his
mentors, Alger sought clues in the classics about how to lead citizens and
influence the popular mind.

Armed with the education and religion of the Harvard elite and imbued
with its mission, Alger joined with that "patrician class giving responsible
leadership to its community."[4] The Boston Protestant clergy "regarded
themselves as rightful leaders of society in time of crisis" and contributed to

12

progressive and social reform voices toward the end of the century. The Unitarian tradition yielded religious leaders who were "activist, sensitive to social problems, receptive to secular ideas, and willing to dissent."[5]

Alger's classics education shaped his view of the importance that the political community be one, not many; that public-mindedness must triumph over selfish and private concerns. It shaped his view that all classes should have, insofar as possible, the same tastes, habits, and interests; that the distance between rich and poor was a danger for the community.

One of Alger's own early mentors, Harvard President Edward Everett, classics scholar, orator, politician, was among those preoccupied with how elites could establish leadership over emerging classes. Emerson, recollecting Everett's influence and rapport with his audiences, wrote: "There was an influence on the young people from the genius of Everett which was almost comparable to that of Pericles in Athens . . ."[6]

As a Harvard student of the classics, Alger occupies a place in a continuing discourse about leading the young. The author of popular fiction and of working-class story paper literature, like Everett as orator, established a credible conversation with an audience outside elite cultural circles. Alger was well aware that pedagogical issues were involved in establishing such a conversation.

THE CLASSICS AT HARVARD

> Those who read what the beginning of Rome was, and what her lawgivers and her organization, will not be astonished that so much virtue should have maintained itself during so many centuries; and that so great an empire should have sprung from it afterwards.
>
> Machiavelli, *The Discourses* [7]

When Alger was born in Chelsea (now Revere), Massachusetts in 1832, New England had already witnessed significant social and economic changes since the time of the founders. At manufactories like the Lowell Works, wage-laborers spoke up for reduced hours, better pay, and about the injustices of the factory system.

But Alger would witness far more dramatic changes in his lifetime. Railroads and telegraphs eliminated distance, generating a national marketplace. Immigration brought those with foreign languages, brogues, different religions and customs to cities and towns in the United States. Industrial development transformed the landscape;

Horatio Alger Jr., early 1870s. (Harvard University Archives.)

city populations swelled. The United States was increasingly seen as becoming a nation of rich and poor. Difference and distance between Americans was ever-more apparent. The Civil War shattered any thought that our differences were insignificant. We were no longer—if we were ever—a nation where all were of one estate.

In the eyes of some elites and moral guardians, the Republic was practically under siege. And if the endurance of the Republic depended on the virtue of its citizens, what would happen when we were made up of a nation of strangers and cast among people who could not be counted on for good moral influence? If family, hometown, and clergy were all declining as persistent influences on the young, what would become of the Republic?

Horatio Alger, Jr., approximately 1890. (Harvard University Archives.)

During this revolutionary time, Alger followed his father's footsteps, both through Harvard College and the Divinity School. The universe in which Alger moved was one of tradition and privilege, confidence and moral clarity. To gain admission to the Harvard freshman class in 1848, Alger had to demonstrate competence in Virgil, Caesar, Cicero's Select Orations, Stoddard's Latin Grammar, Greek, ancient history and geography.[8] Harvard students were not given the opportunity to take a course on the Industrial Revolution until 1880. The staid undergraduate curriculum "operated to create 'a separate and Brahmin class, who could be called gentlemen.'"[9]

Alger's large graduation class in 1852 was virtually ethnically homogeneous.[10] "The boys who composed the members of the Class of '52 were all American born, and with four exceptions all of English lineage."[11] The author could trace his New England roots nearly to the landing of the Mayflower.

Alger's own family was far from wealthy; when young, the future author experienced the effects of his father's financial difficulties, which contributed to the move from Chelsea to Marlborough. He was the recipient of financial assistance at Harvard. And Marlborough, where he grew up, was a small town on the periphery of Boston, that center of the universe. His final years in South Natick were similarly spent on Boston's periphery. Just as his circumstances placed him on the periphery of privilege, Alger occupied a rather contradictory position in American life and thought of the Gilded Age.

At Harvard, the younger Alger excelled in the gentlemanly field of classics, graduating Phi Beta Kappa.[12] His discourse was steeped in Xenophon and Plato, Thucydides and Herodotus; his college writings were a pantheon of Greek and Roman statesmen, philosophers and Sophists, playwrights, sculptors, and painters. Alger wrote prize-winning essays on "Cicero's Return from Banishment," "Athens in the Time of Socrates," and a translation into Greek of "The State of Athens before the Legislation of Solon," from Grote's *History of Greece*.

The Harvard Unitarian moralists who taught Alger père et fils, attempted to resurrect Plato and render his teachings compatible with Christianity. William Ellery Channing was among the most Platonic of the "Cambridge Platonists" in the decades just prior to the younger Alger's arrival.[13] Alger's Socrates "entertained views respecting the dignity of the human soul no less elevated than those which are held by Christians of the present day." The Harvard student added:

> He [Socrates] was no less firmly convinced of the certainty of
> a Divine Retribution, and depicted in fearful colors the punish-
> ment which await those who have given themselves up to the
> dominion of sin on the earth.[14]

In his later fiction, the need to visit evildoers with retribution—now in the secular realm—was compelling.

There was a good deal of consensus in that Harvard community that Hume's skepticism could and should be rejected for the empiricist's claim that observation was the basis of knowledge and that objects of knowledge could be sensible things. They admired Baconian natural science and gravitated to Scottish Enlightenment philosophers.[15] Alger's library charges while a student reveal that he consulted Scottish magazines steeped in common-sense philosophy and that he was prompted to examine Bacon. His readings in Scottish common-sense philosophy also included the work of Thomas Reid.[16] This background contributes to what John Cawelti saw: that in Alger, middle-class respectability equals spiritual grace.[17] Common-sense philosophy prompted its disciples to insist that empirical evidence was reliable and that the material world provided "historical proof of intervention in human affairs by a personal God"; idle speculation was discouraged. Humans could trust their common sense—their perceptions; through these perceptions, they could apprehend God's ways.[18] These self-appointed moral guides were optimistic about human perfectability: virtue was accessible; the classic search could be democratized. The author's optimism was shaped in this context.

After graduation, Alger took up residence in Cambridge. He tutored, wrote fiction and nonfiction, and continued in the footsteps of the Reverend Horatio Alger, Sr. when he entered the Divinity School at Harvard. He shortly departed. According to one scholar, the Divinity School curriculum "never went beyond dry-as-dust church history, homilectics, Hebrew grammar, and textual exigesis."[19] Several years later he re-enrolled, completing the course in 1859.

He took the obligatory gentleman's tour of Europe on the eve of the Civil War, sending back light travel correspondence that was printed in the *New York Sun*.[20] He also sent back an account of the funeral of Eugène Scribe in Paris, the only piece of Alger's that was ever published in the prestigious *North American Review*.[21] Failing to pass muster when he took his physical for the Union Army, Alger served as supply minister and guest minister in the Boston area.

He turned down an opportunity for a pulpit in Ohio. His life and thought were oriented toward New England and New York, and he liked to claim Boston as his residence. Through Alger's eyes, Boston must have looked as it did to Howells even in 1902: "Most of our right thinking, our high thinking, still begins there, and qualifies the thinking of the country at large. The good causes, the generous causes, are first befriended there . . ."[22]

The author eventually accepted a Unitarian pulpit offered in the Brewster parish on Cape Cod. His ordination on December 8, 1864 was presided over by several prominent Cambridge Unitarians.[23] Edward Everett Hale, who himself extolled the virtues of the novel and who later authored one summoning Jesus into modern-day Boston in the guise of a Syrian visitor examining philanthropic agencies, delivered the charge and the address to the people at the ordination of Reverend Horatio Alger, Jr.[24]

In 1865, the Unitarian periodical *Christian Examiner* carried advice from one Unitarian minister, urging his colleagues to generate sermons that were as wide-ranging, polished, and engaging as possible; otherwise "the most intelligent and earnest men and women will go to literature instead of to church for inspiration, guidance, and culture."[25]

In the year of his ordination, Alger's first novel, *Frank's Campaign*, appeared. *Paul Prescott's Charge* soon followed. While still a preacher in Brewster, Alger was chosen for inclusion in Duyckinck's new edition of the *Cyclopaedia of American Literature*. Thanking Duyckinck less than a month before scandal broke, Alger wrote:

> I hope in course of time to be more worthy of such mention . . .
> I bring out in the Spring (Loring, publisher) a novel, under the
> title, "Helen Ford," and in the fall a new boy's book, not yet
> commenced . . .[26]

Clearly Alger intended to write as well as preach. In doing so, he followed the lead of other Boston Unitarians in the field of religious fiction.

RELIGION AND FICTION

The highbrow *North American Review* noted on the eve of the Civil War that "people grow more and more unwilling to swallow instruction, and will hardly take it at all, unless it is cunningly disguised in fiction."[27] Religious figures of various denominations, sometimes familiar with statistics indicating the Protestant church was not reaching the masses or observing firsthand the Protestant churches filled with businessmen and professionals in fashionable Yankee neighborhoods, began to come to terms with the tastes of a secularizing era. They recognized the importance of fiction as an emerging popular genre.[28]

Sermons and lectures incorporated fictional devices, and "secular anecdotes and sentimental embellishments were frequently preferred to theological exposition." Reverend Henry Ward Beecher "theorized at length on the value of colorful illustrations as opposed to dry logic in preaching," and delivered sermons "famous for their lively anecdotes and stories."[29] The permeation of religious tracts with fiction prompted Harriet Beecher Stowe, the Congregationalist minister's sister, to note:

> Hath any one in our day, as in St. Paul's, a psalm, a doctrine, a
> tongue, a revelation, an interpretation—forthwith he wraps it up
> in a serial story, and presents it to the public. We have prison
> discipline, free-trade, labor and capital, woman's rights, the
> temperance question, in serial stories. We have Romanism and
> Protestantism, High Church, and Low Church and no Church,

> contending with each other in serial stories, where each side
> converts the other, according to the faith of the narrator . . . Soon
> it will be necessary that every leading clergyman should embody
> in his theology a serial story, to be delivered from the pulpit
> Sunday after Sunday.[30]

Religious and moral instruction became increasingly a matter for novels
and story papers. Ministers read, and increasingly published, sentimental
tales that emphasized feelings over intellect.[31] The apologia for new forms
of moral instruction was occasionally militant. From the pen of a trained
Unitarian minister close to Alger came this defense of drama:

> The ecclesiastical ideal of life is abnegation, ascetic self-repression
> and denial; while the dramatic ideal of life is fulfilment, harmonic
> exaltation and completeness of being and function. Which of
> these ideals is the more just and adequate?[32]

The serialization of Beecher's *Norwood* was published in the *New York
Ledger* which, in 1867, was the story paper with a massive circulation of
300,000. It appeared in novel form in 1868. *Norwood* was a sentimental tale
of simple, pious villagers in a small New England town. The novel was
selling rapidly the same year as was Alger's *Ragged Dick*. Financially,
Beecher's adult novel was by far the larger success. Beecher received a
$30,000 advance for the manuscript, and Robert Bonner, editor of the *New
York Ledger*, estimated that the serial run of *Norwood* had brought the story
paper $120,000 in new business.[33]

Alger's work had undisputed kinship with this religious fiction, in
which, by the 1850s and 1860s, "the boundary between natural and
supernatural is abolished . . . both worldly success and divine grace merge
into a single mythical process."[34] As secularization proceeded along with
the century, religion was no longer central to the theme of even religious
novels. "To secularize sin and salvation was to make them more manageable,
to retrieve them from the doubtful realm of metaphysics, and to anchor
them in perceivable reality."[35] It was this conjunction of worldly gain and
spiritual growth, so prevalent in religious fiction, that Mark Twain satirized
in the 1860s.

Twain, who had his own sort of rags-to-riches story in *The Prince and the
Pauper*, lampooned the Sunday school fiction of the 1860s in his Good Little
Boy and Bad Little Boy stories of the Civil War decade. Twain's stories make
abundantly clear that this world's rewards and punishments are certainly
not meted out according to desert.[36] The public responded to Twain's
irreverence. Twain may not have had *Ragged Dick* specifically in mind—it
was serialized the year Twain's stories were published—but Alger, too, had

his satirists. William Dean Howells satirized Alger's rehabilitation of young Sam (*The Young Outlaw; Sam's Chance*) in *The Minister's Charge.*[37]

Much religious fiction posed no competition for Alger: it was deadly. It ended up chiefly in Sunday School libraries. One elite publication complained that these distrusted religious novels contained "either an intolerable infusion of doctrinal theology, or a mixture absolutely revolting of earthly passion and spiritual pride, so that it may be deemed lucky, if they are only tedious and uninteresting." Religious novels, it was said, were "too serious for the gay, and too gay for the serious. So they are seldom read . . ."[38]

However, some revival ministers were spectacularly successful in reaching a large audience. Beecher and Moody augmented oratory with new mastery of the print media to extend their large followings. Beecher never wrote a second novel, and his personal morality soon came under public scrutiny in a way that Alger's never did. But by 1872, the highly successful Congregationalist minister could pronounce the conventional pulpit a thing of the past.[39]

Alger joined other moral leaders to a large degree in wishing to "regenerate individuals and change society."[40] Yet these self-appointed moral leaders battled over who would influence and shape the values of the young. The revivalist was one source of competition Harvard elites faced for moral influence over the Republic.

If certain revivalists, developing personal cults, had a striking power to persuade, Alger was certainly not, by temperament, cut out for the stage performance. He was also cut off from the podium from which to wield this potential influence.

An authority on the subject of nineteenth century religious fiction found that "a significant number of those who dealt with affirmative religion in novels were failed ministers or philosophers." He failed to count Alger among these.[41]

ESCAPE TO NEW YORK:
THE DECLINING ROLE OF THE PULPIT

Alger had but a short-lived ministry; he abandoned it precipitously when charged with "the abominable and revolting crime of unnatural familiarity with boys" of the parish, which he did not deny.[42] He left under cover of darkness in the midst of undenied charges leveled by his parishoners in March of 1866. The price for smoothing the matter over was found in his resignation and his father's letter to the Secretary of the American Unitarian Association four days after the charges surfaced:

> I presume you have already received from my son Horatio a note announcing that he has resigned his parish and all intention of ever again entering a pulpit. It is not unlikely that you may have learned from other sources something of the unfortunate circumstances under which his ministry has closed. I am naturally anxious that no unnecessary publicity should be given to the matter. The only desirable end to be gained by such publicity would be to prevent his further employment in the profession, and that I will guarantee that he will neither seek nor desire. His future, at the best, will be darkly shaded. He will probably seek literary or other employment at a distance from here, and I wish him to be able to enter upon the new life on which he has resolved with as little as possible to prevent his success.[43]

Although Alger was forced to give up the attempt to save souls from the pulpit, he did not yield in this task as a writer.

Alger moved to New York in the spring of 1866. In introducing himself that year to the editor of the new magazine, the *Galaxy*, he wrote: "I have established myself in New York with the intention of devoting myself solely to literary pursuits and increasing my acquaintance with publishers."[44] He supplemented his income by tutoring wealthy children such as the Seligmans and Cardozos.[45]

The author submitted his poem "Friar Anselmo's Sin" to the *Galaxy*'s editor a few months after he had been forced from Brewster. The poem has been read as a reference to the episode, along with a resolve to try to make amends in service to others. "FRIAR ANSELMO (God's grace may he win!)/Committed one sad day a deadly sin . . .," Alger begins. The friar, seeking death, is visited by an angel, who counsels:

> Courage, Anselmo, though thy sin be great,
> God grants thee life that thou may'st expiate.
>
> Thy guilty stains shall be washed white again,
> By noble service done thy fellow-men . . .[46]

As Alger continued to write juvenile fiction, at least one member of the Brewster Parish committee was scandalized that this practitioner of unspeakable horrors was publishing pieces standing to influence the young. Solomon Freeman attempted to alert Joseph H. Allen, publisher of *Student and Schoolmate*, to the scandal, so that he would not publish Alger's work. His efforts having failed, he appealed to the Secretary of the Unitarian Society in Boston and was advised that the church had no leverage over the press.[47]

Alger said little if anything about his one-time ministerial career, omitting mention of this training when identifying himself to publishers. Though he appeared in the religious suit of the a card game entitled "Game of Authors," the biographical data Alger provided in 1874 to George A. Bacon for the game narrated this story:

> Graduated at Harvard College in 1852. For several years a teacher in Cambridge & elsewhere. At the same time connected editorially and otherwise with various periodicals. Visited Europe in 1860 & 1861. Returning, was again employed in literary pursuits. Published Frank's Campaign, his first juvenile, in 1864. Removed to New York City in 1866, and still resides there . . .[48]

An 1869 letter acknowledging authorship of *Nothing To Do* concluded: "Be kind enough in addressing me to omit the 'Rev.' as I wish my name identified only with the literary profession."[49] He mentioned instead the poetry and stories contributed to *North American Review, Putnam's,* and *Harpers';* his association with A. K. Loring; and the fact that "Mr. Duyckinck has a brief sketch of me in his recent edition of the 'Cyclopaedia of American Literature.'"[50]

Whatever Alger's view about the pulpit as a vehicle for wielding moral influence prior to the Brewster affair, he would subsequently downplay the role of the clergy and formal religious institutions in moral guidance of youth. *Ragged Dick,* in the stages of conception when he wrote Duyckinck from Brewster in January, 1866, stood just at this transition.

Religious persons and institutions play a role in supporting the virtue of two early heros, Paul Prescott and Ragged Dick. Paul Prescott found in a church sexton an adoptive parent. However, his economic salvation came about because he fell asleep in a Manhattan church; the author tells us that the sermon was boring. When at Harvard, Alger was privately admonished for unexcused absences from prayers.[51]

Ragged Dick is, indeed, one of those boys who attended Sunday School on his route to rehabilitation. He did so with—and with the encouragement of—one of his new merchant-benefactors, Mr. Greyson, who taught the class. Even here, it was the good merchant and layman, rather than a minister, who provided moral suasion. It was a frequently voiced sentiment in the late antebellum era that the mercantile class represented "an aristocracy of gold . . . the best thing of its kind we have had yet, the wisest, the most human"; "the saint of the nineteenth century is the good merchant . . . He is wisdom for the foolish, strength for the weak, warning to the wicked, and a blessing to all."[52] Greyson-like characters attested to the truth of the statement that "there are in this, and there are in every community, men of property and influence, who always stand ready to encourage and assist young men of enterprise and merit."[53] Alger simply moved the locus of their influence to the secular realm.

Beyond the early novels and poetry, there was little overt religious instruction, sentiment, or observance in Alger's tales.[54] If ever asked, Alger heros professed faith and thanked God for benefits rendered. We may meet men of the cloth on a rare Sunday, but church and clergy were not the major formative influences on central characters. If Alger agreed that "The successful men of our country, in every department of labor, accomplished their purpose on principles derived directly from the Bible, or which were in harmony with it," his successful men nonetheless did not carry Bibles or quote from them.[55] Neither did Alger's boys.

Although formal religious language and instruction were downplayed, the influence of the Unitarians of Boston was nonetheless felt. Alger, like his mentors, could easily maintain that love of virtue could be quite separate from organized religion. Heros were naturally or instinctively moral. Doctrinal purity was not the issue: "Our object is not to convert men to our party, but to our principles." And principles could be read from behavior: "A man is not a Christian in proportion to the amount of truth he puts into *creed*, but in proportion to the amount of truth he puts into his *life*."[56]

Apart from the fact that Alger was rarely as transparent in linking story to religious instruction as were contemporaries Oliver Optic and Henry Ward Beecher, there were other real and important differences between Alger and other would-be moral guides.

Alger offered optimism about the future; many other moralists, including Beecher, decried decline. Horace Mann complained: "how few there are among us who would not disparage, nay, ridicule and contemn, a young man who should follow Franklin's example!"[57] Moralists echoed jeremiads of old. The old guard processed forces of change in the framework of declension; the golden era of social relations in America was past, and "the social history implicitly woven throughout the advice manuals was an extended jeremiad on America's declension from a more ordered and virtuous era."[58] Alger did not find appealing the Calvinist's lack of faith in human perfectability.

What alternatives presented themselves for guiding new generations? Many traditional inhibitions and restraints on workers had disappeared— not only because of the absent authority of traditional clerical voices. With the increasing separation of workplace and residence space in the city, employers had less opportunity to supervise workers' leisure.[59]

Revival ministers who converted businessmen and professionals had won considerable success among factory workers since the revivals of 1830–31. These spellbinders supplied one potential basis for controlling workforce behavior—an internalized ethic. Alger was both wary and skeptical of the nature of their influence.[60] Beecher in particular lacked compassion for the poor and laboring classes, evident in his diatribes against unions and labor demands for a living wage; his message, as we will see, was quite different from Alger's.[61]

Some of Greyson's real life compatriots turned to exhortation, prohibition, censorship, Sunday closing laws, and compulsory church attendance at sites of worship specified by manufacturers to effect similar purposes.[62] Alger was also hostile to compulsion.

Ragged Dick's Greyson figure is a different metaphor for moral control over the workforce. A surrogate both for family and for the employer as guardian of the moral order, Mr. Greyson gently leads his impoverished protégé, Richard Hunter, Esq., into the path of righteousness, relying upon neither fear (hellfire) nor compulsion. Only after Dick has been set on the right path is he fit for employment in a business establishment.

The author appeared undisturbed by the declining authority of American clergymen over America's youth; his fiction took most responsibility for influencing the young from their hands. In Alger's view, midcentury moralists, with their advice manuals, sermons, lectures to mechanics, deadly fiction, and sometime prophesies of decline, were not addressing the future. Alger could be seen as seeking to influence classes and youth that might otherwise be lost to virtue as he defined it.

PEDAGOGY

> A writer for boys should remember his responsibility and exert a wholesome influence on his young readers. Honesty, industry, frugality, and a worthy ambition he can preach through the medium of a story much more effectively than a lecturer or a preacher. I have tried to make my heros manly boys, bright, cheerful, hopeful, and plucky. Goody-goody boys never win life's prizes. Strong and yet gentle, ready to defend those that are weak, willing to work for their families if called upon to do so, ready to ease the burden that may have fallen upon a widowed mother, or dependent brothers and sisters, such boys are sure to succeed, and deserve success.
>
> Alger, "Writing Stories for Boys"

Here was fiction that was meant to approximate truth—meant to offer guidance for life. Prefaces to Alger novels frequently articulated his desire that his readers learn and take inspiration from the example of the hero. In a piece published a few years before his death, Alger voiced this didactic purpose:

> It seems to me that no writer should undertake to write for boys who does not feel that he has been called to that particular work. If he finds himself able to entertain and influence boys, he should realize that upon him rests a great responsibility. In the formation period of youth he is able to exert a powerful and salutary influence. The influence of no writer for adults can compare with his. If, as the years pass, he is permitted to see that he has helped even a few of his boy readers to grow into a worthy and noble manhood, he can ask no better reward.[63]

It is clear that the author believed in the continuing relevance of the classics; "at this moment Athens exerts a wider influence and excites a deeper interest than all the great empires of antiquity through the ever fresh and beautiful creations of her intellect." The cultural beacon was Athens, not Rome. The best of Roman literature was "but a reflection of the superior splendor of the age of Socrates." He concurred with Macaulay that from the literature of Athens "has sprung all the strength, the wisdom, the freedom and the glory of the western world," and traced "the effects of Athenian culture in the vast accomplishments" of Burke, Dante, Cervantes, Bacon, and Shakespeare.[64]

Rome was but a shadow, and so, too, in his view, was America. Both could borrow. Both Athens and Rome offered important historical lessons. The causes of Athenian excellence lay not in the work of a single mind or a few great minds; rather, "these were such as arose from the peculiar genius of the people, by which we may understand strong general powers of mind devoted to a particular study."[65]

But if the potential for excellence depended upon the genius of the people, leadership was nevertheless vital. Alger inquired how certain leaders of classical antiquity acquired a natural title to lead, and more broadly, with how one leads and directs a democracy. A self-appointed "natural aristocracy" might well pose these questions as they sought to legitimate their claim to deference by nonelites.

Alger was fascinated with the means by which Pericles "acquired such absolute mastery over the popular mind":

> We must take into consideration his own character, and examine how far it was suited to command the age in which he lived and the people whom he governed. The secret of his success is to be found in the harmonious adaptation of his character to the prevailing spirt of his countrymen. "The supreme power ob-

> tained by Pericles," says a brilliant English writer, "resembled a
> tyranny, but was only the expression and concentration of the
> democratic will." He did not seek to control, but rather yielded
> to and regulated the irresistible current of the popular desire. No
> Athenian ever possessed so many qualities for obtaining great
> and lasting influence over the various classes of the citizens.[66]

Alger noted how Pericles gained the support of various interests in the populace: "By the encouragement which he extended to the various industrial interests of the people, he gained their confidence and steady coöperation in his measures."[67]   Building monumental architecture, encouraging industrial interests, and expressing the democratic will were all part of leading.

In writing about Cicero, the Harvard student again wondered how one acquired authority over the young. But the method is best spelled out in the Bowdoin Prize essay: To lead or guide the young, one must first have their confidence. To lead, one must yield in some measure to popular desire; only then can one regulate and direct it, and acquire the confidence and cooperation of the people. Taking some of these counsels to heart, Alger took stock of the audience he hoped to lead. And in doing so, he found himself embroiled in controversy about standards for literature.

Leadership was not the exclusive province of men of politics. It was also a question of the appropriate literature. To guide young people—or *a* young *people*—one had to begin where they were; in Socratic form, one must understand the nature of the audience. And what kind of reading matter is fit for a young people?

The Harvard student found some literature better adapted to young than old people:

> History from its very nature could not become popular with the
> Athenians. They were yet young; and it is true in the case of
> nations as well as of individuals, that it is the characteristic of
> youth to look forward eagerly and hopefully into the undiscov-
> ered future . . .

Poetic tastes varied with the political development of a people:

> The majestic epic, with its constant reference to the old mythol-
> ogy, replete with legendary lore, sprang up among a people yet
> in the infancy of their political history, whose minds were swayed
> by the wildest improbabilities, with whom physical strength was
> esteemed in proportion as it was often called into exercise in the
> constant struggle for political existence. Subsequently, in the
> more stirring and agitated times which attended the develop-
> ment of Republican governments, elegiac, lyric, and iambic

poetry arose. Then, for the first time, poetry became the expression of individual feeling, and the inmost recesses of the human breast were laid open by its inspiration.[68]

Considering Greek literary productions in this light, the juxtaposition of high art with interest and accessibility to the general reader speaks volumes about Alger's evolving pedagogy. Alger seemed torn between judging most praiseworthy that which appeals to the general reader or that which reveals the greater artistry. The Harvard youth, pronouncing Aeschylus the father of Attic Tragedy, called attention to the "Titan like majesty" of his verse, its "grand and terrible sublimity," and concurred with another analyst that "the passions appealed to are masculine and violent to the exclusion of Aphrodite and her inspirations . . ." And yet, there is merit in Sophocles, with "a closer approach to reality and common life; the range of emotions is more varied" than Aeschylus; there is, in Sophocles, "a comparative simplicity of speech like that of living Greeks."[69] Alger's preference wavered between the "bold and startling metaphors . . . [the] rugged boldness and irregular fire" of Aeschylus and the "elegant but less forcible creations" of Sophocles and Euripides.[70]

The story was similar among Greek historians. If "[Thucydides'] work stands higher as a work of art," the budding author nonetheless asserts that "the narratives of Herodotus are much more interesting." Thucydides' work was "dignified"; "to the politician the work of Thucydides is rich in valuable lessons, while to the general reader Herodotus presents much greater attractions." Alger's Herodotus drew upon travels and practical experiences: "His descriptions have all the vigor and animation of an adventurer and a wanderer. 'He has none of the refining disquisitions that are born of the closet.'"[71]

Alger also read Plato through the filter of Scottish common–sense philosophy. His Socrates, who made his contribution to philosophy when it was in an "unsettled state," "turned his attention chiefly to practical philosophy: speculation and theory, except as connected with practice, he deemed of little value."[72] Everywhere, the author exhibited a marked preference for the practical.

Alger "fitted a great many young men for college—his partiality being for classical studies."[73] But his appreciation of the classics stressed the accessible. Some of his disadvantaged heros acquire the rudiments of Greek and Latin on a course of self-improvement, but he saw that an education in the classics was not available to all members of this Republic. Could the others be improved by literature and by personal influence? The author's pedagogical preference for what was accessible to and appreciated by youth shaped his criticism of other advisers of the young. Alger believed that the characters of religious fiction were altogether too pious to appeal to the young people he wished to reach. Although *Norwood* was a best seller, perhaps owing to Beecher's huge Congregationalist following, if reading it is any indication, Alger could not be more correct.

"A writer for boys," he wrote, "should have an abundant sympathy with them. He should be able to enter into their plans, hopes, and aspirations. He should learn to look upon life as they do." Alger dismisses authors whose heros talk "like a preacher" and who are perfect prigs.

> I have sometimes wondered whether there ever was a boy like
> Jonas in the Rollo books. If so, I think that while probably an
> instructive, he must have been a very unpleasant companion for
> a young boy like Rollo.[74]

Jacob Abbott, author of the antebellum *Rollo* books, constantly preached or had poor Rollo preached to. Jonas warned, for example, never to tarry on the way to and from school—not even to look into a bird's nest.[75] The didacticism and moral propriety of these antebellum children's books is crushing. Alger designed heros to have the imperfections of boyhood as well as "qualities that make boys attractive."[76] He wished to speak to less than perfect youth.

This sentimentalist also thought he could better gain admission to the world of real, human potential readers by introducing the palpable. "I have always preferred to introduce real boys into my stories," he wrote.[77] Personal contact was another means of influence. Friends remembered the contact he had with street boys; the author said that close study of boys was important to his work.[78] Alger wanted very much to be adopted by the young—in person and through his literature; he enjoyed recounting how the boys of New York came to visit him. Personal contact—with his students and with street boys—was part of the process of persuasion.

Alger's Socrates possessed "a kindling and persuasive eloquence, which attracted to his side men of all ages and especially the young." Contemporary accounts engaged in "the enthusiastic veneration for his character." His education of the young was through personal contact. What different would Alger have had said about himself than what he said of Socrates?:

> Over his disciples at least, he exerted an almost boundless
> influence. That the tendency of his instructions was in the highest
> degree salutary no one can entertain a doubt. The object to which
> he chiefly directed his efforts was to prepare his youthful auditors
> to fill creditably the stations to which they might be called in after
> life.[79]

VINDICATING THE SOPHISTS: THE COMPATIBILITY OF VIRTUE AND REPUTATION

There is an uncanny sense in which Alger's reflections on the Greeks foreshadowed the controversy his literary productions would engender. The author's attempted vindication of the Sophists, following Grote's *History of Greece*,[80] reveals much about his own later life course.

As tutor, Alger imparted his educational skills in exchange for money, offering a college preparatory course with heavy emphasis on the classics for the children of the wealthy. As author, Alger concerned himself with the education and moral elevation of average citizens. Alger's material well-being depended in both cases upon the tastes of those who purchased his services and wares. The reconciliation of popular tastes (marketability) and merit takes place repeatedly in his fiction.[81]

And so, Alger came to the defense of the Sophists. Contrary to the typical charge that the Sophists were "intellectual and moral corruptors," who worked "by arguments specious rather than profound to show the worse to be the better reason," the Harvard student saw them as real teachers.[82] "The Sophists were a class of men whose vocation it was to train up youth for the duties and pursuits of public and private life." The young student was impressed with their "ready and impressive elocution," and with "the readiness with which they imparted to others the knowledge they had themselves acquired."[83] He appreciated their emphasis on rhetoric: "One of their leading objects was the cultivation of an easy and graceful style of oratory, an indispensable accomplishment to every Athenian who wished to acquire political consideration."[84]

Alger neglected to note that a popular desire to "acquire political consideration" was one of the chief problems with Sophists and speech makers for Plato/Socrates. What became of the reproach that the many could not tell the difference between seeming and being and the charge that the Sophists helped direct many toward public life who had no business being there?

Alger's defense fell back on the standard of public opinion itself. Had the Sophists been as corrupt and immoral as alleged,

> they would hardly have met with the enthusiastic reception with which they were greeted in the various cities which they visited. Superior knowledge and intellectual force always command respect, when united with elevation of sentiment and correct principles. The state of society in which they command equal

reverence, when unattended by these, must be intrinsically vicious.

Nor would they have acquired their positive historical reputation, for "History affords no examples of men who have acquired a great intellectual renown by teaching a low or corrupt morality."[85]

Alger was dismissive of the charge that Sophists enabled their pupils to pursue unjust designs, and "to make the worse appear the better reason, and to delude the heavens by trick and artifice into false persuasion and show of knowledge without the reality." This same argument was urged against Socrates.[86]

Respect, enthusiastic reception, historical renown, the reputed intelligence and morality of the Athenian democracy (the same democracy, Plato but not Alger remembered, that put Socrates to death): All of these become proof to young Alger of the qualities of the Sophists.[87]

Alger's cousin, with some assistance from our author himself, wrote in defense of the standard embodied in public fame: "It cannot be fairly thought that . . . great place and fame . . . are accidental. Such achievements . . . are the general measure of worth and fitness." Moreover, "a wide, solid, and permanent reputation . . . is obtained only by substantial merit of some kind. The price paid is commensurate with the value received."[88]

Fame was one measure of popular taste; so was what was paid for. One of the chief objections of Socrates and Plato against the Sophists, wrote Alger, "was that they sold their knowledge for money." Alger, whose own livelihood would soon depend upon pleasing the buyer, might understandably wish to vindicate public opinion:

> It is unquestionably true that the Sophists demanded and received payment for their instructions. The price . . . was never, we believe, exorbitantly high. But after admitting this we are at a loss to perceive what conclusion can be drawn prejudicial to the character of the Sophists as a body.

The author concluded that "The laborer is worthy of his hire"; "why intellectual labor should be considered less worthy of recompense we are unable to conjecture."[89]

Virtue was not only compatible with payment and with monetary reward; recognition (expressed in popularity or payment) was, Alger wished to believe, evidence of merit. He conveniently ignored problems raised by Plato: giving to all the same thing, seeking to please those who pay for the good, or the standard of goodness that a money-based market transaction occasions.

Whatever errors, carelessness, and lack of subtlety can reasonably be laid at the feet of "the common mass of the community," the democratic tribute of sustained attention and monetary reward does not err:

> The multitude are abundantly able—none more so—to respond with admiring interest to the impression of original power, recognize the broad outlines of a sublime and fiery soul, thrill under the general signs of genius, and pay deserved tribute to popular exhibitions of skill.[90]

Ultimately, then,

> the great average of the people are better judges, fairer critics, than any special classes or cliques can be; because the former are free from the finical likes and dislikes, the local whims and biases, the envy and squeamishness which prejudice the feelings and corrupt the judgments of the latter.[91]

There is, in short, "nothing in the character or vocation of the Sophists which need expose them to the obloquy which has attached itself to the name." Rather, "the great intellectual activity which reigned at Athens in the time of Socrates is attributable in no small degree to the influence of their teachings."[92]

There was a clear tension. Admiring Socrates, Alger wished to side with him against philosophers who exalted "the material above the immaterial"—the physical universe over the soul. "One great object which he [Socrates] had in view was to expose the 'seeming and conceit of knowledge without the reality.'"[93] Socrates constantly discriminated between seeming and being, opinion and essence; Alger attempted to follow.

In applauding Socrates's conduct at his trial, Alger respected his refusal to pander to opinion: "He disdained to descend to the usual practices of accused persons, who sought to secure the good will of the people by flattery, and to excite their compassion by lamentations." Alger termed this Socrates's "noble independence," and his "indifference to the final issue"; he admired "the boldness of his bearing, and the manner in which he defied [the] authority [of the judges]—a point on which the legal profession are quite as sensitive at the present day as were the Athenian Dicasts of old." His bold stand earns "the respect and admiration of all subsequent ages."[94]

Socrates sided with real standards of excellence. But Alger and his mentors, emphasizing the practical, wished to make virtue more widely accessible: Most, if not all, could partake in Being, immortality. The realm of the material—sense data—was rehabilitated. The Platonic route to understanding virtue was shortened.

CONCLUSION

Pedagogically, philosophically, and economically, Alger grappled with the tension between what was truly the best and what was popular. He found it impossible to concede that popular taste was the ultimate arbiter of value; he constantly approached such a position. The author knew the dangers of popular opinion, referring to "prejudices which had taken deep root in the popular mind," and yet, writing for a popular audience, wished to believe that the public were discerning.[95]

The author was unsure at Harvard, as he remained throughout his career, about the standard of public opinion. He seemed as a moth circling the flame. Constantly teaching the difference between shadow and substance, the author nonetheless retained considerable faith in the people's ability to judge rightly. Dependent upon pleasing the public, he craved signs of recognition from established cultural elites. As the nineteenth century progressed, fewer authors could have it both ways.

Custodians of culture deplored a decline in popular taste. Alger's own work was charged with contributing to that decline and with having misguided the young. What Alger called having "sympathy" with his young readers—entering into their thoughts and desires as a means of entertaining and influencing—was renamed. More than a few late nineteenth and early twentieth century critics who railed against Alger's works thought materialism had won; they shaped Alger's own historical reputation.

Alger, who admitted his modest literary skills, had a ready rationalization for writing popular fiction. He never apparently reacted to charges that he was a corrupter of the young—either in Brewster or during the Comstock era. He might have wished he could have claimed as his own epitaph that which he wrote of the Sophists:

> Stripping the name of Sophists of all that would tend to mislead us, we find them as a class exerting a most salutary influence upon the age in which they lived, promoting the spread of general intelligence, and by their success constantly increasing the estimation in which literature was held. It is to be regretted, that, thorough the force of circumstances, their character has been so utterly misconceived, and the important influence which they exerted upon the culture of the Greek mind so entirely unappreciated.[96]

3

Republican Rites of Passage: Character
and the Battle for Youth

*So far as success in the world is concerned, all depends upon a few short
years—upon the character you form in this spring season of your being.*

Joel Hawes, *Lectures to Young Men* [1]

Were I to define what I mean by character, I say *it is that which
makes free and intelligent beings have confidence in you.*

John Todd, *The Young Man: Hints Addressed to the Young Men of
the United States* [2]

Almost all of the products of Alger's pen featured—and were directed to—
boys and girls on the verge of adolescence. If those addressed stood on the
threshhold of life and their habits were just becoming formed, they
increasingly faced this critical period of life away from home.[3] In antebellum
America, "a number of clergymen, teachers, and sentimental writers
confronted the moral problem generated by . . . mass migration [from the
country to booming cities] in dozens of manuals of advice to American
youth . . ."[4] Alger, too, directed his attention to youth who, leaving familiar
surroundings and community networks for the city in ever-increasing
numbers and at ever-younger ages, were cut adrift from traditional moral
influences of family, clergy, and friends. In dangerous new surroundings,
the young must learn to grow and adapt while keeping their identity as
members of the Republic intact.

33

This transition was of the utmost import for the youth's spiritual and temporal well-being. Moreover, it was crucial for those who believed that the only way to ensure the survival of the Republic lay in preserving the character of the new generation.[5]

Alger's basic story may be read as an allegory. This chapter explores parallels between the rites of passage of young heroes and those of the young Republic. Each seeks to maintain a core of identity and establish its virtue through the dangerous passage. The trials of the young are the trials of the Republic. In the success of the former lies the triumph of the latter. Entering its adolescence, facing Civil War, immigration, urbanization, industrialization, increasing polarization of rich and poor, corruption, greed, materialism and selfishness—all of which threaten to tear it apart— the Republic's triumph lay in the preservation of virtue, meaning its integrity, identity, independence, and freedom. Alger's fiction does battle for the Republic.

Allegory plays an important role in the appeal of the Alger story. Confronting and overcoming the dangers against which many Alger contemporaries inveighed, the young fictional figures offer an optimistic prognosis for the future of the Republic. The boy of good character could prevail; the Republic as growing youth is offered reassurance.[6]

ALLEGORY OF THE REPUBLIC

> Society is a man in a larger form, and we are all members, and must act in concert with the rest, and do our duty to the whole, or we shall find ourselves—like a hand that lies inactively appropriating the life-blood that flows into it, without doing any thing for the whole body—gradually losing our power, and withering away into mental impotency.
>
> T. S. Arthur, *Advice to Young Men on Their Duties and Conduct*
> *in Life*[7]

Alger's most frequent central character is a boy from fourteen to sixteen years old who is thrust into a new environment, almost always the city. The story is a rite of passage from boyhood to manhood during which the youth must undergo many trials. The completion of the passage yields a young adult whose virtue is firm; the adolescent of the Republic attains manhood.[8]

In one variant of the theme, however, a child who is too young to be cast adrift is returned to dependency—to adoptive parents—who will provide the education and moral guidance that will enable the youth to make the rite of passage later. Victory preserves virtue as the youth is saved from having to enter the world of adulthood unequipped for struggle. *Julius, the Street Boy; Mark, the Match Boy;* and *Phil, the Fiddler* are among the stories in which the victory lies in adoption or recovery by surrogate parents.

Female street children are at risk and must be rescued as well. On the streets, they had little to look forward to. According to Brace, who set up a lodging house that provided instruction in morals and in economic self-sufficiency for some of these girls, many female street children could be expected to end up in a life of prostitution.[9] Heroine *Tattered Tom* is, in fact, a young street girl of twelve, posed on the brink of adolescence. Alger rescues her just in the nick of time and returns her to the care and moral supervision of her long lost mother. Better yet, a vehicle is provided for the salvation of more girls:

> For her sake, her mother loses no opportunity of succoring those homeless waifs, who, like her own daughter, are exposed to the discomforts and privations of the street, and through her liberality and active benevolence more than one young Arab has been reclaimed, and is likely to fill a respectable place in society.[10]

One could say of Alger's male and female characters, a few years younger than Dreiser's Caroline Meeber, who entered Chicago in the summer of 1889:

> When a girl leaves her home at eighteen, she does one of two things. Either she falls into saving hands and becomes better, or she rapidly assumes the cosmopolitan standard of virtue and becomes worse . . . Half the undoing of the unsophisticated and natural mind is accomplished by forces wholly superhuman. A blare of sound, a roar of life, a vast array of human hives, appeal to the astonished senses in equivocal terms. Without a counsellor at hand to whisper cautious interpretations, what falsehoods may not these things breathe into the unguarded ear![11]

Excessive materialism was only one of many temptations a boy or girl faced in the city; the threats to character and virtue were legion. "Young people are easily drawn into any scheme, merely from its being new, especially if it falls in with their love of pleasure; but they are almost as easily discouraged from it by the next person they meet with."[12] For the moralist, intervention was critical. The link between individual character formation and the welfare of the community was unquestioned:

"The street-girl's end." (Charles Loring Brace, *The Dangerous Classes of New York, and Twenty Years' Work Among Them.* New York: Wynkoop & Hallenbeck, 1872, reprinted NASW Classics Series, n.d., illustration opposite p. 122.)

> You are . . . soon to be the leading, acting members of society; to
> occupy all the places of influence and trust, and to have at your
> disposal all the great and precious interests of the church and
> state. Consider now, how much depends on the character you are
> forming . . . the welfare of this whole community . . . [depends]
> on your possessing a character of true virtue and excellence.[13]

Since the character of the young and the character of the Republic were
inextricably bound, leaders assumed responsibility for each. If the viability
of the Republic depended upon virtue, character formation was possibly *the*
central political concern.

It was not uncommon, at mid-century, to talk of the Republic as a
growing youth.[14] This language was the heritage of the founding generation:

> "Republicanism was the concomitant of youth . . . Monarchy and
> hereditary aristocracy were deviations from nature, the products
> of oversophistication, of age and decay."[15]

In T. S. Arthur's analogy of individual and society, should the moral fiber
of one decay or atrophy, so shall the other.

Even more deliberate were some parallels drawn between the health and
liberty of the Roman republic and the morals of youth:

> When Cataline [sic] attempted to overthrow the liberties of
> Rome, he began by corrupting the young men of the city, and
> forming them for deeds of daring and crime. In this, he acted with
> keen discernment of what constitutes the strength and safety of
> a community—*the virtue and intelligence of its youth—especially of
> its young men.* This class of persons, has, with much propriety,
> been denominated the flower of a country—the rising hope of the
> church and society. Whilst *they* are preserved uncorrupted . . . the
> foundations of social order are secure, and no weapon formed
> against the safety of the community can prosper.[16]

Alger joined in the venerable tradition of Americans who had looked to
lessons from classical antiquity to discover what strengthens and what
undermines modern republics. His 1852 English Oration Prize essay,
"Cicero's Return from Banishment," highlighted the tension between virtue
and corruption in Rome. Although Cicero had quelled conspiracy and was
loved by "all good citizens," the ill-disposed among the powerful had
succeeded in driving him into exile. Alger's sentimental tale features the
triumphant return of Cicero to Rome, demanded by the popular will. "The
city gates were thrown open," as Rome embraced its preserver. The Roman
people were his "Captives, bound by no unwilling fetters but by the ties of
gratitude and affection." But the oration—and Cicero's triumph in this
account—end on an ominous note, in which the fragility of liberty and civic

virtue are clear: "Thus closed the grandest civic triumph which the world has yet seen! It was one of the last efforts of public liberty to do honor to its patron and defender."[17]

Liberty was fragile, indeed. Henry Ward Beecher and many of his dour contemporaries thought the battle was being lost on these shores in the nineteenth century. For those who issued moral warnings shaped by the language of republicanism,

> The jeremiad—that most American of all rhetorical modes—was merged with the language of classical republican theory to the point where one can almost speak of an apocalyptic Machiavellism; and this too heightened the tendency to see that moment at which corruption threatened America as one of unique and universal crisis.[18]

Middle class moralists in the nineteenth century repeatedly linked their concern for the morals of America's rising generation(s) with their fears for the disintegration and degeneration of the Republic. Their fears rang out in advice manuals, lectures to mercantile associations and mechanics' societies, and sermons.

ADRIFT IN THE CITY: MORAL PERILS AND THE ADOLESCENT OF THE REPUBLIC

> Of all who shall finally make their bed in hell, *they* will have the lowest place, who, not satisfied with being wicked themselves, labor to diffuse the poison of their principles, and lure unguarded youth to the gates of death. To say of any one, *"he is a corrupter of youth,"* is to give him the worst possible character.
>
> Joel Hawes, *Lectures to Young Men*

Advice manuals depicted many power-seeking culprits seeking to influence the young stranger entering the city. They posed the danger of moral and bodily harm. Virtually all manuals advised the reader how to judge knavery and how to deal with strangers.[19] Alger is part of this discourse. The same liminal figures appear and threaten to undo the hero, morally or materially.

Alger's project for preserving the Republic from tyrants, demogagues, and enslavers was, likewise, a *personal* project. Vice is personified in the power-seeking deceiver and manipulator; virtue is personified in the youth who struggles for independence.

The captivating image of the raw country youth standing on the urban threshold, ready to seek his fortune was certainly as old in this country as was Franklin's *Autobiography*.[20] The nineteenth century image, connoting adventure, excitement, and mobility, was not novel, nor were fears for unsupervised youth.

What was, perhaps, unusual was the urgency of the fear and the frequency of its expression in mid-century. The former can be sensed in Horace Mann's words: "Torn from the parental stock and transplanted to a city, who can describe the dangers that encompass a young man during the period of his moral acclimation?"[21]

There was a sense that myriad noises and sensations could overwhelm the malleable youth. "Everything leaves its impress on the young: the countenances they look at, the voices they hear, the places they visit, the company they keep, and the books they read."[22]

It became ever more dangerous to trust. The unsuspecting boy was watched and marked by many eyes, such as "the seducer in the shape of the young man who came before him, and who has already lost the last remains of shame"; the pander to vice "who has as little remorse at the ruin of innocence as the alligator has in crushing the bones of the infant that is thrown into his jaws from the banks of the Ganges"; and "she—who was once the pride and hope of her parents—who now makes war upon virtue and exults in being a successful recruiting-officer of hell." Meanwhile, the youth entering the city was "generous and confiding. He mingles feelings without suspicion and is ready to believe all sincere who proffer him their friendship."[23]

Benjamin Franklin may not have needed an advice manual to help him enter Philadelphia and decode the city, but, for many antebellum authors, circumstances in the mid-nineteenth century city were quite different. Mid-century anxieties reflected an era of marked social mobility.[24] Migration of youth to cities and immigration raised urgent issues of citizenship, along with the moral and political incorporation of strangers. So many were now flocking to the cities, including persons from abroad, whose principles were as yet unknown. Corruptors lay in wait to lure and destroy the young of the Republic.

The confusion and anonymity of the growing city created a rich opportunity to prey on strangers. So did the changing economy, with the early nineteenth century "proliferation of moveable wealth, especially negotiable paper." The combination "made possible for the first time a wide variety of swindles, frauds, forgeries, counterfeiting activities, and other confidence games."[25]

As old patterns of social deference crumbled, peer pressure was seen as a dangerous source of corruption of the morals of the young.[26] "Nothing is of more importance to young men than the choice of their companions."[27] Judging correctly is critical:

> Every young man may see how much depends upon his choice of associates. If he mingle with those who are governed by right principles, his own good purposes will be strengthened, and he will strengthen others in return. But if he mingle with those who make light of virtue, and revel in selfish and sensual indulgences, he will find his own respect for virtue growing weaker, and he will gradually become more and more in love with the grosser enjoyments of sense, that drag a man downward, instead of lifting him upward, and throw a mist of obscurity over all his moral perceptions.[28]

The stranger who approaches the young man fresh from the countryside or small town is a seducer who is attractive because he knows his way around the city, appears to "know the ropes," and because he offers friendship, entertainment, and familiarity "at the precise moment when all familial and communal restraints were falling away."[29] The new entrant to the city was offered a quick social network in a world of strangers.[30] This seducer was frequently termed a confidence man.

The term "confidence man" was probably first employed by the New York press during their coverage of the arrest and antics of an 1849 street swindler, William Thompson, who tricked several citizens out of their gold watches before his capture. Thompson, who had the appearance of a gentleman, approached another gentleman in the street, chatted briefly, and asked "whether he had the confidence to lend his watch to a stranger." Handed his prize, the street artist walked off laughing. The press averred there were other such criminals operating in New York, and a survey of police captains in the 1860s estimated that confidence men represented one-tenth of New York City's professional criminals.[31]

The confidence man was only one symbol of power against which the young needed protection; we will later discover other emerging dangers and sources of illegitimate power in the Republic. But the personified moral corruptor of youth galvanized the attention of a significant number of writers of Alger's era.

Karen Halttunen effectively demonstrates that the recurring focus on the youth's urban companion, the demagogue, and the gambler all represent anxieties about power. Such figures expressed fears about the consequences of major social, political, and economic transformations of the mid-nineteenth century. The confrontation between the virtuous boy and the confidence man symbolizes the struggle for the virtue of the Republic. In the confidence game, "the passive liberty of the American youth falls victim to the self-aggrandizing power of the confidence man."[32]

The fear and its lexicon were holdovers from the eve of the American Revolution, when aggressive, creeping, encroaching power—like the ocean, like a cancer, like jaws, like appetite—too often "destroys its benign— necessarily benign—victim." This victim was "liberty, or law, or right."[33]

The confidence man, in assaulting character, assaults that which guards individual morality and collective virtue.

> There is no charm in free institutions to sustain themselves and to bless a nation. Liberty, where the individual is the slave of his neighbor's opinion, or still worse, of his own passions and appetites, is a mere sound.[34]

The battle for the liberty of the boy was a battle for the liberty of the Republic and its free institutions.

For the most fearful, vulnerability was so serious that even the presence of the profligate could be considered "polluting to the soul"; contamination merely required contact. The imagery of contamination carried over from the cholera years; "the licentious man was said to be 'a pestilence in the community' who could infect everyone around him because 'his breath blights every innocent thing.'"[35] Refusal to associate with corruption was the best safeguard.

As a general rule, Alger's boys keep away from gambling dens, saloons, and the company of the corrupt. One must beware the powers of seduction. If "granny" or a father-pretender is corrupt, the boy or girl of good character tries to escape and find his or her true parents or relations.

However, Alger did not think evil was so readily contagious that good character could be contaminated on mere contact. He did not attempt to keep the boy away from all tempting experiences. One must be wary of boys who smoke, drink, swear, play billiards, or squander money, but these vices are not absolute guides to character, since reform is possible.[36] In Alger's version, the ramifications of contact with vice could be serious: the near-penniless hero might be bilked for a free meal or lose his remaining money. But money and virtue were not the same. In the typical advice manual, contact leads more frequently to a slow seduction into drinking, gambling, theater, and sex.[37]

For these authors, it was clearly important to build lines of defense against potentially corrupting influences. This included learning how to "read" character—to discern the difference between appearance and reality— and how to develop and maintain a firm character oneself.

LESSONS IN SURVIVAL: READING
CHARACTER AND DECODING THE CITY

> [Beware] the goodnatured civilities of persons you have never
> seen before. Gratuitous offers of assistance or advice, or good
> fellowship, are suspicious, to say the least. Do not be persuaded
> to go anywhere with these casual acquaintances.
>
> *Wood's Illustrated Hand-Book to New York* [38]

Alger invariably puts forward some character whose appearance is deceiving,
whether urban confidence man or country squire. The device reveals how
critically important is the separation of appearance, artifice, reputation, and
pretence from nature (being). This concern with hypocrisy was widely
shared. "Archetypal hypocrites threatened ultimately, by undermining
social confidence among men and women, to reduce the American republic
to social chaos." The art of such figures lay in manipulating "facial
expression, manner, and personal appearance in a calculated effort to lure
the guileless into granting them confidence." [39]

Especially when the Alger hero leaves familiar surroundings of country
or small town life, he is at risk among rascals. The world becomes much less
predictable and friendly. The boy is "green" and too trusting upon contact
with the city, falling victim—sometimes more than once. One must be
shrewd and tough to separate friend from foe, appearance from reality. The
hero survives by learning how to decode the city and learning the lessons of
character.

Writers of the romantic period valued transparency of character. Nature,
not artifice, was the clue to good character. One heard that "His face was the
index of his mind" or a boy's eye constituted "the perfect mirror of his
mind" [40] In a simple world, good character can be read off the face.

However, the world has its deceivers—perhaps in increasing number.
Americans no longer lived in a world in which they could count on honesty
and plain-dealing. Too many were obsessed with gain. A businessmen
complements young Ben Barclay in *Store Boy* by telling him: "Your honesty,
my boy, is of the old-fashioned kind. It is not the kind now in vogue." [41]
Because it is difficult to judge those who stand on pretense or contrivances,
the unsuspecting boy would do well to keep up his guard. Signs of
friendship were not always what they appeared, and not all cues were
readily readable. The boy needed to learn how to protect himself. Alger had
learned enough lessons from city life to realize that naturalness could be a
liability. The boy himself must be less forthcoming with strangers than a
simple-natured boy would, without ever actually lying. Somehow, the

Alger hero must participate in codes in which worthy people can read his character off his face and behavior—he must be straightforward, honest, open-hearted and sincere—while learning how to keep manipulators from reading and playing upon him.[42]

There is no genuine privacy for one who is unable to hide his or her feelings. As Alger repeatedly reminds readers through the vehicle of boxing, emotions can get in the way of achieving one's objective; being angry is no way to best an opponent in a fight.[43] Broadcasting feelings and having moods written all over one's face are kinds of involuntary publicity that may prevent one from being in control and realizing one's legitimate purposes. When central characters assume false identities or false missions or conceal their feelings in order to advance the cause of justice, readers learn that performance (of deceivers) may necessitate performance.[44]

If the reader pays close attention, appearances as described by Alger are a giveaway to character in all but a very few cases. The author was interested in both phrenology and physiology, and his heroes are laden with "positive" physical and behavioral attributes.[45] They are generally described as frank, manly, sturdy, stout, resolute; attractive boys usually are given dark hair. Such boys have an open face and an air of independence and self-reliance. Alger finds *physical* clues to the nondepraved natures of some characters, despite their hard lives, crude manner, and bad habits. Villains look mean or ugly and tend to have behaviors and dispositions to match. They are often given red hair and sallow or pock-marked complexions.

Appearance differentiates the evil nature from the character molded by circumstances. Looking at the description of two would-be robbers, we can see that unattractive descriptions suit those whose nature leads them to crime:

> One was a short, stout man, with a heavy face and lowering expression; the other was taller and slighter, with a face less repulsive. The former, in rushing into crime, appeared to be following the instincts of a brutal nature. The other looked as if he might have been capable of better things, had circumstances been different.[46]

Alger teaches an important lesson in notable examples where character judgments are impossible to make on the basis of appearance. In *Adrift in the City*, a well-dressed man "accosted" Oliver Conrad and invited him to lunch at Delmonico's merely for the company. Oliver felt quite lucky indeed, because he was penniless. However, the gentleman lured Oliver home with him after lunch and tried to chop him up in the name of science. In this rare case, there was nothing about the character of the gentleman to tip off the reader. Oliver Conrad could not have foreseen the danger awaiting him after Delmonico's unless he were generally suspicious of unsolicited—*or unearned*—kindness.[47]

This story highlights the author's beware-strangers-bearing-gifts or Trojan Horse message: do not trust people volunteering something for nothing or great deals and tips, even if they look as distinguished as the old physician in the moral story. Occasionally, someone approaching the hero with an offer of a job or seeking a travelling companion to the West is on the up-and-up, but one must be perspicacious. It is understandable that Oliver accepted a meal when destitute, but it is always problematic and often dangerous to accept favors from complete strangers.

The cases in which figures appear good or evil by physiognomy would seem to generate conflict about how much control the individual has over character formation. Popular temperance tract and advice author T. S. Arthur thought that young men came in two classes: one was comprised of those who "feel the force of good principles, and are in some willingness to act from them," and the other was "composed of such as are led mainly by their impulses, feelings, passions, and selfish interests."[48] For Alger, a small number were evil by nature; others simply failed in their duties and had fallen into temptation. Any great concession would have threatened the vitality of the Republic. But what class was it that could not "feel the force of good principles"? Does the *capacity* for goodness reside with some more than others? The question of biological parentage looms importantly in these novels; the author seems determined to demonstrate that the central character (including the orphan) springs from decent stock. If capacity for goodness (or evil) can be by inheritance, there is a dark implication. Capacity is only potential; goodness can be derailed. Alger's guide to character would then be the Yankee self-preservation manual.

CHARACTER: THE ANTIDOTE

> The primary meaning of the word *character* is a mark made by cutting or engraving on any substance, as wood, stone, or metal. Hence, as applied to man, it signifies the marks or impressions made upon the mind.
>
> Rufus W. Clark, *Lectures on the Formation of Character, Temptations and Mission of Young Men* [49]

Filippo [*Phil, the Fiddler*], a rare Italian-American hero, exhibits promising character traits. His good humor and lively disposition, his resilience and optimism contrast with the despair of other boys forced to work for padrones or placed in similarly hard circumstances. His face was often lighted up by a smile, "for in spite of the hardships of his lot, and these were neither few nor light, Filippo was naturally merry and light-hearted."[50] The hero is bold, plucky, courageous, and hopeful. Such traits are expected of an Alger hero.[51] Virtue is active, just as in the republican model. While Phil is too young to attain manhood, he is on the right track, and adoption preserves and enlarges his capacity for liberty.

Character was the key to freedom. Well-ordered character, self-discipline, and honesty were hedges against power-seeking culprits and the corruption of the Republic. Character formation was the nineteenth century version of a self-defense course.

The boy of good character was, in the parlance of the age, manly.[52] When the young "walk in the midst of allurements for the appetite," those who yield are not men but beasts. "He who cannot resist temptation is not a man."[53]

One who would form a firm, self-reliant character must cultivate firm principles early in life:

> ...you are to be, in this life, and in that which is to come, just what your principles make you. These are the foundation and frame work of character; these, the main-spring of purpose and action ...[54]

Character was a sacred obligation: "on the character you are now forming hangs your own eternal destiny." Each must take charge of his or her own moral destiny. "By exercising self-possession, self-government, and, above all, self-reliance, he [the self-made man] placed himself beyond evil influences and became a law unto himself."[55]

Youths with fixed principles could not be led astray by companions. A frequent counsel was that "He who acts from a settled regard to duty is sure to sustain, in the eyes of his fellow men, a character of substantial excellence and worth ... he *will be respected*."[56] Formation of firm principles and manly character were Alger's recipe for gaining respect and having self-respect as well. Advice manual authors articulated a new version of the (self)work ethic: *"you may be whatever you resolve to be. Resolution is omnipotent"*; "real men" were self-made.

Boys who must count only upon themselves develop their manly self-reliance.[57] The presentation of the hero as orphan or apparent orphan, a common nineteenth century romantic plot device, figures in this context. With uncertain parentage and lacking place, station, or fixed identity, the Alger "orphan" creates his or her own identity and selfhood. Ragged Dick becomes, through his efforts, Richard Hunter, Esq. In the case of many of

Alger's orphans, successful creation of selfhood is *followed* by revelation of true heritage and access to material comfort. The hero regains a name and birthright only as a result of producing and owning his identity, proving his character and making his own way.[58]

In Alger's moral universe, all real men were self-made, for one was not born virtuous. Virtue and true manhood required work. Manliness connoted action, duty, and usefulness in the pursuit of some honorable calling.[59] These were not passive or contemplative virtues. Becoming self-made— owning one's own character—entails agency, struggle. This struggle defined the hero's triumph. It is in this sense the author can actually be described as the celebrator of self-made men.

By the middle decades of the nineteenth century, Americans dreamed of self-made men. They surely thought of something other than what the advice manual authors meant. "Surely *no young man* ... can prefer the brute power of money before the moral power of character," speaks the plaintive voice.[60] The complaint persisted: "this inordinate desire for money is the cause of countless failures. . . True manhood and true womanhood are involved in true success."[61] By mid-century, the danger of fascination with wealth would have to be confronted—it could no longer be escaped. Chapter 8 examines Alger's solution to the problem.

WHAT KIND OF SCHOOLING DID MANLINESS REQUIRE?

Alger's heroes clearly exhibit the moral and ethical conscience of the mid-nineteenth century Unitarians. Harvard Unitarians believed that humans were born with a moral faculty—with the potential to make moral judgments; in this sense they were equal. In contrast to the Calvinist doctrine of predestination, Alger's Unitarian heritage offered the universality of grace. And if some few lacked the capacity for virtue, Alger's moral story is nonetheless infused with a sense of possibility.

The obligation of firm character followed from the assurance that "there are such things as truth and falsehood; as right and wrong. These are, in their nature, immutable and eternal."[62] Immutable moral values are discoverable.

However, moral judgments were not mere instincts. The faculty must be made conscious—even possibly trained. Not all used this faculty.[63] What schooling, then, did virtue require? From whence came the Alger hero's firm sense of right and wrong?

Clearly, not from a Harvard education. Alger heros were not terribly reflective and certainly not philosophical. They may have had only rudimentary formal schooling, and most were not under influence of clergy. These adolescents had good instincts and discovered how to trust them. They augmented their common sense through valuable lessons learned in street school and by association with good guides. The education that tends to self-improvement was not monopolized by elites or their institutions: Neither Harvard nor the church mediated access. Alger even provided alternatives to the institution of the common school, which, in the middle decades of the century, was recommended to promote good behavior and moral development. Many looked to the common school for the Republic's virtue and well-being; institutionalized learning and literacy could combat poverty, vice, and crime.[64] But Alger boys and girls were sometimes unschooled, or torn from school in the formative years. If they would not be lost, the institutional pillars of presumed virtue must be replaceable. Benefactors and surrogate parents replaced family and church; home learning replaced formal education. Even the poorest Alger hero was likely to acquire a book to improve himself, learning how to read or teaching himself some other part of the common school curriculum. The most untutored could acquire the moral grammar.

Alger may have modeled his fictional boys on his revered woodsman, Natty Bumppo, unschooled and living apart from civilization. He judged character very well, disregarding social distinctions that did not depend on personal merit.

> A disbeliever in the ability of man to distinguish between good and evil without the aid of instruction would have been staggered by the character of this extraordinary inhabitant of the frontier ... no casuist could have made clear decisions in matters relating to right and wrong.[65]

Catherine Zuckert terms Natty the ideal democratic citizen. He can recognize and respect differences of ability, and he has independence and strong moral sense. "Because he listens so immediately and directly to his own natural impulses and sentiments, Natty is not deceived by appearances or impressed by conventional distinctions."[66]

Unschooled benevolent affections could go a long way toward maintaining the Republic. Alger had faith in the boy of the adolescent Republic and staked some faith in the democratic impulse.

"It is the heart and not the brain/ That to the Highest doth attain," Alger quoted from Longfellow in an ode he composed upon the latter's death in 1882.[67] It is as if, with the ethical sentimentalists of Adam Smith's era, Alger found the moral sense located in the emotional, not the rational part of the soul. Among Thomas Reid's "animal" (i.e., not rational) powers were the affections:

> The benevolent affections were natural and unreflective, seeking
> the good of others without conscious selfishness. Since they
> reflected a mere "instinctive sympathy" they did not partake of
> virtue until blessed by the rational moral sense. Yet the benevo-
> lent affections were beneficial, even essential, to the individual,
> since they provided the basis for society, without which man
> could not exist.

Benevolent affections included "Gratitude, pity, friendship, and parental
and filial love." Malevolent affections, prevalent among Alger foils, included
envy, contempt, and resentment.[68]

However, the Harvard moralists identified the moral sense with the
rational (our conscience "interprets to us God's love of virtue and hatred of
sin"). According to favored philosophers Thomas Reid and Dugald
Stewart, there were two rational powers: prudence and conscience. The
former was self-regarding, and the latter regarded duty and was equated
with the moral sense.[69] Alger's boys acquired both of these "rational
powers."

Alger had been influenced by ethical intuitionists and Cambridge
Platonists who saw "'goodness' or 'rightness' as simple, indefinable ideas,
perceived intuitively by human reason"; right—no less than truth—was
self-evident *if* one would only look. "Good sense is good judgment," Reid
held. Common sense and the moral sense were the tools to discover that one
should promote the general good.[70]

For Alger's Unitarian mentors, sentiments were an *aid* to conscience.
According to William Ellery Channing, "Sentiment is not mere feeling . . .
it is feeling penetrated with thought." Reason and desire were joined when
"the good life meant achieving a delight in virtue."[71] But since virtue
required more than benevolent affections, the Alger hero who chose to
perceive duty joined an elite class.

Selfishness was associated with acting upon desires contrary to the
interests of the community. Self-love was different. Gambling, drinking,
smoking, and self-indulgent spending were merely selfish. In the view of
T. S. Arthur, "Our object is, to make him [the boy] feel that he does not stand
alone in the world, and therefore should never permit himself to act from
purely selfish principles."[72] License is selfish. "Men were not created for
mendicity societies, and almshouses, and the gallows; but for competence,
and freedom, and virtue."[73] Responsibilities and duties the individual
maintained toward society and toward other individuals loomed far larger
in the discussion of these nineteenth century moralists than did rights.

Self-love was prudential self-regard and was generally not at odds with
conscience or duty; the temperance man displayed respect for himself and

also followed the dictates of conscience. Seeking comfort or gratification of desires were not evils per se, but "the appetites required regulation by higher powers."[74] Prudence was consistent with the moderate gratification of desires and appetites; it was inconsistent with violence and self-indulgence.

Temperance, modesty, honesty, restraint of anger, self-improvement, industry, frugality—virtues of Alger's boys and featured in the advice barrage from preachers—all partook of self-love and were components of duty.[75]

The virtuous person had, then, a balanced character; "True greatness... [lay in] self-mastery." Moderation and self-mastery produced *freedom*. "Only when a man was following the guidance of prudence and the moral sense was he free," according to Reid. The corollary was that "the man who was not the master of himself was the servant of sin."[76]

Alger internalized this Christianized Plato. If sophrosyne was the particular virtue of the bronze class in *The Republic*, it was the virtue of the ideal democratic citizen formulated in Harvard Yard.

IMPROVEMENT, OPTIMISM, REFORM

> Beware of companions whose moral character is below your own, unless you associate with them only to reform them. Avoid those who depreciate true worth, and speak lightly of the best class of citizens, and sneer at reforms...
>
> William Makepeace Thayer, *Success and Its Achievers*

Didactic though Alger's fiction may be, he translated much of the moral content of advice manual literature into a more lively and *optimistic* picture. If characters faced all the same dangers, the author nonetheless managed to play the exorcist. Villainous personae of the drama do not ultimately drag down the adolescent of the Republic. Setting the young down virtually alone in the city, Alger found good moral influences for them. Heroes could become men, even in the city of strangers and loose morals.

Those armed with the proper character would help others overcome moral danger. Ragged Dick; Mark, the Match Boy; Tattered Tom; Dodger in *Adrift in New York*; and Sam Barker from *Young Outlaw* and *Sam's Chance* all stand in testiment to the power of reform. Far from model young people, they only progress gradually toward good habits and respectability. Even the hero who steals on the street, from an employer, or from a friend can be rehabilitated through the good influence of another boy, a benefactor, or a lovely little girl.[77] A little moral encouragement and respect goes a long way for the ex-clergyman. Therefore, it follows (in the words of another advice author):

> All good members of society ought to make it an object, to give
> special patronage and encouragement to young men of worth
> and character . . . if young men could once be convinced that the
> patronage and favor of the respectable part of the community,
> and consequently their success in life, depend on their possessing
> a fair, unimpeachable character, it would have the happiest
> influence on their morals and habits.[78]

Since individual example can cure individual vice, the young people addressed should, themselves, "perform the angelic office of guardians and advisers to those who are younger than yourselves, and who look to you for example."[79] Alger's heroes do exactly this. Armed with firm character, they help safeguard the morals of the new generation, promote the interests of the community, and demonstrate that we can become more—rather than less—moral.

When first met, Alger's boy of common sense (wherever this sense is located) has good instinct but not yet virtue. Virtue requires some reflection and choice between good and evil.[80] Young protagonists acquire the capacity to use their rational moral sense only upon confronting and making moral choices. This confrontation requires exposure.

Contact and conflict with evil became the necessary condition of moral effort, thought clergyman Thomas Hughes:

> In that strife, then, the first requisite is courage or manfulness,
> gained through conflict with evil, —for without such conflict
> there can be no perfection of character, the end for which Christ
> says we were sent into this world.[81]

Alger apparently concurred. Innocence may sustain community, but innocence is not virtue. With the transition to manhood, the Alger hero acquires consciousness and conscience.

Alger sometimes remarked that going to the city was a kind of gamble that the young should not make if the odds of a decent life at home were good. Virtue *was* more easily protected, if less constantly tested, in the countryside. If the only way the boy could become "manly" was by having to choose between good and evil, what better choice than the city? Thus, it seems, the dialogue with the city must be joined after all.

The author dealt with this tension by providing a *doubly* happy ending to the rites of passage. One observer found that Alger

> . . . essays a half-solution by representing his heroes as bringing
> to Sodom the leaven of their home-town virtues. They improve

New York's moral tone and in exchange New York makes them rich.[82]

"The city must be recovered, recaptured as the city upon a hill."[83] Alger's youth confronts the perils of the city and both benefit. The hero becomes one of those to whom society can look for its regeneration.[84] By encouraging reform, heroes are actively preserving the Republic.

Character rehabilitation *is* social reform; it *is* the endproduct of political reform. The rehabilitation of Ragged Dick and his confrères suggests something quite different from degeneration. The Republic, through contact and association with vice, has lost its innocence. Only with trial and confrontation, however, can it hope to partake of virtue.

REPRISE

Contemporary jeremiads lamented the corruption that threatened a unique Republic with disintegration and degeneration, but their authors were generally ill-equipped to reach those who dreamed of the excitement of urban life, of opportunities, of the wonder of growth and change. Those lecturing youth—clergymen (John Todd, Joel Hawes, Henry Ward Beecher), educational reformers (William A. Alcott, Horace Mann), and popular sentimental writers (Timothy Shay Arthur) urged the formation of moral character, and, more often than not, feared the battle would be lost.[85] Alger's fiction also recalled the young to their original principles. But the tone of alarm in the face of danger was not there: he expected this battle to be won.

In Alger's allegory, authority of conscience and continuity of character were essential. Some subset of adolescents must win this struggle if the freedom and integrity of the community were to be preserved. However, even those who fell short of true morality but who were guided by good instincts contributed importantly to the task. The "gratitude and affection" with which the Roman people bound themselves to Cicero—benevolent affections, not virtue—would always remain the most powerful bonds in the community. For the optimist, those who were not vicious but who either avoided confrontation with evil or who fell short in the struggle to attain true manhood could, nonetheless, recognize and appreciate virtue. Both classes— heroes and their welcomers—contribute to the happy prognosis for the adolescent Republic.

Alger never wavered in his moral certitude. The principles by which one should live and according to which members of society should treat one another were eternal. At this level, the universe was known and knowable.

On the eve of the twentieth century, most Americans probably still presumed the morality of the universe and felt certain of moral and political judgments.[86]

Religions could adhere to such a worldview in the twentieth century, along with westerns and other genres in popular culture. However, by the end of World War I, men and women in intellectual and literary circles lost this moral certainty.[87] This turning point may demarcate a real end to the illusion of unity between elite and mass culture.

4

———

Guidebooks for Survival in an Industrializing Economy

The times were hard. There were thousands out of employment, and fifty applications where there was one vacancy. Day
after day he answered advertisements without effect.

Alger, *Adrift in the City*

Alger characters have long been seen as symbols of success, but that success
is much misunderstood. What has escaped recognition is the rootedness of
Alger's discourse in the economic transformations of the second half of the
nineteenth century and the extent to which his texts engage these massive
changes. This context is central to the very definition of success.

Alger wrote in—and for—a rapidly changing economic and social
universe. The author was well-attuned to the destruction of the old order
and established a correspondence to the economic environment of the
reader at this level. Tales describe a world full of cares, economic pitfalls, and
anxieties.[1] Hardship, disruption, and uncertainty are central to understanding
the Alger formula. Alger has painted a grim world that is only too real.

These works offer guidebooks about weathering the transitions of the
emerging order. Alger has no recipe for spectacular success; rather, he
presents a map for survival—survival which is *literally* at issue in each story.
Locating and defining failure is also vital to understanding the measure of
economic success.

Like other popular fiction texts, these texts offer "a blueprint for
survival under a specific set of political, economic, social, or religious

53

conditions . . ." [2] Quite a few members of the contemporary audience could respond to the idiom, which fit some important features of its immediate context. And by such measures of the success or failure of a *text*, *Ragged Dick* and its companion volumes were more successful than most of Alger critics have allowed.

FORM AND SUBSTANCE

In Chapter 3, we showed how Alger educated his readers to dangers by teaching them how to read character. While Ragged Dick Hunter escorts Frank Whitney around the city, he explains some of the ruses used in confidence games and petty thievery. Often, however, communication between the author and the reader performs the same function. The style and form of Alger's writing affords insight into the classes and categories of young people the author appeared to be addressing.

Each of these novels incorporates a ritual of trial and transcendence. With only a few basic plots, part of the comfort and hope in these works may come from the mere repetition of the formula. Formulas and stereotyped, one-dimensional characters help simplify a complex world.   The pattern reassures fears: trials can be overcome, fortuitous accidents can happen, virtue can triumph, and quick and clever boys can outwit evil antagonists.[3] Traditional values are reasserted in a rapidly changing environment. The emerging landscape is made more predictable.

Sensational, formulaic plots may be seen as addressing "problems concerning the relations among people of different sexes, races, social classes, ethnic groups, [and] economic levels."   Endless rescue scenes, family separations, and trials that violate laws of probability offer solutions for social and political problems:

> The function of these scenarios is heuristic and didactic rather
> than mimetic, they do not attempt to transcribe in detail a
> parabola of events as they "actually happen" in society;
> rather, they provide a basis for remaking the social and political
> order in which events take place.[4]

Stereotypes serve to identify who is one of us and who is not—they help constitute identity when so many are strangers.[5] Such cultural shorthand helped many Americans cope with the dramatic change in the composition of the population, as roughly 16.7 million persons immigrated in the latter half of the century and non-English speakers rapidly joined the ranks after 1880.[6] In Alger's fiction, some Western

European migrants have come to be "of us"; the Irish, Italians, Germans, Chinese, ex-slaves, and Jews have not. Jews, never formally identified as such, are identified by their names and their relationship to money. Scottish-Americans are sometimes singled out for their thrift.

Stereotypes provide codes for action. In popular fiction, Jane Tompkins has argued,

> stereotypes are the instantly recognizable representatives of overlapping racial, sexual, national, ethnic, economic, social, political, and religious categories; they convey enormous amounts of cultural information in an extremely condensed form ... [they] operate as cultural shorthand, and because of their multilayered representative function are the carriers of strong emotional associations. Their familiarity and typicality, rather than making them bankrupt or stale, are the basis of their effectiveness as integers in a social equation.[7]

Furthermore, formula writing itself affords an important device for addressing a world fraught with uncertainty. It is not only essential that the hero transcend dangers but that readers understand these dangers if they are to act in the face of the unknown. A hero's "greenness" was cured for the reader—a surrogate for experience acquired the hard way. Alger frequently let the audience in on secrets the hero did not know.

Or, the secrets yielded to the reader of multiple Algers. Lessons in survival were available through ritual repetition—formula writing. (Re)readers could become quick studies, watching characters step into pitfalls they themselves have learned to identify. With formulas, the audience can master cues and warning signs from the environment; they can acquire a sense of efficacy and worldliness.

But what cues from the environment must one read in order to survive as an economic actor? This chapter and Chapter 5 examine the kinds of economic dangers and disruptions Alger saw, named, or addressed directly and indirectly. Chapter 4 addresses the discourse of Alger and his contemporaries concerning hardship and dislocation; Chapter 5 turns to the problem of industrial labor. In each of these chapters, we discover that the lenses through which Alger and his contemporaries permitted themselves to see economic changes—and the language they employed to talk about them—were ground by history, class, and culture.

A WORLD OF HARDSHIP
AND UNCERTAINTY

Picturing Hard Times

The panic of 1857 brought an end to the period of economic expansion that prevailed during most of Alger's youth. The panic of 1873, fueled in considerable measure by speculators, occasioned a lengthy ensuing depression. Panics and instability recurring in the final three decades of the century disrupted homes, farms, communities, and workplaces.

Alger's guidebooks reference many anxieties and tensions of this period and do so far more realistically and critically than is recognized. Heroes, families, and friends experience the economic and social fallout of industrial development directly or metaphorically.

Disruption of the family, of traditional means of earning a livelihood— whether through trades and crafts or agriculture—and attrition of small towns are all pronounced. Local boundaries and barriers were breaking apart; the market was extending its domain. The worth of one's "human capital" increasingly depended upon the state of general commerce.

Many heroes began life in a small town in New England, where we are given to understand there were no economic opportunities for advancement or even for adequate existence. These small towns were not vital; those who could stay and survive were heirs to wealth or had relatives who could provide positions. There were a few jobs in the local economy for the boy who must help his family (school janitor, farm hand, dry goods clerk), but these merely permit the hero to modestly supplement the family budget. As city boy *Phil, the Fiddler* discovered, "though there is less privation in the country, there is also less money."[8]

Life is not easy on the farm, where we first meet some characters. We may be told that some can live comfortably by farming through skillful management and luck, but the people Alger introduces us to rarely do so. The hero's family is usually faced with debt and mortgages they cannot pay off. Many houses and farms are foreclosed; families sink deeper and deeper into debt, suffering many privations. Often, no lending institutions exist, leaving the family at the mercy of unscrupulous or usurious individuals.

The fiction approximates a pattern of farm experiences of the period. The 1870s and 1880s witnessed widespread deflation and a worldwide drop in grain prices; farmers faced increasing difficulties and became indebted to eastern banks. Nationally, the percentage of gainful workers employed in agriculture declined from 50% to 37% in the last three decades of the century.[9] In New York and New England, the disappearance of farms was even more obvious. With the exception of Vermont, which retained 42% of its population in agriculture in the 1890 Census, all other states in the region were significantly less agrarian, with agricultural pursuits accounting from between 7.5% and 16% of the population.[10]

Some heroes enjoyed middle- or upper-middle class comfort and a classical education until dispossessed or orphaned near the story's outset. Occasionally, father loses his money in stock swindles, then dies.

In other class settings, father is usually dead. Occasionally, father is a cast as a skilled craft worker, rendered economically ineffectual when laid off or let go because business in his particular trade is slow, or the business fails or is sold.[11] Father absence, in Alger, also means there is no family business or trade into which a hero could step.

By the time the hero leaves home, the traditional family has ceased to be a viable economic unit. Some Alger stories blame outsiders. One of the most common threats to the hero's survival is posed when a widowed mother or father remarries.[12] By forging wills and dominating the real parent, stepparents insinuate their own arrogant progeny into superior economic position in the household. The stepparent then contrives to relieve him/herself of the care of the legitimate heir. Even members of the extended family are suspect, as uncles perform similar roles or defraud their relations. The inevitable consequence of such machinations is that the hero is set adrift in the world—disinherited.

The wealthiest man in town, usually called "Squire," similarly poses a threat to the hero's family. Squires have often acquired their wealth by theft and deceit. Such men hold neighbors at their mercy and contribute to their economic hardships. Attempts to defraud a poor widow of her home are common; sometimes, the squire's object is to pressure the woman into marriage. Squires wrong a family repeatedly to secure ill-gotten gains.[13]

Wherever they are found at the commencement of the story line, virtually all central characters must earn their living or help support the family.[14] Fictitious youth are introduced into the workforce while the number of children engaged in nonagricultural labor was increasing.

Individual migrations figure repeatedly as families and generations are split apart. In private dramas, these stories reflect the pattern of migration from villages and countryside to cities, especially to New York, as the number of people living in cities increased fivefold from 1860 to 1900.[15]

Disruption and dislocation are virtual constants in the Alger formula. These stories are not characteristically rich in detail, but the kind of detail that did capture the author's attention heightens awareness that these are novels attuned to hard times and deprivation. Despite the author's own travels in the West and in Europe, fictional journeys and interludes of high-seas adventure provide rather little to satisfy his readers' curiosity about things exotic. Whether mining for gold, travelling aboard ship to Australia or aboard trains on western adventures, central characters are merely engaged in alternative forms of the struggle for survival.

The struggle for food, clothing, and shelter are major preoccupations. Among the most prevalent details are those concerning restricted diet and the cost of a meal. Great attention is devoted to what is on the hero's table and whether there is enough for him to eat his fill. Many protagonists can be found far from home, with no knowledge from whence their next meal will come. For some characters, being reduced to dining on bread alone is an all-too-frequent occurrence.

Money is a constant topic of conversation or concern. The reader's attention is constantly directed to the cost of making ends meet; to patches on clothing and cheap fabrics the hero and his family don. Buying a new suit, a dress for mother or sister, or acquiring an overcoat are major events. We know exactly what the hero earns per day or per week. We know his expenses and watch him carefully calculate how much he can save—if anything. Central characters can rarely afford niceties or common amusements. When a boy or girl is allowed a trip to the theater or circus, Alger will often turn it into more than mere diversion; the event may become a means of economic salvation.[16]

Whether thrown out into the world by accident or malice, the hero is "freed" from the land, and he is almost always "free" to go to the big city. The family or family fragment, no longer the locus of economic production, undergoes a separation of private and public. The family may remain the locus of affective ties but work—at least for males—takes place in a different space. In the city, only tramp-thieves, poor women, and street children live and work in the same space.

Oliver Conrad "like all boys . . . fancied a change" and wanted to go to New York to obtain a business position in *Adrift in the City*. He thought it would be much more agreeable to live in New York than in a quiet little country village where nothing was going on. The author commented:

> This was a natural feeling, but there was another side to the question which Oliver did not consider. How many families in the great, gay city are compelled to live in miserable tenements amid noise and vicious surroundings, who, on the same income could live comfortably and independently in the country, breathing God's pure air, and with nothing to repel or disgust them?[17]

Although aware that the dream of escape to the big city was linked with excitement for many small town and country readers, Alger frequently remarked that many boys would be economically better off staying in the country, since many do not succeed in the city.

But most heroes have little choice, and once the boy gets to the city, the author provides an introduction to city sights, scenes, and architecture. Some novels take the reader on a guided tour of Manhattan sights, with perhaps even an expedition by ferry to Brooklyn. The streetwise hero is engaged as a guide for a relative stranger; Dick shows Frank Whitney the sights for several days and eight chapters in *Ragged Dick*.

There was sufficient detail that more than one Alger enthusiast has claimed that these books were veritable Baedeker's guides to "Old New York streets and landmarks."[18] A newspaper source eighteen years after Alger's death attempted to demonstrate, by wandering the streets through the eyes of Alger's characters, that "Horatio Alger, jr., has left us one of the few accurate pictures of a great city in the making"; his descriptions were compared with Dickens's London and Hugo's Paris.[19] Because the pre-Civil War city provided the backdrop for some of his stories, an authorial comment frequently noted that a structure is since gone, or that Central Park is now much more complete.

Readers encounter the great hotels, but the lesser hotels around City Hall, which offer the warmth of their heaters to freezing lads in winter, also make their appearance, for Alger's "minute knowledge of the New York of his day was gained from the boys about whom he wrote." The gaze and judgments of the street children completed the portrait of the city's personality.[20]

Urban detail offered most frequently indicates a purpose other than providing a travelogue. According to one historian:

> In large part these books existed and thrived because they provided an easy and terror-free way of making possible rural adaptation to urban life. You could find out *what* to do, *where* to go, *how* to begin, and *how* to proceed in the city. They are effortless guidebooks, not simply to success but to life in the city. They were how-to-do-it books ... A young man from the country could brief himself on transportation around the city, the ways to obtain lodging and employment ...[21]

Only outsiders—newcomers—had a need for guidebooks to the big city, and at least Alger's many city stories may well have served such a function. *Ragged Dick, Ben, the Luggage Boy,* and other such tales offer some kinds of reliable data on the city, its dangers, and its hierarchies.

Alger, who himself lived in boardinghouses during a good part of his thirty years in New York, duly noted the expense and respectability of various neighborhoods in which boardinghouses were to be found. The author "shows himself to be as astute a recorder of the differences between the four or five lowest grades of boardinghouses as Balzac could have wished to be."[22] Readers learned *where* one moved to move "up" in the world as they watched boys moving further uptown to provide more desirable lodgings for their families. The weekly cost of lodging and the type of accommodation one's money would procure are rarely neglected. Alger may warn the reader that the prices mentioned are old—that lodging costs more now—so in case the reader is entertaining thoughts of coming to the city to seek his fortune, he is forewarned.[23] There is an occasional forray into Delmonico's, but the location of clean but cheap restaurants and what a dime will procure on the plate are much more frequently noted.

The guidebook also told of places to be avoided. Fairly vivid portraits of crushing poverty, ill-health, and squalor on the Lower East Side of Manhattan appear. The reader's eyes are sometimes directed down the most impoverished streets and into its tenements. But more often, we glance and pass by quickly. Alger called Baxter Street

> one of the most wretched spots in the city, lined with miserable tenement houses, policy shops, and second-hand stores. Whoever passes through it in the evening will do well to look to the safety of his pocketbook and watch, if he is imprudent enough to carry either in a district where the Ten Commandments are unknown, or unregarded.[24]

And similarly, of Rector Street, near Trinity Church:

> Just in the rear of the great church and extending down to the wharves, is a collection of miserable dwellings, occupied by tenants upon whom the near presence of the sanctuary appears to produce little impression of a salutary character.[25]

This statement is not just about the housing quality and living conditions of a neighborhood; there is a distinct bourgeois gaze. It is a statement about a community and its values—its difference and its apparent removal from the moral universe of decent folk. It is a warning to others. The community has taken on a character, attributed to the morals of its members—this is how difference is understood when a community comes to be a community apart. Other Alger boardinghouse communities may mix characters in the same space, but these spaces have residents whose behavior is unintelligible, different, and ungodly. These spaces, at night at least, are offlimits. Alger does not see them as different *class* spaces but as godless places.

Danger to Property

With increasing privatization of property and decreasing sense of community, violation of liquid or fixed assets generated serious problems of survival. In Alger's fiction, property is always under siege, and danger to life and limb result. Loss of property is, again, generally blamed on evildoers.

All sorts of cold, calculating men and women have designs on liquid and fixed assets; they are happy to rob poor orphans of their last few dollars. Scoundrels and foils practice the arts of fraud and deceit. Bandits, pickpockets, counterfeiters, forgers, and confidence men fill the pages. Characters are robbed at gunpoint, knifepoint, or are bludgeoned for money or other possessions; they are sometimes placed in repeated jeopardy at the hands of the same villain.[26] Pickpockets slip into the hero's wallet on trains and other conveyances, and thieves steal into hotel rooms at night. Often, the overtrusting boy has innocently dangled information in front of the thief.

The outlaw, and especially the road agent, appears in fiction about the time of the railroad strike of 1877. This figure appears in Alger, especially— although not exclusively—in stories involving western travel. Other authors depicted fictional outlaws, such as the popular *Deadwood Dick*, as heroes, akin to the social bandits and peasant outlaws of earlier tales. In the dime novel, "the period which turns institutions like banks into quintessential public villains and bankrobbery into the most readily understood form of robbing the rich marks the adaptation of social banditry to capitalism."[27]

Unlike such portrayals, Alger's outlaw is merely another unsympathetic character preying off value created by others. In confrontation with the outlaw, an Alger hero outwits the villain or forfeits his own slender resources rather than those of his employer.

Kidnapping occurs frequently as some antagonist seeks ill-gotten gains. Wealthy children are kidnapped for ransom; kidnapped children may be used to pass counterfeit money; or a hero may be kidnapped and slated for death because he stands in the way of plans for illicit gain.[28] Kidnapping of a hero prior to the outset of the story is an occasional motif fueling children's fantasies of being adopted (and thus being someone other than who they seem). In a few sensational cases, the boy is really heir to a fortune.[29]

Evil characters intervene in a dying relation's disposition of property. They forge, hide, or destroy wills. Impatient for wealthy relatives to expire to get their hands on a fortune, the unsentimental help relations out of this world.[30] Amid such threats, it is hard for central figures to hold on to what little they have. Deprived by ruse or theft, nothing stands between the hero and starvation except himself—his character—his only valuable property as he seeks work in order to live. And even his character frequently comes under attack. Mean-spiritied co-workers frame a boy for a theft they or their friends committed. Employees contrive to have the hero lose his job because they believe the position should go to a relative (a slacker). Co-workers, jealous of the favor and rewards an employer showers upon a good worker, arrange an incident that costs the hero his job. Employers fire boys on the basis of hearsay and circumstantial evidence when money disappears. The formerly valued and trusted employee finds himself let go without a letter of reference, which would enable him to get another position; he may even be arrested. These attacks, threatening reputation or character, are especially grave. This loss is worse than losing money because one can be deprived of the means of earning a livelihood.

FAILURES

> If I stayed [in New York], I'd be a bootblack all my life . . . There
> ain't no chance for a boy like me to rise. I wouldn't want to be a
> bootblack . . . when I got to be old and gray-headed.
>
> Julius, an illiterate street boy in Horatio Alger, *Julius, the
> Street Boy* [31]

The now-famous boys and girls populating Alger's early Ragged Dick series live hand-to-mouth on the streets of New York, existing by their wits. Each day is an exercise in survival and a scramble for food and shelter.[32]

Benefactors and surrogate parents help some figures escape poverty and the dangerous shoals of adolescence. Not all escape. "Turning bad" is the most frequent scenario Alger envisioned for those who are not rescued. Youngsters who cannot earn a living wage by their labors, who have minimal education, and who develop vices are likely to turn to crime. Crime, prostitution, yielding to strong drink and gambling, homelessness, and long-term economic marginalization are among the ways to fail.

Charles Loring Brace, social worker, author, and provider of some of Alger's source material, included in the "Proletaires of New York" a large class of criminals and paupers, the only saving grace of whom is that this life is not yet "so deeply stamped in the blood" as their English counterparts. The "dangerous classes" of New York " . . . are as ignorant as London flash-men or costermongers. They are far more brutal than the peasantry from whom they descend . . ."[33]

"The fortunes of a street waif, second stage." (Charles Loring Brace, *The Dangerous Classes of New York, and Twenty Years' Work Among Them*. New York: Wynkoop & Hallenbeck, 1872, reprinted NASW Classics Series, n.d., illustration opposite p. 32.)

In addition to vagrants and criminal elements, Brace observed

> still other tens of thousands, poor, hard-pressed, and depending
> for daily bread on the day's earnings, swarming in tenement-
> houses, who behold the gilded rewards of toil all about them, but
> are never permitted to touch them.[34]

Most of the poor Alger displays are widows, orphans, invalids, and those who have succumbed to drink and gambling. Alger's homeless men and women are occasionally glimpsed in ten-cent lodging houses, sleeping *en masse* on straw-covered floors. Others inhabit community poor homes, asylums, or squalid, crowded tenements. There is an occasional glimpse of men walking the streets in search of work, and an occasional male in a ten-cent lodging house has, we learn, grown disspirited and given up.

But how did Alger and his contemporaries view the nonworking, able-bodied male population in this period—or more precisely, how did they understand the emerging phenomenon of mass unemployment? If any spectacle appeared to controvert the "logic" of the self-help formulas, it should be this.

Tramps

The economic slump in the 1870s "created for the first time a national specter of huge groups of workers deprived of their means of livelihood."[35] However, rarely were the unemployed "discovered." What *was* "discovered" during this period was the tramp. "It was ideological naming of the new phenomenon of unemployment."[36]

The noun "tramp" came into vogue after the panic of 1873, with the great increase in numbers and type of jobless Americans, with a concomitant rise in vagrancy. A very early use of the noun "tramp" occurred in the *New York Times* in February, 1875. During the decade, tramps were increasingly discovered in cities, the countryside, and along transportation lines. Magazine, newspaper, and reform interest in tramps rose during economic downturns.[37]

Alger discovered the tramp as well. Serialization of *Tony, the Tramp* began to appear in the *New York Weekly* in 1876. The tramp and his ward-hero are at center stage in this story, and it is considered "one of the earliest appearances of the tramp in fiction."[38]

In Alger's 1876 rendition, the "uncle" voluntarily pursued his life as a tramp; the boy was merely compelled by circumstance. It is not inconsequential that Tony correctly refuses to believe he is related to his tramp-guardian, Rudolph. Character might be inheritable, with tramps passing on their degeneracy to progeny. One influential study released in

1877 traced generations of criminals found in an Ulster County, New York jail; the next year, another author argued that "tramps were actually a tribe that passed 'bad blood' from one generation to the next."[39] Since tramps were frequently depicted as recent immigrants, the notion of inheritable character defects probably added fuel to religious and ethnic group hostilities.

Alger's tramps believe they are owed a living; rather than create value, they live by begging or transferring the property of others into their own hands. They are lazy, thieving, drunken reprobates. On rare occasions, a tramp of some education and intelligence makes his appearance, "qualified to earn a good living in some respectable position"; however, "drink was his enemy and was likely to be through his life."[40] Alger shared with many contemporaries the view that character defects explained the tramp.

In American popular ideology, the vision of the tramp as an adult who would not seek work was pervasive. The tramp was often portrayed as a "lazy, incorrigible, cowardly, utterly depraved savage"; this image has been recycled as part of the American discourse about unemployed urban African-Americans in the late twentieth century.[41]

Linkages between tramping, unemployment, and industrial upheavals occurred to relatively few, and even fewer "mainstream" intellectuals and social reformers. At the 1877 meeting of the Conference of Boards of Public Charities (a section of the American Social Science Association) at Saratoga Springs, "the idea that men *could not* find work was absurd in the judgment of the delegates." An influential scholar and charity organizer defined tramps broadly as "all idle persons . . . not having any visible means of support...wandering about...and not giving good account of themselves."[42]

As the 'science' of philanthropy grew, tramping was often attributed to the effects of indiscriminate charity.[43] Tramps, some argued, were being attacted to the city by excessive generosity without concern for need. Writing of an especially work-averse tramp encampment on the banks of the Schuylkill River, an otherwise sympathetic observer echoed many reform voices: "The almshouse is conveniently near, and these lazy crowds, from some unexplainable reason, are kept pretty well supplied from that institution."[44]

Ragged Dick may have slept under wagons in New York in 1867, but his successors could have had a hard time of it. Confinement was one popular response to the tramp phenomenon, as evidenced by the rise of vagrancy legislation. If Alger's young Italian boy in *Phil, the Fiddler* (1872) wandered unfamiliar streets and roads in the environs of Newark, playing tunes on his violin for a few pennies, he was not likely to do so freely for long. New Jersey passed the nation's first antitramp legislation in 1876.[45] Other northern states in the temperate zone followed.

"Laws making criminal offenses out of begging, aimless wandering, and alms soliciting would allow authorities to jail tramps and to put them to work at hard labor."[46] Such legislation presumed there was ample work for willing, able-bodied men. If vagrancy laws were pervasive, the tramp would find no advantage in moving from one place to another.

Vagrancy arrests in New York City almost doubled between 1876 and 1877. The use of police station house lodging, where tramps had been able to seek warmth on a one-night basis, was cut back. Many reformers claimed the decrease in the number of tramps in New York by 1881 stemmed from the success of the antitramp legislation rather than from an amelioration of hard times.[47] The problem would recur.

The downturn of the mid-1880s brought the focus of charity organizations onto children. Part of the effort was the discovery of imposters; one reformer said people looked upon the New York Charity Organization Society (founded 1882) as an "anti-mendacity league" or a "detective society for preventing imposition and bringing swindlers to justice." Half the respondents to an 1886 questionnaire sent to various societies, organizations, public officials, and philanthropists by the National Conference of Charities and Corrections believed that only one in ten tramps was a genuine workman. "Ninety percent felt that at least one out of every two unemployed was by nature a tramp." In the survey, the major causes of tramping were still seen as personal failure, immigration, heredity, and indiscriminate charity.[48]

With the Paris Commune of 1871 an uneasy memory, the terms "army," "tramp," and "communist" were often conjoined in literature and the press. Some elites posited a connection between the labor violence of 1877 and tramps. Tramps were blamed for railroad violence and other organized, militant acts. For many, the link between tramps and industrial troublemakers was obvious. Professor Francis Wayland of Yale, charity organization president from New Haven, told the Saratoga Springs conference in 1877 that "'the inner history of the recent disgraceful and disastrous riots' in some principal cities revealed how large detachments of 'our great standing army of professional tramps' rather than the 'so-called strikers' were mainly responsible for the destruction of valuable property." Wayland suggested that tramps were at war with all social institutions and implied there was a central agency under which they were loosely organized.[49]

Newspapers were quick to sensationalize crimes committed by tramps, and attack the "tramp evil."[50] In the 1870s, some American newspapers proposed, or applauded, the extermination of tramps: "A wrecked freight car invariably means a dead tramp. It's an expensive but effective way of getting rid of a very undesirable class of nuisances."[51]

It appeared to be a fairly widely shared public perception that tramps constituted an organization. Tramps *were* increasingly found in groups in the 1870s:

> Where they previously existed as single wandering vaga-
> bonds, they now have increased until they travel in herds, and,
> through the dire necessity of their pitiable condition, justly
> create some anxiety and alarm.[52]

In the late 1870s, "communities of outcasts" could be found along the Eastern seaboard states. "In a strip of wood on the Darby road, near Philadelphia, and in a most picturesque spot, is a regular settlement of tramps, who live in the same place winter and summer." Some were more or less permanently established; others formed and broke up like gypsy camps.[53]

Even during the panic of 1893, public imagery, newspapers, and reformers made little if any distinction between the involuntarily unemployed individual and the tramp.[54] Coxey's army of the unemployed, which marched on Washington in 1894, was popularly viewed as composed almost exclusively of tramps. The *Nation* argued, on that occasion, that tramp movements were a national disgrace, only encouraging the "Henrys" who were seeking the fruits of labor, not labor. To allow such disorder to persist without retribution would endanger the country much as France had been prior to the Revolution.[55]

Only after two decades of study following the panic of 1893 did reformers begin to conclude that "most men assumed to be voluntary tramps were on the road because of involuntary unemployment." When the Populist Governor of Kansas set aside the state's vagrancy statute by executive decree in December, 1893, it was "the beginning of a widespread recognition that a connection existed between hard times and tramps."[56]

As the tramp was discovered as a category for relief, charity, study, and legislation, Alger's sympathies were enlisted more than some contemporaries. He sought help and well-placed charity rather than incarceration for young street vagabonds. However, it is probably not accidental that most of his rough street heroes and even *Tony, the Tramp* appear prior to the period of greatest public concern and hostility. After promising the rehabilitation of a baggage smasher, Alger editorializes:

> If the community, while keeping vigilant watch over the young
> outcasts that throng our streets, plying their petty avocations,
> would not always condemn, but encourage them sometimes to

a better life, the results would soon appear in the diminution of
the offenses for which they are most frequently arrested.[57]

Allan Pinkerton, detective and strikebreaker, likewise argued against
severe measures taken to eradicate the tramp problem, because it could not
be done: "Like the poor, we shall always have them with us." Alger puts
the same sentiment in the mouth of the hero's mother in *Luke Walton*.
Pinkerton's 1878 work makes a plea that is practically written into several
Alger works, save for one significant detail:

> During this period, when the hard hand of necessity bears down
> so heavily alike upon business man and workingman, and when
> we, who may be situated in comfort, are so apt to forget the keen
> needs of thousands of our fellows who have fought the fight
> against persistent and relentless misfortune, and fallen, there
> should be a more general leniency towards a class who are made
> up of people often as good as we; and some charity should be
> exercised, rather than a relentless war inaugurated, the result of
> which will only be to reclaim no one of them, and rapidly increase
> crime and criminals.[58]

This plea echoes Alger's appeal for street children like Sam in *Sam's Chance*,
the central characters of *Rufus and Rose* (both of which antedate this
Pinkerton plea), and foreshadows the later speech of young Luke Walton,
who complained about how some of the rich treat poor newsboys in
Chicago.

But once adult miscreants figure instead, Alger's voice falls silent. Never
exhibiting the level of hostility voiced by some members of the community,
Alger finds the adult tramp to be a scourge afflicting decent, hard-working
citizens. A few adult tramps are rehabilitated in Alger; most are not. Only
voluntary self-reform will restore this person to economy and society. The
rootless stranger—whether tramp, bandit, or confidence man—threatened
property and upset the moral order of the community.

Alger's fictional tramps are lone, fleeting, male figures, outside the
community. They were neither representatives of the ranks of the
unemployed nor communists; they did not travel in groups. It is unlikely,
then, that he held tramp armies and gangs accountable for the violence
attributed to them.

If a figure's "outward appearance and shabby habiliments proclaimed
him a tramp," looks may be deceiving.[59] Alger did not begrudge the adult
tramp a meal; Ragged Dick and Tattered Tom could not be judged by their
tattered clothing. Especially among the young, stock must be taken of
character. Given the popular prejudice that the person in rags is a tramp,
perhaps it is especially important that, rarely fashionably attired, a very poor

hero and his family can always take pride in being neat and clean. When on the road or penniless in the city, this boy would be less likely to resemble the tramp.

Tramping or Working?

> Luke Walton: I have sometimes seen gentlemen, handsomely dressed, and evidently with plenty of money, speak roughly to these young [news]boys. It always makes me indignant. Why should they have so easy a time, while there are so many who don't know where their next meal is coming from? Why, what such a man spends for his meals in a single day would support a poor newsboy in comfort for a week.

> Mrs. Walton: My dear Luke, this is a problem which has puzzled older and wiser heads than yours. There must always be poor people, but those who are more fortunate ought at least to give them sympathy. It is the least acknowledgment they can make for their own more favored lot.
>
> Alger, Luke Walton

Two authors gaze at a scene on a New York City Hall Park bench. Alger's Wren Winter of *A Rolling Stone* arrives in the city with little if any money, no job, and no place to go. Pondering his next step as he sits on a park bench, the boy encounters a man. And what kind of adult male lounges on a bench in City Hall Park? He was "a bloated and shabby man of middle age, whose red face indicated that he did not practice prohibition or approve of the prohibitory law." He "was a man who preferred to live on other people's money, rather than work for himself." After being refused the nickel he asks of the hero, he absconds with the boy's entire worldly possessions: "[Wren] saw the tramp, for this term describes him, hurrying across the park with the bundle in his hand." The man is eventually captured and handed to the police.[60]

Pinkerton looked upon such a park bench scene differently as he described the Manhattan migratory pattern of tramp printers in the summer. Pinkerton's tramps hold an identifiable place in an occupational-class structure:

> These careless fellows will hang about the printing-offices, hide about for printers in luck to borrow a "half-case" (a half-dollar) from them, and sun themselves in City Hall Square upon the benches until night. Then the police will drive them out, and, in company with the "pan-jerkers"—all that large class of loafers who subsist by rendering some slight service about restaurants—

they begin "moving on." By eight o'clock, down every approach
to the lower part of the island, will be seen these squads of tramps
straggling along to the Battery; and by midnight hundreds will
be asleep upon the benches, leaning against lamp-posts, stretched
upon the ground, and even lying upon the wharf with their
ragged legs hanging over . . .[61]

In Alger novels, dangerous, unsavory figures wander the streets, the
roads, and countryside. Many are depicted as perennial itinerants; many
are tramps. The thief and his colleague in *Forging Ahead* were introduced in
a way suggesting a systematic danger: "In the summer season, not a few
of the desperate characters who, at other times, lurk in the lanes and alleys
in our cities, start out on vagabond tramps through the country districts."[62]

The migration pattern noted by Alger *was* common—the tramp travelled
in specifically urban patterns and often took to the countryside in the
summer months but returned to the cities in colder seasons. "They used
cities as the hubs of their information networks, travelling back from a farm
to a city, then moving out to another farm or to a forest or another city." "The
essence of a tramp's working career was erratic employment, of seasonal
work overlaid with hundreds of varying jobs and locales." In the spring and
fall, they often worked on farms; in the summer, they might be found
working construction trades, or serving as skilled artisans or unskilled
hands in factories and shops.[63]

Tramps could be found cutting ice, lumbering forests, and shoveling coal
and snow in the winter, but they also followed railroad tracks to the cities
and sought shelter in police stations and charitable institutions.[64] Tramps
filled cheap lodging rooms such as were described by Alger in *Tattered Tom*
and begged on street corners.

Pinkerton reminded readers that tramping could be a rational means of
pursuing one's craft. In Europe,

> after a mechanic of any sort had completed his term of appren-
> ticeship, custom made it imperative that he turn journeyman,
> which is only another word for tramp, and pass from one part of
> the country to another, and often into other countries, to improve
> and perfect his trade by coming in contact with other journey-
> men, observing how work was done in other shops, and generally
> bettering his skill and practice.[65]

The tramp was a man "walking to work"; tramping was "an expected
and rational part of the search for work." Single males, in especially bad
times, were joined by married males wandering for a livelihood.[66] Migration
patterns were linked to rail networks and to regional economic conditions.

Not only the unskilled took to the roads. Workers in construction trades often tramped because their work had different geographical loci; carpenters tramped to find the next job, using networks such as hearsay, information from fellow craft or tradesmen, and advertisements. Late in the century, union publications served as an important information link between the itinerant artisan and potential employers. By the turn of the century, unionized cigar makers tramped.[67]

Miners moved from job to job and between wage-labor and prospecting as new discoveries were made. Many men travelled great distances—and even from Europe—to come to the mines, lured by the West, by high wages, or by the desire to "become rich suddenly" in precious metal mining. High wages reflected labor shortages that persisted in mining in this period.[68] But with mining increasingly tied into the world market and affected by global factors such as the silver panic of 1893 and copper prices in Paris, there was considerable employment instability. Butte, Montana, known for its job opportunities, witnessed such an oversupply of job-seekers in 1885 that "as many as 20 and 30 can be counted at one time round every hoisting work supplicating for work which they cannot get," and were forced to remain because they did not wish to "count railroad ties on an empty stomach ..."[69]

Whatever the reasons for tramping, it was an experience claimed to have had a significant impact on the practitioner:

> The effect of tramping upon any person is to make him keenly alive to the fine generalship of living without work, and existing when work cannot be secured. He cannot but become a sort of guerilla on the outskirts of civilization.[70]

Tramping was, said Pinkerton, an education in self-reliance; among the self-made men are "countless persons who have been made all that they are or have been, by this peculiar educational process." He asserted that "Many of our greatest men ... have either at some time been unqualified tramps, or have done considerable of what might be called real vagabond tramping."[71] Alger also endorsed the education acquired by imposed self-reliance and constantly remarked how many of the most successful men began life poor. But he did not see the tramp as a man "walking to work."

WHY ISN'T ALGER'S HERO A TRAMP?

> Men leaving Eastern cities for Western towns, desiring to econo-
> mize, have pushed their way along afoot, and after having been
> out a half-dozen days on their journey, could scarcely be distin-
> guished from a genuine tramp . . . this necessarily rough out-door
> life often produces the tramp manners and appearance, so that it
> would be almost impossible to select the tramp from among those
> on the road.

> Allan Pinkerton, *Strikers, Communists, Tramps, and Detectives*

Alger stories are filled with itinerant heroes who take to the roads with little
in their pockets. They constitute a geographically mobile population and
often travel on foot. Some boys come from within a fifty-mile radius of the
city, but others travel considerable distances to reach their destination,
whether city or mine site. They may arrive with no money, no place to stay,
and no job. They depend upon the good will of strangers along the way for
food, lodging, and sometimes transportation. Why are they not tramps?

The author certainly could not even fathom the comparison between
hero and tramp.[72] Alger exempts the wandering hero, on the basis of age,
character, and motive, from the community's judgment of many other
wanderers. The attempt to delineate and differentiate appropriate and
inappropriate rootlessness is part of an ongoing Gilded Age discourse about
industrial development, class, and the identification of members of the
Republic.

While heroes might have to live off the local economy, their characters
recommend them to strangers in the local populace, who open their doors.
They either had a bit of change to offer hosts or hostesses, or were able to
perform miscellaneous chores in barter. Willingness to work for a meal or
a bed is the key to their decency.

Alger's heroes also have an end to their travels in view. In one variant of
the formula, boys move as rapidly and purposively as their funds permit
from the small town or countryside in the environs to the big city. Sometimes,
the journey is brief, obviating the necessity of working en route. Frequently,
however, boys accept what they view as short-term employment short of
the city, and continue itineracy as magicians' apprentices, wandering
warblers and whistlers, and assistants to travelling professors. The hero's
aim is to cease wandering and return to the community—sometimes the
very community he has been forced by circumstances to leave. Nonheroes
lack comparable intentions, as they dog the path of the hero and from coast
to coast, intent on living off the wealth of others.

The boy who moves in search of work is making his way, seeking brighter opportunities. The adult who tramps is highly suspect. Both tramp and hero were economically marginalized, mobile figures. It was vital that the two not be confused. Should the young, whatever their station, fail to obtain the community's consideration and assistance, both hero and Republic lose.

Reception of the Unemployed in Countryside and City: A Case of Luck?

Alger's boy-heroes rarely if ever found themselves turned away when they sought food or lodging along their route. The author wished to believe in human goodness. However, the hero was very lucky in his reception.

Unemployed youth, men, and tramps were all the same to farm people of the 1880s. Hamlin Garland and his brother chronicled their 1880s "experiment" in tramping in *A Son of a Middle Border*. They found jobs in the East "exceedingly hard to get," and "the people on the highway suspicious and inhospitable." They came to know the reality of hunger and were forced to assume the posture of tramplike begging. "We looked less and less like college boys and more and more like tramps, and the house-holders began to treat us with hostile contempt":

> No doubt these farmers, much beset with tramps, had reasonable excuse for their inhospitable ways, but to us it was bitter and uncalled for. I knew that cities were filled with robbers, brigands, burglars and pirates, but I had held (up to this time) the belief that the country, though rude and barren of luxury was nevertheless a place of plenty where no man need suffer hunger.[73]

Frosty receptions were not confined to the East. A newspaper reported a Minnesota farmer's murder of two tramps and cited approvingly the intent of a group of farmers to "fertilize their land with their dead bodies... as a radical and permanent cure for the evil complained of . . ." [74] In the Northwest, Garland struck out on his own to seek employment as a teacher. Having spent all his money, he "passed house after house while the water dripped from my hat and the mud clogged my feet," appalled by the "natural antagonism of the well-to-do toward the tramp":

> Once, as I turned in toward the bright light of a kitchen window, the roar of a watch dog stopped me before I had fairly passed the gate. I turned back with a savage word, hot with resentment at a house-owner who would keep a beast like that. At another cottage, I was repulsed by an old woman who sharply said, "We don't feed tramps."[75]

In 1891, Princeton assistant professor of Political Economy Walter A. Wyckoff, supplementing his meager book-learned lore, moved through rural areas as an itinerant unskilled laborer. At one point travelling as a magazine salesman (not unlike one late Alger hero), Wyckoff was dismayed and puzzled by his treatment. Poverty made him "an object of unfailing distrust"; blacks and whites, rich and poor were equally unfriendly. Kindness was the exception.

> My good-morning was not infrequently met by a vacant stare, and if I stopped to ask the way, the conviction was forced upon me that, as a pack-pedler, I was a suspicious character, with no claim upon common consideration.[76]

Wyckoff found job hunting in the countryside infinitely easier than in the city, with its congested labor market. Without money, it was impossible to keep clean, to keep free of lice, to be decently groomed, or to get decent rest. When searching for work, "the actual barriers grow greater, as the outward marks of your mode of life become clearer upon you . . ."[77] While waiting to apply for work outside one factory gate, Wyckoff saw many "in face . . . who, if not already of that class, are approximating to professional tramps."[78] Cut off from the means of survival, he keenly felt his predicament: "You are a superfluous human being. For you there is no part in the play of the world's activity."[79]

"It will puzzle you to decide whether in all the world there is any place for them to go to if they would," wrote Pinkerton, of the collections of tramps he saw in the 1870s.[80] Both genteel moralists and socialists thought they had answers; these answers reflected very different visions of the Republic.

Diverging [Class] Visions of Hardship

> Jesus Christ was himself a tramp. He was certainly one in the estimation of the Jews. His father was a tramp carpenter. But he was more utterly a tramp than them all. No other ancient or modern tramp could compare with him in destitution or homelessness.
>
>   Pinkerton, *Strikers, Communists, Tramps and Detectives*

There was a different discourse. Labor newspapers, too, by the mid-1870s occasionally identified tramps with Christ or drew analogies between tramp armies and "Lincoln's Grand Army of the Republic."[81]

Having once been a poor apprentice and tramp journeyman in Scotland, Allan Pinkerton realized the connection between economic downturns and tramping. Expressing resentment for the attitude of elite reformers and newspaper journalists who "know nothing whatsoever of suffering and privation," Pinkerton took issue with Wayland and the Yale reformers' rendition of the 1877 riots, and with any who condemned "the universal villainy and ferocity of the tramp."[82]

The rapid increase of tramps, so alarming "to certain kid-gloved social scientists,"

> is the direct result of unprecedented hard times and conditions which a great and protracted war has left as a legacy. When these pass away, and brighter days return to our industries, people will see tramps disappear from the highways and byways—not altogether, for this will never be, but the thousands among them who have trades and professions will gradually but surely return to them.[83]

In the aftermath of the Civil War, the majority of those who joined the "brotherhood of strollers" were not there from choice, Pinkerton argued. "If thousands are here from abroad who have been compelled to turn tramp, how many of our own people have been forced into the same kind of life as the only way left to live outside of the poor-house?"[84]

By the 1870s, the labor press and the Populist press concluded that "the tramp is a man, an unfortunate man, who can find no work . . . he [is] a product of the times." Henry George saw the tramp as a symptom:

> Behind [the tramp], though not obtrusive, save in what we call "hard times," there is, even in what we now consider normal times, a great mass of unemployed labour which is unable, unwilling or not yet forced to tramp, but which bears to the tramp the same relation that the submerged part of an iceberg does to that much smaller part which shows above the surface.[85]

A dime novel of 1894, offering a sympathetic depiction of Coxey's industrial army, has the fictionalized Coxey respond to newspapers that term them tramps:

> Many of us look like tramps, it is true; but what has brought us to this condition? What has thrown us out of employment? What has caused our mills and work shops to shut down? What has brought many of us to starvation? These men in Congress . . . the majority of whom are the slaves of the corporations and trusts, who sell their souls for the flesh-pots of Egypt, who shut their ears to the cry of the starving.[86]

Many of the trades and professions from which tramping Americans were liberated were disappearing for good. Pinkerton may not have noticed that the world was changing permanently and profoundly, but for some other observers near the century's end, class differences constituted a chasm.

In many working-class vehicles, tramps did not deny, and were not ashamed of, their status. In fact, the stories may even affirm that "the disinherited tramp is the rightful heir of the republic."[87]

Alger's *Tony, the Tramp* is anxious to escape the position he feels he cannot own.[88] Tony's creator saw, in the tramp, nothing to embrace and little to pity. For this son of the Boston Whigs, the reaction was estrangement from those unlike us, tempered by an offer that they could be like us if only they would. His universe was not divided between tramps and millionaires who, in stories read by the working class, were frequently juxtaposed and brought into confrontation.

Others thought that precisely this conflict was tearing the Republic asunder:

> The fruits of the toil of millions are boldly stolen to build up colossal fortunes for a few, unprecedented in the history of mankind; and the possessors of these, in turn, despise the republic and endanger liberty. From the same prolific womb of governmental injustice we breed the two great classes—tramps and millionaires.[89]

In the story of *Tony, the Tramp*, known in book form as *Tony, the Hero*, Alger bridges the gap between figures who had begun to represent the polarization of American society. He restores the young wanderer to the community of respectable citizens and also arranges for Tony to *become* a millionaire, reclaiming his rightful English estate, negating the meaning of the gulf.

CONCLUSION: SUCCESS AND SURVIVAL

Alger's cheerful assertions that one's exertions are sure to lead to self-sufficiency rest on the assumption of a growing economy with available steady employment and adequate remuneration for those of good character. New opportunities were created and some were made better off, but money wages did not even show consistent growth until 1880.[90]

The tramp presented a specter of economic dislocation and downward mobility. For Alger, this figure was unrecognizable, unlike respectable citizens. Good people may suffer temporary reverses of fortune, but they do not experience long-term downward mobility. Downward mobility is meted out to those who do not deserve to enjoy their property, wealth, or position.

Adults who actively seek work in the city with no place to stay may not be defined as tramps by Alger, but their near invisibility bespeaks his difficulty naming that experience.

Pinkerton's account of the fortunes of a former business manager of a Chicago daily newspaper was antithetical to the truths of Alger's world. Here was a man with much ability and influence, of good education, connections, culture, and friends. Deprived of his job through a change in proprietorship, he was found among the "vast army of newspaper cormorants that was fastened upon the Northern Pacific Railroad just before its bankruptcy," and from there saw his fortunes steadily wane. By 1874, he was a tramp:

> The last time I saw him he was shuffling along a country road, almost shoeless, ragged, dirty, and forlorn, wrapping himself in his skinny arms as if to thus derive some additional warmth—the picture of animated degradation, and yet with a trace of cheeriness and contentment about him, as though he derived some sense of satisfaction from the reflection that he could get no lower.

Pinkerton finds that "among this army of tramps there is a large number of persons of fine minds and attainments"; it is quite possible that "a man may be eminent to-day, and to-morrow a tramp."[91]   Alger does not see or share such disconfirming evidence on the downward mobility of the able with the young.

Alger discovered the tramp, but could only recognize him with old, familiar categorizations. This framework denied the extent to which the tramp demarcated change. The tramp was merely another specter to be avoided by the virtuous.

We have seen some of the most visible classes that Alger's boys and girls stand to join if they are not successful and some of the most-discussed types of failure. But equally ominous is the factory.

5

<hr>

Saved from the Factory

In an Alger story serialized beginning December, 1892, Ben Bruce determines to leave the home of his mean stepfather. Ben meets a friend who is superintendent of a "factory for the manufacture of leather board." The superintendent asks the boy how he would like to work there. Ben Bruce, expressing a desire to secure a better education, nonetheless answers: "If the choice lies between working on a farm and working in your factory, I will work for you if I can get the chance." The starting wage is adequate, and the boy inquires whether he would be preparing himself for "higher" work; the superintendent answers in the affirmative. Just when they are about to strike a bargain, the dam which provides water power for the factory is blown up, apparently by two discharged workmen. Since the factory must be shut down until the dam is rebuilt, the boy's hope of employment there is ended.[1] And so, Alger "blows up" this option rather than forsake Ben there. He is saved!

This dramatic and unusual Alger event disposes of the factory option and reveals a marked aversion to depositing boys and girls in industrial employments. The modern factory was generally absent from his panoply of dangers occasioned by economic and social transformation. What can be reasonably inferred from this silence? What did the author and his contemporaries think of the opportunities and dangers of industrial wage labor?

The factory was already an inescapable presence in the northeastern antebellum landscape in which Alger frequently set his tales. Such boosters of industrialism as Edward Everett (for whom Alger ran

The dam is blown up! (Arthur Lee Putman [Alger pseudonym], "Ben Bruce," *The Argosy* 15, December 10, 1892.)

errands as a Harvard freshman in 1848) could proclaim the factory at Lowell, begun in the second decade of the century, the "fulfillment of the American Revolution and a model of republicanism."[2] But others were not so sanguine. Travellers to England worried over the poverty and moral debasement that accompanied industrialization and wondered whether they were looking at America's future and the demise of republican virtue. "The machine unmans the user," Emerson wrote after his 1847 trip abroad.[3] By 1840, the vision of the American factory as a community was difficult to sustain in light of labor discontent, worker combinations, and analyses of wage slavery.

The number of production workers nearly quadrupled from the eve of the Civil War to the end of the century. In this same period, the number of manufacturing establishments in the United States expanded more than three and a half times; two-fifths of all U.S. industrial establishments were factories by 1899.[4] Employment in transportation, public utilities, trade, finance, and real estate increased over sixfold in these four decades. The number of children employed in nonagricultural pursuits almost tripled from 1870 to 1900; many of these were employed in cotton mills.[5]

The New England states and New York, frequent settings for Alger novels, underwent the same processes of change. The percentage of the population engaged in manufacturing in four of these states was as high as 41 to 52.5% by the century's end; the lowest in the region was 25%; trade and transportation accounted for as much as an additional 21.5% of persons employed.[6]

The rare brick, furniture, or shoe manufactory or mill in Alger stories involved preindustrial skilled craft work; he had not allowed mechanization to appreciably alter the nature of work.[7] At the outset of *Five Hundred Dollars*, serialized beginning 1889, Bert Barton is thrown out of work as a shoe pegger by the introduction of a machine. This was a very rare occurrence in Alger's fiction.

Stories virtually never describe factory work. Often, the reader has no idea what is made and is not taken into areas of production. The author exhibits little or no curiosity about this workplace. Robert Rushton provides the chief support of his family by working in the factory in Millville. Beyond this, one learns only that the brick factory provided about the only employment in town, that Robert was able to earn six dollars a week, and that tardiness resulted in a twenty-five cent docking.[8] And, although a few Alger heroes begin work life in a factory, early in the story circumstances (sometimes, dullness in a trade) quickly conspire to compel them to look for other work.[9] The mechanized factory is kept at arm's length and out of sight.

On first impression, mining is more in evidence. When Alger turns his attention westward, he invents scenarios in which a young boy heads off to dig for gold. The author almost unfailingly sets these California stories during the days of the gold rush and reminds readers it is not as likely they could do the same. But his miners are self-employed, generally toil at or near the surface, and command their own time and actions.

As early as 1856, long before Alger's first trip to the West in 1877, the Sacramento Union noted that there were "few places in Western mining where individuals or companies could make three dollars a day without 'considerable' capital investment." An 1864 Comstock newspaper observed:

> A pick and shovel and sack of flour, though backed up by brave
> heart and willing hands, are hardly adequate to the work of
> driving tunnels and sinking shafts, to say nothing of the mills
> and reduction works necessary to silver mining.[10]

Miners were increasingly paid a wage, subjected to searches for ore stealing, and closely supervised and directed by others. They were lowered hundreds of feet below the surface in steel cages, to work in dark, damp, dangerous environments. Operations became increasingly industrialized and expensive, involving blasting, hoisting, timbering, and milling. Mine owners attracted money from Europe; among the owners and operators of western mining during the Gilded Age were the Dutch, British, and French.[11]

Such changes did not proceed in uniform fashion and pace. Shallow mining employing a dozen or fewer workmen might exist alongside enormous lode operations with several hundred employees; mines with little differentiation of labor might exist alongside those with extensive division of labor and specialization. Miners continued to move from job to job and between wage-labor and prospecting as new discoveries were made. In the major lode mining camps, unions had been formed by 1870, and "had successfully rebuffed several attempts by capitalists to dictate conditions that the workers found offensive." [12]

Unionization, resistance to the employment of Chinese workers at lower wages, and strike activity were also clear indicators that the world Alger described was past. Occasionally, an Alger hero sees a modern mining operation, and even once is lured into a mine shaft and abandoned, but readers do not become acquainted with those working below the earth.

Alger boys exit the the world of industrialized labor; they do not seek to make their way within it.[13] Geographic mobility for young boys is essential to their escape. Only those who confine their search to the local community in which they begin life find themselves dependent upon factory work as the sole available employment. In Alger's city, there are other things to do.

When seeking work, the central character often turns down manual labor or the opportunity to learn a craft or trade. The stinginess of the man to whom the hero would be apprenticed is sometimes adduced as the reason for refusal, or the boy might submit that he does not want to live away from his mother (which he inevitably chooses to do when he leaves for the city). Often, he merely asserts that he does not believe he is cut out for certain types of work or does not think he would like it.

Alger does not always make clear why craft work, farm work, or a life at sea is undesirable. Some employments were dead-end jobs:

> Now, Ben [Barclay] had no objections to farm labor, provided he had a farm of his own, but at the rate such labor was paid in Pentonville there was very little chance of ever rising above the position of a "hired man," if he once adopted the business. Our young hero felt that this would not satisfy him. He was enterprising and ambitious, and wanted to be a rich man some day.[14]

Often, however, the hero simply thinks he would prefer some other trade, even if it does not pay as well.[15] Heroes are clearly destined for another fate. They often have their sights set on business, for which they may have an instinctual bent.

To what length Alger is willing to go to keep the boy afloat and away from the factory gates! Alger's young heroes join a circus, whistle, and give bird imitations on the stage for a living. They also commence working life as magicians' apprentices, circus riders, actors, stable boys at hotels, part-time school janitors, baggage "smashers," newspaper boys, street musicians, or bootblacks. When one nearly penniless boy claims to feel foolish playing the harmonica on stage for money, his companion replies: "it would be more ridiculous *not* playing for money. Whatever talents we possess our Creator meant us to exercise for our benefit and the pleasure of the community."[16] The hero is lucky he lives in an era when he can exhibit his talents on stage rather than in subway stations.

As these young people wander through the city in search of employment, they do not see even those factories found along well-travelled routes, adjacent to shops, horsecars, and residences. To remove even the possibility of exchanging one's labor power for a wage in industry, the factory must become invisible.

Luke Walton, set in Chicago, is deposited for copyright the same month and year that Carrie Meeber comes to Chicago in *Sister Carrie* (August, 1889). Luke sees many of the same new downtown sights Carrie does. Yet Dreiser's Carrie, who trudges the streets in search of work, could

Harrison & Newhall's Sugar Refinery, Philadelphia, 1856. (Lithograph by William H. Rease. Historical Society of Philadelphia.)

not avoid passing and viewing the manufacturing establishments on her long walk from home on the west side of the river to the downtown area. Unable to find a position as a shop girl, she eventually finds a poorly paid, unpleasant position manufacturing shoes. The factory girls she eventually leaves behind have little hope of betterment. Carrie could not help but see men toiling at heavy labor in the streets; poorly clad shop girls who worked so hard and had so little; the pale, ragged creatures in states of mental stupor who walked the streets or held out their hands for change.[17] But when Alger's newsboy walks home to his poor and unfashionable neighborhood, he does not seem to pass any factories or see the ways many people labor. Away from the bustling downtown commercial center, across the Chicago River, there is only the usual Alger drama.[18]

Engels had noted in 1845 that the structure of the city almost conspires to keep the manufacturing establishments and the squalid tenements of the poor out of the view of the untroubled bourgeoisie, lining the streets with tidy shops and concealing what lies behind.[19] Alger found poverty, tenements and ten-cent lodging houses, but when it came to the factory, Alger's boys share the privileged gaze of the bourgeoisie.

Alger's urban world is full of small shopkeepers, merchants, clerks, errand boys; "businessmen" are bankers or merchants and "capitalists" are usually lenders or hoarders. There are many mercantile establishments and counting houses.[20] Rarely do the businessmen described appear to employ manual laborers.

Central characters discover that many urban jobs will not pay a living wage. Yet employers note there are plenty of boys who will take, (for example), two dollars per week. Obviously, our hero calculates, these jobs are for boys who live at home and supplement family earnings. In at least one instance, Alger editorializes that not even a little boy could live on these wages. Alger's young boys walk away from such opportunities. Even when destitute, these characters are never forced to accept anything offered. Something or someone intervenes to obviate the necessity of such a "choice."

As they walk or run away from jobs in factories, crafts, farming, and trades, these boys accept minimal living wages as errand boy, cash boy, or telegraph messenger, hoping to rise through the ranks within their particular business establishment. But career and earning trajectories of Alger characters do not mirror options in the late nineteenth century economy. As late as 1900, 36% of the experienced civilian labor force aged fourteen or older were employed in manual work, another 31% were farm workers, and 9% were employed in service work. All of Alger's heroes find employment in the white-collar workforce, although only 18% of all workers are so classified in

1900. These boys are also found earning at the high end of the scales for average weekly *adult* earnings during the period.[21] Who, then, cannot run away from the factory? As women's work was integrated into the capitalist economy, females in Alger's stories suffer many economic hardships and privations as they seek work in order to survive. These women are engaged in the manufacturing process through either piecework or the putting out system. A kindly character in *Rufus and Rose* has a typical story. She was entirely dependent on her earnings as a seamstress, laboring in her room from early morning until evening and barely earning enough to survive.[22] She clearly was losing her health and could only earn one-third of what Rufus earned selling newspapers. When the boy asks her whether they might pay her any more, she replies: "No, they find plenty who are ready to take their work at the price they are willing to pay. If anybody complains, they take away their work and employ somebody else."[23]

Likewise, in *Helen Ford*, Martha sewed constantly only to find her wages decreased 20 percent because shops were gave out less work and more people seemed to desire it. "Many could not obtain a chance to work at any price." Here, Alger forcefully editorializes, referring the reader to an article in the *Atlantic Monthly* for evidence :

> Perhaps no employment is more confining and more poorly compensated than that of sewing. The narrow choice allowed to women, who are compelled to labor for their livelihood, leads to an unhealthy and disastrous competition in this department of toil, and enables employers to establish a disgracefully low scale of prices.[24]

Less geographically mobile than men and boys in Alger's world, these women have fewer opportunities and are more dependent upon their employers. This grim picture does not allow much hope of success apart from rescue. The best case provides either for marriage or for installation in the home of a successful hero. Production as mindless drudgery has been linked with the female.

FACTORIES AND FAILURE

Literary heritage was not inconsequential as a reason for the invisibility of the factory. As the product of literary traditions that preceded realism, Alger may well have believed some subjects were unfit for discussion. William Dean Howells had to do battle with an earlier faith; "in the strife-torn, graft-ridden years of the late nineteenth century, industrial society had understandably seemed to literary men an enemy, not a subject." Alger expressed respect for Howells, but he greatly admired the author Edmund Clarence Stedman, who expressed a wish to lift readers above the sordid details of contemporary life.[25] Although Alger's most popular works tended to feature neglected New York street urchins, his literary work seems to reflect the views of the *Christian Union*:

> Realism . . . [seemed bent on] crowding the world of fiction with commonplace people, whom one could positively avoid coming into contact with in real life; people without native sweetness or strength, without acquired culture or accomplishments, without the touch of the ideal which makes the commonplace significant and worthy of study.[26]

Alger's heroes did not put such "commonplace" adolescents at center stage. Regardless of economic circumstances, his heroes were always those exceptional boys with whom one was happy to make contact.

But there was much more to the absent factory than the unattractive and uninspiring literary nature of the subject. Alger did not think the factory offered a very good route of mobility. It did not nurture aspiration. It was, perhaps, for those who do not have the right disposition or will to succeed. Alger spent his youth in Marlborough, Massachusetts, which he remembered as engaging in shoe manufacturing. "Though diversified, the local economy was not immune to the cyclical fluctuations which plagued the shoe industry at large." Nearby towns, more dependent upon manufacture than Marlborough, suffered frequent cycles of boom and bust. When forced to shut down temporarily in a glutted market, an Alger shoemaker comments:

> That's the worst of the shoe trade. It isn't steady. When it's good everybody rushes into it, and the market soon gets overstocked. Then there's no work for weeks. If a man manages to save up a little money in good times, he has to spend it then . . . [27]

Alger's "experience" with manufacturing was that it did not provide a reliable income. And crafts and skills could become outmoded. Thus, heroes sought to escape business cycle fluctuations and discover steady work with reliable and rising wages. Boys sought careers at work.

Alger was not as sanguine as some contemporaries about opportunities in the nineteenth century factory. Rosy depictions of factory opportunities were repeated throughout the century by industrialists and their supporters, and even some less biased late-century writers found more opportunities in the factory than did Alger. Among the latter was William Makepeace Thayer, whose advice manual Alger sent to a young friend. Claiming to be "familiar with a wealthy man who left the farm at eighteen years of age for work in a straw-hat factory" despite the wishes of his father, Thayer narrates how the boy "used leisure moments in studying other branches of the business. He . . . was ready, at any time, to perform extra work for his employer." Employees, each of whom had his particular work, reacted with derision, considering this man a fool spending his "time and strength in work you get nothing for." However:

> In three years the young man from the farm was superintendent of the establishment, and a good one, too. That was what he started out for, and he obtained the object he had in view sooner than he expected. He shortened the distance by serving his employer to the very best of his ability, watching for opportunities to learn what he did not know, doing often more than his employer required of him, and proving, by actual service, that he meant to master the business.[28]

One could hope to rise through the ranks in the factory as well.

Supportive evidence for claims such as Thayer's has come from several later historical studies of social and geographic mobility in nineteenth century industrial cities. In one prominent study, the rags-to-riches promise was judged to be no myth in Paterson, New Jersey from 1830 to 1880:

> So many successful manufacturers who had begun as workers walked the streets of that city then that it is not hard to believe that others less successful or just starting out on the lower rungs of the occupational mobility ladder could be convinced by personal knowledge that "hard work" resulted in spectacular material and social improvement.[29]

The likelihood of rising from day laborer, unskilled worker, or skilled artisan to successful manufacturer was small, but it was not so inaccurate to assert that manufacturers who founded new firms in Paterson tended to come from the rank and file.[30]

Other recent historical evidence tends to support Alger's skepticism about rising through the ranks *in* a manufacturing establishment. The route from shop hand to supervisor was neither quick nor terribly likely. If there were some upward mobility through positions, downward mobility was likely as well, and lateral movement from department to department was also common. Patronage played a significant role in explaining advancement.[31] A now classic study of Newburyport, Massachusetts contends that

> most of the social gains registered by laborers and their sons during these years were decidedly modest—a move one notch up the occupational scale, the acquisition of a small amount of property. Yet *in their eyes* these accomplishments must have loomed large.[32]

If laborers believed that their mobility within the working class made them Algeresque heroes, it was ironic that Alger did not concur. These modest gains, however perceived by their achievers, did not generally decrease the employee's dependence upon manufacturing.

The author might have had some sympathy for this response offered in 1889 to factory boosters:

> If you tell a single concrete workman on the Baltimore and Ohio Railroad that he may yet be president of the company, it is not demonstrable that you have told him what is not true, although it is within bounds to say that he is far more likely to be killed by a stroke of lightning. [33]

"We find that *many of our most conspicuous public men* have commenced their careers as newsboys," Alger was fond of repeating.[34] He did not say "factory hands."

While the heroes and friends we meet eventually find white-collar work, there is no indication that *all* do. Alger merely tells us that plenty succeed and his hero wants to be among them (a sentiment expressed by Harry Raymond in *Sink or Swim*).[35]   It was essential to Alger's formula for advancement that character be noticed; it was also critical that character be rewarded. The stakes were higher than money: If not all could escape the factory, not all would achieve equal independence.

The factory system surely did not illustrate Alger's principle that, by application, hard work, cheerfulness, loyalty to one's employer, and honesty, any boy can hope to be noticed for his endeavors and advance. In the emerging industrial order, there was less opportunity for the individual to engage in personal contact with a boss, impress him, or employ his education or wits in new and different tasks. The increasingly impersonal factory wage labor system provided limited scope within which workers could affect their destinies. The equivalents in market exchange were hides, not character.

Other arenas offered better opportunity for personal contact between employees and employers—smaller work settings or those with less hierarchical work arrangements. Alger's boys at work maintain frequent contact with their employers, who, for their part, make frequent appearances among employees. And, although intermediaries may try to interpose themselves between the lowly employee and his employer, the door of the latter opens for all.

If it was essential to Alger's formula for advancement that character be noticed, it was also critical that character be *nurtured*. Boys and girls needed to be uplifted by the good example of their superiors and certainly not corrupted by them or by co-workers. Factory labor was not likely to take Alger's street-hardened hero without advantages and uplift him, exposing him to a better class of people who would encourage him to better himself. Employments in which the employer is so far removed as to approximate the fictional, and where immediate contact may be with hardened companions who may lead the youth astray, are no bargain.

Those with power stood to affect the identity and morals of those over whom they exercised control. In Alger's universe, many individual employers, in their greed, prey on the vulnerability of workers. If capitalists and their factory agents do not stand for virtue, what will become of their employees? Alger's distrust of capitalists and their power will receive further consideration in Chapters 6, 7, and 8.

But the factory should be avoided even where the case is not so sinister. Certain occupations were less desirable than others because they did not allow the youth to grow and improve. Midcentury Harvard Unitarians argued that "man had both a mind (that is, a spirit) and a body, but his destiny clearly lay in developing the power of the former."[36] Physical labor—farming (despite Jefferson), crafts, trades, or factory work—while honorable, might not provide the opportunites necessary to moral development. As one advice manual put it: "Idealess occupations, associates, and books should be avoided, since they are not friendly to intelligent manhood and womanhood. Ideas make the wise man; the want of them the fool."[37] Even if indifferent workers might comply with factory discipline in order to keep their jobs, the work environment did not help make them *men* [or women]—it did not improve them.

Manliness required power over oneself. Retaining power meant having some discretion over one's labor processess and resisting labor that is merely manual. Factory work increasingly entailed steady application to one task, divorce of mental and manual, loss of discretion, and close subjection to the control of others.

Alger clearly values having some discretion over how one's time is expended. Young Paul Hoffman, proprietor of a necktie stand in *Phil, the Fiddler*, spends one early morning helping the young Italian boy escape New York and the exploitive padrone who lives off the labor of little boys. His efficacy established, Paul notes on the morning that he helps young Phil that "it is almost nine o'clock—rather a late hour for a business man like me . . . It is lucky that I am my own employer, or I might run the risk of being discharged."[38] He is not controlled by the clock. Control over time was linked to power. Alger's readers do not feel the tyranny of the clock. Punctuality is held in high regard, but time has not fully acquired a price. Heroes are paid by the week, not the hour. However, a successful boy may purchase or be given a gold watch and chain toward the end of a novel. Its display functions as an indicator of potency, although it is also a harbinger of the new value of time. It is as if the watch bearer controls time rather than being controlled by it.[39]

The chains that bind the Alger hero to a worthy employer are not manufactured of power but of loyalty. The "loyalty to employer" that Alger repeatedly stresses as vital to getting along is already part of the boy's disposition prior to his employment; he simply has to find a good and trustworthy employer whose interest he can take as his own. Selflessness is one of the traits that attracts the benefactor's—and/or potential employer's—attention to the boy in the first place. It is a marriage made in heaven: the employer does not have to work at inculcating this internalized identification with the values and goals of the business.

This relationship begets mutual confidence. In return, the "trusted" employee is empowered to exercise his intelligence and judgment on behalf of the firm. His salaried labor is frequently performed outside the place of business, with variable hours and duties, and without immediate supervision. The boy retains a great deal of control over bodily movements and time and can determine how to perform tasks. He can exercise discretion on behalf of the employer when sent afield as the latter's trusted business agent; when far away, the boy may even be empowered to define the employer's interest.

Although the hero is almost always dependent upon others for his livelihood, he need not renounce his independence of judgment but is instead asked to bring it to the workplace. This judgment is repeatedly validated—virtually never corrected or overridden. The employee progressively builds a stake in the concern. There is little unattractive about this type of labor.

CONCLUSION: THE MEASURE (AND SCIENCE?) OF SUCCESS

After examining the critical moral dimension of success in Chapter 3, Chapters 4 and 5 have offered a reconsideration of the kind of sense Alger's fiction made of the changing economic order. Chapter 4 argued that, far from celebrating streets paved with gold, Alger depicts a world full of economic hardship, dangers, dislocations, and undesirable outcomes. This chapter has shown that the factory is a significant work site to be bypassed; the hero performs neither the role of industrialist nor that of wage slave. The factory is not a setting in which community of interest between employer and employee could endure.

But what, then, is the *economic* measure of success? Two benevolent Alger merchants in New York who started out poor state the success formula particularly well:

> Most of the men in this city who have succeeded in business or in the professions started as poor boys . . . There are the same chances now that there always were. Serve your employer well, learn business as rapidly as possible, don't fall into bad habits, and you'll get on.[40]

They assert the enduring secular relevance of past values and the almost mathematical invariability of opportunity. These merchants offer an ahistorical understanding of the American job structure and an immutable set of rules of the game. Prominence is possible; "getting on" is predictable if one follows the maxims: it is almost scientific. The bold, legible hand, ability to count and figure interest, punctuality, neatness, politeness, loyalty, and honesty are not among the job requirements for speculators and robber barons. They are skills for "getting on."[41]

Aspirations of central characters are pegged to a respectable, comfortable life—a "competence," as it was still sometimes termed by Alger. Most of his boys do not *aim* at wealth, but rather at the elimination of want. The stories end with many figures just escaping economically marginal status or obtaining a modest paying position on the first rung on a career ladder in a mercantile or financial establishment. A small number begin different career trajectories in law or newspaper work.[42] The final page may suggest the boy will likely rise higher. When Alger (especially in his late stories) adds a sensationalist twist, he generally reminds the reader that cases in which a boy promises to become a rich man while still young are unusual.

Although the merchants' formula would reassure the boy that the *world* is still the same, Alger's story can only maintain that (1) rules and values are the same and that (2) opportunities exist as before. On every other economic dimension, a different tale is told. The author repeatedly portrayed a world being turned upside down, fraught with constant dangers. Wits and courage are in high demand. Success cannot be measured apart from its backdrop.

As heroes measure their *economic* success by the distance travelled from their privations and insecurity, they implicitly measure it against failure. Economic failure in Alger is linked with a transition from youth to adulthood without establishing secure, stable employment with opportunities for incremental advancement of one's wage. Failures continue not to know from whence their next meals come. Failures do not establish careers. Failures do not develop personal relationships with employers, nor do they merit the attention of benefactors. Unconnected and alone, they are treated impersonally as labor. Buffeted about by the vicissitudes of the business cycle, such figures are cut adrift in times of depression, without the means to fend for themselves and without skills (or character) in high demand. Failures do not have bank accounts, and they do not own property. Economic success is defined against the twin specters of economic marginalization and proletarianization; both threaten the moral order.

The Alger story takes boys (and occasionally girls) who have been cut adrift from the traditional economy, and thus economically marginalized, and finds specific places to insert them into the new economic world. Merchandising, the growing trade sector, finance, law, and real estate ventures offer routes into middle class comforts for the author's protagonists.[43] Alger does not place his faith in opportunity in the rapidly growing productive sector, but has most boys find their careers and investment opportunities in sectors engaged in the distribution, circulation, and exchange of the new wealth of a capitalist economy.

If economic success is escape from failure, success also maintains, and means, continuity with the past and with the familiar as so many features of the landscape were transformed. The economic agent must be *active*, not passive, and yet his manhood depends upon avoiding the economic sphere most closely associated with production.

6

Technology, Organizations, Corporations, and Capitalists

> The corporate or semi-corporate organizations of society are so numerous and so pervasive of all kinds of social activity that the individual citizen, trying to attain the ideal of personal independence venerated in the theory of the political institutions of his country, finds every avenue under the control of some kind of an association in which he must acquire membership or to whose regulations he must submit . . .
>
> John P. Davis, *Corporations*

As Alger's career drew to a close, one could proclaim the advent of the centralized, bureaucratized, industrial state. Corporations, trusts, pooling arrangements, labor unions, professional and voluntary organizations, and bureaucracies were incontrovertible features of the late-century landscape. In 1897, a leading scholar on corporate form pronounced that "the growth of corporations in western Europe and the United States signifies nothing less than a social revolution."[1]

Specialization invaded politics, business, and charitable activities; the amateur was being replaced by university-trained professionals. They brought their new conceptual tools—and great confidence in their new expertise—to bear on such problems as industrial liability laws, railroad regulation, child labor, tax reform, and transit franchises.[2] As organization and administration pervaded life, "all but the most exceptional individual seemed reduced to impotence and insignificance." Intellectuals began to recognize, "grudgingly, indirectly, and obscurely—what amounted to an organizational revolution, itself unguided and unwanted."[3]

Such were some of the fruits of progress. Invention, technology, rationalization, and science were its companions. In grand expositions in Europe and the United States, "World Fairs of marvels and technological breakthroughs" displayed the wares of progress in "county-fair atmosphere."[4] Observers waxed eloquent about the union of science, art, and technology. The Machine Arcade at the New York Crystal Palace Exhibition of 1853 brought home the role of technological invention in modern American history, leading one reporter to an epic analogy: "The Crystal Palace may be termed the Iliad of the Nineteenth Century, and its Homer was the American people."[5] Alger himself attended the Vienna International Exposition in 1873 on his second European tour.[6] It was a difficult time for those who matured before the Civil War. Alger's generation "did not anticipate the destruction of a way of life by unregulated industrial growth and was appalled by the price computed in human terms."[7]

The spectacle of size and scale was often captivating. But Alger's optimism about technological change and new opportunities for material advancement in an urbanized, industrialized economy, was tempered with fear of loss of power and independence for the individual.

John P. Davis observed: the worker "finds his wages determined by the corporation that controls the business employing his labor, and seeks refuge in a trade union that deprives him of his individuality." Finding railway companies, banks, investment companies, trusts, church organizations, and professional organizations that mediate between person and person wherever they turn, people "begin to realize that they are governed more by corporations than by the state, that they are the major part of the mechanism of government under which they live."[8]

This chapter explores the tension between the delight in homo faber and the fear of what man creates. The impact of invention and technology was not merely coextensive with either progress and liberty. In attempting to name the creation, a generation sought for the boundary between what was natural—and therefore just—and what was artificial, and potentially damnable. There was considerable ambivalence in the prognosis concerning the effects of technology on the Republic.

HOMO FABER

As early as his Harvard days, Alger had exhibited a fascination with homo faber—with the monuments and public buildings which stood as works of art in Greece and Rome. Alger's Pericles had had recourse to *techne* to influence the popular mind:

> He gratified their taste by the erection of those stupendous works of art whose magnificence is attested by the ruins yet in existence. The Odeon, the Parthenon, the Propylaea and numberless other fabrics . . . rose in rapid succession . . . The splendor of the public edifices exhibited a dazzling contrast to the narrowness and irregularity of the streets, and the simplicity of the private dwellings. It was the aim of Pericles to strengthen the patriotism of the Athenian citizen by a pride in her beauty, by presenting to him everywhere objects which should remind him of the majesty of the commonwealth, and symbolize the extent to which individual interest should yield before the all-absorbing glories of the state.

Not only did these public works, on which "no expense was spared," produce their effect upon the citizens of Athens, but the "visible splendor of the city" gave Athens "an appearance of power greater than the reality," and "procured for her an influence—real though unacknowledged—over all others, and inspired an involuntary deference even in those who most hated and feared her."[9]

Alger shared the excitement of the spectacular transformation of the profile of the urban landscape. He told readers about urban transitions—the creation of Central Park and various building projects underway. The great hotels such as the Astor House, "the pivot on which New York life revolved" for Alger and the Fifth Avenue Hotel captivate his gaze; he arranges important fictional encounters in the quasi-public meeting places of hotel lobbies. Alger boasts:

> One of the Queen's Palaces is far from being as fine a looking building as the Fifth Avenue Hotel. St. James Palace is a very ugly looking brick structure and appears much more like a factory than the home of royalty. There are few hotels in the world as fine as this democratic institution.[10]

Like many of his contemporaries, Alger was captivated with the advent of the department store, with its allure of consumption, described as an event in itself in this period. The department store was dazzling and sensuous, "a permanent fair, an institution, a fantasy world, a spectacle of extraordinary proportions, so that going to the store became an event and an adventure."[11] Wanamaker's of Philadelphia, which opened its doors the year of the Philadelphia Centennial Exposition of 1876, was one of these grand stores; it was said to be larger than the Bon Marché.[12]

One senses the excitement generated. Alger writes: "I went into Siegel & Cooper's big store, having a friend employed there . . . It must be larger than Wanamaker's will be. *That* opens next Monday." Munsey, the publisher who delights in new enterprises, "has opened a large department store on the first floor of his building in New London."[13]   Alger even published a biographical sketch of New York department store magnate A. T. Stewart.

The department store was a place of employment and a potential model for modern, judicious employer-employee relations.   One observer wrote that Mr. Wanamaker felt under personal obligation to make his four thousand employees "thrifty, reliable, and happy, if possible."   He has "established a civil service system, and a plan of working by which he knows the yearly, monthly, and weekly record of each one employed."   There was also a profit-sharing arrangement, through which an approximately one hundred fifty thousand dollars were apportioned among employees in addition to salaries.   Wanamaker provided two spacious restaurants, food at bare cost, and plenty of tables, easy chairs, and a large library for the rest and profit of employees with a full hour break.   "By this arrangement, Mr. Wanamaker has accomplished his purpose, secured the most reliable and best working force in any store in the United States.   Magnanimity is the word to apply to the author of a scheme so unselfish and philanthropic."[14]

Many citizens of the Republic were fascinated with what technology and progress had to offer.   "The nation as a whole was seized by a mania for invention."   School children in the 1850s sketched "smoking steam-engines or steam-boats, all in movement."   In the New York State Asylum, lunatics worked on plans "for leather frying pans and elliptical springs to cushion Niagara Falls."[15]

The author seemed to celebrate expanding transportation and communication linkages, which facilitated the exploration and transformation of space.   He and his fictional characters use the telegraph and long distance transportation networks, which increasingly integrate space into the world market.   These networks allow heroes and benefactors to take possession of space (investment; urban speculation) and acquire liquid capital (e.g., gold).[16]   Expansion of world trade carries Alger's characters on merchant ships bound for India, the Orient, and South America; they mine for gold in Australia.

Alger's hero is sometimes an unwilling passenger on ships bound for distant ports, having been kidnapped or lured on board.   Nathaniel Hawthorne's passenger willingly and eagerly boards the "Celestial Railroad" (1846).   Both are transported to unknown regions.   In the first case, the adventure is productive and often materially advantageous.   In the latter, the ride becomes increasingly more sinister.   Hawthorne paves the way to hell with the marvels—and soot and cinders—of progress and invention.

"The modern Moloch. An engine of destruction (off the track)." *(Diogynes, Hys Lanterne*, Volume III, 1853, p. 287. Library Company of Philadelphia.)

The many railroad and steam engine disasters constantly reminded some in Hawthorne's generation of the price of progress; Alger turns technology's wares into unlooked-for advantages.

Alger's writings shared some of one-time mentor Edward Everett's optimism about the alliance between republicanism and technology. Everett liked to emphasize that, in America, the "wheel of fortune is in constant revolution, and the poor, in one generation, furnish the rich of the next."[17] Alger, like Everett, saw opportunity as a constant in human affairs; there was merely a shift from rural toward urban opportunity.

Nonetheless, the appearance of poverty, crime, immigration, and unemployment prompted anxieties as Alger's eyes roved the changing urban landscape. And, apart from his willing reliance on new transportation and communication links, his writings display remarkably little express recognition of the scope and significance of technological change or of the effects of organization.

Was there something new in these phenomena—something connected to progress, technology, and incorporation? Did technology and invention upset received truths about the laws of economic development? Prewar society believed the economy was balanced and diversified, "resting on immutable laws and composed of relatively small units competing briskly for shares of expanding regional markets." It was anticipated that healthy competition and continued parity of wages and prices would bring independence to the American workingman. "Economic distress and social dislocation were seen as transient phenomena beneath which lay a permanent harmony of interests, the substratum of the natural moral order."[18] A popular exhibit at the Paris Exposition of 1867 was the locomotive America, "intended as a statement of both republican engineering and republican machine art." The Philadelphia Centennial Exposition continued the display of technology in 1876. Machinery Hall housed the 39-foot-tall, 680-ton, $200,000 Corliss engine, which provided all the power for the exhibits in the hall. When President Grant and the Emperor of Brazil opened the Centennial by starting the engine, "the audience thrilled to see how a slight human gesture could trigger such vast power." An observer found "Strong men . . . were moved to tears of joy."[19]

The Paris Exposition in *Frank Hunter's Peril* must have displayed marvelous technical accomplishments and inventions; the hero goes there on his European vacation. The only thing readers see is the new farm plow invented by Frank's acquaintance. Most Alger inventors are misfits, estranged from their environment. Robert Ford, inventor, is considered foolish for attempting to fashion a flying machine in *Helen Ford*. Creators rarely realize any money by their inventions, at least during their lifetimes.[20]

American concern about the impact of technological change had been voiced ever since Thomas Jefferson worried about the compatibility of republicanism and virtue with manufacture. When America's next generation of men of letters travelled to Europe toward midcentury, they often visited factories and brooded on the impact of industrialization and technology upon virtue and civilization.[21]

On his gentleman's tour of Europe on the eve of the Civil War, Alger appeared not to notice the impact of technological change. Instead, he wrote travel essays and newspaper copy about tourist attractions, scenery, food, and culture.[22]   A highlight of his literary career was the publication, by the *North American Review*, of his eyewitness account of the funeral of Eugène Scribe in Paris.

Were the machines in the Crystal Palace the *Iliad's* Trojan Horse? The near invisibility of organization, industrialization, and incorporation in Alger reveal something other than Edward Everett's optimism.

COMPETITION AND COOPERATION

One would hardly realize that Alger inhabited the same universe as Edward Bellamy, who published the extremely popular novel *Looking Backward* in 1888, purporting to solve the most pressing issue of the day—the labor problem.   Alger wrote during the heyday of the Knights of Labor; the American Federation of Labor was growing, and organized labor could claim approximately 300,000 members by the early 1870s.

One might forget that this was the era of robber barons, huge corporations, stock watering practices, and industrial strife.   Few industrial magnates litter the pages. Virtually no worker combinations, unions, or strikes appear in even Alger's later novels. While Alger wrote, the violence of 1877, the Haymarket Riot the Homestead and Pullman Strikes took place.[23]   During a time when miners were organizing, Alger's miners dig for gold—alone or with partners. When one labor uprising is mentioned in *A Debt of Honor*, it is a passing reference by someone remote from the action; the destruction of property in *Ben Bruce*, noted in Chapter 5 is extremely unusual.

While the duties and cement of community were vital pieces in Alger's formula for generating opportunity, it was not through *combination* with others that heroes sought to improve their station. In an era of organizations and major social movements, Alger's individual tends to travel alone or engage in informal, noncontractual cooperation. Employers needed the capacity to separate wheat from chaff; employees had to depend upon their character for advancement. We have no idea what governs the partnership that graces many final pages.

Alger's chief biographer believes the author was, in fact, a closet admirer of cooperation.[24]   On two occasions, Alger wrote former pupil Edwin Seligman about cooperative stores, knowing of the latter's interest in socialism. The store in Natick, Massachusetts, where his parents resided,

> has been a remarkable success . . . and paid extraordinary
> dividends. Yet I do not know that there has been anything
> exceptionally favorable in the circumstances attending its forma-

> tion and history.　The secret of its success has been good
> management, and where cooperation fails, I suspect that failure
> is due to poor management.[25]

Alger visited at least one such store—the Zion Cooperative in Salt Lake City—on his way to the West Coast in 1877.[26]

The mention of these cooperative ventures in letters to Seligman—and apparently nowhere else—probably represented more of an attempt to maintain common ground with his pupil than any abiding interest.[27]　Some contemporaries thought worker-run cooperative ventures were the wave of the future, preferable to constant industrial strife. But farmer's cooperatives became important players on the wrong side of some of Alger's favorite political issues.

Did cooperatives coerce? This question would surely be central for Alger. He remained silent, just as he did in the face of contemporary arguments that worker combinations threatened to coerce employers, limit workers' freedom, or tamper with natural and just relationships.

Alger clearly supports *informal* cooperation that is neither organized nor institutionalized, juxtaposing it to uncivilized competitive behavior. Decent Alger street boys behave much better than many "businessmen." Wren, hero of *A Rolling Stone*, lacks work but is befriended by a shoeshine boy of Irish descent who teaches him the trade.　He helps Wren obtain a blacking kit, and they become partners until Wren learns the trade. He receives no money but only instruction while he serves his brief, two-day apprenticeship.　His "patron" did not think of the potential new competition being created, but only of Wren's need for employment.　Collaboration triumps over competition.[28]

This spirit of cooperation is immediately juxtaposed to the attitude of another street boy, Irish Mike, who tries to claim exclusive title to a particular corner he had occupied for a week and who is not impressed by Wren's assertion that "There's room for us both"; Mike argues that "there ain't business for us both, see?"[29]　Wren claims equal right and sticks up for his position, with the support of surrounding merchants who dislike Mike because he is a bully.　Trying to protect one's turf by excluding others from a trade is bullying. The author, however, offers no clues about what workers should do when faced with excessive competition in street trades—the sort which causes *Paul, the Peddler*, to watch helplessly as his necktie prices drop.[30]

The hero of *Luck and Pluck* (1869) is happy to share his father's estate with his disagreeable stepbrother:

> It had never entered his mind to grudge him the equal advantages
> which Squire Oakley, for his mother's sake, had bestowed upon

her son. He knew that his father was a man of property, and that there was enough for both.[31]

The hero is comfortable with equality and has a generous nature; the foil is determined to destroy any competition and win any comparison. A recent study of the genre of the American Western makes an argument about cooperation that appears compatible with Alger's view:

> Efforts to work with a group through mutual support are doomed to failure . . . If an individual—in the generic sense—is to help others, he must be an individual in the market sense; that is, he must depend only on himself and act as he knows best. Reliance and trust in a group will only weaken him . . . Successful acts are individual acts; only the weak and unsuccessful, albeit decent and kind, work with and depend upon a group.[32]

Subscribing to the liberalism of an earlier era, the author sought to perpetuate and enlarge

> the amount of social freedom the citizen has . . . freedom to move in society, to rise and fall upon his own merits, and to be precluded from no advantage and from no employment of his talents or enjoyment of his fortunes, by barriers of caste of social prejudice.[33]

Labor's troubles do not stem from freedom of contract. For "the right of the individual to own himself must not be infringed, and so the right of the individual to sell himself and to be owned by someone else must not be denied."[34] Young heroes sell their labor power cheerfully and assume there is no imbalance in the bargain they have struck. This assumption depends upon another: males (excepting young children) walk away from bad bargains.[35]

Alger's proffered solution is to create labor that is free and mobile—not tied to a particular skill or employment, so that workers can move from branch of industry to branch of industry. They seek employments in which they cannot be trapped.

Rejecting new hierarchies, differentiation, and specialization in the corporate world, Alger's labor market equivalent of Marx's universal labor fills the role of Boy Friday. The author still maintains faith in "the divine amateur of antebellum legend."[36] Alger's leading figures literally come in off the street. His winners are generalists.

But the individual must be able to negotiate from a position of equality: canceling out power requires independence. The graphic account of suffering behind the items displayed in the Chatham Street pawnbroker's shop described in *Phil, the Fiddler*, highlights Alger's hostility to those who would take advantage of those who cannot bargain as equals. The proprietor's "business was a very profitable one, allowing the most exorbitant rates of interest":

> When the poor have occasion to raise money at a pawnbroker's, they generally find little in their possession to pawn except their clothing. Here was a shawl, pawned for a few shillings by a poor woman whose intemperate husband threw the burden of supporting two young children upon her. Next to it was a black coat belonging to a clerk, who had been out of employment for three months, and now was out of money also. Here was a child's dress, pawned by the mother in dire necessity to save the child from starving. There was a plain gold ring, snatched by a drunken husband from the finger of his poor wife, not to buy food, but to gratify his insatiable craving for drink.[37]

There is no overt support for state regulation of conditions, wages, and hours of labor. However, the concern Alger expresses on behalf of seamstresses and working children who cannot obtain a living wage recognizes categories of workers unable to protect themselves against the cupidity of specific employers. Such concern, voiced by some reformers since at least the 1820s, fueled efforts before the turn of the century to introduce protective legislation for women and children.

Alger's biographer has quite rightly found "a critic of sharp business practices and cutthroat competition."[38] Alger fails to give his characters any viable weapons with which to fight them.

MACHINES AS MEN, AND
MEN AS MACHINES

Which corporate rules and practices were machinelike, and which were "natural?" For authorities such as John P. Davis, corporations and machines were both about the control of nature and about the control of men over men. Echoing Marx, Davis wrote:

> Corporations are instruments of control, of social organization, just as machines are instruments of men's control over the forces of nature; corporations are social machines to which the individual has become almost as completely an adjunct in his relations to men as he has become a mere adjunct of the machine in his relations to nature.

Like the leviathan, the corporation is an association of individuals that becomes more than the sum of the parts. There is something very un-human about this association. This association "has reference rather to the corporate property or industry than to the persons associated. The physical element is exaggerated, the human element is depressed."[39]

Competing legal theories contended either that the corporation was merely a mode of organizing a group of persons, or that it was "not simply a group but a 'group' which is recognized and treated by the law as something distinct from its members." And for those who wished to maintain that, even at law, the corporation was a fiction and therefore invisible, only the persons comprising the corporation were real.[40]

By the 1880s, law had given corporations some of the *powers* of persons.[41] Moreover, the corporation acquired privileges and immunities that individuals singly did not have. Individuals, by associating as a corporation, could protect part of their personal assets against liability. The Fourteenth Amendment due process clause was increasingly used to protect removal of corporate property. These artificial beings were becoming quite real.

Through corporations, organization, machinery, transportation, the individual has been removed to a greater distance in both time and space from the forces of nature on which he depends. His contact with nature is more effective, but it is less direct. He has become far more dependent on the artificial physical element (machines, factories, railways) and the human element (organized society) than on nature itself.[42]

Such corporate beings "free" people from much of their dependence on nature; these artificial and owned creations, in turn, exert control over humans and over nature.

As the corporation began to achieve an identity at law as a real entity, Alger was among those who saw it only as a fiction, as nothing other than the individuals who compose it. The corporation itself is virtually invisible; however, the corporation is personified: Individual businessmen become its stand-ins. The corporation that challenges or transcends market rules—through price and rate fixing, monopolies, cutthroat competition, and holding communities hostage—does so in the fictional guise of the activities of individual self-interested villains [businessmen]. If the corporation is becoming a monster—the artificial, intangible person that can transcend natural bounds in an "exhaustless greed for lucre"—for Alger the monster is the person identified as the capitalist. Fiction has translated public events and public entities into essentially private struggles.[43]

The vision of the individual as the corporation may reflect a gnawing awareness among Alger's contemporaries that these Gilded Age corporations did not well serve public purposes. "The purpose of the modern corporation is less plainly to contribute to national development and is apparently confined, to a large extent, to the amplification of the individual."[44]

Alger tries to insist that the corporation either conform to laws and limits of nature or pay the price. Prior to "trust-busting," fictional evil-doers get exposed and fail, upholding the (natural) individual. But the operating requirements of transportation and communication companies in this era "had made obsolete the competition between small units that had no control over prices—prices that were set by the market forces of supply and demand." Monopolies were "no longer regulated by market mechanisms."[45] When it was hard to name a perpetrator or the crime, Alger's powers against the corporation were feeble. And thus, perpetrators of some of the stock watering swindles and phony stock options escape detection and punishment.

MACHINES AND MONEY- MAKING: RULES ARE RULES, BUSINESS IS BUSINESS

> It will be the object of every honest man to render, in all cases, an equivalent for what he receives. Where the market price cannot be known, each of the parties to an honest contract will endeavor to come as near it as possible; keeping in mind the rule of doing to others as they would desire others to do to them in similar circumstances. Every bargain not formed on these principles is, in its results, unjust; and if intentional, is fraudulent.
>
> William Alcott, *The Young Man's Guide*

Alger retained the time-honored notion of exchange of equivalents as the basis of value. Central characters may refuse excessive rewards for services performed. Fair business dealings serve the interest and improve the lot of each party to the transaction; the honest business man "will in no case take even the smallest advantage of his neighbor."[46]

Horace Mann asserted that the boy of good character avoids any occupation "if, with his own weal, they do not also promote the common weal"; and he abhors the idea "that anything can advance the *well*-being of himself which involves the *ill*-being of others."[47]

Beyond activities identified as legally criminal, how identifiable were these occupations? Alger and his contemporaries frequently resorted to cataloguing inappropriate business *practices*.   The list was frequently imprecise as observers sought to determine what practices detracted from the common weal, and what kinds of truck and barter failed to make both parties to the transaction better off.

This common weal was the measure of fairness and underpinned an organic theory of justice. An activity that tends to "the success of the few" is described as a "great temptation." T. S. Arthur instructed: "nearly all speculations are dishonest means, by which one man gains a certain amount of money in a transaction that another loses." But these gentlemen, reared and educated before the war, had trouble locating this transfer from the pockets of one to the pockets of another. Where or how is it announced? One advice author cleverly finesses the problem of detection: "when you hear a man triumph in gaining by another's loss, you may easily judge of his character."[48]

Advice manuals complained of dishonest business dealings throughout the century. These included concealing or misrepresenting facts about value (buying for less and/or selling for more than fair valuation) and selling unsound and defective goods. The merchant who sells cheap goods is usually attempting to pass off merchandise as higher quality than it is by charging high prices. Here was evidence of declension:

> Throughout all trades and professions there prevails a system of fraud upon the public which is becoming apparent in the gradual deterioration of almost every article of general consumption, while the makers stun the public ear with declarations of the superior quality of every thing they produce. Thus the effort of each calling to secure its own interests, at the expense of the whole, has been the effort of all; and the consequence is, that all are worse off for it.[49]

Alger's own Paul Prescott suffers by such a merchant. He is unhappy at work when he discovers his employer would complete a sale at any cost. Clerks are encouraged to misrepresent the quality of merchandise; Paul honestly responds to a customer's query and is discharged.[50] He cannot put forward his best efforts or exhibit loyalty to such an employer. Heroes shopping for an inexpensive suit are steered away from these stores, identified either by the look of the merchant or the location of the shop.

Holding out for the last dollar in a transaction, haggling over price, and negotiating from a low offer are all ungentlemanly. Shrewdness is no compliment for Alger. In a late story, *A Rolling Stone*, a cigar store merchant and would-be San Francisco urban lot owner, who attempts to buy low and sell high, appears as "a man who would be good at a bargain, and whom it wouldn't be easy to overreach."[51] The hero, representing the absentee owner in the transaction, instead sells the San Francisco lots to a different purchaser, who immediately offers their approximate market value, without negotiating and without bargaining. One who is aware of rising values does not misrepresent it or play upon another's imperfect information. Since fair market value is knowable, both parties in a transaction should approximate it. All else is greed.

*　　*　　*　　*　　*

The best tip-off that something is amiss is when an Alger character insists that "rules are rules; business is business." Cold, passionless, machinelike pursuers of profit are barely recognizable as human. These soulless monsters are unnatural persons whose presence pose threats to those of flesh and blood and sentiment.[52]

Alger's biographical sketch of department store magnate A. T. Stewart catalogued Stewart's business principles, from which he never deviated:

> 1) Strict honesty in all dealings with customers. 2) One price for all. 3) Cash on delivery. 4) Business to be done as business, and without reference to any other consideration. 5) Courtesy to all, of whatever rank. In the days of his greatest prosperity a poor Irish woman was as welcome in his large store as a lady dressed in silks, and the clerk who should presume to treat her with impertinence would have been instantly discharged. All these rules I can unreservedly commend, with the exception of the fourth, which Mr. Stewart carried too far.

These principles accounted for Stewart's success. However, Alger was not quite satisfied. Impersonal calculations are inadequate to justice. Stewart was hard and stern: business was business. He failed to temper justice with mercy. Alger felt compelled to add that Stewart engaged in little charitable activity.[53]

While Stewart retains his aura of respectability in the sketch, in Alger's fiction, he would not have fared as well. Here, the term "capitalist" tended to be negatively loaded and was applied to a variety of pursuits. Capitalists may be thrifty, self-made men, but they are also grasping, excessively self-centered individualists. Such is the (rare) industrialist Brantley Wentworth in *A Debt of Honor*. The Wentworths of the Alger universe are depicted as machinelike, ruthless, uncaring, breakers of labor. Like Dan's first benefactor says of Mr. Gripp, a clothing store owner in *Dan, the Newsboy*, "He doesn't deserve to [sleep to-night], for he grows rich by defrauding the poor who work for him."[54]

Capitalists are often provided with only slightly ambiguously Jewish names. A terse description of one such character is memorable for its portrayal of the unsavory capitalist. A minor Alger character seeking to borrow money

> went straightway to a dingy room in Nassau Street, occupied by an old man as shabby as the apartment he occupied. Yet this old man was a capitalist, who had for thirty years lent money at usurious interest, taking advantage of a tight money market and the needs of embarrassed men, and there are always plenty of the latter class in a great city like New York. In this way he had

accumulated a large fortune, without altering his style of living. He slept in a small room connected with his office, and took his meals at some one of the cheap restaurants in the neighborhood. He was an old man, of nearly seventy, with bent form, long white beard, face seamed with wrinkles, and thick, bushy eyebrows, beneath which peered a pair of sharp, keen eyes. Such was Job Green, the money-lender.[55]

A minor character in *A Rolling Stone* seeks payment for some vests his mother had made, only to have the salesman refuse to accept the partial lot ("six or nothing") despite the boy's protestation that his mother needs the money. A customer in the San Francisco clothing store overhears the conversation, and although he has selected a fine suit, decides he will not purchase from the merchant. The customer says "The suit is satisfactory; but I don't care to trade at a store where there is so little consideration for employees."[56] The salesman pleads that rules are rules, but Alger is unsympathetic: one cannot hide inhumanity behind bureaucratic rules and standard operating procedures.

Alger is especially disturbed when a creditor's hardness takes place in the realm of bare necessities, such as lodging. But ability to pay forms no part of the calculus of the man who hides behind "business." Such a man, whether landlord, lienholder, or merchant, insists on payment on the appointed date without exception; he has no compunction about evicting tenants or foreclosing mortgages.

When a minor character in *A Rolling Stone*, unable to get sewing to do, is unable to pay her forthcoming month's rent, the landlord offers her only until the next morning to come up with the full amount. The poor woman (who will be rescued by the hero) protests "...where shall I go. You would not put us into the street?" The landlord's unfeeling response is: "That is not my lookout. I have my taxes and repairs to pay, and I cannot keep tenants that do not settle for their rent."[57] He relies upon his chain of legal and business obligations; other landlords rely upon legal rights.

Although the argument about what *would* be fair under such circumstances is incomplete, Alger's fair price might not be independent of need. Demanding market value from those unable to pay is a form of unfairness—and a moral defect—regardless of contracts explicit or implied. Should merchants or capitalists, then, completely suspend their claims in the face of need? Alger does not seriously consider this option. Taking account of ability to pay does not require cancellation of the debt, but merely suspension of the tyranny of *time*.

Two miners with whom the hero of *Dean Dunham* falls in exhibit a generous, liberal spirit, which Alger believes life in the West tends to breed. They give the boy a good claim so that Dean can mine with them:

> [Dean] might have travelled far enough in the East without meeting strangers so free-handed. Indeed had he met the same parties at home, he would scarcely have found them so liberal. The wild, free life of the West had opened their hearts and made them generous.[58]

Their generosity and fairness contrast with the self-interested "capitalist," and yet Alger shows that these same miners are quite capable of protecting their business interests. When selling their claims, they conduct hard-nosed business the "right" way. "I don't want to be extortionate," says one, "but the claims are good ones, and we don't want to sacrifice them." The results leave them "complacent"; they recognize that, by comparison with what they were worth when they came West, and with what others who have worked their whole lives were worth, they have "done pretty well."[59] Getting the last possible dollar out of an investment is immaterial; it is not the proper measure of performance.

CONCLUSION

Merchants and capitalists who profit from the loss of others, who insist that "business is business," who supply only money-backed "demand," who fail to recognize need in their calculation of price, and who fail to pay a living wage have much in common with machines. One who places money or money-getting at the center of the universe is anything but a success, and anything but a man.[60] For Alger, large fortunes seem often to be built on getting something for nothing.

The creation of unthinkable fortunes had to generate discomfort for those in the Gilded Age who held an exchange of equivalents theory of fair business dealings and those who believed that honest labor was central to the addition of value to the economy.

The successful businessmen Alger praised were not the Rockefellers or Jay Goulds, and indeed, large fortunes may have disqualified capitalists from Alger's high regard; otherwise, Alger would have been more comfortable with Andrew Carnegie. Advice manual author William Makepeace Thayer termed Carnegie's *Triumphant Democracy* "one of the best books published in our country." An immigrant, a self-made man, a philanthropist, and an endower of free libraries, Carnegie advised young men to "Avoid drink, avoid speculation, avoid endorsements. Aim high. For the question 'What *must* I do for my employer?' substitute, 'What *can* I do?' Begin to save early."[61] The steel magnate claimed he engaged in collective decision making with his workers and made professions of great concern for them. He viewed his business as a collective, human enterprise.

At what point do producers cross the line to the sinister—or what is their crime? Alger lacks an analysis of the basis of wages or profits that would stand up to the industrial era. Size and scale of operation and of fortune themselves appear suspect. Where do large profits come from? What is a fair rate of return to the employer? What is a just rent? What is owing to labor?

What the author saw was that capitalists exert dangerous power over others—power that they frequently misuse. Horace Mann articulated the danger from this kind of wealth at midcentury:

> You have power over any quantity of water or steam, and over any number of wheels. You have power, too, over the *bodies* of certain classes of men; but do good with your wealth, and you will become a ruler over all men's *hearts* . . .[62]

The fear of the power capitalists hold over the lives of others and the naming of their crimes against nature is further explored in Chapters 7 and 8.

The human capacity for improvement was a unique and a mixed blessing. If others worried that homo faber had created the monster of Frankenstein, who radically transforms the creator's life, Alger argues for continuity. Industrialization does not create new rules for business dealings. Labor can be rewarded fairly and honestly. There is room for compassion in economic exchanges.

7

======

Natural Aristocracy in a Democracy: Authority, Power, and Politics

> That American citizen who has original manhood and lives a
> fresh, honest life of his own, regardless of the dictation of King
> Caucus or Queen Average,—the most heartless and vulgar
> despots that ever reigned,—sets the bravest of examples and
> teaches the most needed of lessons
>
> William Rounseville Alger, *Life of Edwin Forrest*, Vol. 2

Although the Civil War served as backdrop for several early tales, Alger's fiction is otherwise almost devoid of explicit reference to political figures and conflicts. There are no "party men" and few politicians. Rarely does the author route a hero to a career in politics.

Alger nonetheless maintained a healthy interest in political contests and issues, and his letters display attentiveness to political campaigns and national party conventions. His conception of American candidates and issues was rather pedestrian, and his views unsophisticated; he appears not to have read a great deal of political commentary or analysis; his views seem to have been shaped by his party's advertising and attacks.[1] But Alger was an unabashed and loyal Republican partisan.

Election nights still brought people—whether working, newsgathering, or observing—into the streets. Alger was among the number on the night of the Tilden-Hayes contested election of 1876:

110

Wm. A[lger] and myself were out late Tuesday night. He insisted that we were overwhelmingly defeated, and laughed at me for expressing confidence that Hayes would be elected after all.[2]

He was still caught up in the heat of political contest during the last presidential campaign of his lifetime. On September 9, 1896, he offered that "the next two months will no doubt be full of political excitement, but it seems to me that the issue is not doubtful." Just after the McKinley victory, Alger wrote his young *Tribune* friend, Irving Blake: "You must have worked hard during election week. But it came out all right, and I am rejoiced."[3]

Political sentiments pervade his work. The most direct expressions on political issues of the day are found in his letters and in his juvenile biographies of admired Republican presidents Lincoln and Garfield, and Whig Senator Daniel Webster.[4] But closer examination reveals that Alger's *fiction* also re-enacted important political and economic struggles of the day. Favorite issues included sound money, economic development, and policies encouraging responsible growth; also deserving of attention were spoils, corruption, and the possibility of virtue in politics.[5] All were wrapped up with the issue of power.

RESISTING POWER

Dangerous power was a problem in the workplace and in the economy, in society, and in politics. Much of the counsel about power was directed to youth, but adults who exercised power and influence over others were also reminded of their responsibility. Wealth was one of the most pronounced sources of power.

Wariness of large fortunes was, in great measure, suspicion of the power that wealth tended to generate. Extreme wealth was a danger for the community. Alger was likely to concur that

> vast fortunes are a misfortune to the State. They confer irrespon-
> sible power; and human nature, except in the rarest instances, has
> proved incapable of wielding irresponsible power, without abuse.[6]

Alger boys learn to recognize and avoid certain types of persons and situations where they were likely to yield up power over themselves, whether in gambling dens, factories, or in the political arena. They avoid yielding control over their bodies to another. They run away from those who would compel their labor or compliance; they are liberated from the prospects of indenture or apprenticeship; they flee the authority of evil stepparents and they escape kidnappers. Amateur performers seek to

"Kit's flight from the blacksmith (fleeing an apprenticeship)." (Horatio Alger, Jr., *The Young Acrobat*. New York: Hurst and Company, n.d., p. 62.)

escape the control of managers and handlers. Boys escape the clutches of those wealthy individuals (frequently "capitalists") who manipulate labor and take advantage of those most dependent upon them, and who are equally likely to hold members of the community hostage over loans or mortgages.

The successful resist illegitimate power and help weaker members of the community do the same. Young Paul Hoffman helps Fillipo escape from the padrone in *Phil, the Fiddler*. Conscious and confident of his own strength, Paul says he "should like to see [the padrone] try" to beat him.

> Phil looked admiringly at the boy who was not afraid of the padrone. Like his comrades, he had been accustomed to think of the padrone as possessed of unlimited power, and never dreamed of anybody defying him, or resisting his threats. Though he had determined to run away, his soul was not free from the tyranny of his late taskmaster . . . [7]

Alger liked to brag that this novel helped bring an end to the padrone system in New York. However, the claim is excessive.

Alger's use of the rhetoric of rights most frequently takes place in the context of resistance to abuse of power. When heroes defend their rights, they guard their own power, autonomy, and independence. The Alger hero "had a proper spirit, and did not choose to be bullied"; such a boy "did not mean to be imposed upon, or to have his just rights encroached upon, if he could help it."[8] A boy hero may stick up for his rights, or "claim 'the right of ordinary humanity' to defend others' rights." The hero who struggles to regain his birthright will not agree "to be deprived of his rights."[9]

This posture is not passive, but is defensive only. Central characters do not seek power over others. They never encroach on rights and liberties. Power is a good only when it stays within limits.

Power looked as if it were a zero-sum game, with a natural *balance* of power. Each agent must guard his/her own power to maintain independence. Any change in the equation of power increases the power of some agents relative to others. When one yielded to liquor, gambling, or other vices, one ceded control; they—or those who manipulated—acquired power. One of the most important loci in the struggle over self-determination—and yet one easy enough to overlook in Alger stories—was politics.

Fear of central power was an American legacy. The Revolution constituted additional proof for the founders, should they require more than had been provided by their favorite English and Scottish Enlightenment thinkers, that political power was a tremendous danger. Humans are imperfect; power is a great temptation and very likely to be abused. The danger did not, by any means, disappear with formal independence. European powers lay in wait to insinuate themselves as Americans fought among themselves. There were an increasing number of enemies within.

Political power was, nevertheless, necessary; without order, human existence "is precarious and beset with constant perils."[10] And occasionally, positions of political power were occupied by men who Alger could wholeheartedly admire as models for his audience. Lincoln, without power, could not have preserved the Union. Power, used properly, maintained the independence of the Republic.

Political power must uphold the citizen's capacity to maintain his [sic] own independence. In Alger's eyes, it followed that political power should uphold rightful property. Property was an important means for placing oneself and one's family outside the dangerous power of others. His hero's search for liquid and fixed assets was part of his struggle to retain power. Like property in the self, it was a means to independence. James Fenimore Cooper said it clearly:

> *Property is desirable as the ground work of moral independence,* as a
> means of improving the faculties, and of doing good to others,
> and as the agent in all that distinguishes the civilized man from
> the savage.[11] [emphasis added]

"As property is the base of all civilization," Cooper wrote, "its existence and security are indispensable to social improvement." For Horace Mann, "to the young man without patrimony, there are few higher earthly duties than to obtain a competency."[12] Having enough for one's comfortable existence provided competence, power, independence. A moderate amount maintained the balance of power.

In an expanding economy, the quest for property was a positive sum game. It was a game Alger believed all could play to win. However difficult the view was to maintain in the Gilded Age, Alger argued that property, honestly acquired, was not attained at the expense of others. And, if property helps secure liberty, then the hero, in acquiring property, makes the world safer for democracy.

DEMOCRACY AND THE LIMITS OF POLITICS

> The great immigration of foreigners into the country, and the
> practice of remaining, or of assembling, in the large towns,
> renders universal suffrage doubly oppressive to the citizens of
> the latter . . . it is a painful and humiliating fact, that several
> of the principal places of this country, are, virtually, under the
> control of men of this class, who have few convictions of liberty,
> beyond those which arise from a love of licentiousness, who are
> totally ignorant of its governing principles, and who, in their
> hearts and language, are hostile to the very people whose
> hospitality they enjoy . . . Whatever may be said, on general
> principles, of the necessity of giving to a government the broadest
> possible base, few will contend that circumstances like these,
> ought not to qualify the regulation in practice.
>
> James Fenimore Cooper, *The American Democrat*

Extension of the franchise posed new problems of illegitimate power.
Conservative elites bemoaned the fact that men of worth departed or were
pushed from the public realm, yielding the stage to demagogues courting
an unwise democracy. Not only the manipulators were to be feared: the
lawless were also potentially tyrannical.

Men of education and virtue were not sufficiently aggressive for the new
era:

> Real worth is modest, and always ready to defer to others; in fact,
> often too much so, in society, for the general good, while shallow
> conceit is ever thrusting itself rudely forward, and occupying the
> place of wiser and better men.[13]

Tocqueville's observation of the previous generation sounded equally
appropriate in the Gilded Age: "In our day it is a constant fact that the most
outstanding Americans are seldom summoned to public office, and it must
be recognized that this tendency has increased as democracy has gone
beyond its previous limits."[14]

Yielding political space to men who pandered to the lowest tastes and
who enthroned passion or selfish interest meant that, whatever men were
capable of, *politics* became capable of much less.

The politics of selfish interests could surely undermine the Republic. As
northerners read the causes of the Civil War, selfishness had almost
succeeded in doing just this. Selfishness was not confined to the basest urban
classes and their political lackeys.

Alger probably wondered, along with Henry Adams, "whether any
politician could be believed or trusted," and whether politics could have

anything to do with truth or honor. If Alger held a high opinion of the potential in human nature, when individuals acquired power, it was another matter. "Could one afford to trust human nature in politics? History said not."[15]

If politicians were blamed for contributing to the debasement of the public, so was the partisan newspaper. The press, which occupied a position of public responsibility, was frequently charged with failing in its most minimal obligation not to *further* debase public opinion.

Alger himself had written of the tendency of a popular vehicle to corrupt. Aristophanes satirized "the institutions of his native city and dragged out into open view her political errors and social defects." Was Greek comedy "productive of greater good than evil in its effect upon the public mind"?

> Ridicule is a potent weapon, and when well-directed may serve an important purpose in promoting the cause of virtue and good morals. But when we find it . . . directed against the virtuous and vicious alike,—against the purest and most blameless characters: when it represents vice and corruption as the legitimate consequences of the intellectual progress of the age, its unfavorable influence upon the popular standard of morality and intelligence can no longer be questioned.[16]

Like Greek comedy, the press could undermine public morality by presuming viciousness in public figures of whatever stature. The newspaper press debases merit, and

> assails almost every official in the country with the foulest accusations. Are these writers destitute of patriotism and of faith in humanity? Are they ignorant of the fact that if they convince the public that their superiors are all corrupt the irresistible reflex influence of the conviction will itself corrupt the whole public?[17]

This echoed earlier complaints: "The precipitate manner in which many conductors of papers condemn men and measures, upon slight evidence, is one of the prevailing *evils* or rather *sins* of this very country." Party spirit perverts the press so far that it is difficult to determine whether "the press serves most to enlighten public opinion with truth, or to pervert it with error."[18]

But just as he had wished to believe in the goodness of public opinion when writing of the Greeks and Romans at Harvard, Alger wanted to believe that the modern American public could at least *hope* to judge rightly. As the press attacked his distant relation, Russell A. Alger, for inept prosecution of the Spanish-American War, Alger wrote: "I have felt provoked at the senseless and unreasonable criticisms on your official course, but the public will do you justice in the end." McKinley asked for his resignation.[19]

How, under universal suffrage, could men of education and virtue be heard? The question was of vital interest to the Whigs, the party that Emerson once termed "the active, enterprizing, intelligent, well-meaning & wealthy part of the people."[20] These solid citizens viewed themselves as an objective disinterested aristocracy—unselfish guardians of the public good and the voice of moderation in public life. Edward Everett, one of Alger's Harvard mentors, claimed that the Whigs embraced "an enlightened and liberal conservatism." Jacksonians talked of "equality," Whigs emphasized "duty" and "morality."[21] Alger's political heritage was decidedly Whig.

In journals of Whig opinion, including the *North American Review*, authors lamented "the decline of virtue and principle in American political life since the eighteenth century."[22] The year Alger was graduated from college, Horace Greeley proclaimed that fellow Whigs "prefer the society and counsel of those who walk, so far as we may judge, in the ways of Virtue, to that of the reckless, ostentatious servitors of Vice," with which he associated the "Democratic" party.[23]

Seeking to teach that "liberty has no real value without responsibility and order," Whigs found Democratic voters undisciplined—unschooled in the self-imposition of internal restraints.[24] The Democrats [in antebellum America, the "Democracy"] were even lawless. Horace Greeley observed: "Take all the haunts of debauchery in the land, and you will find nine-tenths of their master-spirits active partisans of that same 'Democracy.'"[25]

Among the Whigs were persistent critics of suffrage extension who were fearful that the people would come to respect no one except themselves. "Because of ignorance or self-interest, dependence of the people upon themselves was as dangerous as their dependence upon landlords or employers."[26] The *vote* could be a dangerous source of power when delivered into the hands of those most unable to discern seeming from being, who were not masters of themselves, and whose difference from the children of the Mayflower was apparent.

Around 1840, when Democratic Party rivals were increasingly embarrassing the Whigs on the suffrage issue, the Whigs gave up the frontal assault on extension of the franchise. In national politics, in one now classic account—despite the anachronistic reference to the Alger type—the Whigs turned defeat into victory by transforming their message:

> If they gave up Hamilton's hatred of the people, they retained
> his grandiose capitalist dream, and this they combined with
> the Jeffersonian concept of equal opportunity. The result was

to electrify the democratic individual with a passion for great
achievement and to produce a personality type that was
neither Hamiltonian nor Jeffersonian but a strange mixture of
them both: the hero of Horatio Alger.[27]

But the Whigs hardly rushed to embrace democracy. Those from Alger's
home state of Massachusetts remained rather effective in constraining the
suffrage. On the eve of the Civil War, taxpaying qualifications to the suffrage
remained in Massachusetts, Rhode Island, Delaware, Pennsylvania, and
New Hampshire. Local government was especially viewed as "a kind of
public service corporation which either was, or should be, non-partisan and
in which only taxpayers should share." Old New England stock in small
towns feared that enfranchisement would increase the political power of
those who did not share its interests and values. The year after Alger was
graduated from college, a mass meeting in Faneuil Hall in October, 1853
narrowly rejected the principle of manhood suffrage that was contained in
the revised constitution; this included state elections.[28]

Obviously elected representatives must be allowed to exercise their
discretion for the good of their constituents, rather than be bound to them.
But Whig sympathizers sought other ways to try to filter opinion and
minimize dangerous sentiment. Democratic harms were also addressed via
electoral tricks. Massachusetts Whigs supported "banker's hours" at the
polls:

> the polls were closed at sunset, to disfranchise, according to
> Democrats, Cambridge laborers who worked in Boston but
> had to vote in their place of residence. When they returned
> home the polls were closed.[29]

If workers were to vote under Sunset Law restrictions, employers might give
workers "time off to vote under the supervision of plant foremen or other
representatives of management." The pressure of watchful eyes again
figured as Massachusetts Whigs, in 1839, managed to pass a law requiring
ballots (which were then party tickets printed in varying colors) to be
submitted unsealed and unfolded. Democrats were unable to force a secret
ballot until 1851. In-person registration and/or annual registration
requirements also worked against some poor or neglectful voters and those
who could not meet residency requirements.[30]

Whigs had to pin their hopes for the preservation of virtue in politics on
more than electoral ruses. But what else could be done? Whigs especially
saw public education and oratory as vital means of leadership in a mass
democracy.

Universal school attendance was, under the circumstances, desirable.
Education was a means of self-improvement and taught self-discipline;

since human nature was most malleable in youth, enlightened guidance would have its greatest payoff here. In school, salutary moral influence took the form of a person and a text. Even in dangerous environments, public education could combat vice's counsel and keep class cleavages from deepening.[31] With so many coming to America's shores, this guidance became all the more necessary.

Oratory was also an important means of social control. Alger's appreciation of orators, from Pericles and Cicero to Webster and Everett, was shared by other Whigs. "Rhetorical ability . . . was crucial in a republic, for free men who could not be coerced had to be persuaded." The orator "must not only defend the people's true interests but show the people themselves where those interests lay."[32] If any were to guide the young, it was because they could persuade others of their entitlement and moral authority, both by their actions and by their words.

Leadership was surely not confined to public space. James Fenimore Cooper saw the private gentleman belonging to that class which is "the natural repository of the manners, tastes, tone, and, to a certain extent, of the principles of a country"; he therefore had a high obligation "to be a guardian of the liberties of his fellow citizens," while avoiding "the cant of demagogueism with the impracticable theories of visionaries, and the narrow and selfish dogmas of those who would limit power by castes." But the rest must recognize and respect quality when they saw it:

> He who would honor learning, and taste, and sentiment, and refinement of every sort, ought to respect its possessors, and, in all things but those which affect rights, defer to their superior advantages.[33]

Alger's heroes were properly attentive and deferential to those fit to lead. They learned from such men and women.

When just entering his junior year at Harvard at the age of eighteen, Alger wrote Cooper seeking an autograph for a collection of American authors of distinction he was forming: "Permit me to take this opportunity to express to you, Sir, the great gratification with which I have perused many of your works—more especially the Leatherstocking Series."[34]

Alger may have appreciated Cooper's demonstration that human life was good by nature. Natty Bumppo embodied "the natural moral standards on which a peaceful, prosperous society could be constructed," and pointed to "natural standards of justice," which included rights of self-preservation and property. Rejecting social conventions and distinctions as the basis of excellence, Cooper maintained that people could "live together in peace... if they learn to tolerate religious, cultural, and individual differences." Men and women who profited by contact with Natty came to appreciate the "value of both self-control and service to others"; they became "fit to govern a democratic people."[35]

Whereas Cooper believed "the physical and moral qualities are unequally distributed," and criticized suffrage reform, Alger was born to a later generation.[36] The day to oppose suffrage reform was past, even had the author been of the fearful temperament. Alger would have to find a balm for the ills in Pandora's box.

Alger, in fact, played optimist to some Whig fears. He was willing to assay the proposition of antebellum suffrage reformers, that men "shared the capacity to improve indefinitely those great moral and rational faculties with which they had been endowed by their Creator."[37] Newcomers could learn the rules of the game and join the Anglo-Saxon Republic of virtue. Nature was *capable* of much more than most settled for. His Republic could endure democratization but required at least noninstitutionalzed leadership by enlightened Whig-Republicans. Natural leaders could hope to prevail over self-interest. People could be swayed by words, by moral example, and by the right kind of literature.

Despite the dangers of misguided and selfish popular power, Alger, with his faith in human nature and the hope that public opinion *could* be properly guided, cautiously embraced democracy.

GILDED AGE POLITICS

> I am almost satisfied with the result of the convention, but, except in Indiana, I think you [General Russell A. Alger] would have been a stronger candidate than Harrison. However, the strongest feeling with me as with you is the hope that our party may win against an Administration which is unAmerican, and hostile to the industrial interests of the people.
>
> Alger to Russell A. Alger, July 4, 1888[38]

Alger's view of the limits of politics were shaped by the quality of the people he saw seeking to wield political power. The Gilded Age hardly offered a promising record.

Young Woodrow Wilson observed, in 1879, that American politics was characterized by "No leaders, no principles; no principles, no parties." Henry Adams thought that "one might search the whole list of Congress, Judiciary, and Executive during the twenty-five years 1870 to 1895 . . . and find little but damaged reputation." According to a later historian, Gilded Age parties "divided over spoils, not issues."[39]

*   *   *   *   *

As a thirty-year New York City resident during the heyday of Boss Tweed, the author's disgust for Tammany Hall helped poison his view of the Democrats, and of urban politicians more generally. New York politics was rife with corruption and bribery, extending to the police and judicial system. And, "like other Harvard-educated patricians, Alger disdained machine politics and unprincipled campaigns."[40]

The Democrats held no monopoly on unprincipled politics. Republican Party politics were rife with factional leaders, bosses, and corruption. Alger sometimes saw this in urban politics. When the Republicans lost the New York City elections of 1897, Alger "consoled" Blake:

> I am not sure but it is better to have Tammany win now. Before the next election it will have made mistakes enough to send voters in disgust into the Republican ranks. Platt and Croker seem to be "birds of a feather."[41]

Republican boss Thomas C. Platt headed a political machine much like that of Tammany, and both appeared to have had close ties with corporate interests. The stakes in the election were control over the city's $90 million annual budget, plus control over the revenues from "rents, fees, fines, interest, assessments for street improvements, bond sales and premiums, ...selling of legislative 'goods'"—everything Tammany knew how to control. The Wigwam also gained control of some sixty thousand employees. "The disreputable classes vociferously celebrated the occasion, assured that the town was once more to be 'wide open.'"[42]

At the national level, the Republican Party "sought actively to strengthen its social base by espousing the policies of American industrialists." Although Alger was less willing to see it, capitalists distributed bribes, fees, gifts, and investment opportunities to Republican politicians to obtain favorable currency policy, exemption from regulatory legislation, and government largesse. Garfield's successor, Chester A. Arthur, had been "the major domo of [Roscoe] Conkling's notorious New York Customhouse machine, a spoilsman's spoilsman." When the Republicans narrowly won the presidency in 1888, Boss Matt Quay quickly noted that Providence had nothing to do with the Harrison victory. The new president would never know "how close a number of men were compelled to approach the gates of the penitentiary to make him President." Harrison lamented to Theodore Roosevelt, "When I came into power ... I found that the party managers had taken it all to themselves. I could not name my own Cabinet. They had sold out every place to pay election expenses."[43]

What Alger *did* understand was that winning the allegiance of voters by intimidation, bullying, threats, corruption, favors, and plying them with liquor was not the stuff of enlightened politics. Here, surely, was an issue of illegitimate power in politics.

"Had Julian Lorimer been older, and in political life, he would have aspired to the position of a boss. He enjoyed power, and desired to have his power acknowledged by others."[44] Alger's street bullies, like the Irish Micky Maguire in *Ragged Dick*, had more than a passing resemblance to the political hack, waging turf battles.[45] Men of wealth, such as Julian Lorimer, also abuse their positions when they seek to obtain power over trusting citizens.

Alger's conflictedness about the capacity of the public to judge its leaders well, and about the quality of public opinion generally, can be seen in his treatment of the man who appears to be public spirited or is charged with the public trust. This theme is usually played out in small towns, where "squires" acquire positions of community and/or political leadership by virtue of their wealth and social status. Such a man is often not what he seems; his wealth is often fraudulently acquired. The squire in charge of the local poorhouse or orphanage rarely takes adequate provision for his charges. He is often "mean" (cheap); he is happy to reap public credit for his service while delivering very little.

Even the relatively homogeneous, small town public has not been a good judge of the worth of such squires. Most people in town are respectful or even obsequious; they fail to see the ongoing abuse of trust. The author intervenes where public judgment fails, and terminates illegitimate power.

A "realist" in an advice manual Alger recommended is made to say that self-reliance is naïve and passé: "It is patronage that does it. You must have some relative or friend to help you up, or you have no chance."[46] Alger's distaste for nepotism and patronage in politics and in the business world, and his belief that this problem had to be rectified, is evident.

The setting for this confrontation is usually the counting room. A frequent device has a senior clerk in cahoots with a young nephew or relative to have the worthy hero lose his job so that the lazy or unreliable relative can get it. In correcting the abuses of nepotism, the spoils system, and patronage politics in fiction, Alger makes merit triumph over favoritism. Here was a voter ripe for appeals for civil service reform.

For Alger, character was strong recommendation for a presidential candidate. Former Civil War general and Michigan governor, Russell A. Alger, made a charitable gift to a thousand poor boys in Detroit. This contribution was all the proof Alger needed to support the 1888 Republican candidacy of one who turned out, upon inquiry, to be a distant relation.[47] Hearing of the generous gift, Alger initiated contact: "Of course I have noticed the prominent mention of your name for a high national office, and should be glad of an opportunity to vote for you."[48]

When Harrison secured the nomination at the 1888 convention instead, Alger conveyed to his relation his scorn for the Democratic incumbent. The author's judgment that the Cleveland Administration was *"unAmerican, and hostile to the industrial interests of the people"* [italics mine], offers a clue about what, besides upstanding character, was salient when Alger made political judgments.

On character, the campaign of 1884 had offered little to choose from. Republican candidate James G. Blaine's lies and questionable financial transactions were placed before the public; meanwhile, the newspapers were publishing accounts of Cleveland's illegitimate child. Moral guardians picked up this attack:

> Republican ministers held large audiences in thrall while with an evangelical fervor and a Victorian profusion of detail they drew lurid pictures of the Democratic leader as a 'libertine' and 'moral leper' who sought to introduce himself into the highest office of the land.[49]

Despite his best biographers' claim that "Alger was a Mugwump, a liberal Republican committed to principles of fair prices and decent wages...,"[50] it is inconceivable, given his thoughts on Cleveland and the Democrats, that Alger joined with liberal Republicans of New York in the Mugwump defection of 1884, abandoning Blaine and helping elect Grover Cleveland. Blaine's 1884 foreign policy plank, which he termed *"American,"* may have shaped Alger's later rhetoric of unAmericanism.[51]

Woodrow Wilson later pronounced that "Cleveland was a conservative Republican," a perception shared by the Mugwumps.[52] But he was not economically conservative enough for some Republicans. Rhode Island Senator Nelson P. Aldrich had called the Interstate Commerce Act, passed during the first Cleveland administration, a virtual revolution that would "cripple both internal and external commerce."[53] Blaine, in 1888, said the "trusts are largely private affairs, with which neither President Cleveland nor any private citizen has any particular right to interfere."[54]

Through later eyes, Cleveland "would defend to the last breath the property rights of corporations under the law, while leading a veritable crusade for reform, designed to regulate a disorderly official corruption."[55] But some perceptions of the era diverged. With uncanny resemblance to the campaign exactly a century later, William C. Whitney, millionaire corporate lawyer with links to Standard Oil, conveyed to Cleveland in 1892 that "the impression of you got by the people is that you do not appreciate their suffering and poverty . . . and have your ideas formed by Eastern money, power, etc.—*the usual twaddle."* Alger wished government to protect legitimate property and business interests, not tycoons, speculators, and stock manipulators. Robber Baron Jay Gould telegraphed Cleveland after his 1892 victory that he felt "that the vast business interests of the country will be entirely safe in your hands."[56]

Alger and Cleveland shared positions on issues the author clearly cared about. The only Democrat to serve as President from the Civil War until Alger's death was notorious for his hard-money stance.[57] The Cleveland administration continued the task of civil service reform, begun with the Pendleton Civil Service Act, signed by Arthur.[58] A light article Alger read pronounced that

> it has been the privilege of President Cleveland to contribute more than his predecessors to the lightening of the President's burdens by reinforcing the merit classes through executive action.[59]

Such reform should have struck a responsive chord. Like a proud father, Alger reported that one of his adoptive sons, some years hence, "passed the civil service examinations and became one of Roosevelt's reform police."[60] Alger reported that he found the article very interesting.[61] It did not soften his dislike for Cleveland. His view of reformers ultimately depended on which party was doing the reforming.

Alger viewed the Democrats as fiscally irresponsible, and thought Cleveland incapable of maintaining business confidence. There was a severe recession during his first administration; Alger believed the downward business spiral following the second election in 1892 vindicated his opinion.[62]

Cleveland's greatest sin in '84, '88, and '92 may ultimately have been that he was a Democrat, associated with the party on which was hung the label of "Rum, Romanism, and Rebellion." Alger could perhaps never forgive the party of the South for their disloyalty to the Republic. For this Harvard Whig with clear anti-Jacksonian, anti-states' rights lineage, dislike for the Democratic Party was visceral. The Democrats pandered to selfish interests and to the base. It was the party of those who were not of good character— of those who were not citizens of the Republic and not American.

While *Ragged Dick'*s creator was not as obsessed about the evil machinations of demagogues and their influence on the morals of the young as were some contemporaries, he saw illegitimate power as a problem to be addressed and redressed. As with corruption more generally, one of the best ways to avoid coming under the influence was avoidance.

POLITICS: CORRUPTION,
SPECTACLE, PERFORMANCE

> . . . I don't care to be mistaken either for a partisan or an office-
> seeker.
>
> Horatio Alger, Jr. to Messrs. Porter & Coates, August 19, 1884.[63]

The author's remarks in letters consistently aver that he relishes his status as a political outsider. He jokes as young *Tribune* correspondent Irving Blake prepares a biographical notice during the course of the 1896 Democratic Convention: "I may add that I never sought a nomination for President at the hands of the Democratic Party. I have no private wire to Chicago."[64] His hero, likewise, rarely sought political office or influence.

Alger's occasional and humorously intended remarks about his own entrance into politics and public view reveal risk-aversion and reticence about taking the public stage. He had a disinclination for "the inevitable vicissitudes of public life" where one cannot control what is thought of one.[65] Reputation is malleable, including a writer's, as Alger discovered.

Shortly before the 1884 election, Alger turned down an opportunity to write another juvenile biography, "a boys' life of the next President, as soon as the matter is settled, whether it be Blaine or Cleveland . . ." Alger claimed that biographies were difficult to write, a sentiment he repeated elsewhere. The reluctant author also again indicated reticence about the public limelight. "It would be a more delicate matter . . . to write the life of a living man, and I should be likely to incur criticism. I think I will stick to stories."[66] He embellished in a letter to his then-publisher, Porter & Coates, as he attempted to obtain some funds from book sales: "It is a delicate matter to write the life of a living man, and I don't care to be mistaken either for a partisan or an office-seeker."[67] Some presentiment of a Cleveland victory may have decided the matter.

When Cleveland was elected, public curiosity was pronounced, as thousands of visitors and office-seekers flocked to Washington. "The sight of a Democrat in the White House seemed to rival P. T. Barnum's circus in popular imaginations," wrote one later historian.[68] For Alger and his Whiggish compatriots, the horror of a Democratic circus may have rivaled that felt by an earlier generation that heard the muddied boots tromping through the White House when General Jackson threw open the doors at his inauguration.

Mass politics was becoming yet another realm of performance, an arena that too frequently involved artifice, deception, and dissimulation. Not only are Alger's heroes not political performers, but they avoid coming under the influence of performers. Performers manipulate appearances, mesmerize others, and plan out their actions and words to gain power over others. To become a performer is to join the ranks of those who lie, commit fraud, and deceive the public.[69]   Most of his fictional characters who seek out public space and recognition are self-serving.

The same could be said of popular preachers and revival meetings: Religion, too had become performance. Unitarian elites were suspicious of the audience manipulation of the revivalists. Religious figures were not necessarily any better guides to moral instruction than the businessmen of Alger's novels who had the good sense to censor themselves from public attention gathering. None of his boys joins the clergy.

Alger's reluctance to route a hero to a career in politics was something other than a mere celebration of business. Too many turned to the public realm for private enrichment; political corruption was so pervasive that the man of good character might make little headway. For most boys, it was best to guard character by keeping away from politics; "there is a gap between the world of persons and the world of politics, a gap that must be left unbridged if persons are to be saved from politics."[70]

When a boy does enter *political* space at the end of the novel, he has already become financially comfortable; bribery and corruption have no appeal. We must presume that his loyalty and feelings, his naturalness remain intact. Political communications by role players in the public realm do not become models for private communication; rather, the private realm—the natural—informs the public.

It is difficult, although not impossible, to be a hero in politics. There must be no divorce between public and private personality—no performance or affectation. In the moral universe of Alger, it may well be that "the primary victims of this world are not its failures but its apparently triumphant artists of performance."[71]

LAW AND THE STATE

> Mrs. Barclay: "The law may be on your side, but the law upholds a great deal that is oppressive and cruel."
>
> Squire Davenport: "A curious set of laws we should have if women made them . . ."
>
> Mrs. Barclay: "They would not bear so heavily upon the poor as they do now."
>
> Alger, *Store Boy*

Just as Alger heroes steer clear of corrupting politics, they often avoid having recourse to the *law* when they have been robbed or wronged. Although policemen may be called to the scene, characters often believe they can settle matters more effectively and justly without such formal intervention. Often, a criminal is let go or merely banished, while the criminal's target notes that it was his *right* to call the law. In other cases, Alger arranges poetic justice for evildoers.

Dean Dunham provides an instructive series of desertions from law. First, a character merely kicks his houseguest out in the middle of the night when the guest tries to effect a robbery: "I was deceived in you, I admit, but now I understand your real character. I won't have you arrested, though I ought, but I require you to leave my house at once."[72] When Dunham and his companion foil a thief who has invaded their Denver hotel room, they again let him go despite the fact that he has a substantial criminal record and they know his character first-hand through previous dealings. The blackguard himself proposes the terms, offering to make it "worth their while" to release him. He would swear before a magistrate the identity of a squire who robbed Dean's uncle of $1000 a year since. This squire is, coincidentally, the thief's captain; the thief rats on his captain because the latter was not treating him right and he has sworn to get even.[73] By releasing the thief, Dean secures a higher-order good, namely, his family's own well-being. Legal recourse could be reserved for the squire.

Something is wrong with law. Squire Davenport, would-be home forecloser in *Store Boy*, follows up his claim of self-interest by saying "The law is on my side." Other cold-hearted men who foreclose mortgages or demand payment regardless of circumstances are often perfectly well within their legal rights.

Alger eschews legal recourse for several reasons. One is that the law may fail to take account of special circumstances, and legal recourse may not be fully equitable. The thief has information of vital importance to young Dean Dunham; the tradeoff provides Dean the information to right another past wrong. Likewise, a poor boy who steals food might be dealt with harshly at law (Alger empathizes with such wrongdoers), where punishment will not rehabilitate him. Or, a perceptive central character may realize who can be turned toward the right path by an act of mercy; the author rehabilitates some errant citizens in this fashion.

There is a further consideration. Just as in the author's criticism of businessmen for whom "business is business" and who demand prompt payment regardless of mitigating circumstances, mechanical application of law without consideration of circumstances is not always just. Too often, as Mrs. Barclay says, the law "upholds a great deal that is oppressive and cruel." The mechanical is not human: justice is a specifically human virtue.

Still another reason to avoid intervention by the criminal justice system was that the law, when right, *was not* upheld. The criticism that New York City politicians intervened to protect friends from justice was widespread, even by the late antebellum era. Politics and corruption permeated law enforcement and the judicial system.

Henry Adams mused in 1862 that "His opinion of law hung on his opinion of lawyers," and that was not positive.[74] Alger depicts sleazy, unscrupulous lawyers, bearing names such as Mr. Sharp and Mr. Ferrett, with some regularity. Yet some of his heroes take up careers in law. If men of firm character enter the law, they may perhaps hope to reform and bring new credit to the profession.

The corruption of law and justice by politics could certainly give an author pause before inscribing recourse to the law in Gilded Age fiction. The types of youth Alger addressed could best guard against irresponsible political power by having as little to do with politics and public space as possible. But the relative invisibility of law and of the state in Alger's fiction should not be read as a flight from all political power. Nor was it an endorsement of laissez-faire economics.

Avoidance of the state was not part of the Whig heritage. *Democratic* pamphlets of Alger's youth argued laissez-faire *against* the Whigs and national economic direction. Whigs favored state policies advancing moderate economic growth, improvement, and development; the party's commitment to "equitable and peaceful progress" required careful and purposeful planning.[75] Protective tariffs, internal improvements, and, for many, central banking were part of the agenda. Whigs had no aversion to using the state for their preferred purposes; Lincoln, attorney for the railroads, continued in the progrowth tradition.[76] Politics should encourage sound economic growth.

"An alderman protecting rowdies from the sword of Justice." (*Diogynes, Hys Lanterne*, Volume II, 1852, p. 28. Library Company of Philadelphia.)

Politics should also foster a morally strong republic, and to this end, it was incumbent upon political figures to lead by inspiring example, by public works that appealed to the imagination, and by rhetoric. The best politics and politicians could creatively attend to the requirements of community.

But *could politics* serve as the improver of men? Experience said no. A few political figures made men like Alger want to believe otherwise, but they were rare. Individuals could improve; the moral tone of cities could improve. But politics in the nineteenth century was not a primary arena for the improvement of character, which alone could bring human progress.

Character building and character rehabilitation take place elsewhere. The real political heroes, for Alger, were more likely social workers who saved the children, the wayward, and the immigrant. With luck, politics could fight corruption and illegitimate power.

Power remained essential to public purposes; the problem was whether anyone but a patrician could withstand its corrupting influences.

THE POLITICS OF A SIMPLE
MORAL UNIVERSE

It will be well for us to remember that "power," as it is used in the American constitution, is but another word for *duty*.

James Fenimore Cooper, "A Letter to His Countrymen"[77]

In Alger's simple moral universe, characters were fairly readily definable as good or evil. If this made him a literary failure by the standards of Howells and the school of realism, Alger was not far removed from the moral universe of political reformers of the progressive era—or in our own.

One of Alger's latter day saints was Teddy Roosevelt. While Roosevelt was highly attentive to showmanship and the creation of a public personality, he was also a well-educated, patrician reformer.

Theodore Roosevelt found the facts of life simple. Roosevelt advocated "clean living and decent politics," and the use of material wealth for ideal ends. He lectured audiences on realizable ideals.[78] Small wonder that Alger enthusiastically supported this patrician politician.[79]

If right and wrong were so clear and so knowable, then all but the most depraved could know one from the other. Evil "was incarnate in extreme inequality, political corruption, and ruthless power..."[80] The commitment to reform and calls to battle against corruption and speculation were not seen as problems likely to undermine the republic, nor systematically related to the ways in which it was changing. The purpose was restoration, driving out despoilers and evildoers.[81]

Progressive solutions to the vexing problem of corporate power, calling for trust-busting, were generally a large-scale version of the solution to economic greed proposed by Alger: destruction of the largest private empires. Like Alger, Progressives had no good answer for dealing with corporate power.

Triumph was not easy: "The silk-hatted and paunchy villains of the progressive cartoons represented real and formidable people, who held power and did not want to let it go." Melodramatically,

> reformers had to face vilification and boycott and blackmail; the
> odds seemed against them, and yet, again and again, the under-
> dog won. The effect was exhilarating and reassuring . . . every
> city cleaned up, every ring exposed was another proof of the
> unfolding morality of the modern world.[82]

The parallel to Alger's world of fiction is striking. With the odds against him, the underdog hero wins out against those who threaten to undo him or to undo the moral universe. In winning, he celebrates the victory of virtue over vice.

If, in the fictional narrative, virtue triumphs without the apparent intervention of the state, it nonetheless required intervention in the form of benefactors to be sufficiently nurtured. The political direction of the Republic required no less if *this* adolescent were to prevail. The Progressives, doctoring the Republic, prescribed a dose of institutional power on behalf of reform. Alger was not adverse to appropriate use of state power. The goals and values of the moral universe were comparable.

Politics, too, required its benefactors. Webster was one from an earlier era. Patrician political guardians such as Roosevelt, like the guardians of culture, struggled to protect the virtue of the Republic. "Naturally such a victory would demand the strenuous effort which was a central ingredient—perhaps the most surely surviving ingredient—of the Puritan heritage."[83]

In the voice of the trust-buster, some scholars have heard conservatism, reaction, and a desire to return to the past.[84] One could alternately identify this posture with Alger's strong desire to maintain continuity of identity and experience while the world was being radically and unalterably transformed. On the brink of the new century, highbrow literature had begun to move beyond the simple moral universe and the confidence that problems had solutions; mass-based politics had not.

The author's optimism was no more naïve than that of many of his contemporaries. His individual understood and believed in an unchanging moral universe. Character was unwavering, and yet this character inhabited a world in constant flux. If, in the Gilded Age and early Progressive era, "the most crucial task for American thinkers was to reconcile a belief in eternal moral truth with the belief in the desirability of change," then Alger's reconciliation remained seductive.[85] Character—and eternal moral truth—could not only coexist with the changing universe; it was precisely what was needed to function in this new order.

At the end of this century, in contemporary political discourse, the world is reduced to the most simple slogans. Good and evil are recognizable and dichotomous. Triumph belongs to resolute virtue, and virtue requires its foils.

But behind the political rhetoric of battle—in which we define our virtue against an adversary—and the military foray that reminds us we are strong and therefore virtuous, something has transpired. National politicians have stopped any pretense of talking to elites and have joined mass culture. Politics is not merely performance; politics has become melodrama.

Just as Alger found a popular formula for putting the best face on the consequences of change, Madison Avenue advertising firms now create positive auras for presidential candidates, knowing that "Optimism Appears a Winner." "Morning in America" in 1984 made regeneration easier than Alger could have. The designers of "The Heartbeat of America" campaign for Chevrolet, hired to create the message for George Bush in 1992, could only dream of finding an image as successful as Alger's. When the day belongs to the most upbeat candidates—when good and evil are polarized and easy to identify—Alger *becomes* politics.[86]

In the nineteenth century, power, agency, and manliness were central in public discourse as many members of the Republic lost the capacity to control their lives and work. At the end of the twentieth century, discourses of power, agency, and gender prevail in a nation losing claim to independence and autonomy in an interdependent global political economy. New confidence men and women—whether Japanese businessmen or American feminists—emerge as threats to power and autonomy of the Republic. Power, modern citizens hear, lies in continuity of principle and moral virtue.[87] The contemporary Republic faces every bit as serious a challenge to its assertions about the relationship between "virtue" and power as did the youth of Alger's Republic.

8

===

Money, Price, and Value: Alger's Interventions in the Market

An Alger hero at the theater for the first time has the satisfaction of a happy denouement: "[He] saw all the bad characters visited with retribution, while oppressed innocence and virtue through much tribulation attained happiness and peace."[1] The hero is not alone. Each story is witness to the same pattern of vindication of innocence and virtue. Alger denouements feature arranged justice on earth and deliver payments due.[2]

Justice pays—literally and figuratively. Payment for character is made in the currency of the new order. By arranging a cash payoff, Alger speaks a language familiar to those whose sights are set in the realm of the material: Justice is profitable. Character is capital.

The locus of this drama is the marketplace. The author yearned to believe that market outcomes were, at least in the long run, just ones. The fact that the author had to resort to so many interventions to make the market "work" indicated otherwise. Through the market, Alger rights a world gone awry. In providing for market justice, the author becomes the *improver* of the market.

This study of arranged market justice explores the relationship between money, price, and value, and reveals the author's perspective on capitalism and economic expansion. We discover that, in the equation of prices and values, although character is capital, capital is not virtue.

This chapter reveals a struggle to identify, define, and classify various activities and the roles they perform in economic development. Alger and his contemporaries attempted to separate the natural and the artificial; to determine which practices were part of the market and which interfered with the market; and to find a terminology for economic transactions in which the loss of some participants constituted the gain of others.

This process of naming, defining, and classifying was central to the effort to talk about what was fair and just. Locating the villainous and the heroic was Alger's attempt to catalogue business practices taking place increasingly among strangers and under conditions of imperfect information. The disjunction of virtue and market justice was portrayed in terms of certain practices and problems that interfered with the information markets could provide. Minus information, goods could not exchange at their value. Corruption, bribery, and nepotism blocked information about prices and value; boys of good character were shut out of employments by those of lesser value. The author and his contemporaries were constituting discourse on human virtue and market relationships at a time when economic relations of the emerging order were being forged and only dimly understood. What was implicit, however, was that money, price, and value must be allied in the marketplace if the Republic is to survive.

MARKET JUSTICE 101—

The Cash Nexus

Alger was far from alone during this period in stressing that virtue made "men" and also had material advantages. As clergy and other would-be moral leaders struggled to be heard in the age of capital, they attempted to infuse their messages with new life. The moral dimension of success was discussed in the *language* of business, and virtue "paid off" in material terms.

Victory, triumph, and success were morally loaded terms when Alger picked up his pen. They became double agents as metaphors from the world of business pervaded nineteenth century moral counsels. Although most guides remembered to argue that "there is something to be saved and gained more precious than even gold or silver," they increasingly claimed that gold and silver followed from virtue.[3]

"Character is like stock in trade; the more of it a man possesses, the greater are his facilities for making additions to it . . . it is like an accumulating fund . . . [4] Or, "Character is . . . a peculiar kind of capital, constantly increasing in value, introducing the possessor to channels of influence and power he had not thought of." Character is "the most valuable possession a youth ever acquires . . . character is also power."[5] A young man's "reputation is better to him than the richest capital. *It makes friends; it creates funds; it draws around him patronage and support . . .*"[6]

> However meagre his stock in trade, if he engages in business, he will not seek to enlarge it by entering Conscience and Honor in his books under the head of "Merchandise;" nor will he begin the sale of goods to customers, by selling his soul to Satan.[7]

Since "acting from a settled and uniform regard to duty, is the surest way to *promote one's temporal interests,*" there should be no incompatibility between religion and principles of good business dealings.[8] "Indeed," a late-century success manual proclaimed, ". . . religion demands success."[9]

The author's Harvard Unitarian teachers were convinced that, as a general rule, the good would prosper in this realm by obeying moral law.[10] The Cambridge faculty tried to avoid making the incentive to morality *rest* on prudence or self-interest. Francis Bowen argued that the utilitarian motto ought to be inverted to read "Whatever is right, is useful." "To say that all virtuous actions are also useful . . . is quite a different thing from saying that actions are right *because* they are useful." This made Bowen skeptical about Ben Franklin, who, in his view, tended to this latter position. But he allowed that

> so far . . . as Poor Richard . . . proves that to be honest and true is the best mode of becoming wealthy and happy, he is a sound moralist. Nor will any great objection be made to his doctrine, if he holds up this fact as *one* of the inducements to virtuous conduct.[11]

Alger's Harry Walton (*Bound to Rise*) resolves upon a course of life after reading Franklin; with book under arm, he sets out in the world.

If "the material and the spiritual were equally real to the Unitarian common sense dualist," it is hardly surprising that one of their pupils could so readily make the route to salvation yield a formula for success in the material world.[12] When entering the realm of fiction, and downplaying catechism and matters spiritual, there is but a small step from the semiofficial consensus of the Harvard Unitarians to Alger's message that virtue pays dollar dividends and that the house built by the undeserving will, like a house of cards, tumble down.

The link between the duty to struggle and its payoff had been made so intellectually clear that many nineteenth century moralists had trouble understanding poverty among men: "Nudity and rags are only human idleness or ignorance *out on exhibition*," said Horace Mann.[13] But poverty became more real and apparent in the Gilded Age. Observation was teaching Alger and his contemporaries that market exchanges were not sure to reward virtue. A late Alger hero says: "I would rather be poor and honest ... than live in a fine house, surrounded by luxury, gained by grinding the faces of the poor."[14]

The changing nature of wealth and growing disparities between rich and poor helped undermine the view that the wealthy members of the community were the men of substance, the repositories of public trust. If would-be leaders could no longer assert that virtue resided with the wealthy, they nonetheless found it almost impossible to embrace the adult poor as true heirs of Christ.

The answer to the dilemma lay in pinning their hopes for virtue upon the *young* among the poor. Alger constantly professes his preference for poor boys: "I never feel as much interest in a rich boy as in a poor boy who has to struggle with circumstances."[15] Garfield reportedly said:

> Poverty is uncomfortable, as I can testify: but nine times out of ten the best thing that can happen to a young man is to be tossed overboard and compelled to sink or swim for himself. In all my acquaintance I never knew a man to be drowned who was worth saving.[16]

Struggle with economic adversity became the externalized site of the struggle against evil that made man moral. Alger's six-volume Luck and Pluck Series was designed "to illustrate the truth that a manly spirit is better than the gifts of fortune.   Early trial and struggle, as the history of the majority of our successful men abundantly attests, tend to strengthen and invigorate the character."[17] Alger made a virtue of necessity, since many Americans in the mid-nineteenth century were "betwixt and between"— lacking fixed social status; in motion, whether up or down; liminal. Transition became a permanent condition.[18] In Alger, being uprooted and mobile— physically and economically—itself became a virtue.

The individual whose status is in flux is much like liquid capital. The value of the individual travels with and is inherent in that person. Foreshadowing arguments against monetary inflation was the assertion that "no man can well be expected to rise higher than his own standard of excellence." Since character requires laboring to own it, whatever encourages such exertion encourages value. "With such [personal] effort, the humblest cannot fail to rise; without such effort, the highest cannot fail to sink."[19] Once acquired, character possesses the property of gold, for like gold, its value is constant and inheres in the mettle/metal. It is of recognized value in any market— just like hard currency.

Market Incentives to Virtue

An important cash nexus binds Alger characters. No matter that readers are constantly reminded that fellow-feeling comes before the self and that one does not risk oneself because one expects to be rewarded: The hero *is* rewarded. The person to whom a needy hero does a service is almost always in a position to express gratitude with money or employment.

An expression of value is always, then, made in cash terms. Grateful parents or soon-to-be-benefactors claim they have debts to the hero they can never repay when they or their children are saved. Yet they always make some kind of pecuniary restitution. When Mr. Roswell's incautious son falls off the South Ferry in *Ragged Dick*, the father exclaims: "My child! . . . Who will save my child? A thousand—ten thousand dollars to any one who will save him!" Dick's determination was, of course, "formed before he heard the liberal offer made by the boy's father"; (in the excitement, he didn't hear it at all).[20] However, even life has been expressed in cash terms.[21]

Even in unextraordinary transactions, money is frequently tendered for kindness or service. A Swiss guide is offered money to search for the hero's body in *Frank Hunter's Peril*, though he would do so otherwise, and the Swiss peasants who nurse the hero back to health are paid for their hospitality at the insistence of its nearly penniless recipient.[22] Incentives to spend for certain kinds of goods are sometimes offered in terms of economic payoff. Richard Hunter, aka Ragged Dick, rationalizes the extra cost of comfortable accommodations by explaining that domesticity pays:

> He had observed that those young men who out of economy contented themselves with small and cheerless rooms, in which there was no provision for a fire, were driven in the evening to the streets, theatres, and hotels, for the comfort which they could not find at home. Here they felt obliged to spend money to an extent of which they probably were not themselves fully aware, and in the end wasted considerably more than the two or three dollars a week extra which would have provided them with a comfortable home. But this was not all. In the roamings spent outside many laid the foundation of wrong habits, which eventually led to ruin or shortened their lives. They lost all chance of improvement which they might have secured by study at home in the long winter evenings, and which in the end might have qualified them for posts of higher responsibility, and with a larger compensation.[23]

Beyond the basic educational skills necessary to garner employment, education is made to pay off in other ways. The utility of education is expressed in terms of the general self-improvement it affords, so books that tend to this end are a bargain at any price. A poor Minnesota farmer says: "books and periodicals we have always classed among the necessities, and I am sure we would all rather limit ourselves to dry bread for two out of three meals than to give up this food for the mind."[24] Those who consider such expenditure a waste know nothing of investment or delayed gratification.

But an indirect market incentive to make this investment is also usually provided.[25] Mr. Whitney, inventor and benefactor in *Ragged Dick*, reports that, while working in a printing office,

> During my leisure hours I improved myself by study, and acquired a large part of the knowledge which I now possess. Indeed, it was one of my books that first put me on the track of the invention which I afterwards made. So you see, my lad, that my studious habits paid me in money, as well as in another way.[26]

The spending that pays is the goose that lays the golden egg; it is folly to refrain. The sale and the Keynesian multiplier effect are similarly marketed as virtuous spending.

Those who perform good deeds without engaging in a rational actor cost-benefit analysis receive rewards of cash value. It is not an economic mistake to ignore market calculations to help one in need. When a hero offers a free ticket to his harmonica performance to a working boy who cannot otherwise attend, it

> proved a stroke of policy. The boy spread among his comrades a highly colored report of Dean's wonderful performance of the harmonica, and the result was a large attendance of young people in the evening.[27]

Altruism links characters in a network of exchanges that pay off the community. Boys helped by those little better off than themselves in turn help others when they are better situated.

A cash reward or transfer cements and reinforces fellow-feeling—that "something extra" inclining people to be virtuous. People *must* be paid for their acts of kindness, or in a world increasingly dominated by the profit motive, acts of kindness and bonds of community will vanish.

This economic incentive to justice cements Alger's tie to the language of the emerging era. Many in his audience would remember the payoff but not the moral message. It was only if the two could be conjoined that the old values could be successfully brought to the new era.

Accidents: Of Chance and Risk

Every Alger story relies in some measure on luck—the lucky accident that links the hero and a benefactor; lucky escapes; lucky meetings. To be sure, there is bad luck as well. Childhood poverty and the loss of parents are unlucky occurrences that could befall anyone. Horses get loose, children stray or fall overboard on the ferry, and train tracks become littered with huge boulders; young wealthy inebriates stand in imminent danger of being robbed or worse. The hero steps into the picture, opportunely placed to intervene in fate, rescuing the benefactor, his or her progeny, or property.

Such recourse to chance led many critics to decry the author's lack of realism. Alger could not seem to make his heroes succeed by hard work in the industrial era; "his stories tell us just as constantly that success is actually the result of fortuitous circumstance."[28] "Ragged Dick and Tattered Tom won success by some sudden stroke, rather than by steady application to business."[29] One of the best Alger readers also claims that "Alger was all but incapable of actually showing the steady, sober advance he talked about so much." The titles (e.g., *Slow and Sure*) and the stories did not mesh.[30] We are told that heroes made no real advance until they met with luck and patronage; "Ragged Dick is not on his way before he saves Mr. Rockwell's son."

> So far from telling of a system so bountiful that any earnest lad could succeed if he tried, Alger's tales implied one that held the disprivileged down so securely that only by the unlikely advent of chance and championship could the impoverished even set foot on the social ladder.[31]

Chance would appear, then, to be a vital element in the Alger formula. But chance is not as accidental as it appears. These "accidents" constitute a marked fusion of sacred and secular language and meanings. In arranging justice, Alger does no more than prove that everything has a cause, and that temporal outcomes reveal the hand of God. Does not God have a moral sense and direct his will toward benevolence? "God and the minds of men . . . supply the power the material world lacked."[32]

The lucky accident is one form of market intervention. It accomplishes several goals. The accident brings a benefactor into the hero's life. It provides a means of relieving a hero of immediate want and makes sure the deserving do not get crushed. It proves the hero a man, not a machine. And it celebrates his membership in the community.

In the accidental encounter, "the philanthropist operates only when virtue presses his spring."[33] Benefactors offer assistance *after* discovering something in the character of the young hero that merits their interest.

A particular kind of risk taking makes the hero worthy of our interest. The hero spontaneously reacts because others are endangered—he takes unreflective, personal risk without knowledge of the outcome in order to prevent harm. This is a particularly elevated notion of duty, demonstrating that "a real sense of one's responsibility as a member of society is indispensable to a true life."[34] One moralist illustrated this principle by drawing upon the John Maynard story that Alger had popularized with his well-known poem:

> True men and women, in the successful discharge of common duties are forced into overwhelming perils. The faithful engineer, on Lake Erie, was congratulated upon both his skill and fidelity, to which he replied, 'I have done only my duty.' Not long after, his steamer took fire, and herculean efforts were made to reach the shore. The fearless man proved true to himself and the men and women on board, standing at his post until the cruel flames roasted him alive. He sacrificed his own life; but the passengers for whom he died were saved.[35]

It is essential that Ragged Dick did not hear and was not swayed by the offer of reward before he plunged off the ferry. Spontaneous response to accident makes the hero human. These characters exemplify C. S. Peirce's understanding of human freedom, requiring some element of "arbitrary spontaneity." Thus, "accidents help to make actions free."[36] "The mere carrying out of predetermined purposes is mechanical"; such behavior characterizes machines—even breathing ones.[37]

Unlike foils who never let concern for others interfere with their plotting for advancement, Alger's boys struggle to succeed without being ruled by planning and rational calculation. Unlike machines, heroes respond to their surroundings with empathy and compassion. They act selflessly and bravely—character traits not found among those who put their own comfort and enrichment first. Accidents not only separate men from machines but highlight a character's affective ties to the community.

These accidents of fortune mark real turning points in the lives of heroes but do not occasion meteoric rise or result in immediate wealth. A near-penniless youth is permitted to weather an economic crisis; the reward provides a cushion against total market dependence. The element of chance offers hope and encouragement to those with few resources; it counsels patience.

The accident results in *personal* contact between economic unequals, essential to ascertaining character worth, as opposed to value measured in terms of job-specific, impersonal labor market skills. Heroes, upholding the equation of price and value, will protest and refuse excessive rewards. They will, however, accept employment.

Ragged Dick is taken into his new patron's counting house at a ten-dollar-a-week salary that is more than he can earn; "he would have been glad, only the day before, to get a place at three dollars a week."[38]   As a perceptive analyst of the Ragged Dick series notes, "Only from parental surrogates who set defiance of the market's determination of wages at 'no consequence' can [the orphans of the city] extract salaries they cannot economically earn."[39] But boys given salaries above what the market would bear represent wise long-range planning investments for their employers, netting savings and returns to the investor far beyond the outlay.   The employer takes a smart risk by entering the bargain.

The author insists that it is *not* luck which causes people to get ahead: the hero has served an apprenticeship. As good Uncle Simon says in *Forging Ahead*, "It's labor more than luck that counts in this world."[40]   Without preparation, material windfalls would be worthless, for "what is thus lightly acquired, is lightly disposed of."[41] Alger *makes* fortune help heroes who are already helping themselves, not waiting for fortunes to drop from the sky. The undeserving lose fortunes. Gifts and legacies arrive only after the hero has manfully struggled and proved his mettle in the world. Even in those few cases where the hero attains great wealth, his windfall comes *only after* he has become comfortable through his exertions.[42] Lasting well-being is never accidental or merely inherited.[43]

Unless one recognizes the centrality of preparation in Alger's moral universe, it is impossible to distinguish between the "accident" through which the hero advances by stopping the runaway horses of a rich woman and the accident of winning the lottery. It is equally impossible to distinguish between the nature of the risks taken by hero, gambler, speculator, financier, and businessman.   Exploring these differences will develop our understanding of vices and flawed relationships to money.

MARKET JUSTICE 201 —
THE ECONOMICS OF PASSIVITY,
RISK-AVERSION, AND GAMBLING

Of Chance and Risk (Reprise)

> A few draw prizes [in the lottery] it has been admitted. Some of
> that few make a good use of them. But the vast majority are
> injured. They either become less active and industrious, or more
> parsimonious and miserly; and not a few become prodigals or
> bankrupts at once . . . It is not given to humanity to *bear* a sudden
> acquisition of wealth. The best of men are endangered by it . . .
> what is gained by hard digging is usually retained; and what is
> gained easily usually goes quickly.
>
> William A. Alcott, *The Young Man's Guide*

The lottery figures importantly by instruction: it is for boys who
expect fortune to drop from the sky. While Alger reminds the reader
of the very slim chance of taking a prize, and what a waste of money
such investment is, the moral of the lottery is more than this. It is a
form of gambling against which advice authors inveigh.[44] Those who
pin their hopes on the lottery are passively awaiting luck rather than
actively engaging in struggle. Dissatisfied with their circumstances,
lottery players are nonetheless disinclined to start at the bottom.[45]
Aspiring to wealth via luck alone is contrary to the message of the
Alger novel. It is not an appropriate route to success. No one with
whom Alger acquaints us is ever permitted to take a big prize.

However, risk aversion—timidity—is also a form of moral defect.
Passivity and lack of courage and resourcefulness draw no
condemnation when exhibited by Alger women, but males who
despair of the future, expect nothing good, give up easily, and
become depressed in the face of adversity are acted upon, rather than
actors on the world stage. They are not men.[46] Those fatalists who
believe struggle is useless "bet" on the status quo rather than upon
progress.

While self-help is active, it is not exemplified by those characters
who actively "help themselves" to what is not theirs. For, in fact, such
characters are blind to their own faults, believe the world is set against
them, lack a sense of the criteria of entitlement, and begrudge the
advancement of others. In a moralistic narrative, Alger says of the
drunken, thieving stepfather of *Rough and Ready*:

> He had a vague idea that the world owed him a living, and that
> he would rub along somehow or other. This is a mischievous
> doctrine, and men who deserve to succeed never hold it. It is true,
> however, that the world is pretty sure to provide a living for those
> who are willing to work for it, but makes no promises to those
> who expect to be taken care of without any exertions of their own.
> The difference between the rich merchant and the ragged fellow
> who solicits his charity as he is stepping into his carriage, consists,
> frequently, not in natural ability, but in the fact that the one has
> used his ability as a stepping-stone to success, and the other has
> suffered his to become stagnant, through indolence, or dissipa-
> tion.[47]

Alger thinks the world has dealt some *boys* a poor hand, but he cannot
recognize in the ragged *man* any relation to Ragged Dick. In fact, such
characters are risk averse.

Where is the boundary between economic passivity and aggression? In
the emerging economic order, what differentiates appropriate from
inappropriate risk—investment from speculation? What engagement with
uncertainty did not constitute gambling? The search for moral and
appropriate economic action was on. Various Alger character foils and
negative role models exist to answer just such boundary questions.

But the issues were far from simple:

> In a market society, a great many actions look like gambling;
> indeed, insofar as the value of commodities or services in such a
> society seems to be determined by factors over which the agent
> has no control (demand, for example), it might be argued that
> every businessman is perforce a gambler . . .[48]

And so, for Henry Ward Beecher,

> speculation is the risking of capital in enterprises greater than we
> can control, or in enterprises whose elements are not at all
> calculable . . . If the capital is borrowed, it is as dishonest, upon
> such [speculative] ventures, to risk, as to lose it.[49]

Alger's melodramas try to balance caution with risk, leaving the
definition of acceptable risk uncertain. A cautious hero puts his money in
a savings account and serves as the model of incremental advancement and
modest success. But an occasionally voiced motto is "nothing venture,
nothing have," and the reader is told that prudent risks help advance the
careers of many young men.[50] Distant land purchases, mercantile ventures,
and occasional stock purchases taken under the advisement of a trusted
mentor are bold but sober risks; Alger defines these out of speculation. By
taking some risk, adolescents, especially in later stories, may rise to

partnerships or wealth.   Nonetheless, even prosperous heroes do not celebrate risk; they have moderate desires in the era of robber barons.

Sober investment, conservative prudence, gradual and incremental advancement, restrained ambition—this is a formula not only for character but for a political response to the expansion of capital.

Economic Growth:
"Slow and Sure"

> The battle for sound money which Mr. Webster fought then has been renewed in later years, as some of my young readers may be aware. In his speeches he showed ... the evils of a debased coin, a depreciated paper currency, and a depressed and falling credit, and it is largely due to his efforts that the country emerged from its chaotic financial condition with as little injury as it did.
>
> Alger, *From Farm Boy to Senator*

Alger waged a lifelong battle against the legacy of restless desire for unfettered expansion in favor of a more cautious and controlled growth espoused by the Whigs. Jacksonian Democrats and their heirs lacked proper perspective on the question of the meaning and direction of expansion; they lacked the New England banker's perspective on growth, credit, and risk. A chief character's frequent motto, and the title of one of Alger's books, was "Slow and Sure." The phrase was no accident.

The difference in perspective between cautious, money-centered interests and the unrestrained ambition of developers of the periphery formed a central tension in American political life.[51] Alger stories *build in* the tension between characters who espouse or embody each of these perspectives. Speculators, spendthrifts, counterfeiters, gamblers, thieves, and boys who tolerate only instant recognition and financial success all stand on the side of chimera and nonsubstance. The hero, family and friends who encourage him, and the sober and cautious Protestant merchant, optimists all, do not take or seek the kind of risks that might bring them to ruin or to spectacular gain. The former scheme to get something for nothing; the latter, in an unarticulated version of the labor theory of value, argue that it is only by steady application and the addition of earnest labor to the economy that value is created. All else is a house of cards.

Jacksonians had cast the war against the monster bank in terms of a struggle of the little man against the moneyed aristocracy. The struggle was one for Old Republican ways, in which power itself was a central issue.[52] As President, Jackson claimed that the bank was founded on "a distrust of the popular will as a safe regulator of political power."[53] His constituency saw their aspirations and economic independence threatened "by an encroaching web of concentrated power—the influence of wealth represented by the Bank of the United States combined with the then-innovative format for organizing economic power, the corporation." These manipulators relied on the federal government to enhance their fortunes.[54]

The bank, "the unnatural creature of lust for wealth and power," thrived on "paper money, the mere specter of palpable value." It existed in "a false, rotten, insubstantial world."

> The bank system suspends the real world of solid goods, honestly exchanged, upon a mysterious swaying web of speculative credit. The natural distributive mechanism, which proportions rewards to "industry, economy, and virtue," is fixed to pay off the insider and the gambler.[55]

If Jackson himself hated debt, for his supporters, the bank issue was a struggle for expansion of credit, waged by optimists about the pace of economic growth:

> The key to preserving republican independence was credit. If the control of credit . . . was concentrated in the hands of a few, then all the variety of individual enterprise would be held in thrall by them.[56]

Strangulation of credit gave preference to the wrong agenda for economic growth. What was, for Whigs, orderly, cautious growth was, for Jacksonians, perpetuation of illegitimate power and missed opportunity for decentralized growth.

In the year of Alger's birth (1832), the voices of caution suffered a major defeat. With the demise of Biddle's Bank of the United States went loss of central control over money and credit. The results were dramatic: "bank failures and collapsed business ventures, outrageous speculation and defaulted loans."[57] In the aftermath of defeat and the Panic of 1837, nineteenth century moralists were prone to find proof of sin and degeneration. Dishonest men swarmed forth from this reverse, "like vermin from a carcass." When the whole people "conspire to defraud public creditors; and States vie with States in an infamous repudiation of just debts," then

> the confusion of domestic affairs has bred a fiend, before whose flight honor fades away, and under whose feet the sanctity of truth and the religion of solemn compacts are stamped down and ground into the dirt . . . The mania of dishonesty . . . is the result of disease in the whole community; an eruption betokening foulness of the blood; blotches symptomatic of a disordered system.[58]

Despite fears and excesses, the 1830s witnessed extraordinary development and a remarkable urban boom—a "reckless, booming anarchy," and "gambles that mostly paid off."[59] "Those who gambled on the future rise of public lands in the West were madmen only in the short-run business sense—only in thinking that future prospects could be realized all at once. . . "[60] As a result of such activity, economic resources began to be transferred from old hands to new. Purchasing power and economic leadership flowed from the hands of New England financial elites into the hands of the evil Brantley Wentworths in Alger's juvenile novels.

If "easy money" stimulated economic growth and spread wealth, "hard money" slowed growth and reconsolidated ownership of new wealth. Under tight money, there would be "permanently high interest rates, and the higher profits naturally flowed to the lenders, the banking system and the owners of wealth."[61] Alger sided with the economic elites.

The Value of Money

> [Garfield] made speech after speech on the finance question, and was a pronounced advocate of "Honest Money," setting his face like a flint against those who advocated any measures calculated to lower the national credit or tarnish the national reputation for good faith . . .
>
> Horatio Alger, Jr., *From Canal Boy to President*

When tampering with value took place in an Alger novel, one entered a discourse not only about credit and easy money, but about inflation, speculation, paper money, and the difference between natural and artificial value.

Alger was a gold Republican. Insofar as the Jacksonians had courted the gold standard, they had been reasonable men. For gold had been "naturally selected" as money, and the "gold-producing power of the earth is abundant and unlimited." The value of gold and the value of money were identical. But whether gold or silver were selected, "neither gold nor silver can be made *fiat* money . . . the amount of labor expended in their production will establish their final and permanent value."[62]

Free silverites were also reasonable men insofar as they identified the value · of money with the value of the material that composed it. Both silverites and gold bugs united in selecting hard money and opposing greenbacks, although the former wanted inflation and the latter feared it.[63] Bryan's position on "hard money" (unlike that of his running mate, Thomas Watson) prompted Alger's remark in 1896 that "The Gold Democrats have nominated a good ticket, and so done something for the credit of the party."[64]

His happiness with the results produced uncharacteristic humor:

> I judge by the papers that McKinley will receive 302 electoral
> votes, and Bryan 300. Both will be elected, and there will be
> three Vice Presidents. We shall have both silver and gold, and
> all will be happy. Our incomes will be doubled, and you can
> drink all the whisky [sic] you want. Perhaps you do now. Let
> us live and hope![65]

But tampering with the natural purchasing power of gold, through
adulteration or substitution, was anything but funny; it was the worst threat

"Milk tickets for babies, in place of milk." Thomas Nast. (From David Wells,
Robinson Crusoe's Money, 1896. New York Public Library.)

to the economy. Fiat or representative money tampered with value just as surely as did forgery or counterfeiting. Representations of value via paper money replaced money as a commodity with money as a promise. This *appearance* of money dupes the unsuspecting, as does the confidence man: the illusionistic goal of both "is to disguise themselves and by looking 'so exactly like the real articles' to 'make the shadow of wealth supply the place of its substance.'"[66]

Perhaps the worst charge was that the value of greenbacks was manipulable. The supply of legal tender could be controlled by the government issuing it to produce either inflation or its absence.[67] Thomas Nast's cartoon "Milk-Tickets for Babies In Place of Milk" scoffs at the prospect of declaring money by government fiat. The cartoon compares such a scheme with trying to make a railroad out of a drawn representation of one and trying to nourish an "inflated" "baby" (actually rag doll) with paper "milk" tickets, declared to be milk. Such tampering with the value of money might as well be anarchy. Government cannot legislate value by mere declaration.

During an era noted for boss rule, political dishonesty, and greed, dealing government into the value of money was alone enough to chill the blood of one such as Alger. Moreover, unlike the earlier National Bank era, when established business interests looked to government to protect growth and investment strategies even against the president, now government was being asked to act as agent for small debtors.

Of Cheap Money and Usury

Alger's biography of Lincoln, *The Backwoods Boy*, makes no mention of the nearly half billion dollars in greenbacks issued by the Lincoln Administration—money backed by nothing but a government promise.[68] The prosperity witnessed by Northern farmers and which stimulated manufacturing during the Civil War took place in an inflationary period during which "sound money" was suspended in order to secure credit for the Union cause.

Subsequent to the war, the Republican Party responded to Eastern financiers' demand for a return to "sound Money." Greenbacks were retired from circulation and the gold standard was reimposed. One ounce of gold would be worth its old, prewar level of $20. "The money supply was, in effect, being shrunk back to its original size—hardened dollars that would buy more for those who owned them."[69] In early 1879, the money stock was only 17% above its level in early 1867, a record repeated only in the 1930s.[70]

The hardship that this policy inflicted was substantial but uneven. As in the 1980s, a period in which some were ruined found others prospering. Industrial development brought expanding output. By the mid-1880s, the national price level resembled that of 1860, and it continued to fall. The frequent destabilization of the national economy was marked by the severe depression of 1873-79, the recession of 1882-85, and bank panic in early 1893, followed by recession lasting until 1897.

The farmer's position eroded, and even when some price stability was restored in the 1885-93 period, farm prices continued dropping. In the Midwest, farmers who began mechanizing not only owed for expensive machinery purchased on credit, but compounded their problems by producing a greater yield, for which there was inadequate demand. During the "Great Deflation," prices on wheat, corn, cotton, and other basic necessities fell to as little as 15 to 33% of their prewar levels. The railroad contributed to farmer problems; arbitrary freight rates were sometimes equivalent to the value of the grain shipped.[71]

Farm debt was especially onerous in the cotton belt. In these southern states, small farmers were reduced to "a state of virtual peonage, their everyday lives held in bondage by the crop-lien system." The "furnishing merchant" took a lien on the farmer's crop as security for staples and supplies and added on commissions and usurious interest rates when crops were sold and accounts were settled. Real interest rates for goods purchased on credit might have approximated 100%. "There was nowhere else to turn; other merchants or banks would not extend credit to someone who was already indebted."[72] When cotton prices fell, farmers were forced to offer the "furnishing merchant" their land as security against purchases. For millions, the result was forfeiture.[73] "Many were compelled to surrender what they thought was their American birthright—ownership of their own modest plot of land," and with it, independence.[74] Not until the end of Alger's life did farmers experienced relief from credit squeeze and from deflation, coinciding with the monetary expansion of 1897-1914.[75]

In the meantime, would-be borrowers found that the money supply under the gold standard could not readily expand. Alger's sympathies for the poor and struggling did not extend to the heretical argument of Populists and the Farmer's Alliance in favor of easy money and greenbacks.[76] Alger was no democrat when it came to expanding access to the money supply: Honest Money must prevail.

Alger, who so frequently depicted the hard times faced by New England farmers, had considerable sympathy but little policy to offer. Foreclosures and usurious interest rates seemed inscrutable apart from the machinations of individuals who took advantage of their neighbors and who valued money too much. These immediate public enemies—the mean squires who hold farm families and small town residents at their mercy—were lenders of last resort where there was no central bank, or gold reserves were absent, to help small owners and local banks through liquidity crises. Such lenders named their own terms, lacking competition for credit. In the countryside, this tended to fuel resentment of Wall Street and the House of Morgan.[77]

Alger's best answer to the usurer who harms others in the course of personal enrichment is summary justice: his life or end fits his crime. Such was the case with Joshua Starr in *Forging Ahead*. Starr was an old man, whose features bore the stamp of meanness (undue economy). He obtained his cook from the poorhouse, later dismissing this underpaid employee because she ate too much and cost too much. Starr had scraped together considerable property, and not always honestly. He cheated his own brother out of $3,000, lent money to his neighbors on usurious terms, showing no mercy when they were unable to pay, and loved money so much he tried to double-collect a note from the hero's family. His end was fitting:

> Joshua Starr was found dead one day in his barn. The property which he had accumulated by miserly ways and unscrupulous dealings, went to a cousin whom he hated. Was his life worth living?[78]

Money: Spending, Saving, and Hoarding, or the Virtues of Participation

> The mere money-maker may grow in shrewdness and worldly wisdom, but his manhood does not enlarge and become enno-bling. His mind must grasp higher themes, that will tax some-thing more than his avaricious nature, to secure real growth. He may become rich as Croesus, but a miser has no real manhood; he is a small specimen of humanity.
>
> William [Makepeace] Thayer, *Success and Its Achievers*

With the triumph of sound money in '96, Alger celebrated: "With the election of McKinley, an era of confidence and prosperity will be ushered in."[79]

> . . . It seems strange to see the Sun and World rejoicing in the election of McKinley, but they regard him not as a Republican, but as the representative of sound money. And what a business boom has followed his election. You know it was the other way four years ago.

He mused about the future of Bryan: "If he hopes to keep free coinage of silver alive for four years he will be disappointed. Already it is getting to be an old story."[80]

The recipe for orderly growth, price stability, and low inflation via the gold standard required an adequate supply of gold so there would be no excessive credit squeeze.[81] At the end of Alger's life, there was some cause for optimism: The world supply of gold doubled between 1890 and 1914, owing to improved mining techniques and the discovery of new gold fields in Colorado, Alaska, and South Africa. "After 1897, 'cheap' gold achieved the objectives that had been sought by the silver advocates. The economic basis for the silver movement was eliminated."[82]

A gold standard economist, writing in 1897 that people were happy to start spending their gold coin after the Bryan defeat, found that there was some unwillingness to do so while the issue remained unsettled: "A certain tendency of hoarding had been developing . . . brought about by the fear of free coinage of silver, and coupled with the hope that later on a substantial premium might be obtained for gold."[83]

Bryanites feared an economy being drained of gold faster than miners could locate it; the supply of gold, they explained, was being lost to other uses, such as jewelry and hoarding. Alger shrugged off the portion of the argument pertaining to discovery. In his mining-for-gold and gold rush stories, heroes and their friends contribute more new gold to the economy.

Nonetheless, Alger's fiction revealed the hoarder and miser to be long-term problems. Whether afraid of free silver, greenbacks, or their fellow man, these fictional figures hoarded through most of his literary career. The author's tales frequently correct the behavior of these misers and hoarders who believed they were avoiding risk by burying gold or hiding it about the house, punishing them with the theft of some or all of their funds. What is the nature of their crime?

Saving per se was not the problem. Alger's most benevolent usage of the term "capitalist" refers jokingly to the shoeshine boy who has a bit saved and who helps another into the business, or to the man who has money available to lend, or who has money accumulated. Alger felt comfortable with an advice manual that argued:

> Savings are the result of labors; and it is only when laborers begin to save that the results of civilization accumulate . . . Thrift produces capital . . . The capitalist is merely a man who does not spend all that is earned by work.[84]

Although Marx would have turned in his new grave at such a definition of the capitalist, it is compatible with at least one Alger sermon:

> Money is said, by certain moralists, to be the root of all evil. The love of money, if carried too far, may indeed lead to evil, but it is a natural ambition in any boy or man to wish to raise himself above poverty. The wealth of Amos Lawrence and Peter Cooper was a source of blessing to mankind, yet each

started as a poor boy, and neither would have become rich if
he had not striven hard to become so.[85]

Accumulation has its purpose:

> Money is science, invention, discovery, enterprise; money is
> the canal, the railroad, the telegraph, the steamship . . . money
> is as essential as light and heat to the world's progress,
> barbarism reigning where it is not.[86]

Saving something (unspecified quantity) is a hedge against uncertainty. But
there is a limit to the value of saving. Once one acquired a "competence,"
more money was superfluous unless planning to start a business venture or
engage in philanthropy.

Economy is a virtue when a necessity, but characters who are too
economical when they do not have to be are guilty of some moral failure. A
young orphan, taken in by an old miserly friend of his father's who covets
the liberal allowance he is to receive for the boy's board, refuses to sleep on
a straw mattress in his new home, saying: "I've got plenty of money, and
I don't see why I shouldn't go in for comfort. I could stand hard fare if there
was any need of it, but there isn't."[87]

Alger's misers lived like the most impoverished of men, pursuing money
as an object at the expense of their own health and well-being. They are
miserable, sour, suspicious, reclusive and lonely, living in constant fear of
losing what they have accumulated.[88] They distance themselves from ties
of affection and from community, often even refusing to marry because of
cost. In *Bound to Rise*, Squire Green attempted to

> convert [his son] . . . into a money-making machine—a mere
> drudge, working him hard and denying him, as long as he
> could, even the common recreations of boyhood—for the
> squire had an idea that the time devoted to play was foolishly
> spent, inasmuch as it brought him in no pecuniary return.

The boy left home as soon as he was old enough; the old man "did not feel
the solitude. He had his gold, and that was company enough."[89]

As orphans Rufus and Rose look for a new home, they are espied by a
childless millionaire, who says "if I only had two such children!" as he passes
with hurried step. Alger preaches:

> His coffers were full of gold, but his home was empty of
> comfort and happiness. He might easily have secured it by
> diverting a trifling rill, from his full stream of riches, to the
> channel of charity; but this never entered his mind.[90]

He echoes boyhood hero Natty Bumppo in *The Pathfinder*, who did not
care for property or money: "I can easily believe, by what I've seen of
mankind, that if a man has a chest filled with either, he may be said to lock

his heart up in the same box."[91] "There is a kind of saving that amounts to meanness; it ought to be avoided . . . If it fill the coffers, it empties the soul of all that is noble."[92] Horace Mann's John Jacob Astor was "hugging to his breast, in his dying hour, the memory of his gold and not of his Redeemer."[93] Love of money is a desire that can never be satisfied.[94] When appropriation becomes a consuming passion, whether exhibited by hoarder or capitalist, it is, for Alger, an unnatural and a destructive desire. The miser is not a man and experiences no moral growth.

To the extent that "the goal of realism, literary and moral, is . . . to minimize excess," Alger shares in the project. His heroes modestly delimit their desires, for in this world "power, happiness, and moral virtue are all seen to depend finally on minimizing desire."[95] But the problem with hoarders was not simply excess desire.

The *crime* was saving with no intent of spending or investing. Misers and hoarders in Alger tales personalize the story about the public consequences of refusal to contribute to economic growth and development. In withholding gold from circulation, these figures refuse to purchase, consume, or invest. Socking money away under the mattress produces nothing; hoarders surround themselves with the mere representation of wealth. Since gold is seen as the foundation of economic growth prosperity, these characters both represent a threat of barbarism and are saboteurs.

Paying off the family mortgage, sending money home to help the family, buying mother a house or sister a new dress are uses of money that sustain economy and community at the same time. Even spending to meet one's needs shares the wealth, for it furthers capital circulation and investment.

Money is an instrument; savings is a means. The hoarder compounds retributions due by trusting no bank or financial institution. Upon relieving the miser of his most valuable prize, Alger teaches a lesson in banking, which serves as apologia for the new order. To make the lesson plain, the author had the hero deliver the argument that the safest place to put money was the bank; he might even take the newly chastened hoarder to this august depository. Hiding evidence of the many bank failures attending each depression in this period and depicting only an occasional heist (which the hero sometimes foils), Alger substitutes certainty for uncertainty.

As moderate savers and bank depositors, owners of money contribute to the growth of the nation as they engage in planning for future ventures. As purchasers and consumers, they also contribute to an economic discourse. Caring for others through money transfers, they allow additional members of the community to participate as purchasers and consumers. Money permits its owners to preserve their independence, to meet moral and physical needs, and to participate in good economic citizenship.

Bad Market Citizenship: Gambling, Speculation, Production, and Capitalism

> He who is accustomed to receive large sums at once, which bear
> no sort of proportion to the labor by which they are obtained, will
> gradually come to regard the moderate but constant and certain
> rewards of industrious exertion as insipid.
>
> William A. Alcott, *The Young Man's Guide*

Street swindlers, speculators, stock manipulators, counterfeiters, forgers, and thieves are interchangeable names for those who create value by fiat in Alger stories. These figures patiently apply themselves to the manipulation of value, profit from creating the appearance of value where it is not, or calculate how to benefit from the real losses of others.

Counterfeiters print money (and even silver coin) and prostitute its value.[96] Forgers tamper with paper transactions, undermining the inviolability of wills, mortgages, and the sanctity of contracts. Gamblers, lottery players, financiers, and speculators all share a faulty relationship to patient industry that places them outside the pale of acceptable economic activity. All violate the social contract.

If commerce bound human society together, speculation tore it asunder. "Commerce" was associated with benevolence, fidelity, confidence, and honesty; "speculation" was associated with wickedness, suspicion, tricks, cheating, jealousy, and fear. Production belonged to the realm of stability, solidity, and caution, speculation belonged in the realm of abstraction, fluctuation, and risk.[97] Speculation was no more palpable to Alger than was speculative philosophy to midcentury Harvard Unitarians. Gamblers ruin themselves with indebtedness. Debt and credit were viewed as moral dangers: They undermined power, virtue, and independence. Here, nineteenth century moralists echoed Franklin. "It is extremely difficult for a person who has ever relied on others, to act with the same energy as those who have been thrown upon their own resources."[98] "Debt—debt! A young man is mad, we had almost said, to go in debt under any pretext whatever."[99] Alger readers could almost hear Franklin's maxims ring out:

> But, ah, think what you do when you run in Debt; *You give to
> another, Power over your Liberty.* If you cannot pay at the Time, you
> will be ashamed to see your Creditor; you will be in Fear when
> you speak to him; you will make poor pitiful sneaking Excuses,
> and by Degrees come to lose your Veracity, and sink into base
> downright lying . . .[100]

By logical extension, it was best to minimize contact with the seductive power of credit.

Risking even one's own property by gambling or speculation had antisocial implications. Henry Ward Beecher argued that such activity threatened to ruin others as well:

> No man could blow up his store in a compact street, and destroy only his own. Men of business are like threads of a fabric, woven together, and subject, to a great extent, to a common fate of prosperity or adversity. I have no right to cut off my hand; I defraud myself, my family, the community, and God; for all these have an interest in that hand. Neither has a man the right to throw away his property. He defrauds himself, his family, the community in which he dwells; for all these have an interest in that property.[101]

Counsels about buying on credit and living within one's means argued, then, *against* much of the behavior that fueled industrial expansion. What defined self-reliance and independence in the nineteenth century business world? Should Franklin's advice against purchasing on credit be extended to trading upon expectation of what one will have in the future?

Even the producer or farmer could be viewed as a gambler, for the futures contract was important to them. The producer could sell his product in advance of having it—protecting himself against a price fluctuation when the good comes to market, and consumers could, by advance purchase, also "gamble" and protect themselves against a future rise in prices.[102] The Farmer's Alliance instituted cooperatives to circumvent usurious lenders and the deflationary tight money squeeze, hoping to recapture their independence. But these cooperatives helped farmers combat negative market effects with a kind of manipulation: They bought the farmers' grain or cotton outputs, stored them in cooperative warehouses, and resold them at optimum prices, "thus protecting individual farmers from the harrowing losses of a glutted marketplace." The cooperatives also purchased supplies wholesale and sold them to the farmer at low interest rates, "insulating them from the ruinous interest rates demanded by merchants."[103]

Gambling interfered with fair market exchange; it was asymmetrical. "The basis of it is covetousness; a desire to take from others something for which you have neither given, nor intend to give an equivalent." If Alger's gambler fleeces victims of worldly possessions, he, too, is a nonproducer:

> In gaming, it is true, property is shifted from one individual to another, and here and there one probably gains more than he loses; but nothing is actually *made*, or *produced*. If the whole human family were all skilful gamesters, and should play constantly for a year, there would not be a dollar more in the world at the end of the year, than there was at its commencement.[104]

Like Michael Milken, Ivan Boesky, modern junk bond dealers, mergers and acquisitions specialists, and insider traders, these earlier figures were seen to be creating money out of paper or illusion without producing anything in the process.

Unlike the calculating farmer or producer who tried to plan for the future by controlling it, Alger's gambler was improvident, spending what would otherwise care for his needs. In his capacity as spendthrift, the gambler, like the miser, attempts "by staging the disappearance of money's purchasing power, to stage the disappearance of money itself." The gambler can be seen as a second figure embodying the fears of those who believed gold was disappearing.[105]

The crimes of the gambler and the speculator were virtually indistinguishable: "Indeed, a Speculator on the exchange, and a Gambler at his table, follow one vocation, only with different instruments."[106] Both are irresponsible and antisocial, destroying rather than creating value.

The speculator was not exactly a new figure in the Gilded Age. Urban speculators were blamed for driving up land prices and disrupting established communities earlier in the century.[107] The term was used broadly. Ragged Dick, an aggressive street salesman, overheard a conversation and boldly inserted himself by offering himself as an urban guide to Frank Whitney: "Being an enterprising young man, he thought he saw a chance for a speculation, and determined to avail himself of it."[108]

However, the speculator came to be identified as plying his trade in the stock market, which was capable of producing wealth out of all proportion to labor or merit. Here, the speculator patiently schemes to bilk many Alger investors of their money. While appearing to sustain a loss himself, it is all merely "paper"—he has, in fact, made a fortune in the transaction.[109] He has shielded himself from risk and barred others from making a sensible determination of risk by concealing information.

Many Alger stories involve losses from speculation—investment in bad stock deals and efforts by officials in a company to deceive investors about the value of their stock. In *The Store Boy* (1883), a naïve foil thinks speculating sounds like an easy way of making money and sees little of the risk. Losing his investment and newly in debt from buying stocks on margin (unwise credit purchasing), he is told that "Keene, or Jay Gould, or some of those big fellows stepped in and upset the market."[110] This followed an infamous case of market plunder of 1879, when Gould had a Wall Street pool, directed by Keene and Cammack, drive up Union Pacific stock:

> With exuberant reports of the company's financial progress being circulated, widows and orphans and lady stockholders rushed to buy the stock. Then Gould, "bowing to public opinion," as he termed it, quietly unloaded upon them some 200,000 shares at a profit of ten millions.[111]

After Gould exited, the stock subsequently crashed.

In *Luke Walton*, a man widely reputed to be a philanthropist has in fact absconded with a dying man's money and has used this money to engage in a major stock swindle. He touted the mythical Excelsior Mine—land which he bought for a song:

> With the ten thousand dollars I hired an office, printed circulars, distributed glowing accounts of imaginary wealth, etc. It cost considerable for advertising, but I sold seventy thousand shares, and when I had gathered in the money I let the bottom fall out. There was a great fuss, of course, but I figured as the largest loser, being the owner of thirty thousand shares (for which I hadn't paid a cent), and so shared the sympathy extended to losers. It was a nice scheme, and after deducting all expenses, I made a clean seventy-five thousand dollars out of it . . .[112]

A widow who thereby lost all of the money necessary to her family's support comes to this "philanthropist" to plead for some restitution; she is callously turned away.[113]

The railroad rebate scandal, revealed by government investigators in 1879, figured by analogy in one fictional work of 1886, *Number ^1*.[114] The scheming housekeeper, like a robber baron, enriched herself by levying "tribute from every tradesman as a compensation for turning the trade in his direction." Her employer—the consumer—

> without being aware of it, paid a larger price than any one else for what articles she purchased, the storekeepers and others compensating themselves in this way for the percentage they had to pay the housekeeper . . .

Upon discovery, the employer "lost confidence" in the housekeeper, telling her "You are not the woman I supposed; for a small gain you have thrown away a great prospect."[115]

Alger would have it that his hero differed radically from the financier. John D. Rockefeller's biographer recounts the thirteen year old's reflection upon the difference between loaning $50 at seven per cent interest and digging potatoes at 37.5 cents per day: "John was impressed by the fact that capital earned money more easily than muscle did." He would let his money work for him rather than be a producer himself.[116] Profit is manufactured without laboring productively; as finance becomes more sophisticated, it looks more like magic—or artifice. "The art of finance is the production of money by 'pyramiding' and 'kiting' instead of investing . . . Money can be in two, three, even four places at one time."[117]

The issue of nonproduction was at center stage. The speculator created fluctuations in prices, purchasing with a view merely to sell again for a large profit, a form of overreaching for Alger.[118] Financiers, speculators, and gamblers generated profits through exchange, but they generated no *use values*. Speculators offered something people would buy but provided nothing they needed. Nothing was added to the community, and a great deal was redistributed upward.

The speculator surpasses the miser as the "cool, calculating, essential *spirit* of concentrated avaricious selfishness."[119] His character, based in desire, was like the prices he commanded: Fluctuating rather than fixed, set free from stable values, reveling in excess. Therefore, this speculator was not a man. This symbol of capitalism for this period "acted more to subvert the ideology of the autonomous self than to enforce it."[120]

Alger gets even with his fictional figures who speculate. Poetic justice awaits an arrogant boy and his unscrupulous father in *The Young Boatman*. Squire Courtney's Wall Street speculations sour and he is undone while the hero's carefully-advised stock investments make him rich. The squire was compelled to accept the post of bank messenger in town, and his son had to go into a store on a very small salary.[121]

The misers, usurers, confidence men, thieves, spendthrifts, gamblers, and speculators of these tales reveal a script about economic dangers and fears surrounding the forces at work in the era of economic expansion in the young Republic.[122] Alger plays exorcist as villainous personae of the drama meet appropriate fates. Despite the constant presence of human menace, Alger's emerging economic order would not become a house of cards.

CONCLUSION: NATURE, ARTIFICE, AND THE MARKET

Alger's modern drama, set in the marketplace, attempts to re-enact the Greek tragedies he so much admired:

> On the one side virtue—on the other vice exulting in conscious strength—are opposed to each other. A terrible conflict ensues between the opposing principles of good and evil which generally terminates in the overthrow of the latter by the interposition of Divine power. A fearful retribution awaits the guilty while long-suffering virtue receives a fit reward. Viewed in this light,

it will readily be seen how far the tragic drama was fitted to promote the ethical study for which this age was so remarkable. The many questions of duty which were raised and left undecided by the tragic poets were not left so by the spectator.[123]

In the market, the classics student and ex-Unitarian minister disposed of Thracymachus' challenge that it is better to seem than to be just. Alger reworked Cephalus' definition, as had Plato, to demonstrate that justice is profitable throughout one's life. Real value promotes one's own interests as well as those of the community. It yields far more than does appearance.

For Alger, nature was not always benevolent. Nonetheless, tampering with nature makes life more cruel and unstable. Alger's foils, including quite a few capitalists, are simply manipulators of natural and just relationships. These figures scheme to control and profit from control over nature and value. They detract from, rather than contribute to, economic growth and opportunity.

But where is the boundary between nature and artifice in market society? Is the "natural" economy the same as the moral economy when it comes to the marketplace? Alger seems to vascillate between thinking business crises and depressions are unpredictable, uncontrollable, and merely natural, and alternately believing they result from machinations of the unscrupulous.[124]

Many authors whose formative years antedated the Civil War shared a vision: "that of a rural republic, pastoral, small-town, run according to village values which . . . [they] considered natural and therefore normal."[125] Their values harkened back to an eighteenth century agrarian or small-town New England world view, where goals were circumscribed. Agriculture was stable; industry was not. In direct, local exchanges, "the maximizing of profit was less important to these producers than the meeting of household needs and the maintaining of established social relationships within the community." Production and consumption generally took place among biologically related persons, or among others nearby who were linked historically over generations; "these men and women were enmeshed . . . in a web of social relationships and cultural expectations that inhibited the free play of market forces."[126]

Like Henry George, Edward Bellamy, and Henry Demarest Lloyd, Alger attempted to adjust and preserve simple agrarian virtues in the new urban industrial era. Finding the tensions and contradictions between old values and new realities beyond reconciliation, reformers more radical than Alger turned to utopias, providing "an alternative model of growth and development . . . comforting in its assurance of the survival of familiar values."[127] In the face of tensions between old and new, Alger offered a construct of a manageable and familiar future. The work exudes faith in the continued relevance of the simple virtues of the past in the age of industrialism. Leading readers away from both crass materialism and selfishness, Alger allowed the justice of pursuing modest material goals, so long as it was not at the expense of others. This cheery message helps explain his appeal: His hero, a prudent investor in the future, profits thereby.

Alger could not maintain the *innocence* of his country boy intact when he seeks his living in the city. Even if the self-sufficiency of Jefferson's rural yeoman must yield, the values could survive. Thus, "manliness, strength, resolution, and independence," key values to Alger, could transcend the demise of the economic base of the republican yeomanry.[128] The hero's fate vindicates old, conservative, solid values against commercialism and the glitterati of the city. Attaining a very nice competence is the reward for steadfastness and golden character. Modern conservatives like to tell and retell this story.

While a strong sense of individual and social responsibility is essential to preserve the Republic, the project for market justice does not depend upon changing human nature. Rather, the community must ensure that solid men of virtue balance out those who are unredeemed or even unredeemable. Alger's boys and girls whose characters allow them to prevail are just the types who can stand up to Mickey McGuire, padrones, and confidence men. Their visible presence and substantial number will keep the men and women without virtue—the real strangers among us—in check.

Despoilers are public enemies. Some of them are capitalists. Alger's naming was not innocent; Brantley Wentworth is given a surname meaning the dissipation of value. Revealing his fears, Alger also gives some who coerce or destroy innocent natures identifiable ethnicities. Jews are overrepresented among usurers, and the Irish are overrepresented among street extortionists and bullies. They are perhaps seen as too impatient for gain to move fairly and slowly to achieve it.

Thus, most of Alger's heroes *were* drawn from strong Yankee stock; the same boys who had kept the Union together might now keep urban America from ruin. Perhaps Alger shared a vision with Bellamy—that the problem was "how to bring this large middle power to the front and send the rest to the rear and keep them there." [129] Old Protestant stock holds its own against immigrants, foreign-born ideas, and robber barons.

Identifiable despoilers are figures who could appeal to a variety of populist, progressive and anticapitalist sentiments. Alger's bad market citizens are crossovers in political discourse. They generally emerge from the pens of antebellum moralists, but come to serve as villains for a whole broader audience—the "little people" who wage war, perhaps single-handedly, against economic giants. Latter-day Jacksonians would have no trouble seeing here the conflict between greed and goodness: The Alger hero *is* the independent agent at war against the corporation. The small town boy or city orphan who makes good testifies against the power of the corporation, the bureaucratic organization, entrenched wealth.

Alger's market interventions right the world. This alignment of price and value bespeaks resistance to the market rather than acceptance of it. However, the critique of the modern market, couched in small, pious mediations (reform), serves to reinforce acceptance of the rules of the new order rather than fuel rebellion against them. The equilibration of price and value, markets and virtue-based notions of justice, conflate sacred and secular meanings and promises. Minus evildoers, there is reasonable hope of just outcomes.

9

========

Levelling and Its Limits

In this model republic, this land of the free—
So our orators call it, and why should not we?—
'Tis refreshing to know that without pedigree
A man may still climb to the top of the tree;
That questions of family, rank, and high birth,
All bow to the query, How much is he worth?
That John Smith, plebeian, who forty years since
Walked Broadway barefooted, now rides as a prince;
Having managed, though not overburdened with wit,
But rather by chance and a fortunate hit,
To take a high place on Society's rounds;
His claims being based on pence, shillings, and pounds.
I admit there's a certain republican merit
In making the fortune which others inherit;
But why should John Smith so completely ignore
The bridge which has brought him triumphantly o'er,
And turn with disgust from the opposite shore?

Alger, *Nothing to Do*

ERASING SOCIAL DISTANCE

As early as 1857, in an anonymously published bound poem entitled
Nothing to Do, Alger assailed the "self-made" men who forget their roots as
soon as they are established, who lack true worth, and who measure others
by their wealth. The poem recounts the story of a wealthy young snob, who

Being taught to consider himself from his birth,
As one of the privileged ones of the earth,
He cherishes deep and befitting disdain
For those who don't live in the Fifth Avenue,
As entirely unworthy the notice or thought
Of the heir of two millions and nothing to do.

The cosmopolitan traveller calls the others "canaille," having absorbed nothing else from his travels. He believes that "much finer clay/Is required for the rich than the general masses."[1]

As Horace Mann argued, an idle person is no man:

No matter what may be the fortunes or the expectations of a young man, he has no right to live a life of idleness. In a world so full as this of incitements to exertion and of rewards for achievement, idleness is the most absurd of absurdities and the most shameful of shames ... the idle man is not so much a biped as a bivalve ...[2]

For Alger, man is meant for higher purposes than idleness; no one should leave the world its debtor.

A fitting reward lies in wait for the idle young man in *Nothing to Do*— a wife who would spend all his as yet anticipated fortune on "dry goods and/bijoux/with all the etceteras thereto attendant." Prior to enrolling a second time at the divinity school, Alger preaches at the close of *Nothing to Do*:

O, ye who in life are content to be drones,
And stand idly by while your fellows bear stones
To rear the great temple which Adam began,
Whereof the All-Father has given each man
A part in the building—pray look the world through,
And say, if you can, you have nothing to do!
Were man sent here solely to eat, drink, and sleep,
And if, as Faith, Reason, and Scripture, all show,
God rewards us in heaven for the good done below,
I pray you take heed, idle worldling, lest you
With that better world should have nothing to do![3]

Many of the themes that would fill the pages of the juvenile novels were already present in 1857: juxtaposition of wealth and merit, the basis of true manliness, the tendency of people to judge a man by his money, opposition to pretense and creation of social distance, assertion of opportunity for mobility; rewards for the worthy and punishments for the unworthy.

These tales consistently address the gap between rich and poor.[4] This chapter explores the creation and negation of social distance. We again

The wealthy young snob. (Anonymous [Horatio Alger, Jr.], *Nothing to Do: A Tilt at Our Best Society*. Boston: James French & Company, 1857. Houghton Library, Harvard University.)

discover the author "righting" a world that is being turned upside down, reconstituting community where chasms had appeared.

In fact, it is possible to read these stories as Leveller tracts. Arranged justice strikes at the would-be aristocrat and mobility raises up the lowly. Those who will not be contaminated by the poor are often forced to join the ranks. Levelling and its limits reveal a great deal about the author's prescription for healthy democracy. While dethroning the oligarchy, he attempts the restoration of the *aristoi*, the best.

SOCIAL DISTANCE AND DEFERENCE

> The code of aristocratic manners, too, has its sinister or false development as well as its true and benign development. The formula which, in its ungenial phase, it is forever insinuating through all its details of demeanor, when translated into plain words is this: I am superior to you and therefore command you! But the real aristocratic behavior does not say the inferior must obey the superior. On the contrary, it withholds and suppresses the sense of superiority, seems unconscious of it, and only indirectly implies it by the implicit affirmation, I am glad to be able to bless and aid you, to comfort, strengthen, and uplift you![5]

Social distance and distinctions are everpresent in Alger stories, with one or more characters insisting on what is due them because of their rank. The value of money to them lies in what it can provide in terms of status, ostentation, and deference from others. They value difference. Examining the lessons taught through these foils allows us to explore the author's response to the gap between rich and poor and to the impact of social distance and differentiation on the Republic.

Discounting the advantages of inherited wealth and cautioning against reliance upon them were stock discourse in advice manuals through the century. When Alger was born, youth could read:

> Thousands of young men have been ruined by relying for a good name on their honorable parentage, or inherited wealth, or the patronage of friends. Flattered by these distinctions, they have felt as if they might live without plan and without effort,—merely for their own gratification and indulgence. No mistake is more fatal. It always issues in producing an inefficient and useless character. On this account, it is, that character and wealth rarely continue, in the same family, more than two or three generations.[6]

And an end of the century guide admired by Alger advised:

> Young people ... should be content to begin their life-work in a
> small way. They must not despise the lowest round of the ladder,
> nor jump it if they can; it is on the way to the top round. The youth
> who aspires to begin where his father left off is at war with history.
> He wants to break up the established order of things ... He does
> not want to pay the price of success; he expects to secure it
> cheaper. As if Providence would make him an exception to the
> rule! ... The sure experience of such a youth is to end smaller than
> he began.[7]

Alger's favorite foil is, perhaps, the rich boy in a small town who expects
both material goods *and* deference to be handed him. This unpopular boy
who puts on airs and fancy clothing because of his father's position is the
most frequent counterpoint offered to the popular hero. This type believes
his father owes him luxuries and unbounded spending money, grumbles
about his allowance, and tends to fall into temptation.[8] He relies very little
on effort and almost totally on status; he is a lazy, poor scholar, and rather
incompetent. This haughty boy continually reminds the less fortunate hero
of his dress, his poverty, the social distance between them, and how,
therefore, the hero ought to behave. The latter is not considered a suitable
companion, unless his fortunes suddenly improve. The boy and at least one
of his parents are indignant that a poor hero is proud and does not know his
place, for the hero will only give deference where it is due.[9]

Some fictional would-be aristocrats are so calloused that they will
not lift a finger to help save the life of a member of the "lower
classes"—which one snob, when pressed, defines as "working boys
and working men, and so on."[10] Snobs articulate the belief that people
are born into their station, and downplay the view that some successful
men begin in these classes.

Wealth itself does not make a gentleman or entitle one to deference.[11] The
poor hero, of course, has the gentlemanly qualities. The author lectured:

> To be born to wealth removes all the incentives to action, and
> checks the spirit of enterprise. A boy or man who finds himself
> gradually rising in the world through his own exertions, experi-
> ences a satisfaction unknown to one whose fortune is ready
> made.[12]

Unbeknownst to the son who "thinks his father a gentleman of wealth
and high birth," embezzlement, theft, duplicity, or arson often underlie the
squire's fortune.[13] The "squire" engages in speculation, usury, or is a hard-
nosed businessman who put money first to a fault. Foils who emphasize
wealth and distinction usually lose them. Alger quite regularly settles scores
with the son by settling scores with the father.

Sometimes it seems the hero's prosperity functions to silence and show up the sneering and jeering hometown snob or dandy, who has constantly looked down upon our hero in his poverty. The hero may deliberately display new and expensive clothing or watches, to the chagrin and irritation of jealous foils.[14] In one late Alger novel, a young boy who has established a modest fortune practically strews money about in demonstration of his good fortune.[15] But, of course, money is not attained chiefly to get even, nor to establish the hero as the town's replacement squire, and this occasional scenario is usually done in humor.

BRIDGING CLASSES

Charity and Paternalism

> . . . it was awful cold, and there was big holes in my shoes, and
> my gloves and all my warm clothes was at the tailor's. I felt as if
> life was sort of tough, and I'd like it if some rich man would adopt
> me, and give me plenty to eat and drink and wear, without my
> havin' to look so sharp after it. Then agin' when I've seen boys
> with good homes, and fathers, and mothers, I've thought I'd like
> to have somebody to care for me.

Alger, *Ragged Dick*

Ragged Dick, who always seems to maintain a cheerful disposition in the face of hardship, admits to Frank Whitney under questioning that sometimes, like once last winter, he has the blues. While Dick is too old to require adoption, he gets an equivalent. After saving Mr. Rockwell's son from drowning, he is taken into his new patron's counting house.

The New York merchant-benefactors and befrienders (occasionally called capitalists) with tastefully elaborate homes know that money has better uses than conspicuous consumption. It can strengthen the bonds of community and family and promote well-placed charity. This claim was hardly news. Preceding Russell Conwell's "Acres of Diamonds" speech and Carnegie's "Gospel of Wealth," antebellum advice manuals intoned: "The greater a man's wealth, the broader may be, if he but will it, the sphere of his usefulness."[16] Ragged Dick's creator absorbed such "self-evident truths." He viewed himself as a philanthropist of sorts, writing a few months before his death: "With such means as I had I have been able to do a good deal of charitable work, but I doubt if I shall be able to very much more [sic]."[17]

Alger claimed two boys as his adoptive sons, providing their education and support. He wrote repeatedly of them and helped them through a commercial college.[18] Alger writes that the Scotch orphan boy who lives with him "was left to struggle alone and unaided till at 15 I began to care for him." "I have helped other boys to the extent of my means," he writes; his will left funds for the care of a total of nine named boys apart from blood relations.[19] He reports of his success in helping several poor young boys from Natick find places in stores in Boston—one in R. U. White's, one in Jordan & Marsh's. His young friend at the Tribune, Irving Blake, was apparently awaiting a loan from Alger to study French when the latter died.[20]

Being of direct and indirect assistance to poor boys helped Alger define himself and to establish connection with others. In 1888, Alger initiated contact with a distant relative, General Russell A. Alger by voicing appreciation of his charitable gift to the poor boys of Detroit:

> Having devoted a large amount of time, and written four-teen books, illustrating the lives and experiences of the street boys of New York, I confess I felt very proud that one of my name should have accomplished so much in the same field.

The praise was reiterated during General Alger's trial by public opinion during the Spanish American War, when the General was serving as McKinley's Secretary of War:

> I think what has interested me most in your career has been your kindness to the poor boys of Detroit. I am sure you will never regret your outlay for them. I wonder how many of those who criticize you would have done the same thing.[21]

Kindness is real value; it remains a marker of character should reputation be questioned.

Alger practiced on a small scale the kind of nurturance recommended for his merchant-philanthropists. The author's benefactors likewise provide for children and send them to school or employ them. Patronage was more than a mere financial transfer; it helped define the man and wove classes together into a community.

The author celebrates those who realize they are blessed with riches and feel truly fortunate to be able to help those in need.[22] As the new economy integrates diverse people into a community of strangers, reciprocity constitutes a strong social bond.

Reconstituting Community

> There is in all large cities, in Boston and New York, as in Paris and London, a city within a city; or rather outside of the city of the educated, the industrious, and the prosperous there is the city of the ignorant, the wretched, the forlorn . . .
>
> Edward Everett, "The Education of the Poor"[23]

By late antebellum era, the shock many Americans voiced upon encountering the city, with its world of strangers and gap between themselves and the poor had been poignantly captured. Lydia Maria Child reported:

> For eight weary months, I have met in the crowded streets but two faces I have ever seen before. Of some, I would I could say that I should never see them again; but they haunt me in my sleep, and come between me and the morning. Beseeching looks, begging the comfort and the hope I have no power to give. Hungry eyes, that look as if they had pleaded long for sympathy, and at last gone mute in still despair . . .[24]

Half a century later, Dreiser's New York circa 1890 is a city clearly divided between the rich and poor. The glitter of Broadway contrasts with the world of the homeless and desperate; the wealthy who fill their days with pleasure and desire are contrasted with striking trolley motormen and their sympathizers who confront police and scabs. The growing gulf between Carrie and Hurstwood parallels the growing gulf between classes in the industrial city. The unproductive, idle rich separate themselves as far as possible from the unproductive, idle poor who can barely exist.

Alger would deny the anonymity, discord, and class segmentation of the city. Characters constantly run into both friendly acquaintances and thrice-met villains on the streets. Classes still meet in a space of accidental encounters in the city. Accidents bring together people from different parts of the city and from different social classes; the impersonality of the city and the faceless crowd yield. Class boundaries are fluid. His characters range freely across urban spaces without challenging prevailing class distinctions.[25]

The importance of patronage in the Alger formula underscores the author's attachment to a world in which classes are not socially or geographically segregated. Contact and acquaintance are vital to the transaction.

Frequently, heroes help reconstitute community among strangers, bridging the distance between classes, replacing family influences, and combating urban isolation. Strangers and parent-surrogates take over the nurturance and support of those who were young, old, or alone.

A novel at the beginning of Alger's career, *Paul Prescott's Charge*, arranges one such reconstitution of community. Paul rescues Aunt Lucy Lee from the Wrenville poorhouse (where he had been a brief inhabitant), gives her news that her estranged brother will now be sending her money, and removes her to New York, where she comes to live with his adoptive parents and himself. All lives are enriched.

At the end of his career, the hero serves as a vehicle for bringing together a lonely, infirm wealthy man with his destitute cousin and her son in *A Rolling Stone*. While his employer, Mr. Gibbon (the older man in question), is disposed to find Mrs. Ransom and help her financially, it is the hero who devises the scheme to constitute them as a household. The "little family" is established in a pleasant home in Detroit. Mr. Gibbon explains the reciprocity of the arrangement:

> If she is willing to be burdened with me, I will establish a home, and see that she and the boy are well provided for. She will suffer no more from poverty and privation. We will live together and make each other comfortable.[26]

Each is happier and better off in their new community of caring.

One perceptive analyst of the Ragged Dick Series claims that almost every character establishes "his connection to others on an axis of caring or being cared for, or defaulting on such fostering duties."[27] Zuckerman also asserts that the happy ending provides an alternative to independence and loneliness in the large city; boys face an independence they did not seek.

However, while the importance of connection and nurture is unquestionable, Zuckerman has drawn some unfortunate conclusions. He argues that the emphasis in these novels is *not* on self-reliance, but rather on dependence, protection, and escape from autonomy. Each hero willingly *renounces* self-employment and autonomy for the protection of a benefactor:

> Beneath his [Alger's] explicit emphasis on striving upward ran a deeper desire for stability and security; beneath his paens to manly vigor, a lust for effeminate indulgence; beneath his celebration of self-reliance, a craving to be taken care of and a yearning to surrender the terrible burden of independence.[28]

An Alger hero's independence is never defined *against* community. As we have seen in earlier chapters, independence is defined by manliness and steadfastness of character. Character permits the youth to avoid being dependent and overpowered. Only extremely young children and heroines are returned to moral safety in dependence. While the hero may be dependent upon personal contacts to have his value recognized, connection to others is part of being manly; individualists are not connected and are not men.[29]

Class Interaction:
Summons and Invitations

Mr. Plank, a middle-aged, honest-looking mechanic, looked up in surprise when Mrs. Hamilton entered the shop.

"You didn't expect a call from me?" said the lady pleasantly.

"No, ma'am. Fashionable ladies don't often find their way over here."

"Then don't look upon me as a fashionable lady. I like to attend to my business myself, and have brought you the money for your bill."

"Thank you, ma'am. *You* never made me wait. But I am sorry you had the trouble to come to my shop. I would have called at your house if you had sent me a postal."

"My time is not so valuable as yours, Mr. Plank . . ."

Alger, *Store Boy*

The true nobility of culture do not merely summon the poor or working classes to them. The benefactress of *Store Boy* not only travels to her carpenter's shop, but, when employing a poor hero, brings him into her home to live. The author addressed a problem.

During early years of labor agitation in the nineteenth century, workers sometimes demanded that owners fulfill the obligations of paternal authority. An operative could complain of the grievous wrongs occasioned by "the difference in caste which employers create between their sons and daughters and the sons and daughters they employ to increase their wealth." Being denied admittance to the parlors of employers seems to be a recurring complaint in the documents of the period: "Do they find admittance into the families of the rich? Certainly not! They are factory girls—her occupation, nay her usefulness, excludes her."[30]

Employers were seen as creating social distinctions; workers saw the industrial system violating family relationships and social integration.

Alger struggled to maintain an identity of interest between employees and honest employers. He applauded the wealthy and substantial citizen who treated any worthy subordinate as an equal. Poor heroes were invited into the uptown parlors and dining rooms of the wealthy without ceremony. They even moved *into* the household as companions for children, or, if educated, tutors or private secretaries. In fiction, employers and their employees at the bottom rung of the occupational hierarchy, wealthy and poor, remained joined—in the same community and even the same family.

Ragged Dick is impressed with the fact that the wealthy Greysons invite another bootblack and himself into their home for Sunday dinner between service and Sunday School. The charming daughter, Ida, allows no sense of social difference to cross her mind. Ida is typical of such progeny ("Rose Gardiner was a girl of good sense, and her estimate of others was founded on something else than social distinction."[31]) Ida offers Dick a five-dollar gold piece upon learning he is poor, at which point her mother interjects: "Dick cannot be called poor, my child, since he earns his living by his own exertions."[32]

In another instructive case of cross-class socializing, Gilbert Greyson attends a Steinway Hall concert at the invitation of his wealthy friends, the Vivians, in *Shifting for Himself*. A young, pretentious foil and his doting mother have arrived with an extra ticket, which they have determined not to offer Gilbert. They refuse to be seen in his company at this bourgeois event: "If it were in a different part of the house, away from our seats, I should not care particularly," this socially conscious mother says, "if he went with us, he might be thought to be a near relative."[33] Veblen shortly wrote of this modern need to display markers:

> In the modern community there is also a more frequent atten-
> dance at large gatherings of people to whom one's everyday life
> is unknown; in such places as churches, theaters, ballrooms, hotels,
> parks, shops and the like. In order to impress these transient
> observers, and to retain one's self complacency under their
> observation, the signature of one's pecuniary strength should be
> written in characters which he who runs may read.[34]

Randolph, the foil, is a classic example:

> Randolph cared very little for the music, which was too classical
> to suit his taste. He did not expect to like it, but he went because
> he knew that the audience would be a fashionable one, and he
> liked to be seen on such occasions.[35]

The hero "had more musical taste, and appreciated the greater part of what he had heard."[36] His appreciation shows him more gentlemanly than his counterpart. The Vivians are true members of the aristocracy of culture for whom a poor boy may be a friend and equal. To reinforce the point, the author places their seats in front of those of the haughty Briggs.

The natural music appreciation of the unsophisticated hero complements the absence of pretense among the worthy members of the bourgeoisie. Musical occasions in their homes remain unaffected and pleasurable, standing in contrast to some emerging bourgeois performance demands. A mid-century London journalist claimed "that many families were putting on concerts in their homes and driving their children to become virtuosi, with the result that 'in families the piano has extinguished conversation and the love of books.'"[37] But in bourgeois American parlors such as the Vivians', poor Alger heroes join in, singing with natural, unaffected voices:

> The piano was in the parlor adjoining. The doors were thrown open, and Laura sat down to the piano. Two or three songs were selected, and Gilbert sang to Laura's accompaniment. He had a good voice, and a correct ear, and the double performance passed off smoothly.[38]

Minus affectation, the poor and rich interact in harmony. They sing the same notes and can speak the same language.

Manners and Class Markers

In the Gilded Age, "manners provided yet another way of avoiding talking openly about the dirty secret of class in America."

> Victorian table manners were designed to set careful limits upon the possibilities of social interaction and communion, to reinforce and justify existing social relationships rather than to change them. They checked any sort of deviation from the paths of social propriety, whether it led in the direction of individual assertion or of communal transformation.[39]

The teaching of manners was an organized assault on newcomers and "part of the struggle against 'objectionable social groups.'"[40] Knives, forks, and spoons were among the barriers to social entry posed for the uninitiated.

But worthy Alger heroes did not study table manners nor did they read etiquette books such as Chesterfield's *Letters to His Son* or any of the other nineteenth century etiquette books middle class youth were reading, "packed with hundreds of detailed rules covering not inner morals but outward conduct."[41] Although an occasional hero took dancing lessons, Alger's boys and girls did not learn proper dress, comportment, or cleanliness from manuals, nor read about how to behave at evening parties. They did not require lessons in how to converse politely, how to carry themselves, or hold their hands.

If "gentility was the exercise of perfect physical and emotional self-restraint," Alger's street boys and country heroes are possessed of it instinctively.[42] In whatever ways instinct required supplement, the young could become quickly studies in the rudiments of civility, emulating new-found friends.

Hostile to artifice, affectation, and pretence in presentation of self, Alger scoffs at characters who would emulate British aristocracy or try to create an indigenous one. The truly royal have manners but are not mannered. Alger concurred with T. S. Arthur's assertion that "A true gentleman—that is, one who really regards with feelings of disinterested kindness his fellow-man—will rarely commit any glaring violation of good manners."[43]

Downplaying mannered, artificial behavior requires that real ladies, gentlemen, and benefactors devalue artificial markers of distinction. The real gentleman does not stand on ceremony:

> A high sense of honor—a determination never to take a mean advantage of another—an adherence to truth, delicacy, and politeness toward those with whom you have any dealings, are the essential and distinguishing characteristics of *a* GENTLE-MAN.[44]

Men and women of worth live out a commitment to democracy. Real genteel culture remained accessible—without manuals and without a Harvard education. We can all be of one estate—albeit a well-mannered estate.

Artifice and Nature: Rejecting Some Implications of the Public/Private Split

> Not long since I went to Railroad Hall (Madison Avenue) to hear Roosevelt speak. He failed to be present, and rather to my surprise I was called upon to speak, as a sort of a stop gap.
>
> Alger to Irving Blake, February 5, 1896

Alger, the leveller, can be taken as a peculiar sort of spokesperson for democracy in a world in which culture is becoming increasingly class-differentiated and hierarchically arranged. He assaults some boundaries of authoritative communication. The values of the private sphere, seen as natural, have not been displaced by the artifice and posturing that increasingly take place in the public sphere.

The author champions the amateur over the professional and downplays expertise or specific skills. Despite the occasional Steinway Hall event, Alger's boundary between spectator and performer is generally fluid; the gulf between consumers and producers of culture has not solidified.

Before locating their true vocations, young characters very frequently spend some time as performers. They are singers, whistlers, actors, and circus riders. Their performance is unaffected, naked, naïve, and essentially untrained. They act with assurance and without clumsiness, and they are quite effective in engaging their audiences. Ragged Dick never takes the stage, but he is a consummate "natural" performer—a practitioner of the art of street theater.

The gift of these performers lies in their lack of affectation and their ability to perform from true feeling. Art cannot be monopolized by experts and authorities. "Art, while it is not pure and simple nature, is not anything substituted for nature nor anything opposed to nature."[45]

Alger heroes do not have special styles, faces, or personalities designed for the era of the crowd. Neither the author nor his heroes required a distinctive signature or marker; they were not headline seekers, nor did they attempt to command the stage. Unlike foils who call attention to themselves at every turn, heroes, even on the stage, do not insist upon drawing all eyes to themselves. Not seeking to be singled out as individuals, they nonetheless achieve public recognition. If there is "magnification of personality under the new conditions of appearance and performance," Alger has—at least in his fiction—tended to reject the game.[46] Only when he has a few boys attain spectacular wealth toward the end of his own career might it be said that he has recognized the power of the spectacle.

Performance in Alger's world of fiction is relatively democratic; the mass is not divorced from the capacity to "produce" entertainment. Although the author's letters reveal that he frequently went as a spectator to world-touring virtuosi performances in Boston and New York, his fiction refuses to yield up the stage to professionals and to grand personalities.

However, grand spectacles, ostentatious consumption, carefully crafted events, staged performances, and cultivated images increasingly differentiated the public personality from the private, and the performer from the spectator in the Gilded Age. The spectacular events of a "melodramatic and political society" were becoming increasingly common, facilitated by the dissemination of newspapers. Teddy Roosevelt, of whom Alger was enthusiastically supportive, was attentive to showmanship and the creation of a personality for the era of the crowd.[47] With the proliferation of inexpensive reading matter, a certain class of authors were also able to become public personae.

Alger's literary career can be framed by Dickens' lecture tours of America (the second occurring in 1867, the year in which *Ragged Dick* was written) and Mark Twain's grand world tour of 1895-96, the time at which Alger effectively retired in ill health. Both Dickens and Twain were effective public figures. Mark Twain cultivated spectacle, with public tours, costumes, contrived gestures, and a carefully groomed public image. He was one of the real self-promoters and public spectacles of the period.[48] Alger wrote a young friend in 1896: "I heard Mark Twain give three lectures many years ago. They were peculiar lectures but interesting."[49]

Alger's face appeared in a card game; his autograph was solicited by young fans; he gave occasional public lectures; he might be recognized by strangers in the street. He reported to a friend at the *Tribune* that one Monday evening in January, 1897

> I gave a talk interspersed with readings from Ragged Dick on the Street Boys of New York. Among the audience were about a hundred boys who were very appreciative. I occupied about an hour. One boy met me in the street the next day and said "yer done good last evenin'. When are you goin' to lecture agin?"

Alger added, "I don't think the boy will soon be one of the editors of the Tribune."[50] He repeated the lecture in Waltham, where

> among the audience were about 100 boys who recd. me with applause and listened with evident appreciation. About a dozen came up to be introduced at the close. What gratifies me most is that boys, though strangers, seem to regard me as a personal friend.[51]

Notice, however, the difference from performance as spectacle. Alger does not court the gaze of a crowd, but the bridging of gulfs: between educated and uneducated; between audience and speaker/performer. His talks were not the stuff of modern performance.

Thus, when the grand showman, public personality, governor, and future president disappointed the New York crowd in early 1896, Alger was an ironic stopgap. He lacked the dynamism, charisma, and public personality of masters of the art. He was essentially a private man.

The distance between performer and audience mirrors the distinction between the artificial (or mechanical) and natural. The "theatrical" signified "something overdone, unreal, turgid, hollow, bombastic." In the Edwin Forrest biography, Alger and his cousin assert that popular interest in drama increased when theaters began to be built on a smaller scale, with actors and stage brought closer to the limited audience, and themes "began to depict ordinary mortal characters and reflect the contents of real life." Acting came indoors—from the ampitheater to the parlor, and from "a city of gazers" to "a company of critical observers." They associated this development with the nineteenth century romantic school of acting:

> The buskins were thrown off and the masks laid aside, the true form and moving displayed, living expressions given to the features, and the changing tones of passion restored to the voice. Then the mechanical in acting gave way to the passionate . . .[52]

Reading the consequences of change in the nineteenth century as tending away from public and toward private space, away from the mechanical and toward nature, the cousins engaged in a reading of history quite different and almost perversely opposed to what many were reading. Their implicit claim that drama improved in some aspect as its themes shifted from "fate and the tragic pomp and grandeur of monarchs and gods" to "ordinary mortal characters" and "the contents of real life" was turned around by critics of the melodrama. And their acknowledgment of a shift from a drama that appealed to the entire city to theater that instead found a smaller and more select audience hinted at the demise of a common language.

The triumph is allegedly one of feeling over theatrics. Alger likewise rejects the demands of appearance and performance in the social world. His boys and young women are not "put on show"—they do not have separate, exhibited surfaces in the realm of social interaction. There is a sanctity accorded the private and the emotional; here one's real worth is always recognized, regardless of one's fortunes in the outside, public world. The author's domestic scenes are open, warm, and protected. There are no displays, no posturing, no pomp or artifice inside. The "real" people we meet in these domestic scenes do not become different personnages in the street.

King, Aristocrat, Plebeian, and Democrat

> The formula expressed in truly royal manners is, I am so contented with the sense of fulfilment and of universal support that my only want is to see every one enjoying the same happiness! In a perfected state the formula of democratic manners will be identical with this. For then the whole community with its solidarity of wealth and power will be the sustaining environment whereof each individual is a centre. But as yet the private fortune of each man is his selfishly isolated environment; and the totality of individual environments bristles with hostility, while every one tries to break into and absorb the neighboring ones.[53]

In a collaborative work, Alger or his cousin wrote, "Kings are all of one family. They are all free, neither commanding one another nor obeying one another, each one complete sovereign in himself and of himself."[54]

However, to *become* one estate, battle must be enjoined—both with the ersatz aristocrat and with a kind of plebeian democrat. If those emphasizing distinction threatened harm to the Republic, so, too, did those who would debase standards and tastes to those of the lowest.

Ragged Dick and his bootblack-compatriots must possess neither the discontented and insurrectionary plebeian manner ("You are superior to me, and therefore I distrust, fear, and hate you!") nor the submissive or cringing plebeian manner ("I am inferior to you, and therefore beseech your favor, deprecating your scorn!") A pernicious form of democratic behavior, which is "too common in American practice thus far," involves

> the insolent casting off of despotic usages and authorities, and the replacing them with the defiant protest of a reckless independence. I am as good as you, and therefore neither of us will have any regard or deference for the other!

Such behavior "would inaugurate a stagnant level of mediocrities, a universal wilderness of social carelessness and self-assertion."[55]

If democracy is to survive, men and women of genuine worth must be acknowledged as such. Otherwise, there will be no leaders, save the demagogue. Tocqueville had company in his concerns:

> In democracies private citizens see men rising from their ranks and attaining wealth and power in a few years; that spectacle excites their astonishment and their envy; they wonder how he who was their equal yesterday has today won the right to command them. To attribute his rise to his talents or his virtues is inconvenient, for it means admitting that they are less virtuous or capable than he . . .[56]

Richard Hunter (Ragged Dick) eschews these various plebeian and democratic vices, which inhibit personal and social progress. He might be said to possess a better sort of plebeian manner: "The plebeian manner, honest, manly, and good, says, You are superior to me, and I am glad of it, because, looking up to you with admiration and love, I shall appropriate your excellence and grow like you myself!"[57] But in a democracy, the institutionalized entitlement of superior ranks fades; Ragged Dick, democratic citizen, and Misters Greyson and Rockwell, royally mannered, can alike agree:

> We are all amenable to the same open and universal standard of right and good, and therefore we do not raise the question at all of precedency or privilege, or conscious superiority or inferiority, but we leave all such points to the decision of the facts themselves, and are ready indifferently to lead or to follow according to the fitness of intrinsic ranks![58]

The democratic citizen "independent and supreme in his interior personal sphere of life," is

> in his social and public life affiliated with endless grades of superiors, equals, and inferiors, all called on to obey not the self-will of one another, or of any majority, but to follow gladly the dictates of those inherent fitnesses of inspiration from above and aspiration from below which will remain eternally authoritative when every unjust immunity and merely conventional or titular rank has been superseded.[59]

Value—eternal and unadulterated—survives only with the participation of possessors and aspirants. For Alger, this, then, is the limit of levelling.

CONCLUSION

> One of the most amiable features of good republican society is this; that men seldom boast of their riches, or disguise their poverty, but speak of both, as of any other matters that are proper for conversation. No man shuns another because he is poor; no man is preferred to another because he is rich. In hundreds and hundreds of instances have men in this country, not worth a shilling, been chosen by the people to take care of their rights and interests, in preference to men who ride in their carriages.
>
> William A. Alcott, *The Young Man's Guide*

This amalgamation of moral and cultural elitism with egalitarianism produces a potentially seductive message. There *are* standards, but the distance between the possessors and nonpossessors is easily gotten over. Gentility does not come from inheritance nor from advice books; relevant skill acquisition is not monopolized in elite educational institutions. Character—the best currency available—is largely under the control of the individual. At least among white, Anglo-Saxon Protestants, differences in station count for naught. Attainment of partnership with one's employer and a hinted marriage with his daughter erases the meaning of class.

This message arranges justice for a world increasingly becoming divided into classes—in space, in consumption capacities, in work environments and life chances. Alger bridges the gap and offers assurances that persons of true merit will not let it grow wide.

Alger's message about the permeability of boundaries and his negation of social distance convey optimism about democracy—a belief in fundamental equality. He anticipates a bright future for the Republic, retains faith in human nature, and insists that the meritorious cannot be priced out of the aristocracy. No artifice nor artificial barriers shall mar the democratic promise that we are all of one estate and that we engage in the same discourse.

Denying the importance of social distinctions by negating them, Alger corrects a world in which wealth and social status are conjoined. In so doing, he denies one very significant measure of the importance of wealth in the world of his young reader.

Alger the leveller offers a palatable message to populists in the audience, which leaves the virtuous securely in possession of the rewards economy and society have to offer. These stories incorporate a script about levelling, but ultimately justify unequal outcomes and deference to the natural aristocrat. Ragged Dick is a democratic hero only by transcending the plebeian.

10

===

Reading Alger: Searching for Alger's Audience in the Literary Marketplace

> Your kind and flattering letter reached me just as I was starting for the Geysers . . . It gives me great pleasure to find that I have friends and appreciative readers among the girls, as well as among the boys, and on the shores of the Pacific, as well as the Atlantic. I hope at an early date to write a story located in California, and I shall be glad if it proves acceptable to my friends here.
>
> Alger to Miss Harriet Jackson, March 3, 1877[1]

The marked surge in the production, dissemination, and reading of literature in the Gilded Age created new readers and new reading tastes. Rising literacy, increased leisure for some, a spreading national network of reading matter available for purchase and loan, and declining price of fiction helped make readers out of new classes. Especially after 1880, these factors worked in conjunction with growing family incomes to produce changes in reading propensities, buying habits, and tastes. Much of the reading was fiction.

But who read *Ragged Dick* or *Sam's Chance*? Discovering the real, potential, likely, and intended audience for Alger's fiction is no simple task. Popular fiction does not yield secrets easily, and "we know very little about the readers of the *New York World*, the *Ladies' Home Journal*, and *Ragged Dick*."[2]

Whereas this book makes many text-based arguments, the object of Chapter 10 is to search for Alger's audience in the marketplace. One course is to follow the production, circulation, and exchange of the reading matter Alger generated. In doing so, Chapter 10 introduces the story papers, magazines, and the book trade through which Alger reached his public(s), along with the stores and libraries that carried his wares.

But the gap between macro- and microlevel data is large. Although we can paint a picture of who might have read Alger, following vehicles of communication to points of distribution cannot definitively identify the Alger reader. And current historians of the book and of other nineteenth century reading matter are highly skeptical of methods and inferences made about audiences in extant secondary sources.[3]

The best available evidence we can supply on who read Alger comes from a child's diary, fan mail, letters to magazine editors, and testimonials. Since the author directed that correspondence in his possession be destroyed upon his death, this important resource on reader response is lost. However, some recipients of Alger's letters treasured and preserved them. The data are supplemented by Alger's own reports about access and readership, and observations made of readers in the public library.

The individual-level data yields a marked class skew toward the middle-class reader. So, too, does clothbound novel pricing data. But there is reason to hold back from the conclusion that this is the best portrait of Alger's audience. Too often, scholars have forgotten that Alger tales appeared in forms other than clothbound novels.

In any investigation of how far Alger's works penetrated the working classes, there are many silences. Many readers left no testimonials, and the story papers through which many came to know Alger, were, like today's newspapers, discarded or recycled.

In only the rarest case can we *will* the reader to pick up the work and read. The sample is too small and not representative. The portrait of Alger's readers must, then, be further sketched by examining access to the different forms in which these stories found their way to their publics. This chapter draws upon a range of available tools and data to begin a sketch of this portrait. Much more detective work could productively be done.[4] However, this endeavor addresses a near void in our understanding and combats facile pronouncements about Alger's audience that are too often taken as fact.[5] Improving our portrait of the real or likely Alger reader by bringing disparate evidence together in the same place will help in the search to understand the locus of these texts in the space of political discourse.

READING ALGER:
THE NORCROSS DIARY

Grenville Howland Norcross (1854-1937), the son of a former Boston mayor, was graduated from Harvard in 1875, acquired a Harvard law degree in 1879, and became a Boston lawyer. He was active in historical and literary organizations around Boston, including the American Antiquarian Society. As a boy, he attended dance school, took vacations with his family to the shore, visited grandmother in Jamaica Plain, studied Latin, and noted his reading habits in diaries.

While the Norcross diary affords evidence only of the reading habits of one middle-class Boston boy, it indicates that more and less reputable fiction are present in the diets of such young people in the early Gilded Age. The diet was a mix of history, fiction writers who would join the canon—Dickens, Swift, Cooper, Defoe; tales of Alger, Optic, Ellis, and Castlemon; dime novels and railroad literature. It also indicates that Alger became known without necessarily being purchased in book form.

In 1874, Alger supplied biographical data and a photo upon the request of George A. Bacon for use in a subsequent edition of the "Game of Authors."[6] The photo, one that Joseph H. Allen supplied gratis to *Student and Schoolmate* subscribers, appeared in the "'Moral and Religious' suit along with Henry Ward Beecher, Edward Everett Hale, and T. S. Arthur, author of the temperance tract *Ten Nights in a Barroom and What I Saw There*."[7] One of Norcross's boyhood games was an earlier version of the Game of Authors. Other boys and girls of his class may have made Alger's acquaintance in this way a few years later.

Alger wrote the popular sentimental ballad "John Maynard" after he heard a speaker recount the tale of "a courageous if mythical sailor on a Lake Erie steamer who steers his burning ship and its passengers to shore and safety just before he is consumed by the flames." Alger went to the reading room of the local YMCA, found and read the story of Maynard, copied it, and then wrote the poem in a single sitting. His "John Maynard, A Ballad of Lake Erie," was published in the *New York Ledger* in 1862, the *New York Sun* in 1866, and in *Student and Schoolmate* in January of 1868; for its publication in this last case, Alger received "the munificent sum of three dollars." It was anthologized, the author reported, at least a dozen times during his lifetime.[8] The poem became a popular declamation piece in the schools. One who declaimed it was Norcross.

Young Norcross probably read it in *Student and Schoolmate*, for his diary of March 19, 1868 contains the entry: "Rehearsed 'John Maynard', which I am trying to speak." On Saturday, April 4, 1868, public day at school, the fourteen-year-old notes: "I spoke 'John Maynard, a ballad of Lake Erie.'"[9]

Had Norcross perused this same 1868 issue of *Student and Schoolmate* he would have found an installment of Alger's serial story, *Fame and Fortune,* a sequel to *Ragged Dick.* Indeed, picking up virtually any issue of *Student and Schoolmate* from 1867 through 1872 would have exposed Norcross or his acquaintances to Alger.[10] *Ragged Dick* had been serialized in this Optic magazine starting in January, 1867. Bound annual volumes of *Student and Schoolmate,* priced at $1.50 in 1865 and $2.00 toward the end of the decade, also contained the serialization of *Ragged Dick* and his companions.

However, the same spring that Norcross declaimed "John Maynard," A. K. Loring issued an expanded version of *Ragged Dick* in book form. In addition to some stories, three novels bearing Alger's name were already published by Loring: *Frank's Campaign, Paul Prescott's Charge, and Helen Ford.*[11] An entry on Alger appeared in the new edition of Duyckinck's *Cyclopaedia of American Literature before* the appearance of *Helen Ford* or *Ragged Dick,* while *Student and Schoolmate* editor, Boston schoolteacher and principal William T. Adams, who was then "author of some twenty popular boys' books" under the pen name Oliver Optic, was omitted.[12]

In advertising the upcoming release of clothbound *Ragged Dick, Student and Schoolmate* readers were told "The story has been carefully re-written and enlarged by Mr. Alger, new and beautiful illustrations are in preparation . . ." Readers of the earlier version were encouraged to become purchasers of the book:

> RAGGED DICK, or Street Life in New York. By Horatio Alger, Jr., is now before us, brought out in beautiful style by Loring, whose "Up Town Bookstore" is so well known to Bostonians. The readers of the SCHOOLMATE looked with too much eagerness for the monthly chapters in our magazine, not to feel a desire to own a book of so much interest, in which *five* entirely new chapters appear . . .[13]

The announcement was in May, 1868; by August, the editors had to apologize for the delay in filling orders:

> The first edition was exhausted, and consequently a second edition must be issued at once. It is gratifying to perceive the great demand for this excellent book, and we shall now be able, from the new issue, to answer orders more promptly.[14]

During this rush on *Ragged Dick* and a few months after declaiming "John Maynard," young Norcross began reading Alger novels. His first was one of the adult novels, published by Loring in 1866. His diary entry for Saturday, July 11, 1868 reads: "Took 'Helen Ford' by H. Alger, Jr.

"Ragged Dick." (Illustration opposite lead page of *Ragged Dick*. *Student and Schoolmate* 19, January, 1867.)

from Burnham's Library and paid 10 cts. for 'Farming for boys.'" Burnham's, a private circulating library, surely operated much like Loring's own.

A. K. Loring's Select Library, begun in 1859, lent volumes for circulation at two cents per day apiece, and sold off surplus books no longer in circulation at cheap prices. Loring began publishing in 1863, and his first Alger novel appeared the following year. *Frank's Campaign*, set during the Civil War and appealing to young Northern boys to help the cause even in their local communities, combined the "action, emotional appeal, and moral lesson," that A. K. Loring made his publishing credo.[15] Loring published Alger titles until his firm collapsed in 1880.

On the 14th of July 1868, Norcross returned to Burnham's and took out *Ragged Dick*. The only indication of his reaction to Alger fiction was that he read a second volume. This was not unusual, because he rarely recorded his reaction to reading, except in a case where he noted that he did not enjoy something and did not intend to finish it; that month, he found "a great many lies in" Dickens's *American Notes* (July 7, 1868). These were among nine books the boy read in July, 1868 and among the eighty-eight books he read during the year.

For Christmas, 1868, Grenville Howland Norcross received from his father a subscription to one of Optic's magazines, *Our Boys and Girls*. Fiction was also arriving in the home by mail, facilitated by the postal rate structures. Other types of reading matter, such as dime novels, were also distributed by mail. This phenomenon did not escape the attention of the Comstock crusaders.

The postal system supplemented the book publisher's established distribution networks. Would-be readers with financial resources could have access to Alger's clothbound volumes so long as they could receive mail. Books included advertisements from the publisher, offering to send a volume or a series, such as the "Ragged Dick Series," "Tattered Tom Series," "Campaign Series," or "Pacific Series." Purchasers got a boxed set, with a specified number of volumes in cloth, sometimes "printed in colors," but no discount.

Readers of the monthly juvenile *Student and Schoolmate* were advised they could order copies of current and previous Alger volumes through that publication, sometimes at below retail: "TATTERED TOM will be mailed to any of our subscribers, *post-paid*, on receipt of $1.05, retail price being $1.25."[16] Book jobbers, clergymen, librarians, and anyone termed a "large buyer" could lay claim to some sort of publisher's discount and continue the process of book distribution.[17]

Young Norcross's family had, by the late 1860s, joined the class of fiction purchasers: Christmas, 1868 also brought the gift of an Oliver Optic novel from his aunt. Nonetheless, even this comfortably circumstanced boy appears to have owned few of the books he read. Not one individually owned clothbound volume of Alger fiction seems to have been in the Norcross home, yet his work crossed the threshhold in magazines and as lending library books. Public and private circulating libraries and borrowing from friends were prevalent means of acquiring juvenile fiction in his circles, so that a single book volume was likely to have multiple readers. The Norcross experience helps explain the fact that, while publishers generally reported no huge Alger sales, reviewers often noted that his stories were hits with the boys.

Many American families were not yet spending for fiction. During the era Alger wrote, "large portions of the public were using printed matter for the first time, magazines at the start and then an occasional bound volume."[18] The most likely books for a family to own at this time were religious books, an almanac, and perhaps a few practical works.[19] There was sustained interest in volumes that helped Americans in burgeoning communities and settlements plan a "design for living." Volumes of plans and designs for homes became popular in midcentury; books on accounting proliferated after 1870. Etiquette books and advice manuals remained strong sellers, with approximately the same number of distinct editions appearing in the thirty years preceding the war as were issued in the thirty years after 1861. The number of titles published in such genteel subjects as philosophy and poetry was in decline; so were drama, geography and travel.[20]

While the total number of book titles published remained roughly constant from 1869 to 1880, annual output practically doubled by 1890 and tripled by the turn of the century.[21] Some of the strongest selling works were works of fiction.

The publication of *Ragged Dick* assured Alger's status as a well-known author. Publishers of the era considered ten thousand copies to be about the smallest edition of a book that would make it a decided hit.[22] Gauged by volume of sales, *Ragged Dick* was apparently Alger's only "major" commercial success. One standard source, defining best sellers as only those volumes whose total sales approximated one percent of the population of the United States during the decade in which it was published, includes *Ragged Dick* for the 1860s; this achievement required sales of three hundred thousand copies. *Fame and Fortune* (1869), *Luck and Pluck* (1870), and *Tattered Tom* (1871) achieved runner-up status.[23]

By such a measure of popularity, a few of Alger's volumes placed him in the company of Charles Dickens, who made a second American tour in the year *Ragged Dick* appeared in serial form in *Student and Schoolmate* (1867), and English romance novelist Charles Reade. Alger was also in the company of female authors Harriet Beecher Stowe, Louisa May Alcott, Mary Mapes Dodge, and prolific sentimental novelist Mrs. E. D. E. N. Southworth, whose works were also widely purchased in the years immediately surrounding *Ragged Dick*.[24] Henry Ward Beecher's *Norwood* was one of the few comparably popular pieces of religious fiction. By 1870, Mark Twain and Bret Harte joined the list of best-selling authors.

But where publishers' records are absent, publication and sales estimates for any volume are necessarily poor. Alger himself made modest sales estimates. He once volunteered, of the six volume Ragged Dick series, that "the large sales, amounting to probably 150,000 volumes, show the public interest in the poor boys about whom the stories are written."[25] His obituary estimated total sales at 800,000 volumes. In 1910, when Alger sales were strong, *Publishers Weekly* reported that one bookseller estimated current sales of Alger books at a million a year, and dismissed such a claim as "probably very greatly exaggerated."[26]

Some members of the American public in the Gilded Age were initiated into book purchasing by "subscription."[27] A form of mass marketing that eliminated the retailer's profit, subscription publishing "reached the vast majority of the population that never entered a bookstore and perhaps did not live within geographical reach of one."[28] Audiences would not have acquired any Alger *fiction*, but if they looked carefully enough, they could have found Alger included in a subscription book on American authors.[29] They may well have made the acquaintance of various Alger publishers beginning around 1880, for quite a few of these generated a portion of their business through subscription volumes. Publishers' selection of authors, just as their selection of titles to go by subscription, underscored their attentiveness to mass audiences.[30]

Subscription books were designed as books of general interest. Drummers (salesmen) would canvas communities, distribute advertising fliers, and sell a volume house-to-house by showing sample covers and a few sample pages. Interested citizens would then "subscribe," entering their name and perhaps some payment in a ledger carried by the drummer.

Offerings included biographies and autobiographies of famous Americans (including P. T. Barnum), travel narratives (e.g., Livingstone's journals), religious works, temperance tracts by T. S. Arthur, and medical or other encyclopedias.[31] The subscription fare included success guides. In 1872, the salesman's prospectus (dummy) for Harriet Beecher Stowe's *The Lives and Deeds of our Self-Made Men* advertised that this volume, sold by subscription only, would contain over six hundred octavo pages and would be sold at $3.50 to $5.00, depending on style chosen. As an added inducement, subscribers were promised as a "Magnificent Premium, Free to All!" a beautiful engraving entitled "After the Nap," which would cost $1.00 if purchased separately.[32] William Makepeace Thayer's *Success and Its Achievers* first circulated as a subscription book in 1891. Alger was familiar with this version, which incorporated illustrations of famous statesmen, inventors, literary figures, and men of business.

Twain was the only fiction author who was a success in the subscription publishing business; during the 1870s, his bound volumes were sold by subscription only, through the American Publishing Company of Hartford. "'No book of literary quality was made to go by subscription except Mr. Clemens' books,'" William Dean Howells noted, "'and I think these went because the subscription public never knew what good literature they were.'"[33] Twain stood out in what has been called "a form of publishing only a step removed from the dime pamphlets and story weeklies."[34]

But the price of subscription volumes was a major liability if the goal were to generate a mass literature. These volumes were considerably more expensive than other books. They were often elegantly produced and contained many illustrations, for "the subscription audience was fond of pictures and not discriminating in its appreciation of them."[35] The base price for Twain's *Sketches, New and Old* (1875) was $3.00; with gilt edges or a more elaborate half-turkey binding, the cost could rise to $4.50. Pinkerton's *Professional Thieves and the Detectives* (1881) sold for $2.75 in cloth, $3.25 in sheepskin.[36]

New clothbound novels published in 1876 that appeared on the *Publishers Weekly* list of popular titles ranged in price from $1.25 to $1.75. The trade publication's survey excluded elaborate bindings and special editions. These prices were comparable to the cost of acquiring books in the antebellum era.[37]

Most of Loring's Alger titles were offered at $1.25; an occasional volume during Alger's lifetime was priced at $1.50. While these prices were certainly moderate, Alger's clothbound books hardly represented an *inexpensive* price to many Americans in the 1860s and 1870s. The cost of such volumes probably placed purchase out of the reach of the families of tradesmen and skilled workers at least until 1880. The outlay easily represented a day's wages for a nonfarm earner.

A publisher's advertised book price did not mean very much, as the *Boston Globe* editorialized in 1876: "a book advertised for one dollar costs one dollar only to an inexperienced customer."[38] This following advertisement from The Troy *Times* (New York) sounds like it came from the now-defunct Crazy Eddie chain.

A CARD FROM THE BUTCHER

In my advertisement in Saturday's Times I advised the people to go to the other booksellers and see the prices they charge, and then to come and see my prices; but to save them the trouble of doing so I have concluded to compare the prices of another bookseller with my own. The following quotations are taken from the advertisement of one of the leading bookselling firms in this city, and published in the Budget of last Sunday. They advertise "'Aunt Louisa's books,' reduced from $2.50 to $2"; my price has never been more than $1.50... "'Robinson Crusoe,' 'The Swiss Family Robinson,' and 'The Arabian Nights,' reduced from $1.50 to $1"; my price has always been 60 cents ... These facts and figures will enable the people to judge where they can buy books cheapest. I never overcharge, therefore I never require to reduce my prices. I strike "rock bottom" every time.

THE BOOK BUTCHER, 281 River Street[39]

Publishers were outraged but apparently impotent.[40] For streetwise city folk, discounting could increase access to fiction and expand the class of book purchasers at the margins.

The $1.25 list price held until the turn of the century, while family incomes were rising. Porter and Coates of Philadelphia bought the stereotype plates and rights to Alger titles after Loring's bankruptcy and published forty-eight of Alger's novels, many of which were reprints of Loring titles.[41] But at the time of Alger's death, Porter and Coates dropped the price of these novels to twenty-five cents. Reincarnated as Henry T. Coates & Co, the firm also "permitted Hurst & Company, of New York, and Donohue & Henneberry, of Chicago, to do likewise. From this it was only a step to paper covers at a dime a throw..." Millions of boys would read Alger titles as dime novels during the next fifteen years.[42]

Prices and Audiences

Went to Cohasset. Bought a book named "Munro's Ten cent novels no 18—'Wild Scout of the Mountains,'" to read in the cars."

Grenville Howland Norcross, July 27, 1864

If clothbound fiction remained too expensive for some would-be readers until late in the century, cheaper forms of fiction were available from midcentury. There were dime novels, railroad fiction, and story papers. There was considerable overlap. Authors and publishers in one of these genres were likely to be found involved in some of the others.[43] Alger did not publish dime novels, and Grenville Howland Norcross did not appear to read story papers, but one of Alger's key publishers was a major player in the production of both.

Ten-year-old Grenville Howland Norcross notes, on April 24, 1864, that he began "The Wrong Men," a "dime novel." He did not relish this book, but the boy appears to have devoured others. At least prior to the explosion of cheap fiction, some young genteel readers could read dime novels without hiding out behind the barn.

Norcross finished *Wild Scout of the Mountains*, the book he began for his July, 1864 train ride and probably purchased at the station or in the cars, four days later. The boy had validated Munro's and other publishers' belief that people would read railroad literature. Railroads carried passengers with leisure time, suggesting an immediate audience for fiction. Inexpensive reading matter designed specifically for train travel began to appear in the 1850s; the volumes were known as railroad novels.

Aaron K. Loring probably earned his designation as "a pioneer in cheap book publishing" for his early foray into paper covers. The term "cheap book," pervasive in the Gilded Age book trade, referred to books that, considering their character, were "conspicuously low in price in comparison with book prices in general."[44] In 1866, A. K. Loring published Alger's *Timothy Crump's Ward* anonymously in paper covers for their Railway Companion Series.[45] Loring's anonymously published Alger adult novella, *The New Schoolma'am* was "of the paper-covered half-dollar variety" in 1877.[46]

After the demise of Loring's firm, the 1883 publication of *Tom, the Bootblack* by J. S. Ogilvie & Company (New York) may have marked the next earliest publication of Alger in paper covers. Although the railway audience seemed not overly fond of the series specifically designed for this purpose, Ogilvie, known as "the largest 'purveyor' of 'Railroad Literature' in the country" in the 1880s, made a large hit with *The People's Library*. Twelve paper-covered Alger titles appeared in this series, priced from ten to twenty cents per issue.[47] There were other such Alger publishers.

On the train, Norcross might have encountered the likes of Alger's young Paul Palmer, *Train Boy* (1883), who sells newspapers and other reading matter on the Chicago to Milwaukee line. His wares include *Harper's*, *Scribner's*, *Lippincott's*, and the *Atlantic Monthly*; he has "All the illustrated papers and magazines . . . [and has] besides some novels." On one better-than-average trip, Paul sold "three bound novels, which sale afforded him a handsome profit."[48] As he worked the aisles, he quite possibly sold Alger novels.

Among Paul Palmer's wares, newspapers, magazines, and story papers catered especially well to short-installment readers.[49] In the 1870s, large-circulation monthlies such as Paul sells on the railroad—specifically *Century, Harper's, Scribner's, and Atlantic*—showed a combined circulation (including overlap) of roughly 150,000, but the price of these magazines was still relatively dear; in Alger's *Train Boy, Harper's* costs thirty-five cents. But Paul also sells the illustrated papers. These were another matter.

In addition to *Ragged Dick,* two other mid-1860s Alger Loring novels had previous serial runs. The Alger pattern of publishing a serialized story prior to the issuance of a bound volume was not unusual. Newspaper and periodical previews of novel material were viewed as potential stimulators of interest in book sales. And, like the successful movie which is subsequently disseminated as a paperback, the timing could be reversed: Many clothbound Alger novels were again serialized, or, toward the end of the century, reprinted in cheaper book form.[50] *Adventures of Huckleberry Finn* was serialized in a highly respectable publication and also circulated as a subscription novel.

But *Paul Prescott's Charge* and *Helen Ford* appeared in a rather different type of publication than *Student and Schoolmate.* The tales appeared anonymously in the story papers *New York Sun* and *New York Weekly Sun* in 1859 and 1860. These serial stories were among nine Alger published in the *New York Sun* between 1857 and 1860; eight of these ran in the *New York Weekly Sun* as well.[51] The *New York Sun* has been described as "a dreadful penny paper for the unwashed masses."[52] Poe wrote that the plan of this paper was to supply "the public with news of the day at so cheap a rate as to lie within the means of all."[53]

In January and February of 1864, the year of his first Loring novel, Frank's Campaign, Alger published his first serialized story for the firm of Street & Smith. The firm had been active and highly visible as publishers of dime novels and the story paper *New York Weekly* long before their foray into cheap book publishing in the late 1880s. The publishers had persuaded Alger to try his hand at a serial for their story paper, the *New York Weekly.*[54] Following "Marie Bertrand, or the Felon's Daughter," seventeen more Alger stories were serialized therein. While the *New York Ledger* could claim the largest story paper circulation, the *New York Weekly* provided Alger a large potential audience.

Story papers, railroad fiction, and dime novels were joined by other kinds of inexpensive fiction by the time Norcross reached adulthood. At the commencement of the fourth quarter of the century, an observer could still claim that "the masses have not the means, if they had the inclination, to buy many papers and magazines"; this condition would soon change. For many publishers, magazine and book pricing became a key to new markets.

There was a tenfold increase in the number of copies of newspapers and magazines issued in 1890 compared with midcentury.[55] Advertising, publicity, and the availability of second-class postage rates played major roles in this phenomenon.[56] But while newspaper and magazine circulation skyrocketed, the combined circulation of *Century, Harper's, Scribner's* and *Atlantic* declined "in the face of competition from cheaper and less genteel magazines such as *Cosmopolitan, Collier's, McClure's,* and *Munsey's.*"[57] Some publications dropped in price to ten and fifteen cents. Different kinds of publications were thriving.

Alger enjoyed a long association with Frank Munsey, a pioneer in cheap pricing of magazines. Munsey's *Golden Argosy,* begun in 1882, was priced at five cents an issue; the paper stock had more than a passing resemblance to newspaper. From early 1886 to mid-1894, Alger published thirty serials in Munsey's magazine under his own name and, when serials overlapped, under pen names. The circulation of the magazine peaked at 115,000 in 1886.[58]

When Street & Smith launched a new serial, *Good News,* on May 15, 1890, it was also priced for the masses at five cents an issue.[59] The lead-off story was by Oliver Optic; Alger's "Only an Irish Boy" also made its debut run.

Street & Smith "concentrated, perhaps more intensely and for a longer period of years than any other firm, in the marketing of ten-cent paperbacks and various cheap 'libraries' and popular fiction serials." Prior to entering this part of the business, they had apparently helped back the firm of J. S. Ogilvie. Advertising several series in 1890, Street & Smith claimed: "They are not cheap reprints, but are all written by popular American Authors... They are not sold in dry-goods stores, are returnable, and Newsdealers should be sure to have a complete stock."[60] The firm was one of the few survivors among the cheap publishers and piratical libraries after the International Copyright agreement of 1891.

Street & Smith issued almost all of Alger's *New York Weekly* serializations as novels; eighteen of Alger's stories were posthumously edited by Edward Stratemeyer for the firm.[61] This house published twenty-seven clothbound Algers, and well over one hundred appeared in five different paperback series after the author's death.[62] Their Medal Library, begun in 1898, sold books at ten cents in 1900; it was advertised as "a series of high-class books for boys and youth, written by the best authors."[63]

But before Street & Smith began to publish such books, Alger had already become a staple of the cheap book trade. "Of all the publishers of cheap books during the 1880's there were few to rival the cheapness of the F. M. Lupton publications," a firm responsible for one clothbound and eight paperbound Alger titles from the late 1880s until 1906. Some were priced at three cents per number, the size of a short "classic."[64] The imprint of the Mershon Company of Rahway, New Jersey appeared on thirty-five Alger reprints (often abridged) and graced many "cheap and nasty" volumes of fiction starting in the late 1880s. Mershon published a great deal of railroad fiction.[65] The United States Book Company issued Alger titles during its short existence, one in cloth and six in paper covers, and planned to issue others in their paperback Leather-Clad Tales of Adventure and Romance had bankruptcy not intervened.[66] G. W. Carleton, publisher of three Alger novels, was "particularly active in the low-price field."[67] Other cheap book publishers issuing Alger titles in cloth or paper included, but were not limited to, A. L. Burt, Hurst, John W. Lovell, Frank F. Lovell, W. L. Allison, DeWolfe-Fiske & Company, and M. A. Donohue and Company.[68] Toward the end of the century, cheap Alger publishing began to take place in new centers of the book trade outside the Northeast. Inexpensive copies of his work were also published in London.[69]

Although cheap reprints did not have an immediate impact on Alger's sagging popularity, there would be a posthumous payoff. Some of the greatest sales of Alger's works occurred in the first two decades of this century, and "more of his books were sold each year during the Progressive era than were sold in total during his life . . ."[70]

Pricing meant accessibility. But if the American public benefited from the low prices, they nonetheless generally received poorly made books that were often abridged and mutilated. Cheap reprints of Alger's works were no exception.

Working-Class Reading

Purchased reading matter in the latter half of the nineteenth century reached the American public through publishers and bookstores, drummers and train boys who peddled their printed wares. City sidewalk stands offered cheap fiction. Drug stores, stationery stores, and fancy goods stores served as retail outlets for the printed word, where books could be found alongside wallpaper and window curtains. And the railroad and postal system took books and magazines published in major northeastern publication centers to regions and communities in which they had not been available previously.[71] But how far did this proliferating and increasingly accessible fiction reach into the laboring classes?

Reviewing *Paul Prescott's Charge* in 1865, *The Nation* thought that "the tale is likely to prove a favorite in spite of occasional 'big words.'"[72] By the time Loring published *Frank's Campaign*, in 1864, the vast majority of the population was deemed literate, although the figure was lower in the South.[73] Reading English at an eighth-grade level was sufficient, except for some foreign phrases and a few large words, for the Alger novels.

This barrier excluded some of the street boys the author immortalized. There were other obstacles, especially for older readers. Until steel spectacles reached working-class audiences toward the end of the century, their prolonged reading, whether of fiction or of other printed matter, may have been unlikely.[74]

When neither of these problems presented itself, Loring and Porter & Coates clothbound Algers were beyond the *purchasing* power of urban newsboys and other young people struggling to earn a living. However, Alger advertised in *Fame and Fortune* that A. K. Loring was authorized "to send a gratuitous copy of the two volumes of the 'Ragged Dick Series' already issued, to any regularly organized Newsboys Lodge within the United States."[75] Some copies of the novels in the "Ragged Dick Series" reached the newsboys' lodges, and some of these passed through many hands. *Student and Schoolmate* reports:

> The manager of the Newsboy's Home in St. Louis writes, "When on East last year, I got a copy of *Ragged Dick*, and the boys have enjoyed it so much, that it will not last much longer, and are continually asking for the second volume. You will oblige us very much by sending us a copy of both *Ragged Dick*, and *Fame and Fortune*."[76]

Unless poor urban youth encountered these stories in newsboys' lodges, or unless they frequented libraries (and Alger gives us no example in which they do), they may never have seen Alger's fiction in clothbound novels. But they had access to Alger in the illustrated papers from the eve of the Civil War.

As Ben, the Luggage Boy, crossed the lower end of City Hall Park and walked up the Park Row side, "he saw a line of street merchants. Most conspicuous were the dealers in penny ballads, whose wares lined the railings, and were various enough to suit every taste."[77] Story papers appeared alongside other cheap printed matter on street corners of major cities. "Our story papers, damp from the press and printed very black, upholster all the news-stands," reports an 1879 observer.[78]

An Alger contemporary describes modes of dissemination of story paper literature for the 1879 *Atlantic*, and also provides a valuable portrait of the audience. Entering a stationer's, where story papers are also found, this author describes the display:

> The story papers, the most conspicuous stock in trade, are laid out on the front counter, neatly overlapped, so as to show all the titles and frontispieces. Ten are already in, and more to come,—the Saturday Night, the Saturday Journal, the Ledger, the Weekly, the Family Story Paper, the Fireside Companion. Near them on the glass case, in formidable piles, are the "libraries." These are, omitting the prominent examples which do the same sort of service for standard works, pamphlets reprinting at a dime and a half dime the stories which have appeared as serials in the papers. There are papers which, finding this practice a diversion of interest, distinctly announce that their stories will not reappear, and that their fascinations can be enjoyed only at original sources.

Purchasers included a middle-aged woman carrying a basket with half a peck of potatoes; a shop-girl on her way home from work; "a servant from one of the good houses in the side streets"; but most of all come the boys—working boys, school boys, street boys.[79] As the information and story functions of newspapers diverged, the story paper came to be identified increasingly with a working-class readership.[80]

If the point of sale differed from the same story in hardback, there were other important differences. The format and surrounding material put the work in a context different from that of a novel sequestered between cloth or even paper covers. In the story paper, Alger, entertainer and moral crusader, narrated alongside sentimental tales and stories of the Molly Maguires, tramps, and highwaymen. Serial publication audiences got only a small piece of the story at a time, although this was not a new phenomenon: American audiences waited for the next installment of a current Dickens novel to arrive by boat and learned installment fiction reading of necessity.

The alternative to installment reading, demanding no delayed gratification, was the dime or half-dime novel. They were sold alongside the story paper. Alger works would have to vie with these novels for poor boys and working-class readers in the street battles and culture wars, and it was with these works that Alger stories were compared toward the end of the century.

Fiction consumption depended upon more than pricing, literacy, and availability. Reading and purchasing habits are factors in any tale of working-class reading. In a provocative study, David Nord probed the readership of popular fiction by sampling one hundred families in the cotton textile industry from the three chief cotton-milling regions in the

United States, examining links between class, culture, and the disposition to read.[81] In doing so, he drew upon data on family spending for newspapers and books in family cost-of-living budgets developed by emerging bureaus of labor statistics.

Families in Nord's sample spent, on average, $4.23 per year for reading materials—about 2.4% of their discretionary expenditure and .75% of their total expenditures. New Englanders in the sample allotted more than 3% of their discretionary spending to reading materials; Southerners spend less than half of this.[82] Of the working-class families 77% reported at least some expenditure for newspapers and books. However, families in which children were engaged in the labor force were less likely to spend for reading matter than families whose children were not contributing to overall family income. Children in the factory made unlikely readers.

The most intriguing finding was that there appeared to be "a connection between reading and a feeling of arrival in a new culture, of involvement with the surrounding community—whether native or immigrant." Avid readers "seem to have been more at home with the institutions of the modern industrial community." Nord's workers who "had not yet acquired a permanent working-class culture"— who were new to the industrial system and who perhaps expected to return to the land—were "cultural transients" and were *not* spending money on reading materials.[83] Identifiable groups of "cultural sojourners," who participated more in traditional activities of family and clan (gemeinschaft) than in modern community activities (gesellschaft) were less likely to spend for reading matter.[84]

Among working-class families whose children were not employed, reading Alger (and any other fiction) might have been more likely the *greater* the sense of belongingness in the industrial community— quite the opposite from what some text-based projections claim.

Age and Gender

When popular fiction did arrive in the home, it is likely that various family members read it. It was not uncommon for adults to read juvenile fiction in this era, and when Alger sent copies of his works to adult correspondents, he surely hoped they would read them.[85] Although most frequently described as an author for boys, Alger aimed a small part of his fictional output at adult audiences, and he wrote several juvenile and adult novels with female heroines. Among these were *Helen Ford, Tattered Tom, The Disagreeable Woman, Mabel Parker,* and *A Fancy of Hers.*

*   *   *   *   *

Oliver Optic's *Student and Schoolmate* advertised Alger's tales as having appeal across age and gender lines. *Paul Prescott's Charge* was described as "Another good book for the boys, and we presume that the girls will not object to reading it." The notice for *Strong and Steady* claimed: "It is not a book for boys—for from grandfather down to the wee ones all cry out for a chance to read STRONG AND STEADY, and all say 'a splendid story.'"[86] The *Student and Schoolmate* statement was probably more wishful than factual, but was there any truth to the portrait? The observer of story paper purchasers revealed that the audience for this class of publication may have been mixed by age and gender, with boys overrepresented.

But what of the more expensive and respectable Alger vehicles? Fan mail and requests for autographs attest to Alger's popularity among young boys. There is at least some evidence that boys were not alone. Bookplates and inscriptions reveal that copies of Alger novels were given as gifts to girls as well; some were owned by Girl Scout leaders. Alger's letter to Miss Harriet Jackson, quoted at the outset of this chapter, reveals that his works were not only accessible in California, but they were being read by at least some young females.

BORROWING ALGER: LIBRARIES

> Though my sales of books have of course fallen off with the times, I am encouraged by my popularity at the libraries. In the Boston public library of over 250,000 vols. the sup^t. reports that last year Optic and myself led all other authors in popularity, and father learned from the Harpers' Boston agent that on a recent Saturday there were 390 applications for my books and 290 for Optic's who came next for that day. It is also very curious that the single book in that library wh. led all others in popularity last year according to the report was "Timothy Crump's Ward" wh. I published anonymously ten years since, and have never acknowledged. Loring always had a prejudice against it, and allowed it to pass out of print—though I had a considerably better opinion of it. I am very much surprised at its popularity at this late day.
>
> *Horatio Alger, Jr. to Edwin R. A. Seligman, August 6, 1877* [87]

National distribution publishers in the Gilded Age were located in New York, Boston, and Philadelphia, as were chief Alger publishers Loring, Porter & Coates, John C. Winston, and Street & Smith. While improved transportation and communication made possible "a far-flung net of travelling representatives and nationwide publicity campaigns," much of the West and the South remained outside main channels of literary distribution.[88] Nonetheless, Alger made his mark in some of these areas.

Fans and autograph-seekers wrote Alger from various points in the United States. A young male college boy in Georgia told Alger of the availability of his works in the library just around the time of McKinley's election.[89] In Portland, Oregon, during Alger's visit in 1877, he notes "I...find myself, rather to my surprise, well known here."[90]

On Alger's first trip to California in 1877, the author was pleased to note his novels in a public school library three thousand miles from the scene of action in *Ragged Dick*. Planning an upcoming visit to a San Francisco area public school, Alger wrote: "I hear the scholars are curious to see the historian of Ragged Dick, whose eventful story, with others of his kindred, is included in the Public School libraries."[91]

It was in no small measure due to the library that Alger was able to reach a book and magazine reading public that was so widely diversified by class and region. Alger proudly cited large Boston Public Library circulation figures for some of his works. His popularity was part of a boom in fiction circulation witnessed by the libraries. Until quite late in the century, Alger's works were widely available to young library patrons.

When Alger began to write, libraries came in many forms. The free reading room housed leading newspapers and magazines of the day.[92] Young Men's Christian Association libraries and libraries established by some manufacturers in working communities afforded additional access to some fiction.[93] There were subscription libraries and social libraries, supported by member contributions of perhaps five dollars per year; these last, generally known as mercantile libraries, were past their heyday by the fourth quarter of the century.[94] Noted an 1876 observer: "To many of these admission is by membership, fee, or introduction, but there are reasons for believing that in a few years public libraries, free to all, will be found in every city and hamlet in the land."[95]

Alger once bragged that "Hundreds of Sunday-school libraries bought them [his novels] . . . and they were read in every State and Territory in the Union."[96] According to one estimate, at least a third of the Alger volumes purchased "found their way into circulating libraries, particularly into Sunday school libraries."[97] Sunday School libraries appear especially important in providing rural youth with access to moralistic tales for youth.[98] Some turn of the century copies were gifts or awards to individuals from Baptist and Congregational Sunday Schools.

The Gilded Age was the era of great expansion for public libraries, a classification that included public school libraries, state libraries, college and university libraries, prison libraries, and theological seminary libraries. A large proportion of these libraries were nevertheless located in urban areas. Data on the distribution of public libraries in the United States circa 1875 are shown in the appendix to this chapter.

The U.S. Department of the Interior *Report on Public Libraries* (1876) included a revealing table entitled "Classified statistics of circulation of twenty-four public libraries in 1874-75." On average, 67.4% of all circulating works in this period were classed as "English prose, fiction, and juveniles"; the range was from 50% to 77.8% fiction. The averages reported by these libraries for some of the "better" classes of materials were 8.0% for history and biography, 6.7% for voyages and travels, 4.4% for science and art, 1.5% for religion and theology, and 1.1% for German and French literature.[99]

The pattern was mirrored at the Boston Public Library. A table of Boston Public Library (Lower Hall) reading for 1868-75 shows a range of 69 to 78.4% of circulating works in the category "prose fiction for adults and youths."[100] One librarian there opined that if novels, stories and jokes were excluded from the public library, this would, "in general, reduce the extent of its use to one-quarter of what it would otherwise be."[101]

The pattern persisted. In 1881, a librarian at Boston Public Library asserted that

> out of 14,950 books bought during the past five years for the Lower Hall,—the popular department of the Central Library,— 10,417, or 70 per cent, were story-books, technically called "fiction" and "juveniles." This, however, by no means represents the whole amount purchased, since it includes only those stories published in book-form and not those printed in periodicals and magazines, of which great numbers are taken.[102]

These books were not collecting dust; in the same five year period, four-fifths of the material circulating from the Lower Hall and branches consisted of "juveniles" and "fiction," including in the category "the stories contained in the magazines and periodicals, and the very considerable number of novels not classified under 'fiction.'"[103]

Those concerned with patterns of library circulation did more than collect statistics: Librarians observed patrons, and provided some idea of who was thronging the halls of the public libraries to consume fiction. In 1876, one reported: "Most of those who read are young people who want entertainment and excitement, or tired people who want relaxation and amusement."[104] One crusader against most fiction circulating from the Boston Public Library thought that library use knew no class bounds: "Every boy and girl in Boston, over fourteen years of age, has free access to a collection of story-books amounting in the aggregate to 50,000 volumes; and a very large proportion make frequent use of the privilege."[105]

Noting the democratization of reading that accompanied universal education, this librarian-critic writes: "Never before have there been so many who, engaged in purely manual labor, turn almost instinctively for their recreation, at the end of the day, to a book or a paper." While this may be the case, he nonetheless observes that the chief part of the patrons "who throng the Lower Hall and Branches afternoon and evening" were not "poor persons, who must either have their reading free or go without it... but in fact they appear to be principally persons in apparently comfortable circumstances or the children of well-to-do parents."[106] If the laboring classes are beginning to make use of the library, they are doing so shoulder to shoulder with children of the elite, or of the middle classes, who appear to outnumber them as patrons.

TEXTS AND AUDIENCES: CLASS, CULTURE AND ALGER READING

Most text-based projections of Alger's audience claim that the predominant voice in Alger's tales spoke *most* coherently to and for an audience that had *not* been incorporated into the industrial life of the antebellum era. However, even the texts can reveal a more incendiary discourse, as we saw in Chapter 9. This chapter sought to be especially wary of "purely text-based projections of implied readers."[107]

Text-based projections about readership presume, in Stanley Fish's terminology, that there is *one* "text in this class." In the Alger case, it is readily apparent why there is not. Clothbound novels priced at $1.25, juvenile magazines, cheap magazines, Alger reprints, and story papers were not clearly the same texts.

Reading publics were becoming more segmented as they became class diversified. In developed markets of the Northeast, "the reading public became fragmented by sex, class, and religion in the face of the onslaught of new titles."[108] The expanding Gilded Age publishing industry began to target its audiences: "The varied components of the reading public began to be recognized and the mechanisms for the production and distribution of the staple commodity, fiction, were adjusted more precisely to the demands of the market."[109]

From the late 1850s, Alger had been able to sell story after story to the *New York Sun*, the *New York Weekly Sun*, the *New York Weekly*, the *Golden Argosy*, and other inexpensive publications. He was clearly successful enough that penny papers and cheap magazines continued to pay him for new and recycled stories. The mere appearance of an Alger story in a magazine or story paper does not tell us who read it. While pricing made it possible for a broader audience to read Alger, it could not compel their response. During the period Alger generated so many serials for Munsey, *Golden Argosy* circulation dropped to nine thousand.[110] Such evidence, accompanied by Alger's declining economic fortunes, has led one critic to conclude that, although Alger had the vehicles for reaching working-class audiences, his moralism fell upon deaf ears.[111]

This, too, is projection. Publishers made errors: Loring went bankrupt, and every indication was that he was overextended. Copyright books faced stiff competition from other and cheaper forms of fiction; living on copyright book royalties as well as one-time payments for stories, Alger was not likely to grow rich given the type of fiction and where and how it was produced.

We simply cannot know why the reader of these works did so, nor how actual Alger readers produced meaning. We can only speculate on how they "responded to" the author. The literary text is neither irreducibly given nor is it coercive or controlling of reading. Rather, reading is production. It is a process "governed by reading strategies and interpretive conventions that the reader has learned to apply as a member of a particular interpretive community."[112] Readers bring cultural codes to the task.

Reading matter is not always simply taken or left. If it *is* picked up, many things can occur, for "people do not injest mass culture whole but often make it into something they can use." Mass fiction readers were not "passive, purely receptive individuals who can only consume the meanings embodied within cultural texts, . . . powerless in the face of ideology."[113]

Grenville Howland Norcross's family did not object to Alger reading, and they did not appear unusual. But by the time F. Scott Fitzgerald read a cheap reprint of Alger's *Ralph Raymond's Heir* and Carl Sandburg read *Tom the Bootblack* (the reprint title of *The Western Boy*), Theodore Dreiser had to read *Brave and Bold behind a barn*. This way is precisely how some late Alger antiheroes would read dime novels and melodramas.[114]

Alger and Optic tales would only become "trash," or morally suspect, in broader circles beginning in the late 1870s. Many middle-class youth profess reading Alger tales in the late nineteenth and early twentieth centuries; some of them were engaged in clandestine or questionable activity. It is in the context of the rise of working-class reading and the booming dissemination of fiction of all sorts that the battle over fiction in the closing decades of the nineteenth century would take shape.

If purchasers of illustrated papers and cheap monthly magazines read his tales, then there is evidence of a wide class span for Alger's fiction. If one author reached both Grenville Howland Norcross's circles and working-class readers, he accomplished something that many moral reformers could not. To the extent Alger had the attention of the working-class story paper audience, one might at least *believe* that readers were united in the same universe of discourse.

With Gilded Age pleasures becoming increasingly class specific, if different classes read Alger stories through different vehicles, they were likely to be reading quite different stories. The same words could be transported to different worlds.

Ch. 10 Appendix: Public Libraries in the United States, 1874-75

State/Terr.	Population in 1890:		Libraries with:	
	000s	per sq. mi.	300+ vols.	10,000+ vols.
Alabama	997	19.4	31	1
Alaska	33	--[a]	1	0
Arizona	10	0.1	3	0
Arkansas	484	9.2	6	0
California	560	3.6	87	10
Colorado	40	0.4	8	0
Connecticut	537	111.5	125	10
Dakota Territory	14	0.1	4	0
Dist.of Columbia	132	2270.7	57	12
Florida	188	3.4	6	1
Georgia	1184	20.2	44	3
Idaho	15	0.2	1	0
Illinois	2540	45.4	177	6
Indiana	1681	46.8	133	6
Indian Territory	n.a. [b]	n.a.[b]	4	0
Iowa	1194	21.5	79	1
Kansas	364	4.5	19	1
Kentucky	1321	32.9	72	5
Louisiana	727	16.0	31	4
Maine	627	21.0	85	6
Maryland	781	78.6	77	12
Massachusetts	1457	181.3	453	43
Michigan	1184	20.6	89	4
Minnesota	440	5.4	39	2
Mississippi	828	17.9	23	1
Missouri	1721	25.0	87	6
Montana	21	0.1	2	0
Nebraska	123	1.6	14	1
Nevada	42	0.4	6	0
New Hampshire	318	35.2	86	4
New Jersey	906	120.6	91	8
New Mexico	92	0.7	4	0
New York	4383	92.0	617 [c]	44
North Carolina	1071	22.0	37	3
Ohio	2665	65.4	223	14
Oregon	91	1.0	14	0

Ch. 10 Appendix (cont.)

State/Terr.	Population in 1890:		Libraries with:	
	000s	per sq. mi.	300+ vols.	10,000+ vols.
Pennsylvania	3522	78.6	367	29
Rhode Island	217	203.7	56	4
South Carolina	706	23.1	26	4
Tennessee	1259	30.2	71	3
Texas	819	3.1	42	2
Utah	87	1.1	5	0
Vermont	331	36.2	65	3
Virgina	1225	30.4	63	8
Washington Terr.	24	0.4	2	0
West Virginia	442	18.4	23	0
Wisconsin	1055	19.1	71	3
Wyoming Terr.	9	0.1	3	0

[a] Represents zero.
[b] Not available.
[c] Of these, 123, or 19.8%, have New York, NY addresses.

Source: *Public Libraries of the United States of America*, 1876, pp. 762-773 and 1012-1142; *Historical Statistics of the U.S.—Colonial Times to 1970*, Series A, 195-209.

11

The Mass Fiction Writer As Producer and Consumer: Power, Powerlessness, and Gender

At the time Alger came out here he had published all his important books. He came out here to write a book on the gold mining days, and I cannot remember the name of it, but it never was of much importance. He was a slight man with gray hair, and a gray mustache. He seemed quite elderly to me, but perhaps he was not sixty at that time. He rented a room in a hotel on Sansome Street, between California and Sacramento where the Security Building now is, right across the Street from Wells-Fargo Express. It was a third class hotel, as I remember, and not having to work in the Library some mornings, I would spend the mornings with him. He sat at a small marble topped table, writing on small sheets of paper. The room was terribly cold. He would write a certain length of time and complete a certain number of sheets and then we would go out to lunch. In about two weeks, he had exactly one-half of the book finished, and I remember going over to the Express office while he sent it back to the publisher. Some evenings we would walk around the lower part of town, and he would stop before some of the cheap stores and examine the goods that were on display and inquire about the prices. He had New England characteristics. He was a bachelor.

Joy Lichtenstein to Joseph P. Loeb, May 15, 1939[1]

The foregoing reminiscence of Alger in San Francisco, apparently during his second trip there, effectively draws our gaze to the author's place in the market. The popular fiction writer, producing rapidly for the market, occupied a precarious, unestablished position in society and economy.[2] In this reminiscence, Alger's own position at the margins of the economy is highlighted: His slight frame and his slight late literary accomplishments; his drabness and that of his terribly cold, third-class hotel room all indicate his status as a producer. Staring into the cheap stores and attempting to determine the prices of ordinary goods displayed there, Alger gathers "data" for his literary productions in the marketplace. But the image of Alger's attentiveness to mass consumption also underscores how essential *being* consumed was to the author's survival. The popular fiction author wrote in a marketplace increasingly yielding up goods for mass consumption, including reading matter.

Alger's letters exhibit his engagement with the consumption of culture and the culture of consumption. In addition to his fascination with the department store, the author recounts attendance at many middle class concerts, plays, lectures, and musical events; he chronicles his consumption and response to reading matter; and reports (sometimes for money) his summer vacations and occasional travels to Europe and throughout the United States. His heroes and heroines, too, seek opportunities to consume. Economic rewards permit them to spend their way out of privation and permit them modest comforts and amenities.

Nineteenth century popular fiction authors, including ministers and females, "showed an extraordinary degree, even by Victorian standards, of market-oriented alertness to their customers. They had a great deal in common with them." This literature, according to Ann Douglas, "was revealing and supporting a special class, a class defined less by what its members produced than by what they consumed." Authors were, as Washington Irving once said, "Unqualified for business in a nation where everyone is busy"; those producing fiction for a living depended upon the creation and elevation of leisure and expansion of light reading.[3] They were read by consumers who were not at work, or who read in small installments when they were not working. The *New York Times* would say, when reviewing Alger's adult novella, *The New Schoolma'am*, along with two other paper-covered novels (one a juvenile): "These works are meant to read languidly in a hammock, and to be dropped at any moment without a thought of the unfortunate author, who has been doing his best to please."[4]

Stressing consumption and dependent upon being consumed, Alger occupied a place in the newly "feminized" culture. Along with many contemporary authors, including sentimental writers and clergymen, Alger was being distanced from vital centers of power, influence, and activity in society. With limited resources and little power, these authors attempted to influence culture.

The author in the marketplace must function as a producer. Walter Benn Michaels has recently argued that, if writing is work in the market, necessarily involving risk taking and production without knowing a certain outcome, then writing is a kind of speculation. The author's production is designed to be consumed; in the process, the self is a commodity. The writer producing for the market is not only creating something, but is producing his or her identity—the self.[5]

Here is met yet another meaning of the "self-made" man. If "being oneself depends on owning oneself, and owning oneself depends on producing oneself," then the origins of the author's title to property can be seen as paralleling the title of Alger's hero.[6] The self is a property by virtue of laboring to produce it. By producing oneself—being responsible for the development of one's character and maturation—one has a title as producer. This property in the self (independence) must be closely guarded, and then one kind of property (character) can beget another. By the logic of Alger's universe, the author who properly produced the self could hope to acquire adequate remuneration.

But authors of popular fiction in late nineteenth-century America had a difficult time establishing property in the self. Attempting to survive by their words, these authors were dependent upon publishers and audiences and would seek to please. Their power and independence were delimited. Dependence upon the market shaped literary output and popular fiction authorship itself.

By focusing upon Alger the producer of mass fiction, we can explore how the relationship between production and consumption, power and powerlessness, was being reformulated in the Gilded Age, and how adult male identity was shaped in this context.

WRITING MASS FICTION

> In these days authors and publishers are mutually interested in
> each others' welfare and prosperity. There is not that natural
> antagonism which was once supposed to exist.
>
> Alger to Mr. [William] Lee, November 15, 1872.[7]

Disclaiming an attempt to curry favor with the publisher who was just about to commence a term as chairman of the executive committee of the American Book-Trade Association, Alger's 1872 letter puts the most optimistic cast on the world. At a time when "The variety and complexity of author-publisher contracts in ninetetenth-century

America reflected the as yet tentative nature of the relationship between them," Alger voices the greatest of certainty.[8]

Alger was not financially independent and had to make a living at his craft after the ministry was closed off to him. He did not find sufficient reception for his "serious" work and admitted that he chose his branch of literature because it paid him. Writing E. C. Stedman in 1875, Alger explained his decision to turn to juvenile fiction in market terms:

> The *res angusta domi* of which Horace speaks compelled me years since to forsake the higher walks of literature, and devote myself to an humbler department which would pay me better. The decision was made when for an article in the North American Review on which I had expended considerable labor I was paid at the rate of a dollar per printed page. From that time I leased my pen to the boys, and the world has been spared much poor poetry and ambitious prose.[9]

Even so, he was not successful enough or compensated well enough to escape financial worries. When he began his association with Loring, the publisher gave Alger "ten free copies, a $50.00 advance, and a royalty of 5 cents for each copy sold."[10] After the "Ragged Dick Series," he would not have it so good.

Alger was an author with admittedly modest literary abilities. But more than talent was at issue in determining his market capacity. Book underpricing was one possible problem for an author attempting to live by the pen. When retailers offered books as a loss-leader, it was no bargain for the author and publisher. *Publishers Weekly* carried a letter from an anonymous author, identified by the editor as "one of our best juvenile authors," protesting the underselling of books at cheap bazaars:

> A friend, wishing to please me, told me that my last book was selling very rapidly at a certain store in New York, where every thing can be bought, from furniture to dolls' shoes. I was surprised to hear that it was for sale there at all; but my surprise turned into indigniation when the same friend said, "Yes; you can buy all the new publications for children there at a wonderfully cheap rate. Your book is offered for one dollar and eight cents, which is forty-two cents less than it can be bought for at any bookstore in town, and all the books are as much lower in proportion . . . ."[11]

This writer suggests that the underselling of books "does pay the toy dealer, for it is the bait which attracts the crowd," but it apparently does not pay the author. Discounting cut profits and may have meant lower royalty rates. Aside from the ignominy of having one's literary product sold alongside doll shoes, this was a serious issue.

Alger attributed his own fortunes in part to the state of copyright law, once noting parenthetically: "(An author in this present lack of an international copyright law is not likely to have a large income)."[12] A. K. Loring copyrighted Alger's novels in accordance with antebellum copyright law and the new Copyright Act of 1870. And when Porter & Coates of Philadelphia bought the stereotype plates to Alger's work for a very small fee, the copyright passed with the plates.[13] Those works appearing originally in novel form were at least protected within the United States.

Serial publication was not adequately protected by nineteenth century copyright law. It appeared that only if each issue of the periodical had been copyrighted, or if authors had copyrighted each chapter or installment, would they be protected; this defect was not remedied until 1909.[14] Some book and serial story publishers of Alger may have accessed their wares in this manner while the same titles, carried by Loring or Porter & Coates, were still carrying copyright protection. If pirating was a testimony to Alger's popularity, it did nothing for his pocket.

But the largest financial problem for an American author prior to the International Copyright Law of 1891 was that foreign authors could not obtain protection for their works in the United States. Nothing prevented an American printer or publisher from reprinting works of English authors without compensation.[15] The prospects for profit from these unprotected works brought quite a few publishers to the venture. There was so much unscrupulous reprinting in the 1870s and 1880s that "even the big houses felt it necessary to enter extensively into the cheap reprint field in order to maintain their markets." Bitter, widespread price-cutting wars ensued. "Entire novels were printed on the cheapest paper in miserable print, often in the form of serial issues and at ridiculous prices."[16]

Cheap domestic reprints of "imported" English language works competed, in certain segments of the market, with the American author's novels, which were retailing at $1.25 or $1.50. The proliferation of ten-, twenty-five-, and fifty-cent books in series or "libraries" was marked by the 1880s as paperbound books flooded the market. Small wonder the American author worried about sales and remuneration.

Alger's letters are replete with comments about the state of the book trade, complaints about slow times, and the state of his income.[17] Late in life, he recounted the story of his Garfield biography in terms of production and consumption: "I wrote a boys' life of Garfield just after his death . . . I wrote it against time in 14 days. Twenty thousand copies were sold, and so of course I was quite handsomely paid."[18]

The author frequently lamented the impact of his declining health on his productivity because of its effect on his income. He awaited royalty checks and periodically wrote Porter & Coates, seeking funds from book sales.[19] More often than not, he found the state of the book trade "dull."

Writing for the market, Alger tried to attend to what readers and publishers wanted. Publishers exercised considerable control over what most popular fiction authors produced. Even Alger, who was one of the "stars" in the business, received "suggestions" by his publishers concerning the settings or contents of his work. Market information influenced story lines. Alger's "Pacific Series" may have come about as Loring noted that Alger's popularity was weakening in the East but improving in the West; "he advised his star author to reverse his procedure and write stories about the West for boys in the East."[20]

In Alger's case, dependence upon the market bred risk aversion. If the self-sufficient late nineteenth century author could be viewed as a "speculator" in the market, Alger writes much more like the sober, cautious investor.[21] He was not a gambler. As he sought audiences, he frequently borrowed from popular English and American authors. Alger sometimes compared himself to Dickens, longed for his success, and borrowed some of his plot devices. *Oliver Twist* looms in the case of Alger's poorhouse boys who are treated to unappetizing and skimpy food, and may even ask for more; he also drew upon *Great Expectations, David Copperfield,* and *Nicholas Nickleby.*[22] He once complained of a printed criticism that he had modeled a black character's speech on Topsy in *Uncle Tom's Cabin.*[23] Alger borrowed from Twain when he wrote *Tom Brace* (1889) and *Bob Burton* (1886-87).[24]

While looking to other authors for ideas and models, Alger stressed his own independent identity. In advice to a would-be author, Alger recounted:

> When I commenced writing for young people my publisher recommended me to read "Optic's" books (he had been in the field ten or a dozen years) and judge for myself what made the boys like his books. I did so, but retained my own individuality, so that there are marked differences between my books and his. My present taste inclines me to to prefer the juvenile books of J. T. Trowbridge to any other.[25]

The story papers and dime novels represented a new culture industry in the nineteenth century, providing new opportunities for those seeking sustenance by writing. A librarian, writing in 1881 in disapproval of the democratization of authorship and the low standards of readers, linked the dilution of the literary profession to the proliferation of such literature:

> A generation ago comparatively few showed ability to write, and fewer still made a profession of authorship. Now, in the smallest community, there are probably one or more persons either

> amusing their leisure hours by writing, or earning a livelihood by
> it. From this calling none are debarred save by absolute incapac-
> ity. A quire of paper, a pen, and a bottle of ink constitute abundant
> capital for a trade which can be prosecuted anywhere. The
> production of light literature, being the easiest form of literary
> work, is naturally preferred by the great majority of writers,
> while fame and money come more speedily and surely from a
> successful story than from anything else in literature . . .[26]

An author struggling for a mere living can hardly resist the temptation
to win favor by pandering to the demand of the young and simpleminded,
who have virtually unlimited access to sensational reading matter.[27]

Since these light, sensational novels require but little time to write and
have a good chance of success, "who can wonder that the choice is quickly
made?" These novels are cranked out with little regard to quality. Moreover,

> the low price which is paid for the work of all except a few writers
> tends also to affect unfavorably their character; and the rapid
> production, which is partly owing to this cause and partly to the
> keen competition between editors, publishers, and writers, has a
> still more deleterious effect. A successful novelist of the present
> day is urged by his publisher or by his own necessities to ceaseless
> production.[28]

Rapid production of later Alger works meant poor literary quality and
frequent errors, even in remembering characters' names. New tales reworked
old ones with minor variations. If the production was reckless, the formula
writer's investment was nonetheless cautious. A poor entrepreneur, Alger
did not find the formula for popular success easy.

One Alger story in which a writer of cheap fiction figures provides useful
insight into Alger's understanding of the production of this literature.
Sylvanus Snodgrass, a boardinghouse acquaintance of the hero in *Ben Bruce*,
writes serialized stories such as "The Ragpicker's Curse" for the *Weekly
Bugle*. He fashions himself an important writer and claims a popular
following. Yet it is clear Snodgrass makes very little from his novelettes; he
complains of the low prices and borrows money to pay back rent. It is also
apparent that Snodgrass's publisher regards him as expendable or
interchangeable: "He could get along without me, and could easily supply
my place." Thus, it is hardly surprising that Snodgrass's big coup places him
squarely in the ranks of fiction production: "The next day Mr. Snodgrass
received an order for six dime novels from a publisher of that class of fiction,
and it exhilarated him immensely."

Snodgrass exults not only because of the economic aspect of this coup,
but because this unsolicited offer comes from a different publisher. "The

editor of the *Bugle* has thought he owned me, but his tyranny is over." The writer-publisher relationship here resembles the capital-labor one: "I furnish the brains and he furnishes the capital. That's about the way the matter stands."[29]

Alger puts this statement in the mouth of this somewhat laughable character at a time when much of this sort of writing approximated "fiction factory" production. Many authors working in story paper and dime novel genres were reduced to anonymous, undifferentiated literary labor power. These authors were often treated as interchangeable by publishers. A few were able to establish themselves as "stars," but in many other cases, authorial designations such as "Old Sleuth" or "Bertha M. Clay" became the property *not* of a specific author but rather of the publisher. A writer who changed publishing houses could, then, lose his or her "identity." Late in the century, a publisher might use house novelists interchangeably to produce under a certain identifiable name or pseudonym.[30]

Despite the emergence of the fiction factory engulfing many story paper, dime novel, and melodrama authors that he himself depicts, Alger was sometimes blissfully naïve. He was, himself, just successful enough to escape the fiction factories. Scholars are uncertain just how much of the eleven "Alger" works released after the author's death were in fact Alger productions, and one standard bibliography considers several volumes "fakes"—not written by Alger at all. Evidence indicates that Alger arranged for Edward Stratemeyer to complete works of his that were at least partially sketched out.[31] What is clear is that Alger owned his name better than many others working in the field of popular fiction. He could lay claim to this sort of individuality.

ALGER MARKETS HIMSELF

A man can't do business without advertising

Daniel Frohman, *Hints to Advertisers*, 1869 [32]

It is hardly surprising that Alger's chief literary contacts appear to have been writers and publishers in the realm of juvenile fiction. He claimed toward the end of his life that he wrote about thirty letters per week.[33] Many of his correspondents were young boys and former pupils; in 1862 and 1863, he wrote frequently and sent news from Boston to a young soldier, Joseph F. Dean.[34]

Almost all heard from Alger about his communications with literary figures. He apparently maintained regular correspondence with juvenile authors Louise Chandler Moulton, J. T. Trowbridge, and Edward Ellis, and expressed jealousy over Ellis' rate of production.[35] Letters reveal he considered William Adams (Oliver Optic) a revered friend. He communicated with publisher Frank Munsey and maintained friendly correspondence with the editors of the *New York Weekly*.[36]

The most distinguished intellectual figures with whom Alger could claim acquaintance were perhaps William James and Henry James, Sr. Alger apparently confided in William some private matters rarely voiced. The elder Henry James wrote Henry James, Jr. in the spring of 1870 that Horatio Alger "talks freely about his own late insanity—which he in fact appears to enjoy as a subject of conversation and in which I believe he has somewhat interested William."[37]

Alger sought eagerly for signs of recognition—from critics, from prominent authors of his day, and from the public. With his poetry especially, but also with his adult novellas, he attempted to build more substantial literary credentials. He recognized the importance of self-marketing and wished for the reputation and readership recognition could bring, even though he shied from a life in the public gaze.

Remarking once on his own achievements relative to his father, Alger reveals how close was the link in his own mind between striding forth in the world and self-promotional activities. "My father was kept in the background by his own modesty. His son, on the other hand, has not been bashful but made the most of his abilities and opportunities."[38]

While advertising and promotion fell partially in the realm of publishers and distributors, authors advanced their own wares. Some went on lecture tours, while Alger, an occasional speaker, travelled to collect data for his works, arranged some events en route, and managed to gain notice in the papers in the course of his travels. Sending out free copies of books was a form of self-advertisement.

Alger engaged in not a little self-marketing as he sought a place in the literary community. He had a habit of sending copies of his volumes to literary figures of slight or no acquaintance. When he received polite acknowledgment of his gifts, he often took the occasion to write again, meanwhile basking in whatever complements were given.

Flattery, to the point of embarrassment, was part of the arsenal. Upon arrival in New York in 1866, Alger submitted his newly composed poem, "Friar Anselmo's Sin," to editor William Conant Church of the *Galaxy*. Alger congratulated Church on the first issue of the new publication, adding: "You have succeeded in producing something unlike any other American magazine, wh. was a difficult thing to do. Judging from the initial no. I cannot doubt its success."[39] Church presumed the sender was Alger's cousin and sometimes poet, Reverend William Rounseville Alger, author of "Alger's Oriental Poetry." The author quickly cleared up the mistake, but failed to place his poem in the *Galaxy*.

In 1875, the author sent his former Harvard professor Longfellow an inscribed copy of *Grand'ther Baldwin's Thanksgiving*, a book of poetry that included his most well-known poem, "John Maynard." When Longfellow wrote thanks and apparently some words of praise, Alger attempts to use the entré:

> It is hardly necessary for me to say how much I am gratified by your words of approval. Years since, when at college, I remember calling upon you with a classmate, and I shall not soon forget the kindness with which you received the two inexperienced boys whose visit might have been regarded by many as an intrusion.
>
> If you should find any of my pieces available for the collection you refer to, I shall be only too happy to have them used.[40]

The same year, he sent a "little volume," surely *Grand'ther Baldwin*, for which he was trying to obtain some literary recognition, to Mr. Edmund Clarence Stedman, a sort of predecessor to Howells as dean of American letters. To make the contact, Alger had the volume transmitted to Stedman's hands through another.[41] Alger responded to thanks with alacrity:

> I am afraid you do me too much honor in calling me a fellow craftsman, but I am glad to accept the pleasant title . . . I inclose a notice of your Victorian Poets from the Boston Christian Register. It may perhaps be new to you. I congratulate you on the brilliant success which the book is achieving. The combination of high poetical and critical gifts is so rare that the possessor may well be regarded as fortunate. In this respect you stand side by side with Lowell, and there is no third,—at least in American literature.[42]

Using one new acquaintance by correspondence to attempt to make another, Alger concludes his letter to Stedman: "I observe in Bayard Taylor's *Home Pastorals* a sonnet addressed to yourself. I will esteem it a favor if you will give me his address, that I may send him my little book. Some of his lyrics I particularly like."[43]

He was obsequious again when, years later, he prevailed upon Stedman to assess the promise of former pupil Lizzie Cardozo, sister of the legal scholar and jurist, who Alger also tutored.[44]

In self-advertising, Alger circulated quite a few copies of his books, having them sent from his publisher and possibly paying the cost. He passed along copies to relatives and to young boys with whom he corresponded: "I shall write in this mail to my publishers to forward you my

'Ragged Dick Series,' in six volumes, and shall be gratified if you will accept them," he volunteered to distant relative and presidential hopeful, General Russell A. Alger of Michigan. He continued sending his works to the General at precisely the time the latter was in the throes of a crisis in McKinley's cabinet, riding a crest of unpopularity for his handling of the Spanish-American War.[45]

Constantly seeking literary respectability, he would frequently be dismissed or condemned by literary critics. Authors were becoming highbrow or lowbrow specialists. Genres, writing techniques, themes, characterization, and form of publication would all diverge and offer clues about literary status. Ministers, female authors, and popular writers shared a proclivity for light production, writing "poetry, fiction, memoirs, sermons, and magazine pieces of every kind."[46] Although he could not give up his literary aspirations, Alger was becoming a specialist in mass culture and would increasingly be treated as such by critics and prevailing elites.

When he settled in New York in the spring of 1866, and in later self-introductions and biographical sketches, Alger would identify himself as a novelist and as a contributor to *Harpers' Weekly and Magazine*, the *North American Review*, and *Putnam's Magazine* "in its last days."[47] Like his newsboy heroes who rarely hawk the story papers, Alger did not advertise his own considerable story paper literature.[48]

If he was reluctant to advertise this class of literary production, it was clear that the crossover of class vehicles posed problems for one seeking literary legitimation. Meanwhile, story papers were unabashed in seeking *their* audiences:

> The means taken to bring the papers to notice are often as enterprising as their contents. Copies of the opening chapters are thrown in at the area railings, and printed, regardless of expense, to pique curiosity, in the daily papers. The attention of the households of upper New York was widely awakened recently by an invitation telegram, sealed and addressed, the envelope and message-blank exact, saying, *"The child is still alive. You are personally interested in all the details of A Sinless Crime, to appear in to-morrow's _____."* [49]

Could a Gilded Age fiction author still find a disparate class audience? Mark Twain was probably the most successful author of the period in bridging the gulf increasingly separating audiences of the highbrow novel and the dime novel.[50] With calculated attire and attention-grabbing techniques, Twain was one of the real self-promoters and public spectacles of the period. He stressed, rather than hid, his connection to the masses, writing in 1889, the year after his honorary Master of the Arts from Yale:

> I have never tried in even one single instance to help cultivate the cultivated classes. I . . . always hunted for bigger game—the masses. I have seldom deliberately tried to instruct them, but have done my best to entertain them . . . My audience is dumb, it has no voice in print, and so I cannot know whether I have won its approbation or only got its censure.[51]

Twain insisted he did not wish to morally rehabilitate his audience. While he had his own sort of rags-to-riches story in *The Prince and the Pauper*, he lampooned the Sunday School fiction of the 1860s in his "Good Little Boy" and "Bad Little Boy" stories. These stories made abundantly clear that this world's rewards and punishments are certainly not meted out according to desert. Though Alger read Twain and heard him give several lectures, he could not tolerate such a message in his fiction.[52]

Yet Twain scorned the penny papers. He wrote in 1867 that he would not write for the *New York Weekly*, the paper so important to Alger: "Like all other papers that pay one splendidly, it circulates among stupid people and the *canaille*."[53] Twain's idea of the masses more resembled Nixon's silent majority than it did the working classes or audiences for cheap fiction.

While Twain attained literary acceptance and gave calculated performances to well-heeled audiences on the lecture circuit, Alger wished for such acceptance while spending time with some of his literary subjects, who were rougher around the edges. Whether street children read his fiction or not, there is evidence that they gravitated to him. Alger sought out the spots frequented by young street urchins and sometimes treated them with money or candy; the result was that his room became "a veritable salon for street boys." His sister, Augusta, reported that

> nothing delighted him more than to get a lot of boys between the ages of 12 and 16 years in the room with him, and while they were cutting up and playing about he would sit down and write letters or a paragraph of a story.[54]

One street boy was quoted as claiming that "Mr. Alger could raise a regiment of boys in New York alone, who would fight to the death for him."[55] Alger himself, late in life, reported that many young street boys heard him speak in Boston and Waltham about the street boys of New York, and sought out an opportunity to meet him on those occasions.[56]

Twain was more the bold, literary speculator whose speculations paid off in both literary and public acceptance. His aggressive self-promotion revealed this temperament. Alger was not as bold as author or actor. He was more easily marginalized.

No one could reasonably maintain that Alger was "better literature" than Twain. But if Twain scorned the penny papers, Alger could not afford to. Twain was not as frequently the object of the moral crusades against dime novels and sensational literature waged by the guardians of culture as Alger was.[57]

CHARACTER, MALENESS, AND MORALITY: CHANGING EXPECTATIONS AND THE DELINEATION OF HIGHBROW AND LOWBROW

> I judge a book by the impression it makes and leaves in my mind, by the *feelings* solely as I am no scholar.—A story that touches and moves me, I can make others read and believe in.—What I like is conciseness in introducing the characters, getting them upon the stage and into action as quickly as possible.—Then I like a story of constant action, bustle and motion.—Conversations and descriptive scenes are delightful reading when well drawn but are too often skipped by the reader who is anxious to see what they do next ... I like a story that starts to teach some lesson of life [and] goes steadily on increasing in interest till it culminates with the closing chapter leaving you spell bound, enchanted and exhausted with the intensity with which it is written, the lesson forcibly told, and a yearning desire to turn right back to the beginning and enjoy it over again. ... Stories of the *heart* are what live in the memory and when you move the reader to tears you have won them [sic] to you forever.
>
> A. K. Loring to Louisa May Alcott, 1864[58]

Publisher A. K. Loring saw in Alger the kind of author he wished to represent. Loring aimed to bring fiction with a moral message to a mass audience.[59] The publisher sought to win readers with lessons of life couched in appeals to the heart, and with "constant action, bustle and motion." But the lesson-teaching and the action-bustle would frequently come to blows in this era; the formula itself was supplanted in genteel circles by new literary standards. The fate of Loring's publishing firm, which went bankrupt in 1880, was itself testimony to the increasing difficulty of walking a line between mere fiction and salutary reading.

Young readers and working-class audiences might prefer their action and excitement without the moral message, but this distinction became a relatively uninteresting one among elite arbiters of literary standards. The author's vehicles of communication, the identity of a publishing house, and new expectations for literature established by writers, reviewers, and cultural elites in the age of realism all impacted on an author's literary reception, identity, and even readership.

Alger's recourse to story papers, cheap magazines, juveniles, sentimental tales, and formula writing certainly eliminated his chance for serious notice among literary critics. Moreover, the combination of action with moral lesson was increasingly unrecognizable. Emphasis on action and adventure contributed to the fact that, in the Comstock era, many would stop noticing him at all. When they did react, two of the most common lightning rods were character and realism.

Reviewers appeared to be delimiting the meaning of "story," coterminous with the split between story and information functions of newspapers and the rise of the dime novel.[60] Fiction with serious merit would be called something else; stories had nothing good to do with life. And, if "stories" were being read by children and the working classes, perhaps one ought to worry about what was filling their heads.

New definitions of the adult male, and of what constituted strength and activity, were in the making. In the process, the working classes were joined with children and adolescents. In this context, the literary values, forms, characterizations, and style of Alger's fiction not only diverged from emerging literary tastes and expectations, but they increasingly became morally suspect.

Alger was pleased to note favorable reviews, such as that offered by the London Academy for *The New Schoolma'am* in 1877—"a sparkling American tale, full of humor . . ."[61] His early reviews tended to be mildly positive, though rarely were they comparable to notices in *Student and Schoolmate*, which trumpeted Alger's new works until its demise.

His moral reform was not lost on the reviewers who saw Alger's boys' fiction positively; they contrasted it with the kind of sensationalist drivel that young people might otherwise read. When Alger later wrote more "sensational" fiction to try to bolster his audience—incorporating robber barons and some huge fortunes, pointed guns and bandits—reviewers were more consistently hostile.[62]

But Alger's demands of character placed him at odds with the tastes of American literary critics. By the time he began to publish juvenile stories, critics were developing a new interest in character, forming expectations quite different from what Alger and his publisher, Loring, valued. The Alger-Loring concentration on juveniles was serendipity, for they were progressively cut off from the very language of adult literary discourse.

By midcentury, American and British reviewers had distinguished better from worse novels according to the criterion of perceptive characterization; character supplanted emphasis on plot.[63]   The *North American Review* of October, 1856 pronounced:

> It is in this absolute creation of character, that our modern
> novelists so far exceed all that their predecessors were able to
> accomplish. In variety of individuality, in successful delineation
> of the action of one character upon another, or of internal will
> upon external circumstance, or in the struggle of earnest natures
> against adverse influences,—in these, the themes of the modern
> novel, nature herself is almost rivalled . . . . It is now. . . the
> development of character which commands attention.[64]

Verisimilitude in characterization demanded that character be "mixed"— compounded of good and bad qualities. Faithful imitation of life required natural admixtures of faults; perfection or complete consistency was often criticized; characters should be "shaded." Reviewers did not demand that character *change* in the course of the novel, but rather that character unfold. The novel would become a process of character revelation.[65]

By these criteria, Dickens—a model for Alger—was faulted for crudeness by the 1850s. His "characters do not present the mixtures of good and bad in the same proportions as we find in nature." Some characters were "thoroughly and ideally perfect," others were "thoroughly and ideally detestable."

> Our first sight of Dickens' characters makes us perfectly ac-
> quainted with them, and we can know nothing more about them:
> they are shown to us over and over again, but always the same
> . . . It is this permanence and fixedness of character which makes
> it necessary for Dickens to introduce new personages continually
> to keep up the interest of the reader.[66]

Alger drew characters from an earlier epoch. They were easily enough known through their actions—if not by their physiognomy alone.[67] Only when a hero fails to "read" some other character correctly does that character "evolve." They were not like boys around them, but this was not sufficient to grant their individuality. These protagonists possessed inner strength and resolution, but lacked rich inner lives at a time when "passions, motives, and impulses become increasingly important in the lives of strongly marked characters."[68] They were not "individuated" in the language of the day. The self-made man was a very different kind of "individualist."

Protagonists experienced adventures, while external behavior became less important a field of action than inner life for cultural arbiters. For literary arbiters, they were inadequately differentiated.

The Alger action-achievement axis has produced at least one twentieth-century reading in which Alger boys are manly, indeed. "Alger's young readers identify with Our Hero and vicariously through him win 'grit,' 'pluck,' and other symbols of manliness and potency." The author gratified a boy's wish to become a man.

Heroes supplant their fathers economically. Not only are they more successful, but they also become providers for mothers and siblings, and perhaps nurture a father.[69] In this regard, Alger characters speak of potency in the new industrial era.

But *was* this "manly" fiction? Shifting nineteenth century standards are highly revealing: On the dimension of character, Alger boys are losing male identities. Characterization increasingly aligns the Alger hero with the wrong gender and wrong class.

Characters who were simple, transparent, and one-dimensional had not become merely uninteresting. For cultural elites, Alger's characters came to look like the female characters that prevailed as the "natural" or accurate portrayal of women in the second quarter of the century.[70] Simple, undifferentiated persons who tended more to action than to introspection were closer to the realm of nature than to that of convention and civilization. Such characters were more allied with the female. They were, likewise, allied with the young, and with the working classes.

Workers were dissociated from emerging class-based images of manhood by their dependence on employers; loss of control over their activities; intemperance, violence and unrestrained passion; performance of simple, manual labor; absence of cultural refinement; and restricted ability to consume. They were even often exchangeable in the workplace with women and children. Engagement in production itself seemed to estrange one from manhood. Producing the *self* made one a man; producing *goods* made one not-a-man. Antebellum workers who demanded that employers fulfill obligations of paternal authority and who noted "Observe how poor and dependent are the producers, and how rich and powerful the consumers of wealth" sensed the association of manhood, independence, potency, and capacity to consume.[71] Rather subtly the world was inverted: The idle capitalist was a male because he was potent, while the worker-producer was not a man, because s/he was not.

This dissociation of productive labor from manhood became a theme in Veblen's end-of-century *Theory of the Leisure Class*. "Virtually the whole range of industrial employments is an outgrowth of what is classed as woman's work in the primitive barbarian society," he wrote. The division of labor between the sexes is a distinction between exploit and drudgery. Possession of wealth and industrial exemption were cultural measures of prowess; manners, breeding, domestic music, and sports are among the branches of learning that manifest leisure and worth. From the time of the predatory culture, "labor comes to be associated in men's habits of thought with weakness and subjection to a master. It is therefore a mark of inferiority, and therefore comes to be accounted unworthy of man in his best estate."[72]

But with the midcentury rise of the dime novel, new working-class symbols of potency and maleness were created. *John Armstrong, Mechanic* was a muscular, virile, simple, active, hard-working class hero. Learning some rudimentary educational skills helped him rise, but his manliness was not in question.[73] Armstrong was in the company of many more working-class heroes in a battle to retain control over the very definition of maleness in the Gilded Age.

As doers, not thinkers, as characters who are neither introspective nor complexly drawn, Alger heroes share something with working-class John Armstrong. However, consistent with Alger's Whiggish emphasis on temperance and suppression of passion as the route to civilization, his boys neither drink nor do they yield to angry outbursts of verbal or physical violence.[74] And Alger heroes are preserved from mature employment that directly engages in production, often attaining symbols of a heightened capacity to consume. The hero's independence and consumption capacity identify him with power and potency. As gendered characters, Alger's heroes were transitional—perhaps even in no-man's-land.

Mature male development was being claimed and reclaimed. The authors of more "masculine" fiction, such as Melville, Hawthorne, Cooper, and Whitman, "wrote principally about men, not girls and children, and they wrote about men engaged in economically and ecologically significant activities."[75] Alger's central characters are children, adolescents, and women. His absent or failed fathers and his nuclear families consisting of mother and children keeps stories centered on domesticity and consumption, even while heroes must go out into the world to secure these goods.

Alger's boy heroes intend to take their place in the world of men, but they maintain community and nurturant values. Alger not only shared the sentimental author's emphasis on faith, family, and community, but he was an upholder of morality in the Republic. Both were increasingly the domain of women. In the hemaphroditic tale, the author resists what "masculine" is coming to be. The manly boy in a sentimental tale is a wish—and a misfit.

Some Alger contemporaries watched and commented upon shifting gender identities in fiction and other forms of nineteenth-century discourse. Henry James found emerging tastes and standards at midcentury already less male. He marked the decline of masculine religion (stern, Calvinistic): "Religion in the old virile sense has disappeared, and been replaced by a feeble Unitarian sentimentality."[76] The same might have been said of the light fiction of sentimental authors of the era, a point underscored by the success of sentimental fiction among female readers. Another, reflecting more upon the action-adventure emphasis of the generation prior to literary realism, contrasted the new emphasis on inner life and subjective character with "a kind of masculine excellence and robust healthiness [that] is claimed for the novels our fathers read and liked."[77]

As Alger's works were associated with the unreflective and uncultivated, so were their readers. *Publishers Weekly* noted books for youth in their "Christmas Bookshelf" section. Of the 1889 publication of *Luke Walton*, they wrote:

> PORTER & COATES' name immediately suggests Harry Castlemon, Horatio Alger, and Edward S. Ellis, story-tellers dear to the heart of healthy, active boys whom no amount of coaxing can induce to join a Chautauqua course or to care for the many books now published to make learning slip into their little brain-boxes disguised as fiction approved by librarians and teachers.[78]

This was innocuous adventure; but it was seen, by this point, as story telling, not learning. *Publishers Weekly* exhibited slight disdain for the audience, while nonetheless deriding the efforts of the moral crusaders. Here were boys concerned with action, with no evidence of a rich inner life at this point in their young lives. *They* did not yet approximate the men of character reviewers now expected from fiction authors. But since the young could later grow and mature, let boys be boys.

Publishers Weekly's brief notice of *Struggling Upward* in 1890, as with other Alger notices, hits on the naïveté of the work, its poor construction, poor dialogue, and lack of realism. But realism was not here seen as a moral issue: Alger's new novel sounds like *Pilgrim's Progress*. The story "takes up a boy's life at school and carries him through the trials and temptations he encounters in his contact with the world. The boy is poor, but bright and honest."[79]

But representation was also becoming a matter of morality. Reviewers often asserted that more truthful representations of character were in fact more *moral* than idealized ones.[80] In this, they foreshadowed later contentions made by Howells. *Realism* would keep audiences from making mistakes between fact and fiction—all the more vital as the working classes became fiction readers.

What kind of impressions would unrealistic stories form on the mind of the reader, worried the *Nation*: "For a thousand years, we suppose, we shall have books like Mr. Alger's 'Rough and Ready,' and, as they say in the South, for our own part 'we have no use for them.'" The *Nation* voiced its low opinion of newsboys, and feared that "master 'Rough and Ready'. . . is going to deceive many who believe in him. He is a most noble, generous, just newsboy—full as he can hold of good thoughts and good works." If Rough and Ready came into contact with the boys of City Hall Park or Printing House Square, it would "certainly, in a very brief time, cause a temporarily complete and painful change in our clean young wayfarer's views of life." Newsboys "would far rather see virtue defended up in the Bowery Theatre" than rescue little girls from abusive stepmothers.[81]

Like romances and melodramas, the story is not truthful or realistic. And what effect will *Rough and Ready* have? "The layman will . . . form false notions of the being which it is intended to depict; and that is never well." Furthermore, those most needing moral rehabilitation will surely not choose to profit from Rough and Ready's example:

> The newsboys who read "Rough and Ready," however they may approve it as a work of fiction, will say "my eye" when asked to lay it to heart and make it a practical guide. So, them the author has not benefited.[82]

In reviewing *Risen from the Ranks* in 1874, *The Nation* takes issue with advertisements that claim that such "stories exert a healthy influence, and are of immense service to ambitious boys anxious to make their mark in the world." The editors dismiss the connection between fiction and fact and doubt any salutary mental effect, adding: "It is to be conceded that naturally clever boys, if they are only young enough or ignorant enough—and of the latter there are countless numbers in country districts—do and will absorb this sort of pabulum."[83]

When the *New York Times* noticed Alger, it tended to emphasize the lowbrow nature of the entertainment. *The New Schoolma'am*, an adult novella in paper covers, had "a suspicion of thinness about [it], and a certain evident want of knowledge of the world. But to many thousands of readers that will be a matter of little account."[84] For the *Times*, the author did not understand the world and the readers did not care to know the difference between truth and falsehood. Such fiction was mere entertainment, meant to be picked up and put down, like story papers, railroad novels, [and modern tabloids].

Alger readers were progressively depicted as gullible and unable to discern the difference between fact and fiction. If the young and the infantilized working classes could form false pictures of the world, it is not surprising that their reading matter came under increasing scrutiny.

By the mid-1880s, Alger's reputation had taken a decided turn. Many publications failed to note his new works at all or simply scoffed. Even some of the better magazines that had published Alger stories began to ignore him.[85] For some, Alger's fiction had become harmful.

Prior to the mid-1880s, the price of Alger *books* gave little clue about quality and moral rectitude. But other forms in which these tales appeared simultaneously made them suspect. At the end of the previous century in England, sedition and libel trials tended to focus on works that were *not* confined to a small audience, and often "estimated intellectual understanding by a financial scale. . . . An inexpensive price was evidence of the author's malicious intent because it established that the books were addressed 'to the ignorant, to the credulous, to the desperate.'"[86]

Price and audience also figured in the mid-1880 attacks against certain fiction writers launched by Comstock and continued by other cultural conservatives.

The concern on the part of reviewers and genteel moralists that readers know the difference between fact and fiction leads us to Chapter 12 and "culture wars." For we must examine a final part of the struggle to retain influence over the habits, tastes, and identity of the young Republic—the war over entertainment.

CONCLUSION

Alger, failed Unitarian minister, moved into an occupation that was closely akin and temperamentally related to his earlier one. Employing sentimental tales for moral suasion, seeking to uphold traditional moral values, the minister and the popular fiction writer marketed their wares in a domain increasingly divorced from what was defined as the adult male. Economically, politically, and intellectually divorced from his masculine heritage, "the liberal minister was pushed into a position increasingly resembling the evolving feminine one."[87]

In an era when maleness and adulthood were being redefined, both in literary tastes and in the political culture, Alger's figures look less like men in the making. His readership among adolescents and the working classes contributed to the view among literary critics and cultural guardians that the author specialized in writing for not-men: Those requiring guidance and protection. This was almost sufficient to determine the author's stature.

As a producer of highly mechanized fiction, dependent upon the market, Alger struggled to retain some vestige of traditional notions of authorship, ownership, power, and independence. But like the worker, his capacity to consume depended upon being consumed. If his comical character, author Sylvanus Snodgrass, supplied the brains and his publisher the capital, Alger had more in common with Snodgrass than he would like to admit.

Alger's understanding of the relationship between authors and publishers exhibits a cavalier disregard for the facts—or a tendency toward wish-fulfillment—reminding one of Garry Wills' analysis of Ronald Reagan's appeal to the American public. Reagan exhibited a capacity to disregard the facts and rewrite his own history.[88] Alger, like Reagan, can convincingly convey an image of America as we would *like* it to be—because he himself believed it. Alger's skill as a writer, like Reagan's as a politician, was to convey these simple truths, embodying past, present, and future. He sold reassurance and an image of continuity. We remain of one estate.

12

Culture Wars

The ancient mode of dramatic representation differed altogether from that which exists at the present day. All classes of the citizens were admitted to this entertainment, and thus was fostered that love of the beautiful and harmonious which formed a leading trait in the Athenian character.

Athenaicus (Horatio Alger, Jr.), "Athens in the Time of Socrates"

ARE WE ALL OF ONE ESTATE?

The themes Alger pursued in the Harvard essay "Athens in the Time of Socrates" remained lifetime preoccupations. He applauded the unification of classes in the audience of classical tragedies and noted "the strict propriety and moral purity which are always maintained in ancient tragedy."[1]

Alger's essay described the staging and arrangement of the thousands of seats in the theater of classical antiquity. It was impressive that this took place under nature's skies—no gas lighting or artificial settings. Classes were united in the same space and in the same civilized discourse:

> It must have been an impressive spectacle—that vast multitude—seated tier above tier, bench upon bench, occupied by one common subject of interest, with their passions alternately soothed and excited surrendering their whole souls to the absorbing interest with which the poet had invested the brilliant creations of his fancy.[2]

227

The author sometimes compared modern literature and drama unfavorably with Greek tragedy. Theater of today, Alger said, is more contrived.

But many in Alger's generation looked with hope upon "the American stage, an institution which, being yet in its infancy, has capacity for good or evil, the development of which rests upon the present generation." "It is impossible that the people should witness such a performance as that of King Lear [with Edwin Forrest] without elevation and purification of character."[3] Alger's cousin, Unitarian minister William Rounseville Alger, undertook a commissioned, multivolume biography of America's foremost midcentury tragedian, Edwin Forrest; Alger had a hand in the task. If the church attempts to teach, impress, persuade, and command directly,

> the theatre aims directly to entertain, indirectly to teach, persuade, and impress. It often accomplishes the last three aims so much the better because of the surrendered, genial, and pleased condition of soul induced by the success of the first one.[4]

The pulpit cannot compete with the theater in terms of charm, scenery, music, light, shade, color, costumes, or variety. When the theater attempts to educate or influence, "it does it without the perfunctory air or the dogmatic animus or repulsive severity of those who claim the tasks of moral guidance and authority as their supernatural professional office." The minister concedes,

> purified from its accidental corruptions and redeemed from its shallow carelessness, the theatre would have greater power to teach and mould than the church. Aside from historic authority and social prestige, its intrinsic impressiveness is greater. The deed must go for more than the word. The dogma must yield to the life. And while in the pulpit the dogmatic word is preached in its hortatory dryness, on the stage the living deed is shown in its contagious persuasion or its electric warning.[5]

Could it not be claimed that the theater was more *democratic*, and the church more *aristocratic*, and that the former would be the moral educator of a democratic citizenry? The very words for the church "signify a portion selected or elected and called aside by themselves for special salvation, apart from the great whole who are to be left to the general doom." Despite the democratic example of Christ, the church "has been made an exclusive enclosure for a privileged class of believers. In it their prejudices are cherished and their ascetic ideal glorified and urged on all." "But the word theatre in its etymology implies that the world of life is something worthy of contemplation, beautiful to be gazed at and enjoyed."[6] Little more than a year before Alger penned his reflections on Athenian drama at Harvard, popular dime novel author Ned Buntline (E. Z. C. Judson) participated in leading the Astor Place Riots of 1849. This event helped demarcate a new era:

> One theater was no longer large enough to appeal to all classes.... One roof, housing a vast miscellany of entertainment each evening, could no longer cover a people growing intellectually and financially more disparate.[7]

Working classes would increasingly constitute audiences for the melodrama.

The new Astor Place Opera House of 1847 was an elegant, refined structure. There were boxes for the wealthy, reserved subscription seats, and approximately 500 gallery seats for open admission, most with obstructed views. There were dress codes, and no unaccompanied women would be admitted.[8] Class audiences were separated in space, and audience discipline was expected.

But the sorts who populated the gallery were not about to concede their prerogatives. Their theater was one of freedom and informality; they would not be gagged. "Theatergoers occasionally joined in famous speeches and familiar songs, and they delighted in beating actors to the punch lines of old jokes." They talked, ate, booed, cheered, stamped, hissed, jeered, and threw things at performers. They were used to demanding particular pieces and the repetition of scenes. When the catalyst of the Astor Place Riot, English aristocratic actor William Charles Macready, played Hamlet in Cincinnati, a gallery spectator "heaved half a raw sheep's carcass onto the stage."[9]

Such audiences occasionally engaged in more pronounced interventions. The antebellum era was witness to a number of theater riots, often against English actors. Appointing themselves "the public," and proclaiming their "sovereign rights as theatergoers," "rioters dispensed rough justice by chasing offenders off the stage and breaking a limited degree of property, usually within limits set by the elite."[10]

American tragedian Edwin Forrest (1806-72) had fanatical partisans among the American working classes, despite a scandalous divorce and an otherwise dicy reputation. He won a mass following "by his passionate, intensely physical acting, his fervent nationalism, and his exemplary rise from working-class origins to international celebrity," wrote his Alger biographers.[11] Forrest's fans also stamped, clapped, shouted, joined in choruses, and occasionally hissed.[12]

Passionate acting called forth passionate response. If Forrest's portrayal of Iago in *Othello* prompted a canal boatman to shout: "You damned-lying scoundrel, I would like to get hold of you after the show and wring your infernal neck," unreformed audiences in their *own* theaters continued to respond in this manner, even to Shapespearean productions at the end of the century.[13] Middle-class patrons of the arts had become, during the century, reserved, refined, disciplined. Even when, on occasion, the play remained the same, the language was different.

Forrest, the home-grown actor was termed "American every inch," embodying natural and physical robustness, activity, and making connection with genuine feelings; he was seen as contributing to the development of an indigenous school of acting that was neither classical nor melodramatic, combining "the physical fire and energy of the melodramatic school with the repose and elaborate painting of the artistic school."[14] His performances would exhibit "earnest realism ... [and the] native boldness and resolution of his character."[15] Although wanting in beauty, charm, grace, poetry, and polish, he was not deficient in strength, nobleness, sincerity, eloquence, power, grandeur, or sublimity. He was a "great democrat." If Forrest was a "rough jewel," Macready was a "paste gem, polished and set off with every counterfeit gleam art could lend." "The fire of the one was said to command honest throbs and tears; the icy glitter of the other, the dainty clappings of kid gloves."[16]

Forrest's English counterpart, William Charles Macready, also had his partisans among antebellum audiences and critics, who had had the opportunity to see him during his 1843 tour. Macready was described alternately as refined, aristocratic, or classical; he "coveted social preferment and shrank from the plebeian crowd." The biographer found that Macready "was not popular with the multitude, but was favored by the selecter portion of the public." Forrest's biographer fingered the "many Englishmen connected with the leading newspapers in this country," who advanced Macready's cause as their own.[17] Furthermore,

> By natural affinity the English party drew to themselves the
> dilettante portion of the upper stratum of society, the so-called
> fashionable and aristocratic, while the general mass of the
> people were the hearty admirers of Forrest.[18]

The tension between partisans of Macready and of Forrest was highly politicized. The contest upon the particularly high level of audience response at the theater when expressions of political opinion or patriotism were called forth.[19] In 1846, Forrest had seen Macready play Hamlet in Edinburgh and hissed the performance from his box. Forrest also played "against" the English actor in competing productions at some of the cities on Macready's 1849 tour, including New York.[20] Claims of aristocracy, taste, and refinement were pitted against democratic, nativist, and nationalist claims. Posters put up just prior to Macready's visit to the Astor Place Opera House read:

> WORKING MEN,
> shall
> AMERICANS OR ENGLISH RULE
> in this city?
> The crew of the *British Steamer*
> have threatened all Americans who
> shall dare to express their opinion
> on this night at the English
> Aristocratic Opera House!!!
> We advocate no violence, but a free
> expression of opinion to all public men!
> WORKING MEN! FREEMEN!
> Stand by your
> LAWFUL RIGHTS.
> American Committee.[21]

Forrest and Macready were speaking different languages, even when performing the same roles. Some of the London newspapers wrote that Forrest provided a "coarse caricature of Lear," and that his portrayal of Richard the Third was yet another of his "murderous attacks upon Shakspeare [*sic*]," in which, for nearly every scene Forrest "blazed forth in a new and most oppressively-gilded dress." The passion he exhibited in Othello "is a violent effort of physical vehemence . . . Even his tenderness is affected, and his smile is like the grin of a wolf showing his fangs."[22]

And yet the reception Forrest received for his classical roles was favorable by comparison to his more romantic ones. The *London Observer* said of Forrest's American Indian, Metamora:

> His whole dramatic existence is a spasm of rage and hatred, and
> his whole stage-life one continuous series of murder, arson, and
> destruction to life and property in its most hideous form. What
> a pity he could not be let loose upon the drab-colored swindlers
> of Pennsylvania![23]

For Forrest's critics at home and abroad, he was a melodramatic actor. "In melodrama the action is more physical than mental, the exertions of the actor blows of artifice to produce an effect rather than strokes of art to reveal truth." But for his sympathetic biographer,

> The prejudices against him as a strutting and robustious ranter
> who shivered the timbers of his hearers and tore everything to
> tatters were largely unwarranted at the outset, and for every year
> afterwards were a gross wrong. In the time of his herculean glory

with the Bowery Boys it may be true that his fame was bottomed on the great lower classes of society, and made its strongest appeals through the signs he gave of muscle, blood, and fire; yet there must have been wonderful intelligence, pathos, and beauty, as well as naked power, to have commanded, as his playing did at that early day, the glowing tributes paid to him by Irving, Leggett, Bryant, Chandler, Clay...[24]

What *was* a truthful, dignified, or worthy performance? Those London papers attacking Forrest depicted him as "screaming, roaring, bellowing, and raving"; at the same time, a paper supportive of Forrest recalled and missed his former "rough and somewhat extravagant energy."[25] Meanwhile, the *Democratic Review*, an American paper said that

Mr. Macready, an admirable performer, succeeds by subduing all of the man within him; because he ceases, in the fulfilment of his function as an actor, to have any fellowship with the beatings and turmoils and agitations of the heart. He is classical in spirit, in look, and action.

Whereas Macready renounces his manliness, Forrest never forgets that "it is he, a man, with men before him, who treads the boards, and asks for tears, and sobs, and answers of troubled hearts."[26]

Many distinguished players have trodden the stage as gentle-men, Forrest trod it as man. The ideal of detachment, authority throned in cold-blooded self-regard, has been often set forth. He exhibited the ideal of identification, burning honesty of passion and open fellowship. The former is the ideal of polite society. The latter is the ideal of unsophisticated humanity.[27]

This large-hearted man "is upon a large scale, expansive, bold, gothic in his style"; it is no wonder that he has encountered, both in America and abroad, "the hostility of simpering elegance and dainty imbecility." This real man was the creator of "the true Democratic School of Nature."[28]

The night Macready took the Astor Place stage in *Macbeth* in May, 1849, Forrest was a few streets away acting the muscular, pugilistic *Gladiator*, by American playright Robert Montgomery Bird (who authored several other plays as vehicles for Forrest).[29] Forrest apparently gave no support to the disruptors. At the Astor Place Opera House, most of the seats had been secured by "the hard-handed multitude, who had made the strife an affair of classes and were bent on putting down the favorite of what they called the kid-gloved and silk-stockinged gentry."[30]

Macready's entrance was met by a chorus of heckling: "'Three groans for the codfish aristocracy!' and 'Down with the English hog!'" Eggs, potatoes, apples, coins, pieces of wood, a shoe, and gallery chairs finally drove

Macready from the stage.[31] When prominent New Yorkers prevailed upon him to assay a second performance, determined that the mob not prevail, those outside the theater threw paving stones and tried to rush the entrance. The performance went on, and the militia fired on the mob. "The law by its armed force vindicated its authority at the cost of this frightful tragedy, and taught the passionate and thoughtless populace a lesson which it is to be hoped no similar circumstances will ever call for again."[32] In the meantime, Alger was at Harvard, nostalgic for tragedy performance in ancient Athens.

It was hardly accidental that a cherished dime novel author figured in the Astor Place Riots, highlighting as it does the association between story paper, dime novel, and melodrama genres. For the story papers frequently engaged in "the utilization, by paraphrasing them, of pieces which are having a successful run at the theatres... Reversing a common process, they are not 'dramatized for the stage,' but narrativized for the story paper."[33]

The crossing of theatrical melodrama and dime novels meant that "reading became a way of preserving and recapturing a public moment or a favorite performance." Melodramas, dime novels, and story papers shared common audiences and often a common body of stories. And the split that was emerging between melodrama and legitimate theater was reproduced in the split between sensational and genteel fiction.[34]

For antebellum advice manual authors, the theater was often taken to be a categorically evil influence—a school of vice, where those, especially of the feebler sex, listen to the suggestion of the seducer; and where, even the mere presence of crowds was likely to produce disease from the impurity of the atmosphere.[35] For other members of the middle classes in midcentury, it was the working-class theater that constituted the problem. "Art and cultural consumption . . . [were] fulfil[ing] a social function of legitimating social differences."[36]

Just as the author disapproved of and rectified habits and speech patterns that, in his view, demarcated differences in life chances, he tended to boycott the melodramas. The boy who goes to the Bowery or other place of amusement in lower Manhattan is usually drubbed. At best, it is a waste of money for poor boys who would do better saving. The message about delayed gratification is given at a time when working-class audiences were often passionately involved in the theater; toward the end of the century, "some men and women who earned only ten dollars a week in the sweatshops reportedly spent half of it on tickets."[37]

When *Paul, the Peddler* takes his mother and invalid brother to Barnum's Museum, they see what Alger considers a good class of play—*Uncle Tom's Cabin*. "Niblo's Garden, the New York Circus and Wallack's, where a gallery seat cost thirty cents and London successes were often performed, were places occasionally visited by the boys."[38] However, boys attending the theater more frequently go to the Old Bowery or Tony Pastor's, a somewhat different class of establishment. And Tony Pastor's was early vaudeville, considered by many to be morally inoffensive.[39] But here, in *Alger's* Pastor's, "from his seat in the pit," the unreformed hero "indulged in independent criticism of the acting, as he leaned back in his seat and munched peanuts, throwing the shells about carelessly."[40] Critics had been complaining of "the music of cracking peanuts" in American theatrical performances since at least the 1830s.[41]

When a late Alger hero decides to indulge himself by accompanying a friend to one of these suspect theater establishments, he is the ingenue who cannot separate fact and fantasy. When the stage villain throws the heroine from a bridge into the water, the hero is ready to jump onto the stage to save the fair maiden and "punish the brutal ruffian"; he finds it difficult to believe the characters are friends in real life. His accomplished companion knows it is merely play-acting, but points out another in the theater who "believes in it as much as you do," and who is crying. The companion says to Dean: "I envy you, Dean. You enjoy the play much better than I do, for you believe in it while I know it for a sham—that is, I know t's merely play-acting," but Dean does not, in fact, enjoy the world of fantasy.[42] For the hero, it is a "problem" to think the things on stage real. The hero does not participate in the realm of the audience nor they in his. He is of a different class.

Such audience response replays that of an infamous midcentury French "heroine," Emma Bovary, at a considerably more respectable performance. Attending *Lucia di Lammermoor*, Emma

> thought [Edgar] must have inexhaustible supplies of love in
> him to lavish it upon the crowd with such effusion. All her
> attempts at critical detachment were swept away by the
> poetic power of the acting, and, drawn to the man by the
> illusion of the part, she tried to imagine his life—extraordi-
> nary, magnificent, notorious, the life that could have been
> hers if fate had willed it. If only they had met! He would
> have loved her, they would have travelled together through
> all the kingdoms of Europe from capital to capital, sharing
> in his success and in his hardships, picking up the flowers
> thrown to him, mending his clothes . . . She longed to run to
> his arms, to take refuge in his strength, as in the incarnation
> of love itself, and to say to him, to cry out, "Take me away!
> carry me with you! let us leave! All my passion and all my
> dreams are yours!" The curtain fell.[43]

Alger's advice to readers not to spend their money at the Old Bowery or other theaters where melodrama played can be seen in light of his early views, expressed in "Athens in the Time of Socrates." Alger objects to these melodramatic performances just as he and others would object to dime novels, precisely because they encourage their [class] audience to make mistakes between fact and fiction. People who live in the world of fantasy play the lottery and blame others for their bad luck. Fantasy tends to passivity or even criminality—it is not part of a world in which active individuals take responsibility for improving their chances.

Worse than mere amusement, melodrama encouraged sensationalism, pandered to the lowest tastes of the masses, and occasioned mistakes between fact and fantasy. By contrast to tragedy, melodrama's "theme and scene lay in the middle or lower class and in a limited sphere." The Melodramatic Medley, a degenerate branch of the romantic school of acting, "has a nameless herd of followers . . . it has no system and is but instinct and passion let loose and run wild"; it yields "its mushroom crops of empiric sensationalists."[44] Such amusements are not like harmless circuses and magician shows. Alger's objection to the theater is reserved for the theater of the lower classes.

Alger refused to grant the differentiation of class audiences, habits, and tastes that was increasingly visible in theater and literature. The battle over entertainments was part of a broader struggle over culture—a battle in which Alger's fiction became embroiled. Difference posed a challenge to the assertion that "we are all of the same estate."[45] The author of *Ragged Dick* was far from alone in this attempt to make out of many one; it became a central battle of the age:

> Cleavage of classes, cleavage of races, cleavage of faiths! an inextricable confusion. And the voice of democracy, crying aloud in our streets: "Out of all this achieve brotherhood! achieve the race to be."[46]

CONSTRUCTING A COMMON DISCOURSE: EDUCATION, ETHNICITY, AND LANGUAGE

> If two men belonging to the same society have the same interests and, to some extent, the same opinions, but their characters, education, and style of civilization are different, it is highly probable that the two will not be harmonious. The same observation applies to a society of nations.
>
> Alexis de Tocqueville, *Democracy in America*, Vol. 1

Unity of culture implied the construction and maintenance of a common discourse, a discourse of shared language, values, and understandings. Culture was essential to the unity and continued virtue of the Republic; it must therefore be transmitted to the young. Culture was "an idea of how they [people] ought to behave and did not." Culture included "polite manners, respect for traditional learning, appreciation of the arts, and above all an informed and devoted love of standard literature."[47]

Education was a major battleground in the fight for unity of culture in American democracy. "All our material advantages would be worth little without a moral and intelligent people to make a proper use of them," proclaimed a turn of the century high school text.[48]

If not all would acquire classical education in the new era, they at least must know value when they saw it; they must acknowledge and strive to make contact with genteel culture. Alger's street youth must either have an instinctive sense of high and low, or else undergo conversion. For Alger treats the emergence of class differences as problems of habit and character formation. The struggle over [class] habits is viewed as a threat to character development that furthermore threaten to break the Republic into many parts.

The young who fail to modestly prosper may have acquired bad habits that make them unworthy of notice. If these bad habits include gambling, drinking, smoking, theft, and lying, they also include use of improper English, bad reading habits, and selection of questionable theatrical entertainments. Alger's editorial comments, exhortations to moral reform, and declamations against selfishness sometimes address these problems. Those who frequent class-specific amusements, violate genteel morality, and who use (or consume via reading) a private language of shared meaning that excludes outsiders are thereby kept from rising in the world. Their habits constitute their class, are the explanation of their class.

Here is the palliative for the growing disparities of fortune and culture in the Gilded Age.[49] All other indicators of class position—occupation, the relationship of labor and leisure, one's relationship to the clock, and to an employer—are fluid.

But what *kind* of unity was to be achieved? The general presumption was assimilation, conformity, and inculcation of the values of elites. Educated members of the community would be standard bearers for the rest. The past and its values were considered indispensable in the modern world; what was to be taught was virtually unquestioned, immutable. If some in the latter part of the nineteenth century had doubts about "traditional humanistic education as snobbish, useless, and out of keeping with the modern age," Alger, the Harvard-educated classics scholar was not a likely educational reformer.[50]   The recipe for erasing difference lay in the maintenance of standards.

His democratic hero pays his respects to traditional elites. Those Alger boys who have pursued college preparatory coursework at private academies before being thrown onto their own resources may triumph by going to college. They invariably attend seats of liberal arts education such as Yale, Harvard, and Columbia.

When Alger's fiction attempted to expand his audience's educational horizons, it was through the incorporation of classic literature, foreign language lessons, foreign phrases, and puns requiring some cultural literacy to capture. On the eve of the new century, the author advised a young *Tribune* friend: "I decidedly recommend your learning to read French easily. I can't remember the time when I couldn't read it with ease after 13," and offered to lend the young man the money to study.[51]

All central characters acknowledge and defer to the values and standards of moral—not financial—elites. Expansion of wealth does not generate an alternative set of values. Even boys without college prospects acknowledge the value of a classical education and attempt to acquire some of the rudiments. Boys seeking to improve themselves study at night, buy books, learn Latin and French and other liberal arts subjects. They also work on penmanship, grammar, writing, and mathematics, which frequently help them obtain employment. Humanistic education, however acquired, is valuable education, and yields that self-improvement, which is a moral obligation.

"It is no good pretending," Tocqueville wrote after his first American tour, "that the English race has not established an immense preponderance over all the other Europeans in the New World. It is far superior to them in civilization, industry, and power."[52] But what will become of America as these other Europeans become more numerous? Tocqueville, in 1854, thought that the increase of those "not of the Anglo-Saxon race is the great danger to be feared in America—a danger which renders the final success of democratic institutions a problem as yet unsolved."[53] Like most of his contemporaries, Alger accepted the superiority of the Anglo-American in an age of increasing ethnic heterogeneity.

Alger's heroes almost inevitably have impeccable white, Anglo-Saxon, Protestant backgrounds, as evidenced by their unmistakable names.[54] The world his characters encounter is witness to Western European immigration, but there is rather shallow stereotyping of most immigrants. Irish boys and women (especially in the New York stories) are often drunken or thieving and lacking in ambition; Scottish accents are inevitably accompanied by comments about thrift. The Jews do not appear as recent immigrants, but they are routinely cast as wealthy money lenders or villains.[55] There are occasional appearances by formerly enslaved blacks, Italian boys who have barely begun to be assimilated, American Indians, and Chinese in the western stories. Blacks tend to be heavily stereotyped, treated as decent though simpleminded children, often owning awkward Latinate names. Although he displayed empathy toward his rare Irish or Italian hero and toward Chinese characters who figure in some western stories, Alger nonetheless felt compelled to erase difference.

Heroes are not just "any boys" but boys who still lay claim to America. They are the culturally or ethnically privileged. The author, who could almost date his lineage to the Mayflower, appears attuned to preserving their opportunities in a time of rapid change. Only by becoming like *his* Anglo-Saxon Protestant heroes can newcomers hope to rise.

Language was another means of promoting homogenization of culture, and Alger was a participant in the battle over language. Through language, one exhibited a powerful sense of loyalty to a group and its aspirations, and potentially expressed conflict with other social groups with different linguistic forms.[56] Only liminal characters in Alger's fiction retain noticeable dialects or jargon. Language was a class marker.

In one of the rare cases where Alger's hero is other than a native-born American boy of Anglo-Saxon heritage, standard English is at issue. Andy Burke, *Only an Irish Boy*, "always indulged in the brogue more than usual under exciting circumstances." He otherwise tends to speak standard English with only a few "speech-tags" thrown in. Although Andy's education is improved, he never completely loses his brogue, the mark of difference. We are told by a republican-minded wealthy man that "Some of our most distinguished men have been Irish boys or of Irish descent"; however, Andy's own advancement comes largely through a bequest from this very-same friend.[57]

Alger was most popular when writing of the newsboys and bootblacks of New York in the "Ragged Dick" series. He prided himself on bringing the plight of these street children to the attention of the public and to reformers. In doing so, he attempted to approximate their street language and lifestyles. Observation of life makes better fiction:

> I hold that a novelist, or writer of fiction, is best situated in a large
> city, where he has an opportunity to study life in many phases,
> and come in contact with a large variety of types of character. The
> experience of prominent American and foreign novelists, nota-
> bly of Charles Dickens, will bear me out in this statement.[58]

But Alger was no Dickens. Twenty years his junior, Alger lacked Dickens's powers of aural and visual observation: "Dickens' greatest natural gift was his ear." The English author had an intense interest in spoken language, and his idiolects were private, character-specific, speech patterns.[59] Dickens's characters exhibit many idiosyncratic speech patterns; Alger has a few stock patterns of nonstandard speech to which he constantly recurs. These reflect ethnic stereotypes and class.

Moreover, when Alger uses street children in his stories, their rough edges are shown in much the same way as were those of *Pygmalion*'s Eliza Doolittle. Children who spoke vernacular, slangy, "street" English always learned standard English on the path to rehabilitation; success required the acquisition of speaking patterns characteristic of a higher class.

On American shores, Mark Twain is sometimes credited with the revolutionary accomplishment of downwardly transcending the genteel tradition. Vernacular spokesmen take over the narrative as straight characters drop out. In *The Adventures of Huckleberry Finn*, academically correct, exalted speech was systematically linked "with hypocrisy, self-dramatization, fraudulent claims to status, cynicism, and cruelty, all radiating outward... from the institution of slavery."[60] Alger's endorsement of correct and even stilted English stood in stark contrast to the language of the dime novels, and in contrast, too, to Mark Twain.

What were, in Alger's lifetime, skirmishes would soon erupt into warfare. In a few short decades, American colleges abolished Alger's language of discourse. Greek and Latin requirements fell; accepted moral philosophical truths disappeared.[61] The behavioral revolution's search for a value-neutral social science was followed by deconstruction of texts and by multiculturalism. As difference and distance deepened in America, the battles over standard English, English first, cultural and ethical relativism spilled outside the academy and became increasingly politicized.

Entertainments

Authors are quick to see in what direction public taste secretly inclines, and they trim their sails accordingly. The drama, which first gave an indication of the literary revolution in store, soon brings it to completion. If you want advance knowledge of the literature of a people which is turning toward democracy, pay attention to the theater.

Tocqueville, *Democracy in America*, Volume 2

Entertainment was a battleground of culture and class. Forms of amusement—from circuses to evening parties to theaters—were much discussed by the guardians of culture. If parents, guardians, clergymen and other traditional representatives of the moral authority of the community thought that the young were *theirs*, ownership was nevertheless being challenged by "that whole race of men, whose camp is the Theatre, the Circus, the Turf, or the Gaming-table . . . a race whose instinct is destruction . . ."[62] This battle against power and seduction was also a battle about class culture.

Alger was an active participant in this struggle over pleasure. He is not, however, a critic of mere amusements that he considers innocent; one youth is a circus rider, others sing for their living, and a few take part in (legitimate) stage performances. Alger heroes attend magic shows, circuses, evenings of music performed by whistlers or bird imitators, and picture shows put on by travelling professors with stereopticons. Most tracts raising the subject of recreations and pleasure were not concerned with any simple repression of recognised pleasures, but with defining, regulating, and locating them in their appropriate sites. One frequent concern was to shift pleasures from the site of mass activity (fairs, football matches with unlimited players, carnivals verging on riot) to the site of private and individualized activity.[63]

For Alger as well, the pleasures of hearth and home, of a good book and good companionship were better than public spectacle. Good entertainments frequently take place in the parlor. Heroes who gravitate to the city retain a suspicion of the city's pleasures; as another noted, "The 'pleasures' associated with the city have been historically dubious, to say the least."[64]

Certain types of musical performance, appreciation, and instruments differentiate classes in space and taste. In *Shifting for Himself*, a very young boy of a wealthy family, eschewing parlor music, voices his preference for the hand organ. His sister taunts him: "Shall you go around with it . . . or only keep it in the parlor for the entertainment of visitors?" As her brother defends his taste, Laura asks Gilbert "Did you ever see such a barbarian?"[65] This instrument of street musicians is not part of the discourse of middle-class music. The boy will surely become properly socialized.

Some entertainments are more edifying than others. In an early Alger tale, *Ben, the Luggage Boy* is welcome to attend a sacred concert with his sister at Steinway Hall, located in the Bowery.[66] When the music is divested of its religious trappings, Gilbert Grayson is ushered into a classical music concert at the same hall in *Shifting for Himself*. Classical concerts were becoming important public occasions, linking the bourgeois family to bourgeois society:

> Shared tastes became symbolic of shared class interests, and concerts were public displays of a particular sort of exclusive community. (And thus they provided a suitable setting for courtship—all the young people on display could be guaranteed eligible.) Artistic judgments were, in other words, tied up with questions of status.[67]

It is surely not because the ticket was free that Gilbert was at liberty to attend the Steinway Hall amusement. Heroes, invited to theater entertainment by boys not much better off than themselves, frequently decline. The quality and perceived moral effect of the entertainment are at issue. A classical concert in a hall with reserved seats—all markers of middle- or even aristocratic class amusements—make this the proper form of amusement for Gilbert. Attending *and* appreciating a classical music performance in such a setting reveals Gilbert to be a member of the natural aristocracy.

FICTION WARS

I wish I had something to read . . . some nice dime novel like 'The Demon of the Danube.' That was splendid. I like it a good deal better than Dickens. It's more excitin'.

Sam in Alger, The Young Outlaw

One of the most important Gilded Age struggles over habits, tastes, morals, and class markers took place in the arena of reading. Expansion of literacy, proliferation of newspapers and magazines, extension of the market for literature created new readers and new opportunities for the reading public to shape their cultural universe. In the struggle over reading, many guardians of genteel culture found it difficult to recognize and impossible to accept that we were no longer—if we had ever been—of one estate.

The advent of nationally distributed, inexpensive, mass-produced literature was a dubious blessing. As audiences were increasingly differentiated by place, taste, and status, a common response to the "threat" of differentiation was to attempt to suppress or obliterate that which did not conform to the expectations and moral universe of genteel custodians. The antidemocratic response of a paternalistic elite purported to guide the malleable toward a better life. Alger's own difficulties with the guardians of culture point up his different—and more democratic—posture toward moral leadership.

Some of the discourse about the place of fiction in the reading diet of average Americans appears to be a continuing dialogue with Rousseau and, for that matter, Plato. The argument about the potential harm of fiction—especially sensational fiction—is an argument about virtue and citizenship. The corrupting fruits of the same progress that brings popular fiction include luxury, vice, artificiality, and longing for the newest fad. How does one educate Emile, the simple but virtuous citizen? What are the effects of sentimental or sensational fiction upon the tastes and morals of the citizen? How can community be preserved? How can the Republic maintain unity, a hierarchy of values, public-spiritedness?

Perhaps virtue would be more secure if average citizens had no fiction at all, for they seem not to be able to differentiate between fact and fancy. It stimulates them to seek excitement and adventure rather than cultivate solid virtues. This was, in fact, the posture of the most conservative and fearful cultural guides.

Fiction Pure and Simple?

Certain reading was a bad habit, threatening to become a class marker. The terms available to identify this fiction reading included false, unrealistic, cheap, low quality, harmful, and sensational.

When Alger introduces Sylvanus Snodgrass, who writes serialized stories such as "The Ragpicker's Curse" in *Ben Bruce*, "Ben was not much of a judge of literature, but it didn't seem to him that this title suggested a high order of literary merit." Snodgrass haughtily asserts that [William Dean] Howells "couldn't write a story for the *Weekly Bugle*. There isn't excitement enough in his productions . . . They lack snap and fire."[68]

The claim is that story paper audiences would find highbrow fiction—especially the output of an author becoming noted for literary realism—lacking in excitement. Story paper audiences wanted action, passion, and sensationalism. In one of Snodgrass's serialized stories, "there were no less than fifteen murders."

Although Snodgrass says "I know just what the public want," this time, the standard of public opinion is found lacking. Just as Alger had hinted when he wrote of Greek comedy, American newspapers, and Eugène Scribe, he disapproves of pandering to the lowest tastes of the public.[69] And yet, he is patronizing and laughs at Snodgrass, rather than condemn him.

Snodgrass fails in his attempt to get Ben to invest some of his new fortune by starting a new literary weekly after the style of the *Bugle*. While Ben's primary excuse is "I don't believe in going into any business which I don't understand," there is no evidence he understands any business at this point besides selling newspapers and possibly acting in plays.[70] The objection is surmountable when someone of admirable character makes the investment proposition. Ben does not find this undertaking worthy and will not encourage the proliferation of such stuff. *Ben Bruce* appeared in Munsey's *Golden Argosy*, an inexpensive juvenile magazine with a newspaper-like texture. It did not appear in the story papers.

Moral leaders advised readers to avoid literature that inclined them toward bad company or to resort to haunts of vice and dissipation; "a person may be ruined by reading a single volume."[71] Good company in books was as important as good company in persons. History and biography could be recommended. History was still about teaching morality and culture.[72] The classics served the same purpose.

Reading for improvement, then, was far differently viewed than reading for amusement. As T. S. Arthur counseled:

> Self-education is something very different from mere reading by way of amusement. It requires prolonged and laborious study. The cultivation of a taste for reading is all very well; but mere reading does little toward advancing any one in the world—little toward preparing him for a higher station than the one he fills.[73]

Alger heroes' reading tends to their self-improvement. They read works of history and biographies of famous Americans such as Franklin. Boys would also be improved, Alger thought, with his own fictionalized biographies of Webster, Lincoln, and Garfield. Real heroes deserved to be imitated, pirates and outlaws did not.

The boys also read what the author considered high quality fiction. They read works such as "*Pilgrim's Progress, Robinson Crusoe*, the novels of Scott and Dickens, and the juvenile works of Oliver Optic and Horatio Alger, Jr."[74]

But what demarcated high quality fiction? Fiction that participated in the "real" was distinguished from fiction pure and simple. To illustrate, let us look in on a late Alger hero's crusade against poor literature.

Hero Frank Hardy is a travelling book salesman in *The Young Book Agent*. He attempts to save Bobby Frost, a tired and hungry boy who is running away from his good and comfortable home to make his fortune in the city. Bobby wants to imitate the hero of "A book they called a five-cent library. It had a colored picture on the cover. The story was called 'Clever Carl; or, From Office Boy to Millionaire.'"[75] Carl "went to the city and helped a Wall Street man, and got to be worth three million dollars." Frank responds: "Don't you know *all such stories are fiction pure and simple*" (italics mine).

This is clearly news to poor Bobby, who responds: "Fiction? What do you mean?" He is completely crestfallen when told:

> They are not true. If Carl went to the city it's more than likely he'd have to work as hard as anybody to make a living. Of course, he might, in the end, become a millionaire, but the chances are a million to one against it.

In New York, Bobby will be lucky to find any sort of job at two or three dollars per week; "thousands of boys are looking for work every day without finding it." Frank continues: "My advice to you is, to turn around and go home . . . If you get to New York more than likely, unless you have money, you'll starve to death." Bobby returns to home and school. Some time later, when Frank re-encounters the prodigal, he tells Bobby: "I think you'll make more of a fortune around home than in the city." When the boy admits that he has "given up reading those trashy five- and ten-cent libraries," Frank responds, "that's a good job done."[76] Bobby needs a lesson in the difference between truth and fiction.

This literature was not designed to be "fiction pure and simple." The author made repeated claims of relevance for his fiction, just as he made claims about its truthfulness to life. Alger frequently prefaced his works with the hope that the experience of his hero would serve as an example to young boys. Readers are expected to believe that some part—in fact a great deal—of the hero's experience is relevant to their own life experiences. Alger frequently reminded his young readers that characters were drawn from real life. *Student and Schoolmate,* the journal for boys that first serialized early Alger stories such as *Ragged Dick, Fame and Fortune, Tattered Tom, Rough and Ready, Rufus and Rose,* and *Paul, the Peddler* would echo him, fondly advertising how true to life Alger stories were.

In one of the few articles the author wrote about his own work, he responded to the question "Are My Boys Real?" for *The Ladies' Home Journal*:

> The idea is suggested that young people will be interested to learn whether the boy characters in my books are taken from real life. I answer in general terms that I have always preferred to introduce real boys into my stories, and have done so in many instances where it has been possible for me to find a character suited to a plot.[77]

In writing the "Ragged Dick" series, "The materials were gathered by myself at first hand."[78] Alger avers that he knew the Johnny Nolan and Micky Maguire characters from *Ragged Dick,* changing the name of the latter, and that there was a boy with the name "Ragged Dick," but he did not know the boy who bore it. Similarly, he claims he knew the heroes of *Rough and Ready; Ben; the Luggage Boy;* and characters in other of his novels. "I had conversations with many street boys while writing 'Ragged Dick' and 'Tattered Tom' series, and derived from many of them sketches of character and incidents." *Phil, the Fiddler* is not only flesh and blood, but was even photographed for the novel by a Broadway photographer. "I have, by request, given to many of my characters the real names of young friends without necessarily making them portraits."[79]   In Alger's work, current events, real personages, and real locations interlope on fictional journeys.

This kind of veracity, however, did exempt Alger fiction from the same criticism with which story papers were met. Story papers and dime novels deliberately blurred the distinction between fact and fiction, somewhat like the modern tabloids and television tabloids. Many dime novel authors were newspaper reporters and editors, and frequently constructed plots from events reported in newspapers around the country.[80]

Street & Smith, publisher of many Alger novels, suggested to one of their dime writers (as they sometimes suggested ideas to Alger) that he "in future stories make no special effort to produce an unusual plot, but stick closer to the action and incident, taken as much as possible from newspapers, which are teeming with material of this character." The author subsequently kept careful files of newspaper clippings for raw material.[81]

An Alger contempory noted that one attribute of story paper literature provided a "model in boldness to over-timid romancers at large":

> It is the actual introduction of living persons, whose names and addresses are in the directory, selected from any that may be prominent before the community. Sometimes the adventures in which they figure are said to be facts, but oftener they are as the chronicler pleases.

Handsome actors, child actresses, police officials, and even "the resident Turkish minister" have figured in such stories.[82] Alger himself admitted, "I am often indebted for characters and incidents to paragraphs in the daily press.   Whenever I find one that seems available, I follow the example of Charles Reade, and cut it out for future reference."[83]

The story paper audience was invited to believe—or was not discouraged from believing—the veracity of the tales that filled the pages. Story paper literature, Alger's included, blurred the distinction between fact and fiction just as did melodramatic theater.

When Life Imitates Art

Following in the footsteps of Peter Parley's [Samuel G. Goodrich's] earlier tales for children, Alger sought to ensure that young people knew the difference between "fact and fancy" in their world.[84] Otherwise, they might do foolish things.

Alger drew the distinction between an interesting story and a sensational one, inveighing against the latter. While noting that there is "no objection to healthy excitement,"

> sensational stories, such as are found in the dime and half-dime
> libraries, do much harm, and are very objectionable. Many a boy
> has been tempted to crime by them. Such stories as "The Boy
> Highwayman," "The Boy Pirate," and books of that class, do
> incalculable mischief. Better that a boy's life should be humdrum
> than filled with such dangerous excitement.[85]

Foreshadowing the contemporary debate about violence on television, critics often held that stories affected behavior. Because boys are impressionable and identify with heroes and adventures, they run off from good homes to have adventures. The author of an 1879 *Atlantic* piece on story papers recounts several real cases in which boys foolishly imitate story paper heroes:

> Such stories are common. One day, it is three boys who are
> arrested in Patterson on their way to Texas, on the proceeds of a
> month's rent they have been sent to pay, but have appropriated
> instead. Another, three Boston boys do us the honor to believe
> that more adventures are to be found in New York than at home,
> and arrive with a slender capital of four dollars and a half to seek
> them; are robbed of even this by more knowing gamins of the
> place, and spend several nights in the station-house before they
> can be reclaimed . . .[86]

As early as 1865, Alger's readers watch in bemusement as minor figures model their lives and actions after characters in the story papers and dime novels. Paul Prescott's co-worker fashions his feelings about love on the model of a character in "the great story that's coming out in the Weekly Budget." His stilted language of love, his loss of appetite, his emotions are based on what he reads. As the young man reads passages from the paper, Paul, unfamiliar with the story, is amused.[87] The young man reminds one of a famous character from the previous decade, Emma Bovary. Needless to say, such affectation does not help the young man woo his beloved.

A few years later, *The Young Outlaw* (1875) was an unlikely Alger hero. Sam has so many bad [class] habits that his resurrection requires a sequel, *Sam's Chance* (1876). One of Sam's bad habits is dime novel reading. When first we meet him, his new, straight-laced guardian asks him if he had read the Bible. Sam retorts: "No, but I've read the life of Captain Kidd. He was a smart man, though." A pirate is, to Sam, a great man. When bought a catechism, Sam is disappointed that there are no pictures, and says he would rather the deacon get him that book, "pointing to a thin pamphlet copy of 'Jack, the Giant-Killer.'"[88] Sam has obviously acquired very bad literary habits. Unhappy with having to work hard, Sam regrets the absence of a dime novel to read when released to his room under pretense of illness (quoted at the outset of the Fiction Wars section). The influence of a good boy of strong character finally turns him toward the path of rehabilitation—a journey that even brings him into contact with the boys of Harvard College.

Alger's fiction is replete with such examples. New York street boys heading west for resettlement by the Children's Aid Society discuss the dime novel "Pathfinder Pete; or, The Wild Hunter of the West." They are ready to take on wild animals, armed with the "superior knowledge" of the comrade "who had had the great privilege of reading the instructive story of 'Pathfinder Pete.'"[89] Such stories arm them with much misinformation and false bravado.

More serious is a later case, Guy Gladstone, a boy from a good family who runs away from home to hunt Indians in the West in *Dean Dunham*. He is imitating "Daredevil Dick, the Young Hunter of the Rio Grande." In search of excitement and glory, Guy says: "They'll [my parents] be proud enough of me, when they read about my exploits. Maybe there'll be a play written about me. When I get home I shouldn't mind going round, playing in it myself."[90] Guy is later found selling papers in Denver without money enough to go home.

This boy's conflation of dime novels and melodramatic plays is reinforced in *The Young Book Agent*, where we meet another boy whose head is filled with the nonsense of cheap fiction, this time, the melodrama. He is studying to be an actor by learning and acting parts from "a three-act melodrama called 'The Lost Pot of Diamonds; or, Adrift on the Streets of London.'" The farm boy tells Frank "It's a corker," which is Alger's way of telling us the boy does not speak proper English—he speaks slang. The piece he is "speakin'" is a book he bought from another for ten cents: "It's a great theater piece." Frank advises: "Better give up acting and take to minding the cows," but the stagestruck boy does not listen.

Although his mother destroys this theatrical melodrama as "worthless trash," clearly Alger blames her for poisoning the family. She brings out "half a dozen cheap cloth-covered novels" for Frank to examine for possible repurchase. They belong to a class of literature Frank would not touch ("They would not be worth twenty-five cents to me, madam"). Bad family habits have exerted their influence on the young son.[91]

Alger exhorted his audience to a better class of literature. Alger heroes would not be caught dead reading dime novels. They are not swayed by story paper fiction. In an unusual case in which Alger lets pass unnoticed an admission by one of his boys of good character that he read the story papers, it is clear that the boy did not confuse fact and fantasy:

> When I used to read the stories of high life in England in
> some of the New York story-papers, I never imagined that
> it would be my lot to become acquainted with any of the
> English aristocracy, but it has come about.[92]

Alger recognized that common readers—members of the lower orders—
tend to model their lives after characters in melodramas, dime novels, and
story papers. He warns readers not to do so on the basis of cheap fiction. And
yet, he seems to be counting on almost precisely this reaction.

Alger's output remained essentially in the *genre* of the melodrama, with
its stark contrast between good and evil and in which the virtuous triumph
and wicked characters are defeated. However, he proffers only morally
upright heroes. If the audience models its behavior upon that of the hero—
and he repeatedly urges them to consider the hero an inspiring example for
their lives—then could he not reinforce traditional values and/or reform
individuals in his audience?

So long as the forces of law and morality were at center stage and won
out against the criminal element in action-packed adventure, was this not
enough to be on the right side of the moral battle? Alger's works stood at the
boundary of what constituted safe reading; they were not alone. Publishers
might market their sometimes voyeuristic volumes as a way to *avoid*
harmful reading matter. In 1881, a subscription publisher advertised Allan
Pinkerton's *Professional Thieves and the Detectives* to potential subscribers as
"The Most Thrilling, Exciting and Fascinating Book of the Age," claiming:

> The old and young seek books of adventure, and if those of a
> truthful character are not found, they are apt to read TRASHY
> LITERATURE. In this view this work has a purpose which will
> commend it to every family. The adult can read it with profit, and
> the rising generation, by its pages, can see the value and necessity
> of avoiding the PATH OF EVIL. The name of PINKERTON is a
> WORD OF TERROR to the violators of the law throughout the
> land . . .[93]

The "truth" value of the Pinkerton volume lies in its moral message.
When Alger deplored fiction that seemed to offer "false pictures of life," he
was surely in earnest. For that which is most false leads people away from
virtue. As an advice author wrote, "Books are good or bad in their tendency,
as they make you relish the word of God, the more or the less after you have
read them."[94]

Manipulating the boundaries of fact and fiction, Alger hopes readers will
be inspired to virtue (character) through imitation. These stories are
designed to help readers "suspend their disbelief" and take their fiction out
into the world.

Alger has rather astutely been called "a ventriloquist using the dime format in order to reform working-class reading and culture." While using story papers, cheap magazines, and paper-covered books popular with the working classes, Alger was not so much speaking *for* readers of these vehicles as attempting to "recapture and reorganize working-class culture."[95] The language and voice are different, which stood to affect the success of Alger's moral enterprise.

More than the reformation of individuals was at stake. Could not fiction also reform *society*? Alger claimed, in the preface to *Phil, the Fiddler*, that he was the first to bring the attention of the plight of the children of the padrone system before the public; in fact, the New York press treatment of its horrors began around March, 1868 (*Phil* was published in 1872).[96] When Alger claimed that the padrone system "was effectually broken up, not only in New York but in all the large cities of America" within six months of publication of *Phil, the Fiddler*, he was fantasizing. Despite more than one statement Alger made claiming credit for the destruction of the padrone system, no contemporary source concurred, and there is evidence the system persisted for years.[97] Often, Alger seems to believe what he wishes were fact. Was the case of his hope for reforming readers comparable?

One modern critic argues that, though the working classes increasingly had access to Alger's work through the vehicle of cheap fiction, his later stories were far less successful in garnering a mass public than his more respectable "Ragged Dick Series" had been.[98] The working classes preferred stories such as *John Armstrong, Mechanic; Nemo, King of the Tramps; The Molly Maguires*, stories alongside which Alger's own appeared. Alger's declining sales and remuneration may tell us more about what the author was getting paid in an era of declining prices for magazines and cheap reprints than about who was doing the reading. If it were true that Alger had little influence over late-century working-class readers, then it was ironic that librarians and moral crusaders were so determined to remove his influence as reading became democratized.

Libraries: "a mere slop shop of sensational fiction"?

To say that calls for books should be accepted as the indications of what should be furnished, is to make their office [the office of the managers of the public library] a merely mechanical and perfunctory one.

In such communities as we are especially considering, adherence to such a principle as *this would make the library a mere slop shop of sensational fiction.*

William I. Fletcher, "Public Libraries in Manufacturing Communities"[99]

But what was the appropriate recourse? It was extremely unlikely that readers would willingly read that which they did not like. *They* retained some control over their own reading habits. A reader of the Department of the Interior's 1876 report on public libraries would learn, if they did not already know, that "Some of the larger manufacturing corporations have established extensive libraries for the use of their employés." One specifically mentioned contains 6,000 volumes, among which is to be found volumes of light reading as well as some of the best works in all departments.[100] But it was also clear to many of the reformers that the working classes suspected libraries of capitalist philanthropists; the mill workers of Pittsburgh raised questions about who would control the library Carnegie offered the city. Workers were not ready to cede control over culture to the genteel classes and were likely to "avoid a paper bearing the stamp of capital."[101]

Although Comstock fought for higher postal rates, a form of control over the use of the mails for dime and half-dime libraries, there appeared to be little control over what people read, apart from the internal scruples of publishers.

Some guardians of culture inside and outside the church continued to condemn all fiction during this era. There remained a residual distrust of all fiction, but these voices were receding. Religious leaders had conceded a place for moral fiction earlier in the century. The new tone is symbolized in Reverend William Rounseville Alger's apologia for writing the biography of Edwin Forrest.

If novels did not necessarily have a pernicious influence on morals, they were generally a waste of time. For many moral leaders, the best rule of thumb was:

> To make a proper selection in the midst of so much trash and
> poison, is so difficult a matter, especially to young and inexperi-
> enced persons, that he acts wisest, in my opinion, who inscribes
> upon this whole class of books, *touch not, taste not, handle not.*[102]

Alger himself shares some of the concerns of the famed moral crusader,
Anthony Comstock, who attacked dime novels and story papers as "a
symbolic universe so potent as to erase the real world from the minds of
readers, leading them to act out the scenes depicted in dime novels." But
Comstock went further than Alger's humor and exhortation, making God
the ally of censorship:

> The editor of the blood-and-thunder story papers, half-dime
> novels, and cheap stories of crime . . . [is] willingly or unwillingly,
> [among] Satan's efficient agents to advance his kingdom by
> destroying the young.[103]

With the moral panic concerning sensational fiction in the 1870s and
1880s, Alger's critics came to equate him more with the dime novelists and
story paper authors he attacked. The Comstock Crusades and American
Library Association waged war on writers such as Alger, Optic, Castlemon,
Ellis. Not all appreciated Alger's design for rehabilitating the boys of the
dangerous classes. Increasing attention to the reformation and direction of
reading habits accompanied the great expansion of libraries in the final
decades of the century. Whereas a range of opinion existed about what kind
of fiction should be permitted in the libraries, there was a rough consensus
that librarians should attempt to supervise and guide the reading of patrons,
minimizing the likelihood of harmful reading. Librarians were self-appointed
moral and cultural custodians of the Gilded Age.[104]

Among those most in need of direction were impressionable juveniles.
The American Library Association took up the subject of children's reading
in their annual meetings starting in 1882; the annual report of 1883 literally
declared war upon Alger, Optic, Castlemon, and Ellis: "Librarians must
therefore continue to carry the war . . . into the enemy's camp, and by their
very intrepidity enlist parents and teachers to their standard until the day
is won."[105]

Examining this discussion and debate in the *Library Journal* from 1876-
1904, one historian concluded that the majority of middle-class public
librarians "embarked upon an anti-Alger crusade." The crusade to remove
Alger's works from public library shelves scored some its first victories as
early as the late 1870s.[106]

If the era had had the literary equivalent of the movie rating system to
mark these works "PG" or "R," Tipper Gore's rock music warning labels, or
rules confining certain types of shows to late-night television, librarians

might have breathed more easily: "The public library ought not to furnish young persons with a means of avoiding parental supervision of their reading."[107] In an 1894 survey, some libraries reported issuing Alger books to adults only.[108]

Lurking behind these fears was often a belief, reiterated in recent years, that public institutions were undermining parental values and moral authority. Providing trashy and potentially harmful fiction sanctions the activity of reading it, just as sex education in schools suggests that public authorities are condoning adolescent sexual activity. Public distribution of the means of inflicting moral harm (popular fiction) encourages it, and is the nineteenth century equivalent of sterile needles for drug addicts and condoms for sexually active teens. Should the state, the Department of the Interior 1876 report on *Public Libraries in the United States of America* asks, provide citizens with the means for their own undoing? More than a mere survey of what people were reading and where, the Department of the Interior report had posed a question about the uses of *public resources* in the service of reading:

> Should an institution, supported by tax-payers to promote the general interests of the community, hasten to supply any books which people can be induced to ask for by unscrupulous puffs with which publishers fill the papers?[109]

Some contributors directly addressed the issue as one of government *subsidy* of indiscriminate or trashy published matter, prefiguring Jesse Helms's and Patrick Buchanan's indignation about federal support of "immoral" art. The mission of guardianship is unquestioned:

> Surely a state which lays heavy taxes upon the citizen in order that children may be taught to read is bound to take some interest in what they read; and its representatives may well take cognizance of the fact, that an increased facility for obtaining works of sensational fiction is not the special need of our country at the close of the first century of its independence.[110]

Where limited resources prohibit exhaustive inclusiveness, libraries "seeking only to adapt their supplies to a temporary and indiscriminating demand" are blameworthy.[111]

Sounding themes that would be echoed by opponents of bilingual education and multiculturalism in the public schools, some raised issues about the values the United States was promoting through its public expenditures for schooling:

> If it is held to be the duty of the State to supply boys and girls with dime novels, and the business of the schools to tax the

people that they may be taught to read them, public education is not quite as defensible as many persons have supposed.[112]

The 1875 examining committee of the Boston Public Library proclaimed: "The sole relation of a town library to the general interest is as a supplement to the school system; as an instrumentality of higher instruction to all classes of people."[113]

The preoccupation with reading habits extended to those impressionable newer readers of the working classes, who needed guidance every bit as much as did young readers. The "slop shop" image was invoked by a librarian writing about libraries in manufacturing communities in the 1876 government report. A Germantown, Pennsylvania librarian excluded *all* fiction from the library, fearing that factory girls would be be injured "by their false pictures of life."[114]

One complaint emphasized the "lite" nature of this reading matter; reading looked too much like entertainment and not like education. Furthermore, the reader is drawn away from demands of community; the craze for light reading leads to neglect of home and school:

> One teacher said to me . . . that her greatest bane in school was library books, she having to maintain constant warfare against them . . . she had frequently wished that there was not a public library within fifty miles! . . .[115]

The literary quality of the work was surely one issue. Echoing tastes of the literary realists, librarians pointed to the "melodramatic plots, wooden and incredible characters, and an absolutist conception of human nature." But mere juveniles, even of good quality, did not provide stimulating enough mental food for the young. The works were no improver of readers; they were for daydreamers. But, in general, standards for the inclusion or exclusion of works of fiction were based on moral, not aesthetic, judgments.[116]

Youth were also in danger from books which *did not* have "directly injurious tendencies":

> Many of the most popular juveniles, while running over with excellent "morals," are unwholesome mental food for the young, for the reason that they are essentially untrue. That is, they give false views of life, making it consist, if it be worth living, of a series of adventures, hair-breadth escapes; encounters with tyrannical schoolmasters and unnatural parents; sea voyages in which the green hand commands a ship and defeats a mutiny out of sheer smartness; rides on runaway locomotives; strokes of good luck, and a persistent turning up of things just when they are wanted,—all of which is calculated in the

> long run to lead away the young imagination and impart
> discontent with the common lot of an uneventful life.[117]

The lack of literary *realism*, so often noted by reviewers, influenced librarians' hostility to Alger and Optic. This literature painted false notions and impressions in the minds of malleable readers. If readers imitated art, they should only imitate what was highest and most real. Crusaders were afraid of the effects of this literature on behavior. But those who sought to censor it were fearful for *virtue*.

Frequently, the librarians claimed that the hero was too self-reliant, which threatened the family and the social order. Thus, "These books are likely to leave the impression upon the minds of the young that they can get along by themselves without the support and guidance of parents and friends."[118] These words are reminiscent of antebellum advice manuals written by the clergy, railing against those who would destroy the influence of the family and community upon the young boy—attacking the strangers among us and the confidence men in the big cities.

Librarians often viewed Alger heroes as too materialistic, too self-interested. Depicting phenomenal success (as would occasionally appear in Alger's later fiction) was not merely unrealistic. Readers would be made unfit for dealing with life's hard realities: "They are always waiting for some great and unexpected turn of fortune which will place them beyond their present surroundings in some lofty imagined sphere." These books place too much emphasis on selfish schemes to get rich quick, encouraging that "lack of honor which prompts the older person to make all he can at the expense of people less sharp than himself."

> Unless we realize that our children are absorbing from the very
> air to-day the false and debasing idea that "success" means
> "making money" . . . we shall not be the nursery of good
> citizenship we are meant to be.[119]

Some of the more liberal voices were reluctant to censor tastes when the reading matter did not endorse or tend to crime: "If those who cannot make use of any better reading than novels and stories and jokes are not furnished with these, they will not read at all, and this is a worse alternative."[120]

Young people must be admitted to the library, for "exclusion from the library is likely to be a shutting up of the boy or girl to dime novels and story papers as the staple of reading."[121]

A remarkably colorful point on this theme was made by the librarian who authored the "slop shop" remark at the head of this section. Writing of libraries in *manufacturing* communities, he insisted that patron calls for books need not constitute the criterion for what is to be furnished. Still, the conclusion was notably moderate:

. . . But in avoiding the Scylla of unlimited trash, the Charybdis of too high a standard must be equally steered clear of. Those who deprecate the free supply of such fictitious works as the public demands, are generally in favor of the entire exclusion of fiction of a sensational cast, a course which will unavoidably result in alienating from the library the very class most needing its beneficial influence. The old recipe for cooking a hare, which begins with "first catch your hare," may well be applied to the process of elevating the tastes of the uncultivated masses. Let the library, then, contain just enough of the mere confectionery of literature to secure the interest in it of readers of the lowest—not depraved—tastes; but let this be so dealt out as may best make it serve its main purpose of a stepping stone to something better.[122]

How can the elite "wean" young readers and working-class readers "from a desire for works of fiction," or from popular fiction? The Germantown, Pennsylvania librarian whose public library was founded in 1868, and who was cited a great deal in the report on *Public Libraries in the United States of America,* thought he knew. The juvenile section of his library "does not contain children's novels, Sunday school or others:"

On first joining the library, the new comers often ask for such books, but failing to procure them, and having their attention turned to works of interest and instruction, in almost every instance they settle down to good reading and cease asking for novels. I am persuaded that much of this vitiated taste is cultivated by the purveyors to the reading classes, and that they are responsible for an appetite they often profess to deplore, but continue to cater to, under the plausible excuse that the public will have such works.[123]

Readers seeking relaxation could read travel books. Librarians would substitute for parents:

As to the question of inducing readers to substitute wholesome reading for fiction, there is not great difficulty about it. It requires a willingness on the part of the caretakers to assume the labor of leading their tastes for a time. A very considerable number of the frequenters of our library are factory girls, the class most disposed to seek amusement in novels and peculiarly liable to be injured by their false pictures of life. These young people have, under our State laws, an education equal to reading average literature . . . According to our gauge of their mental calibre, we offer to select an interesting book for them. They seem often like children learning to walk; they must be led awhile, but they soon cater for themselves: we have thought but few leave because they cannot procure works of fiction.[124]

This view reflects a strong conservative tradition in library history, in which the library was seen as "a custodian of what was deemed to be worthy of preservation in life, literature and culture." In an era of rapid change and class diversification, these librarians talked of elevating tastes and of refusing to pander to demand. They claimed "that culture could be democratized without being vulgarized."[125]

But where were the parents, and why should it have fallen to public institutions to instill societal values? If we look to Alger's fiction for the kind of answer it provides to this question, we find that children with problems have poor parental role models. Mother reads cheap fiction, granny is a thief, father defrauds poor widows, or stepfather has yielded to alcohol. But even more frequently, the parent(s) are absent due to death or physical distance.

Unwittingly attesting to the "success" of the anti-Alger movement, a 1917 newspaper story caption claimed: "To-day a search for his stories is almost fruitless. Libraries everywhere have thrown out his works or are rapidly eliminating them from their shelves."[126] In an 1894 survey, "of 145 libraries, 34 did not carry Alger and 18 were allowing Alger books to wear out without replacement."[127]

How ironic that Alger employed character foils who wait for money to drop from the sky and who make money the measure of success. Alger had, himself, levelled this charge against bad fiction. It seems a striking irony that Alger, whose fiction so strongly argued *against* passivity, who rewarded the boy who remembered duties to family and community, and who reminded readers that great fortunes were unusual, had become a menace to the Republic.

Book removals did not always take place without protest in the press or protests reported in the press.[128] The removal of Alger novels from the Carnegie Free Library in Allegheny, Pennsylvania in 1896 provoked comment in the *Nation*, which had been critical enough of the quality of Alger's fiction, and in the *Library Journal* itself. The offending librarian defended himself:

> The books were the literary pablum of our fathers and mothers, perhaps, and hence are endeared by memory, but . . . it is a waste of time . . . to read them . . . their literary value is null, and . . . if they do not directly corrupt the morals, they certainly tend to corrupt the manners of the young and to give them false views of life.[129]

The American Library Association conventions continued to denounce Alger novels as "softening the brains" of even the wisest of men. By 1902, their offensive had been sharpened to the point that they would start claiming the novels were "harmful" and "bad".[130] However, just when the public library voted itself out of the slop shop business, sales of Alger novels began to increase rather appreciably, as dime and quarter prices were established. It was impossible to close Pandora's box.

The revival of Alger's works would be a relatively short-lived one, although there have been, in the twentieth century, other periods of briefly renewed interest. A 1917 source claimed: "To-day the name of Horatio Alger, Jr., has almost completely disappeared from the rolls of American writers." Few could even be found in new or second-hand book stores.[131] Beginning about this period, articles and surveys note—or bemoan—the fact that boys do not read Alger and may not even recognize his name. A 1950s author who believes his was the last generation brought up on Alger books and Alger virtues, argues that Alger, although a bad writer, has become "unreadable": "He no longer makes sense. The entire Alger success mythology, which we like to think a permanent part of the American character, is as dead as feudal chivalry."[132] Unread, perhaps, but now a symbol about America.

COERCED TASTE: ARE WE ALL ONE ESTATE?

> Could you, said he [Polemarchus], persuade men who do not listen?
>
> Plato, *The Republic*, Book I[133]

This fight may seem incomprehensible to modern readers, who find Alger's heroes bland and model boys. Most literary critics of the day did not question the *virtue* of Alger's heroes. But the genre, action-adventure formula, and vehicles of dissemination were red flags. And although Alger's fiction upheld many declining classes' values, the invocation to virtue employed the language of dollars. Standing at the margin between respectable and unrespectable literature meant standing in the middle of the battle.

The issue was how to exercise leadership in a democracy, and how democracies deal with cultural defection. The dilemma could be expressed as: Reason, force, persuasion, or end of conversation?

In the wars over theater and reading, the chief culprit was, again, the market. What could be done about culture and public virtue when the market respected tastes expressed as demand? Did not writers, publishers, advertisers, theater owners, and other purveyors of leisure owe their community the elevation—and surely not the debasement—of taste? How and where might elites intervene in the market, rather than allow people to "be induced to ask for" trash by "unscrupulous puffs with which publishers fill the papers?" How could they prevent demand from standing as the arbiter of value?

This felt like a desperate battle, indeed. As class differences were increasingly apparent, the anxiety increased. Could we all still be one estate? For those who felt a vital stake in the outcome, there were several possible responses. One was coerced tastes and standards, including demands for moral conformity, prohibition, and censorship—the route of the library movement.

One of the easiest answers, was, perhaps, expressible in market terms: Low price equals low value. Consumers get what they pay for. But if librarians used book *price* as an indication that cheap reading was aimed at the dangerous classes and the ignorant, their crusade was begun before Alger's works were widely available in paper covers or cheap reprints. Only cheap periodicals and story papers would yield obvious clues.

Conservative elites were quite willing to use the state as an instrument for the enforcement of morals and standards. Although the formulation was often negative—getting the public sector out of the business of subsidizing trash, either through libraries or through low postal rates—the state could make paternalistic determinations about value, teaching the fledgling child to walk. The 1992 presidential campaign rhetoric about the institutionalization of national standards and tests to cure the ills of the public education system continues this discourse. So, too, do the drug wars that seek to change tastes and behavior by removing evil influences.

Is a democracy obliged to give people what they want to hear or consume? For the moral guardians, the state is surely under no obligation to pander to the lowest tastes, and those in the private sector who do so are enemies of the Republic.

Not all were comfortable with censorship. There were growing efforts in this period to save the unredeemed through social reform, charity work, education and attempts to bring the uninitiated some small taste of the higher things of life.

Alger's solution was in part found here. Rather than tamper with the market, one should engage in consumer education. Sell candy but teach children to avoid junk food. Thus, teaching consumers to boycott the melodramas and dime novels would surely reduce the supply. And firm character is like an inoculation against such pestilence; mere contact would no longer cause infection.

Others, conceding the battle for unity and virtue, sought to insulate themselves into segmented societies of like-minded persons of taste or character.[134] They were, after all, the true citizens of the Republic. Those who emphasized class markers and difference in Alger's fiction were among such people; for Alger, they were would-be aristocrats and frauds. Dress, manners, residential neighborhoods, places of entertainment, and other indicators of difference could be used to identify those with whom one was safe; others would be screened out and off. Those truly worthy of respect kept up contact and conversation with any from the other orders who would listen.

The most optimistic believed we could be one estate, and that most humans were alike in seeking self-improvement, sharing the same desire as themselves. The right-thinkers constituted a critical mass and were not going to be undermined by the profligates. Danger did not justify exerting power over those who must ultimately build their own character. Here was Alger.

And in practice if not in rhetoric, here was Ronald Reagan, taking relatively few steps to use government to enforce moral rectitude, while offering verbal support to the moral majority's concerns. Like Reagan, who needed to retain the votes of young urban professionals who liked tax cuts but were unsympathetic to the moral agenda, Alger had to be purchased and heard in the marketplace. A leader in a democracy must also know how to follow.

Critics who feared the moral effects of sensational fiction or who argued for the removal of Alger's works from library shelves were more fearful for the Republic's virtue than was Alger. Unsure of the steady principles of their increasingly class-diversified readership, they echoed fears that sinister influences from without could—or invariably would—corrupt the young. They were more than agents of genteel culture; they were guarding the Republic against vice.

These librarians campaigned to preserve the purity of the Republic, fighting diversification of class, language, and culture by forceably demanding homogeneity. *They*, the natural elite, would lead where others proved unwilling.

The modern enemies of this Republic include the advocates of bilingual education or of multiculturalism, and the "politically correct." What all these have in common is that they challenge the values, culture, and language of privilege. Virtue is not predicated upon unity, nor does equality demand sameness.

That some discounted or misunderstood Alger's purpose—which was not so very dissimilar from theirs—was not just a question about how to read. It reflects two related differences.

First was their own pessimism that virtue could prevail. Alger was considerably more optimistic about the endurance of virtue—at least enough men of character could persevere to ensure the continuity of virtue in the Republic. Those who exhibited desirable moral qualities could continue to instruct by example and encouragement.

Second was a disagreement about whether natural elites need to coerce. Stern warnings, incarceration, and censorship were not part of his repetoire for the young. Fiction could, in Alger's view, educate and elevate the tastes and morals of readers through other means. But this fiction had first to begin with an understanding of the boys (and girls) whom it sought to reach. Alger prided himself on an ability to talk to youth with a natural love of adventure and excitement, and scoffed at model boys. The pedagogical point was that, to lead, one must begin where your audience is, demonstrating sympathy for them. Rollo can jettison Jonas.

Alger's fiction is paternalistic in its encouragement of virtue. But it is virtue by example, kindness, and occasional sermon—not force. Alger was, then, ultimately more committed to democracy: Citizens could be persuaded or encouraged to virtue without coercion, and would be better citizens for retaining their power and liberty.

Alger's engagement in the battle for genteel culture and morality has a democratic flair. Almost any boy (or girl)—unless depraved by nature—can participate in this culture if only they will. They can be heirs to the middle class. At a time when classes are being increasingly differentiated in wealth, life chances, residence space, language, culture, amusements, and reading tastes, we are all of one estate.

In the culture wars, the language at Alger's disposal to define the laudable or acceptable was largely forged by reference to what these were *not*. What *was* in good taste was still rather amorphous: *King Lear* and *The Gladiator*, Howells and Optic each had dignity in the dominant culture. In Alger's view, while there were gradients of quality, these were not principally about class. Those who insisted on exclusive or overly refined standards were merely pseudo-aristocrats and Eurocentric imitators. Indigenous literature and drama at least did not suffer from the sin of Anglo- or Francophilia.

Alger's fiction sought to bridge the gulf between classes in culture, society, economy, and polity. He interposed genteel culture *between* twin adversaries of selfish materialism and working-class culture. In doing so, he had to confront each. This task entailed the reconciliation of performance with nature, a redefinition of manliness and power, and a battle over the politics of theater and literature. Alger reworked social texts without supporting or legitimating the claims of working-class cultures, meanwhile lampooning aristocratic claims based on wealth or a culture of consumption.

13

The Fictional Republic: Alger's Appeal to the American Political Imagination

> Every fiction is supported by a social jargon, a sociolect, with which it identifies: fiction is that degree of consistency a language attains when it has *jelled* exceptionally and finds a sacerdotal class (priests, intellectuals, artists) to speak it generally and to circulate it.
>
> ... each jargon (each fiction) fights for hegemony; if power is on its side, it spreads everywhere in the general and daily occurrences of social life, it becomes *doxa*, nature: this is the supposedly apolitical jargon of politicians, of agents of the State, of the media, of conversation; but even out of power, even when power is against it, the rivalry is reborn, the jargons split and struggle among themselves. A ruthless *topic* rules the life of language; language always comes from some place, it is a warrior *topos*.
>
> Roland Barthes, *The Pleasure of the Text*[1]

Alger's fiction is replete with tension between industrialization and community, between glitter and substance, between self-interested men and those who recognize duty, and between those who attempt to make something out of nothing and those who make something of real value. These works act out economic, moral, social, and political struggles of the period. The spectrum of responses to disruption of lived experiences and understandings of the world—in these stories and in other narratives—

blend reactionary and potentially progressive critiques. Some responses are mobilized into politics, others are not; since classes are made, not found, it is not obvious in advance where apparently reactionary responses to industrialization may lead. E. P. Thompson discovers the sense of lost status and community, memories of a "golden age," value placed on independence, and social egalitarianism that shaped the worldview of radical leaders among the weavers in early nineteenth-century England.[2]

Classes and class fractions "remembering" traditional rights and values may use this language of tradition in forging a new oppositional perspective. For Thompson, one of the chief factors mobilizing remembrances into radical, political expressions of a new working class was the segregation of workers into separate communities—a system of apartheid and alienation of classes.[3] In the United States, many genteel moralists fought to retain these people who threatened to become a class apart. If some attempted to build bridges by lecturing to mechanics' societies or building libraries, writing religious tracts or leading revival movements, Alger built bridges with fiction.

The battle for the Republic had two domestic fronts in the Gilded Age. On one front was a struggle over culture, social distance, difference, and the grounds of discourse. Those who did not choose exit struggled over the terms on which common discourse could be maintained—terms on which all who wished could be part of the Republic. The other front crosscut the first. It was about the terms of participation in the emerging industrial order. The struggle, with a continuum of responses from accommodation to resistance, pitted independence and potency against dependence and powerlessness. Definitions of manliness were at stake.

As Alger and his contemporaries struggled to define and contain the terms on which these battles for the Republic would take place, they fought the politics of class in the language of virtue. And in the arena of production, the discourse, still morally charged, turned to power and gender.

Change, in the form of difference and distance, hierarchy and inequality, was addressed in at least four ways in the Gilded Age: by insulation and segregation, compulsory conformity, moral reform, and levelling. Some simply sought to isolate themselves into communities apart; we were not one estate.

In hands other than Alger's, the insistence that class distinctions of taste, habit, and culture be rendered meaningless could and would become an imperative—"Americanism."[4] Conformity to the standards of genteel culture, and to its morality, was required of an American. As industrial development helped shape the *unrecognizability* of some classes of citizens, those demanding conformity demanded that these classes make themselves recognizable—or alternately, they would simply not exist.

Alger, too, yearned for the world in which classes occupied the same theater and engaged in the same discourse. But his particular vision of unity brought the theater closer to ordinary lives. The discourse should have the moral tone of the Cambridge elite, but the voice and fire of Edwin Forrest.

Although the effort to negate class and cultural distance through moral reform was a significant piece in Alger's repertoire, it was not staged alone. Respectable culture—redefined and broadened—was accessible to nonelites. The Republic would have to give up any aristocratic pretense. Those who would engage in affectation, class markers, make money the measure of the man, and demand deference from others would yield the stage to Ragged Dick. Here spoke a kind of resistance to class differentiation, to crass materialism, to the growing gap between rich and poor, and to the breakdown of community. Here was an author who brought down the mighty, challenged power and social hierarchy, performed miracles of levelling, and insisted that nature could triumph over artifice.

Alger resisted surrender of power by the individual, and by the Republic. This fiction could potentially speak to class fractions threatened by the changes industrialization and urbanization were bringing to the United States. Some were increasingly becoming differentiated as classes apart and losers in the development of capitalism.

There was something in Alger for genteel boys from Boston, as there was for those who read the penny papers. And, in a nation where difference poses a threat to identity, a story that can be embraced by different classes is, itself, taken as a kind of vindication that we are of one estate. There are not too many of these myths of unity left.

While this Gilded Age narrative was one kind of reconciliation of fact and fiction, it was not *non*sense. But why should American audiences continue to find this particular set of symbols constitutive of reasonable discourse?

For most scholars who use "Alger" as a construct—as shorthand for a set of beliefs in American political culture—Alger is a set of propositions about self-help and individualism, hard work, defense of property, and permeability of economic and social structure. American political stories, language, myths, symbols, and metaphors pay homage to Alger despite massive social and economic changes in the century since Alger died. Understandings of how the political economy "works" appear highly static, and conflate aspiration and economic explanation. Self-evident truths look like myths, or false consciousness.

Were it reasonable to "read" Alger as an apologist for capitalism, it would be a serious mistake to treat Alger's stories, as most scholars have, as mere tools of the capitalist class, selling promise of riches and obtaining the complicity of subordinate classes in the race for wealth. In Louis Hartz's reading of the wedding of Horatio Alger to the liberal Lockean creed, the Whig-Hamiltonian-capitalists were allowed to "throw a set of chains around" the American democrat in a blend of Hamilton and Jefferson, peasant and proletariat. By latching onto equality of opportunity, the American Whigs sold the American democrat a bill of goods—an ideological straightjacket.[5]

In this view, we are all simply hoodwinked by the Whigs, who woo us with equality of opportunity while themselves winning the race. Political discourse as a product of relations among social classes (Hartz), myth invocation, and false consciousness look identical. Such readings neither do justice to Alger nor to people who use language to think with.

Confronted with an Alger-centered discourse in late twentieth century America, and the prevailing ways in which this has been explained, it is tempting to borrow from Clifford Geertz a very different sort of claim: that ideologies are most prevalently expressed when things don't work—when they don't make sense. Ideological formulations are adduced when the world is changing, and no longer corresponds to one's expectations.[6] Alger wrote in—and for—an era experiencing disruptions and changes in lived experience. Could not old doxologies simply be dragged out during other such times? In this functionalist view, the discourse need not maintain material groundings.

But this study suggests some material connection. The greatest similarities between the world of the Alger heroes and that of the latter day believers lie at the level of economic fears and dislocations inherent in a capitalist economy—an economy in which the creation of new wealth and new consumption capacities for some take place alongside deindustrialization, unemployment, poverty, and non-European immigrations. In a society where stations are not fixed by birth and where a dynamic economy has brought massive change if not always improvement in well-being, the Alger formula counsels patience, preparation, and optimism. A set of ostensibly timeless propositions is built upon the *rejection* of stasis and decline in economy and society.

The tension between the belief that individuals could produce their own economic security or well-being and the phenomena of poverty and mass unemployment may have emerged in particularly stark form for the first time during the Gilded Age, but it was repeated during twentieth century recessions and depressions.

Reagan and Bush paeans to the formulas associated with Alger re-emerge during the era of deindustrialization and massive change in where and how people work. The argument that struggling manfully against adversity "pays off" materially is a hard times message. After all, who needs success stories in an economy that vindicates the model? In this view, success stories are most useful when extensive social mobility is *scarce*—not when it is widespread. The narratives are about how to *avoid* filling the undesirable positions in the economic order. Alger heroes succeed because they avoid economic marginality, starvation, and depersonalized work environments. No one needs formulas to attain the lot that will otherwise fall to them by default.

In an era of erosion of real wages, fiscal retrenchment, a debt that makes a lie of independence, and uncertainty about the meaning of America, the narratives continue. In an economically interdependent and increasingly integrated world, the hope of independence and self-reliance—and of stable, fulfilling work with rising wages—may be all the more seductive.

Structuralist historical materialists have claimed that ideologies must "make sense" of the system in which classes participate, directing them to places to be occupied in that system if the system is to be reproduced. Classes must have some means of understanding and legitimating their role in the social structure to perform these roles. In this view, if there are mismatches between rules and values, on the one hand, and conditions of lived experience on the other, either these rules and values will change or the system will cease to exist.[7] But a notion of "correspondences," while better than invocations of "false consciousness," still requires better conceptualization and exploration of the relationship between words and deeds—or between worldviews and politics to make sense of the American case.

If an Alger-based discourse tends to reproduce the social relations of corporate capitalism, it is no *explanation* of how and why this grammar of American politics is affirmed and reproduced. People are not merely passive bearers of structure; they construct worldviews and meanings that make sense to them. Social contextualization is essential.

Fictions, myths, and stories are forms of discourse about tensions in the society in question. These scripts offer a variety of texts and subtexts, but they remain historically grounded. For Levi-Strauss, narratives are myths seeking to resolve conceptual contradictions in a particular society; narratives have a social function.[8] Frederic Jameson elaborates: One can examine "the various semantic tokens, the various mechanisms for the production of meaning, or *codes* as they are currently known, the various binary oppositions, out of which the narrative is constructed." Oppositions can be constructed and characters "read" in the context of codes. The narrative serves as "a representation. . . of a struggle going on in the real world of history itself."[9] Stories may address—and even resolve—contradictions that, in life, remain unresolved.

It is sometimes possible to see beyond traditional debates when we free up our language. This study proposes that political discourse participates in the realm of texts. In discourse, as in texts, there are reconciliations of fact and fiction. Fact and fiction must be woven together to construct a narrative. Discourse is the product and process of struggle; there are struggling forces within any text. "On the stage of the text, no footlights: there is not, behind the text, someone active (the writer) and out front someone passive (the reader)."[10]

As we transcend dualisms such as actor-recipient, it is no longer acceptable to suggest that the readers and public were sold a bill of goods and were co-opted by Alger (or by other romances, tales, and promises). It does not advance our understanding of the persistence of Alger to claim an author merely misread his surroundings; it is a mistake to pronounce readers *mis*readers. Locating Alger amid the tensions and anxieties produced by the rapid industrialization of America, we see that the narrative is neither simply pro- nor anticapitalist. Alger was a creature *of* the emergence of nineteenth century American capitalism. He could not possibly stand outside it. Expressing both fears and desires that emerge from the logic of capitalism, Alger was embedded in a system of representation; ". . . that, producing objects of approval and disapproval both, is more important than any attitude one might imagine oneself to have toward it [capitalism]."[11]

The Alger symbols may be frequently woven into a specific class dialect—a doxology—but there are others. People appropriate texts—political and literary—to their own uses. Just as the historical Alger was appropriated differently by various audiences and critics, there is a continual struggle over meaning and symbol in language.

Just as readers constitute texts, they confer meaning on the symbols they use. The Alger hero is *available* for appropriation by different communities. The enduring appeal of this formula is explained in part because the meaning of the foils and juxtapositions is *adaptable* to a variety of American political and cultural conflicts. While the narrative conveys different meanings to different users, "the differences in the meanings we attribute to the symbols tend to go unrecognized, and the myth of their common meaning is preserved." To understand the power of political symbols, one must discover "how they become the focal points of diverse meanings and commonly salient objects condensing and indexing different experiences, fears, apprehensions, hopes, and interests."[12]   The social variability of meaning gives symbols their peculiar potency.

Is the Alger hero a symbol about equal opportunity under capitalism, or is it a symbol about bringing justice to the market? Is it a symbol of laissez-faire individualism or of the triumph of community and character over impersonality, selfishness, and corruption? Does it celebrate economic growth or fight a rear-guard action against differentiation of economic fortunes and of habits, taste, and culture? It can incorporate all of these.

These formulas became identified with a predominant grammar of American politics because they managed to accomplish several things that successful worldviews do.   Political discourse does not merely reflect conditions of material life, but mediates these conditions. Just as ideology never works when it is a complete or accurate representation of the changed world, the Alger amalgam of fact and fiction found continuities between traditional values and understandings of the world and new environments. Political language creates national stories about our experience, and in so doing, helps constitute future experiences.[13]

Alger's selective portrait of the transformations of the political economy wrought by the Gilded Age manages the scope and pace of change in such a way as to mediate disorder, uncertainty and transition.   There is accommodation to the new order; travel and adventure, hope, and new opportunities appear. Heroes improve their standard of living and generally acquire business-related careers. The centrality of private property and of market relations were underscored, but so, too, were values and virtues of the past as the Alger story turned away from capitalism's less attractive features. Neglected or denied are certain troubling or unintelligible activities; others are named and defined out of community-sustaining behavior. Foils are lightning rods for a variety of populist and anticapitalist discontents. This particular articulation of the transforming economic environment framed industrial age problems and solutions in a potentially compelling manner.

The formula also succeeds by narrating its ambivalence toward capitalism, much as does a political discourse stressing individual opportunity, mistrust of big business, and divisions between haves and have-nots. By making justice pay in dollars, Alger acknowledges the importance that materialism has come to have. Generally, however, the wild dreams entertained in these stories are, as in the case of Darnton's seventeenth century peasants who fantasize about a full belly, about attaining stable, salaried positions, with cordial personal relations with an employer. His reconciliations of price and value leave tradition and modernity in uneasy tension.

The author who rights the scales of justice and restores the equation of price and value as Alger does exhibits loyalty to the system. Constant interventions in the market demonstrate that this version of market justice was fundamentally at odds with science—or economic science. But instead of concluding that the market exists in disharmony from the values he would promote, Alger draws a different lesson. Change and tradition are reconcilable; character, virtue, power, independence, and individual agency can triumph in the age of capital. Not only can community be rescued in the face of the economic and social dislocations occasioned by capitalism, but the individual can remain the locus of responsibility, morality, and activity. Stories can have happy endings. Alger may have diffused frustration; since the formulas can be used to participate in the modern capitalist era, they may have played a role in demobilizing and depoliticizing resistance to the emerging order.

But the melodrama and symbols he created, incorporating ambivalence, accommodation, criticism, and resistance to the new order, generate space for some incendiary meanings. Had these been either simple morality tales or simple celebrations of the new order, they would have been far less serviceable as the components of political grammar.

Political formulations, as representations, are always in some sense "fictions." But they remain ways of connecting the past, present, and future. But when political discourse loses the capacity to connect experience and symbols, it loses its capacity to persuade. Fiction pure and simple loses its power to integrate, just as when politicians are perceived as liars, the public perceives the gap between words and deeds.

Another aspect of American experience permits the Alger story to weave this version of a past, present, and future into a plausible narrative. Many scholars have found a fusion of sacred and secular meanings to be characteristic *of* American political discourse—a peculiarity in the language and rhetoric of American politics. Religious meanings may be inseparable from the very language and style of political exhortation we use.[14] Emphasis is on community, purpose, and virtue; a fused religious and secular compact pervaded language as it pervaded politics.[15] Garry Wills found this strain in the Nixon-Wallace backlash, and in the morality of the market.[16] Michael Kammen found it to be part of America's "contrapuntal civilization."[17]

The close linkage between religious thought and American political discourse points, for Sacvan Bercovitch, to the Puritan heritage. Puritan theology originated a special American telos, which he calls the myth of America. Puritans expected their community, the New Jerusalem set apart physically from the sins of Europe, to be the locus of the final confrontation with God. Collective covenant fulfilling was essential in order to reap the rewards God promised (as he had promised the Hebrews): Material rewards, worldly protection, power and privilege.[18] The idea of a "city on a hill" captured the sense of collective mission and helped foster the sense, in 1787, that "the eyes of the world are upon us".

In this Puritan narrative, there is a collective obligation to prosper—an obligation to perform this, and not some altered contract. And so, in a nation founded on the rhetoric of social contract and the right to revolution, there was a peculiar fear of change.[19] Change could take the form of republican reform and restoration, but popular pressures for change threaten the very "truth" of the revolution—that God approved of our design, or even created it. Guarding American liberty entailed a relationship with the natural and divine order. The public interest takes on a meaning in which there can be no fundamental conflict of interest.[20] Failure was a matter of personal culpability and collective treason.[21]

America was a promise and a destiny as well as a place; past, present and future were fused as secular heroes were invested with sacred purpose.[22] The historical was not merely man-made but part of the natural (God-given) order of things. As the American Jeremiad evolved as a political form, language reflected this fusion.

Alger's fiction merges mid-nineteenth century Unitarian tenets concerning character and lived ethics with secular success stories. The "art" of this sacred-secular fusion is that it is *less* transparently materialistic than a Conwell "Acres of Diamonds" sermon or Carnegie's "Gospel of Wealth," and yet *more* secular than religious fiction and the Oliver Optic stories of the period that so often involved a stronger dose of religious education. And yet, the proposition that rewards come to those who persevere and who make themselves "men" is a religious—not finally an economic—one. If those who heard the message that justice pays confused earthly and heavenly rewards, Alger had invited them to.

Conflating sacred and secular rewards, merging fact and fiction, history and telos, and individual and republican stories, a key to Alger's success lay in devising a formula better-suited to those who wanted to have the new world without losing anything in the process.

Alger's story about the youth's rite of passage served as an allegory of the adolescent Republic, in which individual and collective pilgrimages, sacred and secular meanings were indistinguishable. However, Alger's republic is not the same as the New Jerusalem, and the product of these fusions is not merely another jeremiad.

In contrast to overtones of declension and apocalypse in the jeremiads of the period, Alger told a far more optimistic story and exhibited more faith in democracy. The optimism and good cheer of Alger's adolescent hero are never seriously shaken by adversity—a real moral for the Republic under siege or experiencing identity crisis.

Is the Alger hero, then, another Candide? Does he continue to believe, with Pangloss, that everything is for the best in the best of all possible worlds? Alger's heroes, like Candide, constantly faced challenges to their view of the universe and its belief in progress, design, intelligibility, and goodness. Candide's experiences are disconfirming; he finally settles down and reaps a share of happiness with his entourage in a spot rather far removed—even untouched by—the ravages of the age of reason. The Alger hero's optimism fares a little better. The dangers, greed, hardship, cupidity, and selfishness encountered never shake his philosophy. Happiness remains possible. If it is not the best of all possible worlds, there are still many good people in it. Despite—or even through—travails, the basic order of the universe is confirmed.

The Alger hero leaves the Garden of Eden (which no longer supports him and thus is no more) and goes to Sodom and Gomorrah, where he will almost invariably remain. There, he replicates the community that has been lost. If he cannot return to the garden, he can have the next best thing. If Adam and Eve receive knowledge, then Alger heroes receive manhood— self-sufficiency in the marketplace. Leaving behind lost innocence and economic autonomy, man as citizen may become an intelligent and moral being; he becomes free and a member of a community. This is more Rousseau than Voltaire.

Alger's fiction does not exhibit the disenchantment of Beecher and others about the direction of historical change in the nineteenth century. If Henry Ward Beecher would remark in *Norwood* that "The steps of decline are melancholy and instructive," Alger would have none of it.[23] Vice was deplorable and created many innocent victims, but it was not allowed to become the undoing of the Republic. He was not party to Calvinist assumptions about human depravity, and, whatever his apprehensions about the future, he did not believe in the likelihood or inevitability of decline. True to his Harvard Unitarian heritage, Alger displayed an optimism about human nature and was more inclined to think the human personality perfectable.[24]

Jeremiads recall the nation to its original principles, from which it has diverged. The alternative is self-destruction. Less certain that disaster waits in the wings, Alger is more forward-looking, allowing the nation to grow and mature. Nations that struggle with adversity acquire power, independence, and virtue.

It is almost as if America could evolve toward near-universal morality. Out of chaos comes order. Almost all the characters whom the hero touches are improved by the time we leave them—even villains are often poorer but wiser. If the universe is not evolving toward economic, political, and moral improvement, neither is it backsliding into ruin. There is plenty of room for virtue to flourish.

Alger created a fictional republic. In it, there were no classes. All decent citizens spoke the same language and recognized the same values. Men produced themselves; they were not controlled by others. Proletarianization was escapable, and character was universal currency. The story of the fictional adolescent in the Republic and the narrative of the adolescent Republic were made one.

With such a combination of religious and secular formulations, of affirmation of tradition and stepping forth with courage into the unknown and dangerous waters of the industrial era, Alger may have inspired readers of the late nineteenth and early twentieth centuries. But he also seems to have stumbled upon a formula that works well as a political grammar. With this set of tools and symbols, we reaffirm something essential about who we think we are, face the unknown, and prepare to remake the unknown to fit our prior experiences. As we do so, we reconstitute both our prior and our current experience—our "truths" about the order of things.

Horatio Alger, Jr. unwittingly derived a formula to deal with hopes and anxieties in a rapidly changing world. He captured a form of discourse that not only spoke to many in the era in which he wrote but could still be spoken by later generations. The story, "fiction" by the time the ink was on the page, touched something vital. The narrative about our future and our past—and the relation between these—constitutes political identity. In it, Jeffersonian virtues meet the industrial era and survive. The country meets the city, and both win: Virtue and economic opportunity are wedded. The American jeremiad exhorts its audience to stand true to its principles and meet the forces threatening to undo the grand experiment. And the Republic of the creator, emerging from its rite of passage, triumphs.

Notes

PREFACE

1. Louis Hartz, *The Liberal Tradition in America* (New York: Harcourt, Brace & World, 1955), pp. 111-12.

CHAPTER 1

1. Horatio Alger, Jr. lived from 1832-99. *Ragged Dick* was serialized in 1867, more than a decade after the appearance of his first literary work, *Bertha's Christmas Vision* (1856), a collection of short stories. Eleven Algers appeared after his death, completed by Edward Stratemeyer. See Ralph D. Gardner, *Horatio Alger, or the American Hero Era* (New York: Arco Publishing Company, Inc., 1978) and Bob Bennett, *Horatio Alger, Jr.: A Comprehensive Bibliography* (Mt. Pleasant, Mich.: Flying Eagle Publishing Co., 1980) for the chronology of Alger works relied upon here. Gary Scharnhorst and Jack Bales, *Horatio Alger, Jr.: An Annotated Bibliography of Comment and Criticism* (Metuchen, N.J.: Scarecrow Press, Inc., 1981) has also proved extremely helpful.

2. Samuel Eliot Morrison and Henry Steele Commager, *The Growth of the American Republic*, Vol. 2 (New York: Oxford University Press, 1938), pp. 287-88.

3. *Publishers Weekly*, quoted on frontspiece to Edwin P. Hoyt, *Horatio's Boys* (New York: Stein and Day, 1974).

4. Hellmut Lehmann-Haupt, with Lawrence C. Wroth and Rollo G. Silver, *The Book in America* (New York: R. R. Bowker Company, 1951, 2d ed.), p. 201.

5. Only *Ragged Dick* was enormously successful, but the number of volumes, reprints, and various editions of Alger's approximately 125 novels are a testimony to his tenacity. On later sales, see Gary Scharnhorst, *Horatio Alger, Jr.* (Boston: Twayne Publishers, 1980), pp. 141-42. See Bennett, *Horatio Alger, Jr.: A Comprehensive Bibliography*; Gardner, *Horatio Alger, or the American Hero Era*; and Scharnhorst's Chronology in *Horatio Alger, Jr.*

N.B. The abbreviations AAS, A-H, CU, HL, HO, HUA, MI, NYPL, NYPLc, NYPLd, UVa, and YU are explained at the beginning of the References section.

6. Fredric Jameson, "Ideology, Narrative Analysis, and Popular Culture," *Theory and Society* 4 (1977): 543; see also Will Wright, Sixguns and Society (Berkeley, Calif.: University of California Press, 1975), p. 200 on myths and reasoning.

7. See Jane Tompkins, *Sensational Designs* (New York: Oxford University Press, 1985).

8. For such views of Alger, see (1) Herbert Mayes, *Horatio Alger: A Biography without a Hero* (New York, 1928; reprinted with a new introduction by the author in Des Plaines, Il.: Gilbert K. Westgaard II, 1978); Hartz, *The Liberal Tradition in America*; Russel Crouse, introduction to Alger, *Struggling Upward and Other Stories* (New York: Crown, 1945); (2) John Cawelti, *Apostles of the Self-Made Man* (Chicago: University of Chicago Press, 1965); Michael Zuckerman, "The Nursery Tales of Horatio Alger," *American Quarterly* 24 (May, 1972): 191-209; (3) Scharnhorst, *Horatio Alger, Jr.*; and (4) Dee Garrison, *Apostles of Culture* (New York: Free Press, 1979); Esther Jane Carrier, *Fiction in Public Libraries 1876-1900* (New York: Scarecrow Press, 1965).

9. This image of Alger is inherent in Louis Hartz's famous characterization of "Americanism" as liberal Lockean, Horatio Alger atomistic individualism in The Liberal Tradition in America. The "Alger" of Hartz's account is apparently an amalgam of popular mythology and the Mayes hoax. The only reference Hartz makes is to Russel Crouse's introduction to Alger's Struggling Upward and Other Works, an introduction in which the only citation is to "Mayes's thorough and sympathetic biography" (p. ix).

10. Ellen Wilson, "The Books We Got For Christmas," *American Heritage* 8 (December, 1956): 120.

11. Richard Huber, *The American Idea of Success* (New York: McGraw-Hill, 1971), p. 46.

12. Herbert Mayes, *Alger: A Biography Without A Hero*. The hoax was exposed with recantation by the author in Scharnhorst and Bales, *Horatio Alger, Jr.: An Annotated Bibliography*. The Mayes biography was the chief source for the John Tebbel, *Rags to Riches* (New York: Macmillan, 1963) biography characterizing Alger's own life as a road from rags to riches, and for the Alger entry in the *Dictionary of American Biography*. Mayes only recently admitted the fabrication. See his "After Half a Century" in the 1978 Westgard edition of his Alger biography; Mayes's introduction to Scharnhorst and Bales, *Horatio Alger, Jr.: An Annotated Bibliography*; and the preface of Gary Scharnhorst with Jack Bales, *The Lost Life of Horatio Alger, Jr.* (Bloomington, Ind.: Indiana University Press, 1985). Scharnhorst points out that the cheap reprints that appeared in the 1900-1920s revival often abridged the moral purpose, and were also often his late, most sensationalized novels. This "unrepresentative sample" may have contributed to the image of Alger as the "rags to riches" author (Scharnhorst, *Horatio Alger, Jr.*, pp. 135, 142-3).

13. Tales may be set ten or twenty years in the past. Some early stories feature the Civil War; others use the California gold rush. Sometimes the earlier time frame is only made explicit when the reader is warned that prices mentioned are old and thus inaccurate.

14. See especially Cawelti, *Apostles of the Self-Made Man*. One of the most recent opportunities to rethink the Alger message was provided when the newly published "lost" Alger novel, *Mabel Parker* (Hamden, Conn.: Archon Books, 1986) was reviewed: "The Tattered Toms, Ragged Dicks and Matchboy Marks seldom rise in life beyond a comfortable respectability;" and further, "The Alger books ... do not endorse industrial capitalism, nor do they attribute success to untrammeled individualism." See Nina Baym, "A Boy's Book for Adults," *New York Review of Books*, (July 20, 1986): 10. See also Zuckerman, "The Nursery Tales of Horatio Alger."

15. Cawelti, *Apostles of the Self-Made Man*, Chapter 4. See also Scharnhorst, *Horatio Alger, Jr.*

16. The heroes tend to become the wealthiest after 1889, when Alger resorted to sensationalism in an apparent attempt to prop up sagging popularity. Scharnhorst, *Horatio Alger, Jr.*, p. 135.

17. "His heroes come from another time, another society, another reality. Rather than extolling the dominant values of his day, he was reacting against them." Richard Weiss, *The Myth of American Success* (New York: Basic Books, 1969), pp. 59-60; see also Scharnhorst, *Horatio Alger, Jr.*, p. 124.

18. Cawelti, *Apostles of the Self-Made Man*, p. 120. See also Zuckerman, "The Nursery Tales of Horatio Alger," 196, who argues that Alger's "comprehension of capitalistic individuals was no clearer than his conception of capitalist institutions," and concludes that virtually nothing in Alger supports the image of him as apologist for capitalism.

19. See Cawelti, *Apostles of the Self-Made Man*; Scharnhorst, *Horatio Alger, Jr.* (1980); Baym, "A Boy's Book for Adults"; Daniel T. Rodgers, *The Work Ethic in Industrializing America* (Chicago: University of Chicago Press, 1978); Richard Weiss, *The Myth of American Success*; and Zuckerman, "The Nursery Tales of Horatio Alger."

20. Scharnhorst, *Horatio Alger, Jr.*, 1980, preface.

21. Rodgers, *The Work Ethic*, pp. 136, 142, 143.

22. Rodgers, *The Work Ethic*, p. 141. See also Malcolm Cowley, who argues that the format is basically that of the Greek myth of Telemachus, supposed orphan forced to leave home, who goes in search of his father. The father's power eventually restores him to his rightful place. He speaks of the "fairy-tale logic of the story," where the hero is "a prince in disguise." "Horatio Alger: Failure," *Horizon* 12 (Summer, 1970): 65.

23. John Cawelti, *Adventure, Mystery, and Romance* (Chicago: University of Chicago Press, 1976), p. 38; Jameson, "Ideology, Narrative Analysis, and Popular Culture," 545.

24. Is the Alger story a Cinderella story? See Vladimir Propp's *The Morphology of the Folktale*, edited with an introduction by Svatava Pirkova-Jakobson. Translated by Laurence Scott (Bloomington, Ind.: Indiana University, 1958). See Jameson, "Ideology, Narrative Analysis, and Popular Culture," 550.

25. Russel Crouse, Introduction to Alger, *Struggling Upward*, vi.

26. Colin Mercer, "A Poverty of Desire," *Formations of Pleasure* (London: Routledge and Kegan Paul, 1983), p. 99. On this theme, see also Pierre Bourdieu, *Distinction* (Cambridge, Mass.: Harvard University Press, 1984).

27. Both were Harvard graduates in the 1850s. Like Alger, Adams watched Civil War regiments form ranks in front of the Boston State House; unlike Alger, who was in Europe when the war broke out and returned a few months later, Adams was soon to go abroad as personal secretary to his father as Minister to England. Both Alger and Adams valued moral standards, gentlemanliness, reform of politics, and hard money. See Henry Adams, *The Education of Henry Adams* (New York: Modern Library, 1931), pp. 145, 314, 336.

28. See Cathy N. Davidson, "Towards a History of Books and Readers," *American Quarterly* 40 (March, 1988): 11, 14.

29. Stanley Fish, *Is There A Text in This Class?* (Cambridge, Mass.: Harvard University Press, 1980), p. 11 and passim. Roland Barthes would go further, asserting the radical subjectivity of the "meaning" of the text, and at one point suggesting a psychoanalytic typology of "the pleasures of reading—or of the readers of pleasure." Roland Barthes, *The Pleasure of the Text*, translated by Richard Miller (New York: Hill and Wang, 1975), pp. 63, 10-12, 39-40.

30. Mercer, "A Poverty of Desire," p. 88.

31. Annette Kolodny, "The Integrity of Memory: Creating a New Literary History of the United States," *American Literature* 57 (May, 1985): 303, 293 and passim.

CHAPTER 2

1. Junior Class Bowdoin Prize, Harvard University, 1851, p. 5.

2. The Harvard University Archives retains "Cicero's Return from Banishment," "Athens in the Time of Socrates," and a translation into Greek of "The State of Athens before the Legislation of Solon," from Grote's *History of Greece*, Vol. 3, Chapter 11, pp. 93-95 in the 1851 edition.

3. Daniel Walker Howe, *The Unitarian Conscience* (Cambridge, Mass.: Harvard University Press, 1970), p. 43.

4. Howe, *Unitarian Conscience*, pp. 7, 11.

5. Arthur Mann, *Yankee Reformers in the Urban Age* (Cambridge, Mass.: Harvard University Presss, 1954), pp. 100-1; second quote, p. 74. Edward Everett Hale was one such leader.

6. Ralph Waldo Emerson, quoted by John Kasson, *Civilizing the Machine* (New York: Penguin, 1976), p. 44. See Perry Miller, *The Life of the Mind in America* (New York: Harcourt, Brace & World, 1965), pp. 298-300, on Everett's mediocre attempts to adorn the industrial revolution, as well as the submerged incredulity evidenced by his *Arabian Nights* imagery.

7. Niccolò Machiavelli, *The Discourses*, Book I, Ch. 1, p. 105 in *The Prince and Discourses* (New York: Modern Library, 1950).

8. Harvard College Catalogue, 1848-49, HUA.

9. Arthur Mann, *Yankee Reformers*, pp. 103-4.

10. *Boston Daily Advertiser*, August 9, 1895 in the Horatio Alger, Jr. file, HUA.

11. Grace Williamson Edes, *Annals of the Harvard Class of 1852* (Cambridge, Mass.: Privately Printed, 1922), p. 330, HUA. Of the remainder, two were of French extraction, one was of Scotch descent, and the parents of the final student emigrated from Ireland around 1830.

12. According to the obituary and funeral notice in the *Natick Bulletin* for July 21, 1899, "Throughout his Harvard course he devoted himself chiefly to the languages"; HUA.

13. See Howe, *Unitarian Conscience*, especially p. 43. William Ellery Channing was noteworthy among these, although he was no longer present when Alger attended. Alger's father was a Harvard graduate of 1825.

14. Alger, "Athens in the Time of Socrates," p. 28. Henceforth, "Athens."

15. See Howe, *Unitarian Conscience*, pp. 27-31.

16. Library Charging books, HUA. Alger charged several issues of the *Quarterly Review* and one issue of *Blackwood's Edinburgh Magazine*. He also charged Bacon's Works in 1851. See also Howe, *Unitarian Conscience*, pp. 30, 32.

17. Cawelti, *Apostles of the Self-Made Man*, p. 110.

18. Howe, *Unitarian Conscience*, pp. 31, 35, 38.

19. Arthur Mann, *Yankee Reformers*, p. 104.

20. This travel correspondence is reproduced in Jack Bales and Gary Scharnhorst, "Alger's European Tour 1860-61: A Sheaf of Travel Essays," *Newsboy* 19 (April, 1981): 7-26 and "Horatio Alger, Jr. and the *Sun* Travel Essays,"

from the Collections of Jack Bales and Gary Scharnhorst," *Newsboy* 20 (December, 1981): 11-14. Alger published under the name Carl Cantab.

21. *North American Review* 201 (October, 1863): 325-38. The best biographical information on Alger comes from Scharnhorst with Bales, *The Lost Life of Horatio Alger, Jr.*

22. Howells, *Literature and Life* (1902), quoted in Henry F. May, *The End of American Innocence* (New York: Alfred A. Knopf), p. 52.

23. Alger to Mr. Chaney dated November 25, 1864, HO. On Hale's participation, see ordination ceremony program, A-H.

24. Ordination service of Reverend Horatio Alger, Jr., Thursday evening December 8, 1864, Brewster; A-H. See David Reynolds, *Faith in Fiction: The Emergence of Religious Literature in America* (Cambridge, Mass.: Harvard University Press, 1981), pp. 200, 203-4.

25. Quoted in Ann Douglas, *The Feminization of American Culture* (New York: Avon, 1977), p. 134. Her citation of 1862 *Christian Examiner* does not match the date in her text.

26. Alger to Duyckinck dated 28 January 1866 from Brewster, Mass; NYPLd. Alger suggests, in the same letter, that the exclusion of J. T. Trowbridge (Paul Creyton), William T. Adams (Oliver Optic), the widely read author of juveniles, Boston schoolteacher and principal, and editor of *Student and Schoolmate*, and Gail Hamilton (Miss Abigail Dodge) must have been in error. He corrects Duyckinck on the title of his 1865 novel, *Paul Prescott's Charge*.

27. Reynolds, *Faith in Fiction*, p. 209, quoting the *North American Review*, 1856.

28. Arthur Mann, *Yankee Reformers*, p. 75; on fiction, Reynolds, *Faith in Fiction*, p. 200.

29. Reynolds, *Faith in Fiction*, pp. 197 and 210 respectively.

30. Harriet Beecher Stowe, *My Wife and I*, p. 2 (New-York: J. B. Ford and Company, 1871).

31. Douglas, *Feminization of American Culture*, pp. 282-83.

32. William Rounseville Alger, *Life of Edwin Forrest, the American Tragedian* (New York: Benjamin Bloom, 1972; reprint of the 1877 edition), Vol. 2, p. 689; it is possible the passage was written by Horatio Alger, Jr. himself. Which sections of the biography were written by each is not always clear, and none of it is attributed to Alger. See Scharnhorst with Bales, *The Lost Life of Horatio Alger, Jr.*, pp. 106-8.

33. Reynolds, *Faith in Fiction*, p. 206. He reports in the same place that "In the 1860s and 1870s the Presbyterian Bonner commissioned eleven other clergymen to write one novel each for the *Ledger* in an effort to increase the magazine's profits while enhancing its respectability." On Beecher's *Norwood*, see also Henry Nash Smith, *Democracy and the Novel* (New York: Oxford

University Press, 1978), p. 57. Alger never wrote for the *Ledger*.

34. Henry Nash Smith quoted in David Reynolds, *Faith in Fiction*, p. 201.

35. Reynolds, *Faith in Fiction*, quote p. 211; p. 201, citing a dissertation by Elmer Suderman.

36. In Twain's story, the one little boy's virtue nets him no earthly rewards, no recognition, and no place in the Sunday school books for his tragic/comic death; meanwhile, the bad little boy gets along in the world despite his vices. *Sketches New and Old*, Vol. 19 in *Mark Twain's Works* (New York: Harper & Brothers Publishers, 1904).

37. Scharnhorst, *Horatio Alger, Jr.*, p. 106.

38. Reynolds, *Faith in Fiction*, p. 199, quoting the *North American Review*, 1847; 198; see also Reynolds, p. 210.

39. Reynolds, *Faith in Fiction*, p. 211.

40. Reynolds, *Faith in Fiction*, p. 208.

41. Reynolds, *Faith in Fiction*, p. 212, adding that they were not infrequently "people with severe personal or spiritual problems."

42. Letter from Solomon Freeman, Elisha Bangs, and George Copeland, Committee of the Brewster Unitarian Church, to Reverend Charles Lowe, Secretary of the American Unitarian Association, dated March 19, 1866; A-H.

43. Reverend Horatio Alger, Sr. to Charles Lowe, March 22, 1866; A-H. The son's actual letter of resignation is not in evidence. Possibly the father's entreaties were unnecessary; the Unitarian Society resolved upon a similar course of action, including official silence, just prior to its receipt.

44. Alger to William Conant Church, April 20, 1866; NYPLc.

45. Alger's letters to Edwin R. A. Seligman, especially those dated 1 July and 14 July 1885. Upon learning from Bennie Cardozo of Seligman's appointment as Professor of Political Economy at Columbia, Alger writes: "A distinguished professor of Political Economy will be a notable addition to the list of eminent lawyers, scholars, and business men whom I have instructed"; CU.

46. Alger, "Friar Anselmo's Sin," pp. 51, 53-54 in *Grand'ther Baldwin's Thanksgiving*. (Boston: A. K. Loring, 1875, reprinted by Gilbert K. Westgard II, 1978.) Scharnhorst has read the poem as a plan for expiation.

47. Solomon Freeman to Reverend Charles Lowe, September 1, 1866 and Lowe's reply to Freeman of September 7, 1866, pertaining to the publishing activity of the former Brewster minister. Freeman, having attempted to alert the publisher of *Student and Schoolmate* of Alger's moral record, obtained no satisfaction by this route. The secretary of the Unitarian Association, while regretting that Alger's name has been "connected in our papers with moral teachings to youth when it is

so freshly associated with such moral *perverseness* of life," replies that he does not think he would have any more influence over the editor of *Student and Schoolmate* even if he were to agree to try. A-H.

48. Biographical sketch enclosed with letter to George A. Bacon, Esq. dated Jan. 26, 1874. Alger claims the year of his birth as 1834. Horatio Alger, Jr. Papers (#6398), UVa.

49. Alger to W. A. Wheeler, January 2, 1869, UVa.

50. Alger to William Conant Church, April 20, 1866; NYPLc. Church persists in believing him to be his cousin, William Rounseville Alger, author of "Alger's Oriental Poetry."

51. Harvard University Records, Faculty Records, Vol. 13 (1845-1850), p. 127, faculty meeting of Monday, May 3, 1852; HUA.

52. Anne Norton, *Alternative Americas* (Chicago: University of Chicago Press, 1986), p. 48, quoting Reverend Theodore Parker. William Ellery Channing and Lyman Beecher expressed similar sentiments.

53. Hawes, *Lectures to Young Men*, 7th ed. (Hartford, Conn.: Cooke and Co., 1834), p. 112.

54. Malcolm Cowley found "there is hardly a trace of religious feeling in his [Alger's] novels." "Horatio Alger: Failure," 64.

55. William Makepeace Thayer, *Success and Its Achievers* (Boston: A. M. Thayer, Publishers, 1891; also Boston: James H. Earle, 1896). Quote is p. 626 in 1891 ed.

56. Howe, *Unitarian Conscience*, p. 7, quoting James Walker of Harvard in the *Christian Examiner* for 1830, and a sermon by Walker.

57. Horace Mann, *A Few Thoughts for a Young Man* (Boston: Tichnor, Reed, and Fields, 1850), pp. 28-29. Many advice manual clergy, however, found Franklin dangerously worldly in his goals.

58. Karen Halttunen, *Confidence Men and Painted Women* (New Haven, Conn.: Yale University Press, 1982), p. 21. For a good example of the declension framework, see Timothy Shay Arthur, *Advice to Young Men* (Philadelphia: John E. Potter, 1847), Chapter 2.

59. Ira Katznelson, *City Trenches* (New York: Pantheon, 1981); Halttunen, *Confidence Men and Painted Women*, p. 13.

60. See Paul E. Johnson, *A Shopkeeper's Millenium* (New York: Hill and Wang, 1978), pp. 4-6, 46-48, 103-15. But, as Daniel T. Rodgers argues, the work ethic itself did not become the gospel of the urban working classes; *The Work Ethic in Industrializing America*, pp. 14-15.

61. A review of Alger's *Ben, the Luggage Boy* had appeared in Beecher's religious periodical, the *Christian Union* in 1870. Scharnhorst thinks Alger

may have engaged in veiled criticism of an article of Beecher's on labor unions and a living wage when he was writing *Mabel Parker*. Scharnhorst points up that, in *Mabel Parker*, Alger clearly did not believe that a dollar a day was enough for a family to live on.

62. On antebellum manufacturer practices regarding compulsory church attendance among Protestant men and women, and among Catholics, see Anne Norton, *Alternative Americas*, p. 51.

63. Alger, "Writing Stories for Boys," *The Writer* 9 (March, 1896): 37. Henceforth, WSB.

64. Alger, "Athens in the Time of Socrates," Bowdoin Prize essay of 1851, submitted by Athenaicus, pp. 68-69, 82; HUA. Henceforth, Athens.

65. Alger, "Athens," pp. 75-76.

66. Alger, "Athens," pp. 4-5.

67. Alger, "Athens," p. 5.

68. Alger, "Athens," p. 47. ". . . age finds its chief enjoyment in recalling the scenes of the past, in dwelling fondly upon the high hopes and noble impulses of youth—the activity and energy of manhood." Second quote, p. 54.

69. Alger, "Athens," pp. 56-58, discussing and quoting an unnamed recent English author.

70. Alger, "Athens," p. 57. See how this influences views of Macready and Forrest in Chapter 12.

71. Alger, "Athens," pp. 52, 50; Alger does not give a source.

72. Alger, "Athens," p. 26.

73. Biographical sketch, "Horatio Alger, Jr.," *The Golden Argosy* 49 (October 17, 1885); HUA.

74. Alger, "WSB," 37.

75. Jacob Abbott, *Rollo At School* (New York: Thomas Y. Crowell, 1855).

76. Alger, "WSB." 37.

77. Alger, "Are My Boys Real?," *The Ladies' Home Journal* 7 (November, 1890): 29.

78. Alger, "Advice From Horatio Alger, Jr.," *The Writer* 6 (January, 1892): 16, offers advice to a would-be author of juveniles.

79. Alger, "Athens," pp. 33, 53.

80. Alger, "Athens," p. 39.

81. See below, Chapter 8.

82. Alger, "Athens," pp. 38-39.

83. Alger, "Athens," pp. 38-40.

84. Alger, "Athens," p. 41.

85. Alger, "Athens," pp. 44-45.

86. Alger, "Athens," pp. 42-43, quoting an unnamed modern writer.

87. Alger, "Athens," p. 44 tries to use Plato's *Republic* to *defend* the Sophists on the grounds that a vicious society will have vicious teachers and that even the best teachers will not produce a good effect in a vicious society.

88. W. R. Alger, *Life of Edwin Forrest*, Vol. 1, pp. 17-18; henceforth, *Forrest*.

89. Alger, "Athens," pp. 41-42. For Alger's dependence upon his earnings as a writer, see Scharnhorst and Bales, *Lost Life*, especially Chapter 1.

90. W. R. Alger, *Forrest*, Vol. 1, p. 18.

91. W. R. Alger, *Forrest*, Vol. 1, pp. 18-19.

92. Alger, "Athens," p. 40.

93. Alger, "Athens," pp. 38, 25-27, 29.

94. Alger, "Athens," pp. 31-33.

95. Alger, "Athens," p. 37.

96. Alger, "Athens," p. 46.

CHAPTER 3

1. Hawes, *Lectures to Young Men*, p. 113.

2. Todd (1850), p. 76. Quoted in Halttunen, *Confidence Men and Painted Women*, p. 47.

3. Hawes, *Lectures to Young Men*, pp. 97-98: "More is done during this period [from fourteen to twenty-one years of age] to mould and settle the character of the future man, than in all the other years of life."

4. Halttunen, *Confidence Men and Painted Women*, p. 1. Halttunen's work provides a superb discussion of antebellum advice manuals.

5. See Halttunen, *Confidence Men and Painted Women*, pp. 10, 15.

6. The Alger hero will be referred to as "he" since young boys were the chief heroes. However, *Tattered Tom, Helen Ford, A Disagreeable Woman, Mabel Parker,* and *A Fancy of Hers* all feature heroines.

7. Timothy Shay Arthur, *Advice to Young Men on Their Duties and Conduct in Life*, p. 56.

8. Joseph Kett's *Rites of Passage: Adolescence in America, 1790 to the Present* (New York: Basic Books, 1977) argues that early nineteenth-century American culture has no clearly defined rites of passage to manhood; it is unclear at what moment a boy becomes a man. See also Halttunen, *Confidence Men and Painted Women*, p. 27.

9. Charles Loring Brace, *The Dangerous Classes of New York* (New York: Wynkoop & Hallenbeck, 1872; reprinted NASW Classic Series, n.d.), pp. 300-1. Brace wrote of their fourteen to eighteen year old constituency, "... a more difficult class than these to manage, no philanthropic mortal ever came in contact with. The most had a constitutional objection to work; they had learned to do nothing well, and therefore got but little wages anywhere ..." (pp. 307; 303-15).

10. Alger, *Tattered Tom* (Philadelphia: Henry T. Coates & Co., n.d., copyright Horatio Alger, Jr., 1899), p. 282.

11. Theodore Dreiser, *Sister Carrie* (New York: Modern Library, 1917), p. 2.

12. William A. Alcott, *The Young Man's Guide*, 16th ed. (Boston: T. R. Marvin, 1844), p. 139.

13. Joel Hawes, *Lectures to Young Men*, p. 114.

14. Halttunen, *Confidence Men and Painted Women*, p. 10.

15. Gordon S. Wood, *The Creation of the American Republic, 1776-1787* (New York: W. W. Norton, 1969), p. 100.

16. Joel Hawes, *Lectures to Young Men*, p. 1.

17. Alger, "Cicero's Return From Banishment," HUA.

18. J. G. A. Pocock, *The Machiavellian Moment* (Princeton, N.J.: Princeton University Press, 1975), p. 513.

19. See, for example, Alcott, *The Young Man's Guide*, pp. 133-40.

20. Halttunen, *Confidence Men and Painted Women*, pp. 3, 27.

21. Horace Mann, *A Few Thoughts For A Young Man*, p. 7.

22. Halttunen, *Confidence Men and Painted Women*, pp. 3-4, quoting David Magie, *The Spring-time of Life*.

23. Halttunen, pp. 2-4, quoting respectively John Todd's *The Young Man* and Jared Bell Waterbury, *Considerations for Young Men*. She points out that Franklin had his share of confidence men and women to deal with; the *Autobiography* is, itself, an advice manual.

24. Halttunen, *Confidence Men and Painted Women*, p. 3.

25. Halttunen, *Confidence Men and Painted Women*, p. 7, citing Lane, *Policing the City*.

26. Halttunen, *Confidence Men and Painted Women*, p. 13.

27. Hawes, *Lectures to Young Men*, p. 102.

28. T. S. Arthur, *Advice to Young Men*, quote p. 55; see Chapter 5 generally. See also Alcott, *The Young Man's Guide*, pp. 133-40.

29. Halttunen, *Confidence Men and Painted Women*, p. 11.

30. See Alcott, *The Young Man's Guide*, p. 139. Halttunen, *Confidence Men and Painted Women*, pp. 2, 12-13, makes this point effectively.

31. Halttunen, *Confidence Men and Painted Women*, pp. 3, 6, 7.

32. Halttunen, *Confidence Men and Painted Women*, pp. 9-11. I argue against the notion of passive liberty below.

33. Bernard Bailyn, *Intellectual Origins of the American Revolution* (Cambridge, Mass.: Harvard University Press, 1957), pp. 56-57. See also Halttunen, *Confidence Men and Painted Women*, p. 38.

34. Artemus Bowers Muzzey, *The Young Man's Friend*, quoted in Halttunen, *Confidence Men and Painted Women*, p. 9.

35. Halttunen, *Confidence Men and Painted Women*, pp. 4-5, quoting Rufus Clark, Beecher, *Seven Lectures*, and citing Charles E. Rosenberg, *The Cholera Years*.

36. Alger played billiards. He wrote Edwin R. A. Seligman from California on 13 March 1877: "As to billiards, I have played about eight games with a Philadelphia gentleman, at the Palace Hotel, and that is all. Still I can probably discount you when we play again." CU.

37. Halttunen, *Confidence Men and Painted Women*, p. 2.

38. *Wood's Illustrated Hand-Book to New York and Environs* (New York: G.W. Carelton, 1873), p. 27.

39. Halttunen, *Confidence Men and Painted Women*, preface, xv.

40. T. S. Arthur, *Advice to Young Men*, p. 18.

41. Alger, *Store Boy* (Philadelphia: John C. Winston, n.d.; copyright Porter & Coates, 1887), p. 257.

42. On reading character off the face and on the importance of straightforwardness, see, for example, Hawes, *Lectures to Young Men*, p. 77.

43. Heroes frequently study boxing, and Alger himself was versed in this gentlemanly skill. "Two boys knocked at my door the other day and asked if I would teach them to fight—I declined—I don't give free lessons in fighting any longer." Alger to Edwin R. A. Seligman, March 13, 1877 from California; CU.

44. See Chapters 7 and 9 in this book on the avoidance of performance in other circumstances. See also Philip Fisher, "Appearing and Disappearing in Public: Social Space in Late-Nineteenth-Century Literature and Culture," in Sacvan Bercovitch, ed., *Reconstructing American Literary History* (Cambridge,

Mass.: Harvard University Press, 1986), p. 185.

45. See Scharnhorst, *Horatio Alger, Jr.*, p. 89, on Alger's interest in phrenology and physiology.

46. Alger, *Rough and Ready* (Philadelphia: Porter and Coates, 1869), p. 244.

47. Alger, *Adrift in the City* (Philadelphia: John C. Winston, 1895), pp. 151-64. After his ordeal, he does accept an envelope, given "in reparation for the danger" to which he had been exposed, by the son of the mad physician. The destitute hero later opens it to find $100—quite a cushion against any future need to accept a stranger's invitation to lunch.

48. T. S. Arthur, *Advice to Young Men*, p. 3.

49. Clark, p. 28, quoted in Halttunen, *Confidence Men and Painted Women*, p. 4.

50. Alger, *Phil, the Fiddler* (Chicago: M. A. Donohue, n.d.), p. 1, although heroes are not usually termed "light-hearted."

51. See R. Richard Wohl, "The 'Rags to Riches Story': An Episode of Secular Idealism," pp. 501-6 in Reinhard Bendix and Seymour Martin Lipset, eds., *Class, Status, and Power* (New York: The Free Press, 2d ed., 1966), p. 503. See also Chapter 8 below.

52. Hawes, *Lectures to Young Men*, p. 69: a life spent in diversion, pleasure, and amusement is "utterly inconsistent with all manliness of thought and action."

53. Horace Mann, *A Few Thoughts For A Young Man*, pp. 13-14, 70.

54. Hawes, *Lectures to Young Men*, p. 65; subsequent quote p. 116.

55. Halttunen, *Confidence Men and Painted Women*, p. 25.

56. Hawes, *Lectures to Young Men*, pp. 74, 83; Lecture III in general.

57. Here, the message seems compatible with Carnegie's advice to wealthy men not to leave their sons too well provided, because they will lack industry in "The Gospel of Wealth". See Rychard Fink's introduction to *Ragged Dick and Mark, the Match Boy* (New York: Collier, 1962), pp .25-27 for a discussion of similarities and differences in the positions of Alger and Carnegie. The case that Alger's position is antithetical to Social Darwinism is made in Scharnhorst, *Horatio Alger, Jr.*, and Zuckerman, "Nursery Tales."

58. See Walter Benn Michaels, *The Gold Standard and the Logic of Naturalism* (Berkeley, Calif.: University of California Press, 1988), pp. 9-10. Henceforth, *Gold Standard*.

59. Hawes, *Lectures to Young Men*, p. 69.

60. Horace Mann, *A Few Thoughts for a Young Man*, p. 65.

61. Thayer, *Success and Its Achievers*, pp. 272-73 (1896 ed.).

62. Joel Hawes, *Lectures to Young Men*, p. 80. See also Lecture IV.

63. Howe, *Unitarian Conscience*, p. 54, discussing the views of Channing and Walker, President of Harvard.

64. See Lee Soltow and Edward Stevens, *The Rise of Literacy and the Common School in the United States* (Chicago: University of Chicago Press, 1981), pp. 85-86, 190 and 197. Edward Everett, "The Education of the Poor," Remarks at the examination and exhibition of the Everett School, 20th July, 1863, in *Orations and Speeches on Various Occasions*. 4 Vols. (Boston: Little, Brown, 1868).

65. James Fenimore Cooper, *The Pathfinder* (New York: Modern Library, 1952), p. 121.

66. Catherine Zuckert, *Natural Right and the American Imagination* (Savage, Md.: Rowman and Littlefield), p. 48.

67. Alger, untitled poem dated Dec. 18, 1882; UVa.

68. Howe, *Unitarian Conscience*, p. 58, discussing the Harvard lectures of Levi Frisbie. According to Howe, Frisbie followed Reid's system and his distinction between malevolent and benevolent affections. In the first quote, Reid is represented by Frisbie.

69. Howe, *Unitarian Conscience*, p. 53, quoting William Ellery Channing; p. 58.

70. Howe, *Unitarian Conscience*, p. 46; Thomas Reid quoted p. 48; see also p. 56. On the general good, see Henry Ware, Sr.'s lectures discussed p. 50.

71. Channing quoted in Howe, *Unitarian Conscience*, p. 62; Howe, p. 63.

72. T. S. Arthur, *Advice to Young Men*, p. 19.

73. Horace Mann, *A Few Thoughts for a Young Man*, p. 12.

74. Howe, *Unitarian Conscience*, p. 58 discussing the lectures of Levi Frisbie. See Howe, pp. 58-64.

75. Alcott, *Young Man's Guide*, pp. 62. 93, 108. T. S. Arthur, Chapter 4.

76. Howe, *Unitarian Conscience*, p. 61, quoting William Ellery Channing; p. 60.

77. Some older characters appear evil but mend their ways and live modest, decent lives, usually because of the influence of the boy. Occasionally a hero's soon-to-be-mentor has vices such as gambling, drinking, or playing billiards; he is saved from robbery or even murder by our hero, who happens upon the scene. The wealthy (young) man generally becomes reformed and more careful of his money and his life through contact with the hero, who he may even adopt, as in *Tony, the Tramp*. The motif of the virtuous little girl (as in *Sam's Chance*) resembles Oliver Optic's more moralistic tales, where a young girl is responsible for the reform of the hero and his exposure to the Bible.

78. Hawes, *Lectures to Young Men*, p. 60.

79. Hawes, *Lectures to Young Men*, p. 61.

80. On this theme, see Howe, *Unitarian Conscience*.

81. Thomas Hughes, *The Manliness of Christ*, pp. 5-6. The English clergyman's work was printed in Boston and New York: Houghton Mifflin Company, n.d. [lectures dated 1879].

82. Clifton Fadiman, "Party Of One," *Holiday* 21 (February, 1957): 118.

83. Alan Trachtenberg on Alger's *Ragged Dick* in *The Incorporation of America* (New York: Hill and Wang, 1982), p. 107.

84. T. S. Arthur, *Advice to Young Men*, p. 3: "society looks to the [young men who feel the force of good principles] . . . as her regenerators."

85. Halttunen, *Confidence Men and Painted Women*, p. 28.

86. Henry F. May, *The End of American Innocence*, pp. 9-10.

87. See May, *The End of American Innocence*, pp. 7-9.

CHAPTER 4

1. I am indebted to Robert Darnton's "Peasants Tell Tales," in *The Great Cat Massacre* (New York: Basic Books, 1984), for a view of hardship in the world of eighteenth century peasants' tales.

2. Tompkins, *Sensational Designs*, p. xvii, xviii.

3. On the significance of formula writing, see John Cawelti, *Adventure, Mystery, and Romance*, and Janice Radway, *Reading the Romance* (Chapel Hill: University of North Carolina Press, 1984). The A-Team, Thomas Magnum, "Miami Vice," and current weekly television dramas provide modern incarnations of formula writing and ritual repetition. The functionalist reading of formula writing derives from Cawelti. Jameson, "Ideology, Narrative Analysis, and Popular Culture," 547-48 critiques Cawelti's approach.

4. Tompkins, *Sensational Designs*, p. xvii, for both quotes. The second refers to several novels prior to 1860.

5. See Jane Tompkins' discussion of stereotyping Indians in Cooper's works; *Sensational Designs*, Ch. 4.

6. United States Department of Commerce, Bureau of the Census, *Statistical Abstract of the United States*, 1985, 105th ed., Table 123. *Historical Statistics*, Bicentennial Edition, Series C 89-119. (Washington, D.C.: Government Printing Office).

7. Tompkins, *Sensational Designs*, p. xvi.

8. Alger, *Phil, the Fiddler*, pp. 173-74.

9. United States Department of Commerce, Bureau of the Census, *Historical*

Statistics from Colonial Times to 1970, Series D152-66. (Washington, D.C.: Government Printing Office).

10. United States Department of Commerce, Bureau of the Census, *Twelfth Census of the United States Taken in the Year 1900*, Statistical Atlas, Plate 93. (Washington, D.C.: Government Printing Office).

11. There appears to be a rough correspondence between the timing of Alger's attention to these depressions and their actual occurrence. See *Five Hundred Dollars, Bound to Rise, Jack's Ward, Rufus and Rose*, and *From Farm to Fortune*. Alger "at least mentioned in his fiction every major economic catastrophe which occurred during his life . . ." Scharnhorst, *Horatio Alger, Jr.*, p. 128.

12. I am aware of only one case in which a stepparent is other than unsavory. This is a stepmother in *Tom Tracy* (New York: John W. Lovell, 1889, under pen name Arthur Lee Putnam). At the end of *Adrift in the City*, the hero's friend and benefactor is likely to *become* his mother's new husband, but the hero is already on his own and successful.

13. In *Brave and Bold* (New York: A. L. Burt, n.d.), Squire Davis attempts to brazen out the hero's assertion that his father deposited a large sum with him before going off to sea, presuming the receipt lost with the ostensibly dead captain. He later attempted to have the hero drowned when the boy went searching for his father.

14. I am aware of one exception. In *Frank Hunter's Peril* (Philadelphia: Henry T. Coates, 1896), the hero has to rely upon himself briefly after being cut adrift during a European vacation.

15. Occasionally, a hero escapes from the city to the healthier environment of the West. In *Julius, the Street Boy* (New York: Hurst, n.d.) an orphan is relocated with the help of the Children's Aid Society. In 1860, just over five million people inhabited American cities (with populations of eight thousand or more), and in 1900, the number was twenty-five million. A record 788,992 immigrants arrived in the United States in 1882, a number not surpassed until 1903. See Kirkland, *Industry Comes of Age* (New York: Holt, Rinehart and Winston, 1961).

16. See *Helen Ford, Young Acrobat*, and *Jed, the Poorhouse Boy*.

17. Alger, *Adrift in the City*, pp. 105, 108.

18. Ralph D. Gardner, introduction to Alger's *A Rolling Stone* (Leyden, Mass.: Aeonian Press, 1975), p. ii. See also Harold Harvey, "Alger's New York: A Story For Old Boys," *New York Tribune* (January 28, 1917), header, section 5, 3: "In his stories of newsboy life he has preserved New York of the late fifties with the descriptive detail of a Baedeker."

19. Harvey, "Alger's New York: A Story For Old Boys," 3-4.

20. Harvey, "Alger's New York," 3.

21. Warren Susman, *Culture as History* (New York: Pantheon, 1984), p. 244. Susman overstates the case by neglecting the fact that Alger often explicitly states the past setting of the book.

22. Michael Moon, "'The Gentle Boy from the Dangerous Classes': Pederasty, Domesticity, and Capitalism in Horatio Alger," *Representations* 19 (Summer, 1987): 97. Moon notes Alger's attention to male-male domestic relations.

23. "It needs to be mentioned that this was in a day of low prices, and that such an apartment now [renting for $5.50 per week], with board, would cost at least twelve dollars a week," *Rufus and Rose* (Philadelphia: Porter and Coates, 1870), p. 28.

24. Unnamed Alger source quoted in Harold Harvey, "Alger's New York," 4.

25. *Ben the Luggage Boy* (Philadelphia: Henry T. Coates, n.d.; copyright A. K. Loring, 1870), p. 70.

26. *From Farm to Fortune* (New York: Grosset & Dunlap, n.d.; copyright Stitt, 1905), one of the Stratemeyer-completed Algers, contains an interesting twist: one must even be wary of potential employers. Nat Nason gets rooked out of $100 by one who poses as an employer who claims to need this large deposit from his prospective clerks. *The Young Bank Messenger* (Philadelphia: John C. Winston, n.d.; copyright 1898 Henry T. Coates) offers a good example of multiple threats from the same tramp plus other defraudings.

27. E. J. Hobsbawm, *Bandits* (London: Weidenfeld and Nicolson, 1969), p. 153. See also Denning, *Mechanic Accents* (New York: Verso, 1987), p. 163.

28. Often, kidnapping becomes the vehicle of travel and adventure. Young Harry Raymond is lured aboard ship, drugged, sent off for China, and eventually thrown overboard in *Sink or Swim* (Chicago: M. A. Donohue, n.d.). See *Rufus and Rose*, *Adrift in New York*, *Timothy Crump's Ward* and its later variant, *Jack's Ward* for some of these different motifs. Zuckerman, "Nursery Tales," offers a fine discussion of the problem of proper parentage and the motif of reclaimed kinships.

29. In *Tony, the Hero* and *Jed, the Poorhouse Boy*, the boy is restored to his estate only after he has risen through his own efforts. There is a bit of Twain's *Prince and the Pauper* in all this: one must learn important lessons before resuming one's proper position.

30. Alger heroes and their mothers may speculate whether news of the death of a relative means money for them, but they never demand it. See *Tom Turner's Legacy* and *Forging Ahead*.

31. The speaker is Julius, an illiterate street boy. *Julius, the Street Boy*, p. 40.

32. Zuckerman, "Nursery Tales," 203 notes that "in the Alger novels of New York a steady undertone of desperation resonated beneath the scattered cries of lucky triumph."

33. Brace, *The Dangerous Classes of New York*, p. 27.

34. Brace, *The Dangerous Classes*, p. 29.

35. Gordon, Reich, and Edwards, *Segmented Work, Divided Workers* (New York: Cambridge University Press, 1982), p. 53.

36. Denning, *Mechanic Accents*, p. 149.

37. Paul T. Ringenbach, *Tramps and Reformers* (Westport, Conn.: Greenwood Press, 1973), pp. xiv, 4, 36.

38. There is some evidence that Alger preferred the title *Tony, the Hero*, but the story paper was aware of current attention to and controversy over tramps, even prior to the 1877 labor struggles. See Denning, *Mechanic Accents*, pp. 149, 151.

39. Ringenbach, *Tramps and Reformers*, pp. 18-19, quoting the *New York Times* (1875) and citing the widely quoted study of Richard T. Dugdale (1877) and that of Brewer (1878). Alger, sometimes accepting the inheritability of character traits, had this figure in his treatment of tramps; Tony was convinced he was not the actual son of Rudolph the tramp because they had different aspirations.

40. James Skerrett in Alger, *Making His Mark* (Des Plaines, Il: Gilbert K. Westgard II, 1979; reprint of edition Philadelphia: The Penn Publishing Company, 1901), pp. 36-38.

41. The Dean of the Yale Law School, speaking before the American Social Science Association in 1877, cited in Denning, *Mechanic Accents*, p. 150.

42. Ringenbach, *Tramps and Reformers*, pp. 16-17, italics in the original. Professor Wayland, "Paper on Tramps," Ringenbach, p. 18; Conference of Boards of Public Charities Proceedings (1877) quoted by Ringenbach, p. 19. Charles Loring Brace also believed that the tramp refused to find work.

43. Ringenbach, *Tramps and Reformers*, p. 17 and footnote 37, page 32.

44. Allan Pinkerton, *Strikers, Communists, Tramps and Detectives* (New York: G. W. Carleton & Company, 1878), p. 62. He did not wish to convey the impression that this disposition was typical of tramps, and appends stories of some hanging themselves or otherwise expressing their desperation.

45. Denning, *Mechanic Accents*, p. 150.

46. Ringenbach, *Tramps and Reformers*, pp. 19, 23.

47. Ringenbach, *Tramps and Reformers*, pp. 11, 23-24. The homeless could subvert the one night limit by moving from precinct to precinct, remaining one night at each; these became known as "revolvers." One found warmth wherever one could on a cold night, and not infrequently went, about midnight, to the station house for lodging, Wyckoff remembered (Walter Wyckoff, *The Workers, An Experiment in Reality: The West*. New York: Charles Scribner's Sons, 1904, pp. 2-3, 35-42). Police station lodgings came under reformers' attacks, partly due to foul

conditions and the mixing of tramps with indiscriminate unfortunates. With the opening of a lodging house established by reformers, the police station lodging declined dramatically.

48. Ringenbach, *Tramps and Reformers*, pp. 25-26, quoting Amos Warner and citing National Conference of Charities and Correction Proceedings for 1886, pp. 192-95.

49. Ringenbach, *Tramps and Reformers*, p. 13; p. 14, quoting and paraphrasing Wayland.

50. Denning, *Mechanic Accents*, p. 150; see Robert Bruce, *1877*.

51. *The Railroad Gazette*, 1879, citing an article from the *St. Louis Times-Journal* and reported by Monkkonen in Erik H. Monkkonen, ed., *Walking to Work: Tramps in America, 1790-1935* (Lincoln: University of Nebraska Press, 1984), footnote 7, p. 16. The same *Railroad Gazette* called on local authorities years later (1888) to "exterminate these pests."

52. Pinkerton, *Strikers, Communists, Tramps and Detectives*, p. 42.

53. Pinkerton, *Strikers, Communists, Tramps and Detectives*, pp. 58, 60.

54. Ringenbach, *Tramps and Reformers*, pp. 38, 39. Sources include the *Yale Review*. The Greenback Labor Party and many Christian Socialists also made the connection, as did John R. Commons.

55. Ringenbach, *Tramps and Reformers*, pp. 44-45, paraphrasing the *Nation* (1894). "Henrys" referred to Emile Henry, Parisian anarchist and dynamiter. Emma Goldman and others had been urging the hungry to "go and get" bread.

56. Ringenbach, *Tramps and Reformers*, pp. 36, 42. Henry George's *Progress and Poverty* and Socialist newspapers discovered this much earlier.

57. Alger, *Brave and Bold*, p. 211.

58. Pinkerton, *Strikers, Communists, Tramps and Detectives*, pp. 66, 66-67.

59. The quote is from Alger, *Making His Mark*, p. 36.

60. Alger, *A Rolling Stone*, pp. 20-23. See Chapter 7 for Alger's reticence about having recourse to formal legal procedures.

61. Pinkerton, *Strikers, Communists, Tramps and Detectives*, pp.55-57.

62. Alger, *Andy Gordon* (New York: A. L. Burt, n.d.), p. 73; originally published as *Forging Ahead*.

63. Monkkonen, pp. 3, 5 in Monkkonen, ed., *Walking to Work*.

64. Ringenbach, *Tramps and Reformers*, p. 5.

65. Pinkerton, *Strikers, Communists, Tramps and Detectives*, pp 39-40. He writes at length about tramp printers in the United States; "tramping . . . is a recognized pleasure and necessity among printers" (p. 53).

66. Monkkonen, *Walking to Work*, pp. 2, 5. Some women also tramped.

67. See Jules Tygiel, "Tramping Artisans: Carpenters in Industrial America, 1880-90," pp. 87-117 in Monkkonen, ed., *Walking to Work*. This evidence on cigar makers comes from the turn of the century. See Patricia A. Cooper, "The 'Traveling Fraternity': Union Cigar Makers and Geographic Mobility, 1900-1919," pp. 118-38 in Monkkonen.

68. Mark Wyman, *Hard Rock Epic* (Berkeley, Calif.: University of California Press, 1979), pp. 28, 42; p. 35, quoting letters from miners; the first is dated 1885. Wyman (pp. 35-36) documents mining wages that frequently exceeded $2.50 to $3 per day in the West; hard-rock miners on the Comstock Lode received a standard $4 per day. Mining wages therefore "contrasted dramatically with the national daily average for nonfarm labor of $1.04 to $1.57 in the 1870-1899 period; for carpenters, $2.23 to $3; wool manufacture, $1.42 to $1.47; shoe manufacture, $1.67 to $1.80; and iron manufacture, $1.99 to $2.03."

69. Wyman, *Hard Rock Epic*, quote p. 14; p. 15.

70. Pinkerton, *Strikers, Communists, Tramps and Detectives*, p.45.

71. Pinkerton, *Strikers, Communists, Tramps and Detectives*, pp. 34-36. He names names and includes Benjamin Franklin and Charles Dickens. He includes under the rubric "tramp" all those who break away from elegant surroundings to go strolling for a period of years.

72. Walter Wyckoff also took great pains to draw the distinction between a tramp and a man wandering and working the countryside in *A Day with a Tramp and Other Essays* (New York: Charles Scribner's Sons, 1901), noting that his university acquaintances were as likely to use the term "tramp" for one as the other.

73. Hamlin Garland, *A Son of the Middle Border* (New York: Macmillan, 1924), pp. 287-88.

74. Monkkonen, *Walking to Work*, footnote 7, p. 15, citing the *Minneapolis Tribune* July 30, 1878, reprint of an article from a *Chicago Tribune* article.

75. Garland, *Son of the Middle Border*, pp. 251-52.

76. Wyckoff, *The Workers, An Experiment in Reality: The East* (New York: Charles Scribner's Sons, 1899), pp. 5, 6, 16, and Chapter 1 generally.

77. Wyckoff, *The Workers . . . The West*, pp. 70-71 and pp. 23, 61.

78. Wyckoff as quoted in Ringenbach, *Tramps and Reformers*, p. 42.

79. Wyckoff, *The Workers . . . The West*, pp. 1-2.

80. Pinkerton, *Strikers, Communists, Tramps and Detectives*, p. 64.

81. Denning, *Mechanic Accents*, p. 150, drawing upon Herbert Gutman (1976) and Michael Davis (1984).

82. Pinkerton, *Strikers, Communists, Tramps and Detectives*, p. 41; preface, p. xi; pp. 31-33.

83. Pinkerton, *Strikers, Communists, Tramps and Detectives*, p. 66.

84. Pinkerton, *Strikers, Communists, Tramps and Detectives*, pp. 47-48.

85. Ringenbach, *Tramps and Reformers*, quoting *The National Labor Tribune*, 1875, and Henry George, *Social Problems*, pp. 37 and frontspiece.

86. "On to Washington; Or, Old Cap Collier with the Coxey Army" (1984) quoted in Denning, *Mechanic Accents*, p. 154.

87. Denning, *Mechanic Accents*, pp. 151-52, drawing upon Captain Frederick Whittaker's *Nemo, King of the Tramps* (Beadle's Dime Library 132, May 4, 1881) for the attitude of the tramp described here.

88. *Tony, the Hero*, the reprint title (New York: A. L. Burt, 1890).

89. Ignatius Donnelly, Preamble to the 1892 Omaha Platform of the People's Party, quoted in John D. Hicks, *The Populist Revolt* (Minneapolis: University of Minnesota Press, 1931), p. 440.

90. Real annual earnings for nonfarm employees declined from $457 in 1860 to $375 in 1870, rose only to $395 by 1880 and then began to show more marked growth, reaching $519 by 1890 and $573 by 1900. Available figures indicate daily wages for nonfarm employees in real dollars rise from 1860-65, decline slightly and stabilize in the period 1865-72, and decline to 1862 levels for the 1872-80 period. (*Historical Statistics*, Series D735-8; index: 1914=100.)

91. Pinkerton, *Strikers, Communists, Tramps and Detectives*, pp. 50, 31-32; 51 respectively.

CHAPTER 5

1. Alger, *Ben Bruce* (New York: A. L. Burt, 1901), pp. 9-11. The first serialization of this story began in *The Argosy*, 15 (December, 10, 1892) and continued into 1893. Here is a case where workers will be thrown out of work through no fault of the employer; some of their fellows are to blame.

2. Kasson, *Civilizing the Machine*, p. 86.

3. Kasson, *Civilizing the Machine*, Chapters 2-3, and Ralph Waldo Emerson quoted in Kasson, p. 127.

4. *Historical Statistics of the United States, Colonial Times to 1970*, Series P1-12; figures are 1859-99. The number of manufacturing establishments doubles from 1879-99. See also Kirkland, *Industry Comes of Age*, pp. 325-6.

5. Kirkland, *Industry Comes of Age*, pp. 325-26; 332, 349, 173. See also *Historical Statistics*, Series D152-166.

6. *Twelfth Census of the United States Taken in the Year 1900,* Statistical Atlas, Plate 93.

7. On the nonmechanized nature of this work see Scharnhorst, *Horatio Alger, Jr.,* pp. 124-25.

8. Alger, *Brave and Bold,* pp. 7, 10-11, 23, and passim.

9. Daniel T. Rodgers claims that it is as if Alger was "desperate for some contrivance to expel [the boy] as quickly as possible into the world where a man could make his mark." *The Work Ethic,* p. 39.

10. Quoted in Wyman, *Hard Rock Epic,* p. 17.

11. Wyman, *Hard Rock Epic,* pp. 9-10, 19; see pp. 80-81 on ore-stealing conflicts and management strategies.

12. Wyman, *Hard Rock Epic,* pp. 12-14; 28 and 42; 14. Quote p. 29. See pp. 38-39 on conflict with Chinese labor.

13. The central character in Alger's *Herbert Carter's Legacy* (New York: New York Book Co., 1908) ends by entering the manufacturing establishment of his benefactor as an office clerk.

14. Alger, *Store Boy,* p. 125. The aspiration for wealth is voiced in 1887.

15. A conversation between the central character and Mr. Forge, the blacksmith in *Tom Turner's Legacy* (New York: Hurst & Company, copyright 1902 A. L. Burt, 176-77) is revealing. Although looking for work, Tom refuses the offer of apprenticeship that could eventually lead to a reasonably lucrative business of his own. He claims he would like some other trade better, and Forge suggests it is because the work is dirty. Tom says he has never thought of that, but never comes up with a real answer. We are left with merely the assertion that he believes himself better adapted to some other work. He handles the rest of the interview as a diplomat and humorist. See also *Dean Dunham,* where the hero turns down a chance to be a shoemaker, and *Wait and Win.* The hero also avoids going to sea and farming.

16. Alger, *Dean Dunham* (Leyden, Mass.: Aeonian Press, 1975), p. 156. See also Alger's *A Rolling Stone.*

17. Dreiser, *Sister Carrie,* p. 160 and passim.

18. Alger's *Luke Walton* (Philadelphia: John C. Winston; n.d.; original copyright Porter & Coates, 1889) was serialized in the *Golden Argosy* in late 1887 and into 1888; his *Train Boy,* serialized and published in 1883 and also set largely in Chicago, exhibits the same pattern of selective blindness.

19. Friedrich Engels, writing of Manchester in 1845, but noting that the plan tends to be common to all major cities, *The Condition of the Working-Class in England* (Moscow: Progress Publishers, 1973), pp. 85-86.

20. Cawelti was among the first to notice this in *Apostles of the Self-Made Man*.

21. *Historical Statistics*, Series D182-232. Looking at average daily wages, available for 1860-80 only in statistical series D728-34 and 735-8, we would conclude that the twenty year range of a week's earnings—if someone worked full-time every day for *six* days per week—would be as follows: $6.54-6.96 for all nonfarm employees; $6.18-7.92 for laborers; and $9.72-13.56 for skilled laborers, which includes blacksmiths, carpenters, engineers, painters and machinists.

22. Miss Manning in Alger, *Rufus and Rose*, p. 72.

23. Alger, *Rough and Ready*, p. 97.

24. Alger, *Helen Ford* (Boston: A. K. Loring, 1866). Both quotes are from p. 255. Scharnhorst (*Horatio Alger, Jr.*) reads such evidence to claim that Alger had closet labor sympathies.

25. Henry F. May, *End of American Innocence*, p. 16.

26. Hamilton Wright Mabie, critic for the *Christian Union*, quoted in Trachtenberg, *Incorporation of America*, p. 182. Alger's appreciation of Stedman in letter to him dated November 29, 1875; YU. On Howells, see an Edward Stratemeyer-completed Alger, *The Young Book Agent*, and the earlier *Ben Bruce*.

27. Scharnhorst with Bales, *Lost Life*, p. 13. Alger, *Bound to Rise* (Chicago: M. A. Donohue & Co., n.d.), p. 155.

28. Thayer, *Success and Its Achievers*, quote from pp. 172-73 in the 1896 edition. The 1891 subscription version was the one with which Alger was familiar. For Alger's gift of this work to Irving Blake, see letter of December 18, 1896 and subsequent mention; HL.

29. Herbert Gutman, "The Reality of the Rags-to-Riches 'Myth'," in *Work, Culture and Society in Industrializing America* (New York: Vintage Books, 1976), p. 232.

30. Gutman, *Work, Culture and Society*, pp. 224-25 and 232-33.

31. Tamara Hareven, *Family Time and Industrial Time* (New York: Cambridge University Press, 1982), p. 259 and Chapter 10 in general.

32. Stephan Thernstrom, *Poverty and Progress* (Cambridge, Mass.: Harvard University Press, 1964), pp. 164-65.

33. Richard T. Ely quoted in R. Richard Wohl, "The Rags to Riches Story," p. 504.

34. Alger, *Rufus and Rose*, p. viii, italics in original.

35. Alger, *Sink or Swim*, p. 111.

36. Howe, *Unitarian Conscience*, p. 42.

37. Thayer, *Success and Its Achievers*, 1896 edition, p. 380.

38. Alger, *Phil, the Fiddler*, p. 153. While self-employment is an expression of independence from control as well, few Alger heroes persist in this route to independence.

39. See, for example, *Dean Dunham*, pp. 186-87. Its value is expressed in its metallic element, being superior to a silver watch. Alger left his "calendar gold watch" to his niece's son in his will of February 15, 1898 (HUA). See Michael O'Malley, *Keeping Watch* (New York: Viking, 1990) on the struggle over control of time and resistance to its standardization as unnatural during this era.

40. Alger, *Tom Turner's Legacy*, p. 230.

41. See Cawelti, *Apostles of the Self-Made Man*.

42. In at least one Alger novel, *Ralph Raymond's Heir* (New York: Hurst and Company, n.d.), the hero may not take up *any* business. Young Robert, having recovered his patrimony, retires to a beautiful country seat on the Hudson.

43. Daniel T. Rodgers: "Nineteenth-century success writers talked of many avenues to the top, but the one they were most familiar with was the mercantile path that led from clerk to junior partner to merchant capitalist." *The Work Ethic*, pp. 38-39.

CHAPTER 6

1. John P. Davis, *Corporations* (New York: Capricorn, 1961; reprint of 1904 edition), Vol. 2, p. 261. See also Michaels, *The Gold Standard*.

2. John L. Thomas, "Utopia for an Urban Age: Henry George, Henry Demarest Lloyd, Edward Bellamy," in Donald Fleming and Bernard Bailyn, eds., *Perspectives in American History*, Vol. 4 (1972). (Harvard University: Charles Warren Center for Studies in American History), p. 138.

3. R. Jackson Wilson, *In Quest of Community* (New York: Wiley, 1968), pp. 173-74.

4. Philip Fisher, "Appearing and Disappearing in Public," p. 163.

5. Kasson, *Civilizing the Machine*, p. 147, quoting the *New York Illustrated News*.

6. Alger to Irving Blake, July 10, 1896; HL.

7. Thomas, "Utopia for an Urban Age," pp. 136, 138.

8. Davis, *Corporations*, Vol. 2, p. 268. The eventual result of this process will surely be an extension of state power: ". . . It would be against the teachings of history to expect that now the state will stop short of the complete absorption of the governmental features of corporations."

9. Alger, "Athens," first quote, p. 6; subsequent quotes, p. 7.

10. Alger quoted in Harvey, "Alger's New York," 3 and 4 respectively.

11. Written of the Bon Marché in Paris. Fisher, "Appearing and Disappearing in Public," p. 167, quoting Michael B. Miller, *The Bon Marché*.

12. Fisher, "Appearing and Disappearing in Public," pp. 163, 167 on opening of Wanamakers. See Alger letters to Irving Blake of November 10, 1896 and November 23, 1896, HL. The claim about comparative size comes from Thayer, *Success and Its Achievers* (1896), p. 137.

13. Alger to Irving Blake, November 10, 1896 and November 7, 1897; HL.

14. Thayer, *Success and Its Achievers* (1896), p. 137.

15. Kasson, *Civilizing the Machine*, p. 41.

16. The importance of the geographic occupation of space and the annihilation of space by time in the nineteenth century receives superb treatment by David Harvey in *Consciousness and the Urban Experience* (Baltimore: Johns Hopkins University Press, 1985), especially Chapter 1.

17. Quoted in Hartz, *The Liberal Tradition in America*, p. 112.

18. Thomas, "Utopia for an Urban Age," p. 137.

19. Kasson, *Civilizing the Machine*, pp. 155, 162; quote pp. 162-63. Reporter to the *New York Herald* quoted in Kasson, p. 164.

20. See *Herbert Carter's Legacy; Helen Ford*. The European vacation in *Frank Hunter's Peril* (first serialized in 1885) was a very rare occurrence in an Alger story.

21. See Kasson, *Civilizing the Machine*, Chapters 2-3.

22. *Newsboy* has reprinted these travel pieces in two of its numbers. Bales and Scharnhorst, "Alger's European Tour 1860-61," and "Horatio Alger, Jr. and the *Sun* Travel Essays." There is some mention of Garibaldi when Alger was in southern Italy; Alger may have once carried a message from Garibaldi.

23. Kirkland, *Industry Comes of Age*, pp. 357-58.

24. Scharnhorst and Bales, *Horatio Alger, Jr.: An Annotated Bibliography*, pp. 15-16.

25. Alger, letter to Joseph Seligman, 14 November 1884; CU.

26. Alger to Edwin R. A. Seligman, 15 February 1877, Joseph Seligman Collection, Rare Books and Manuscripts, CU. See also Scharnhorst and Bales, *Horatio Alger, Jr.: An Annotated Bibliography*, p. 16.

27. Scharnhorst and Bales, *Horatio Alger, Jr.: An Annotated Bibliography*, p. 16, do not seem to know quite what to make of Alger's remarks, noting that "Despite such intellectual flirtations, he usually endorsed the programs and candidacies of liberal Republicans."

28. According to Scharnhorst, *Horatio Alger, Jr.*, p. 126, Alger's street boys

generally help each other and do not enrich themselves at each others' expense, exhibiting the type of bonds discussed here. However, there is an interesting anomaly in *Rough and Ready* (pp. 18-19). A would-be bootblack is engaged by an Alger hero who pays for the equipment and reaps half the profits of the enterprise, "going whacks," as the street boys call it (apparently, a common enough practice). Rufus Rushton becomes this sort of "capitalist" while a newsboy. Since bootblacks certainly hold an economically precarious position, it is hard to imagine how the newcomer made a living wage. We are left to assume he merely worked harder.

29. Alger, *A Rolling Stone*, p. 49. While *A Rolling Stone* was first published in book form posthumously, the story appeared in *The Argosy* in 1894.

30. The point is made by Scharnhorst, *Horatio Alger, Jr.*, pp. 121-22.

31. Alger, *Luck and Pluck* (Boston: Loring, 1869), pp. 18-19; also p. 24.

32. Will Wright, *Sixguns and Society*, p. 148.

33. Bellamy, "America the Only Land of Freedom," editorial in the *Springfield Union* [Massachusetts], July 8, 1876.

34. Michaels, *Gold Standard*, p. 133.

35. This is true for major characters, but *Rupert's Ambition* (Philadelphia: John C. Winston [1899], copyright Henry T. Coates, 1892; and first serialized 1894) tells of a father whose wages are reduced by an unscrupulous dry goods merchant, who knows the employment prospects are bad and that the poor man must acquiesce because his family depends on him. Through a new friend, Rupert finds him a better job.

36. Thomas, "Utopia for an Urban Age," p. 138.

37. Alger, *Phil, the Fiddler*, pp. 137-38; second quote pp. 130-31.

38. Scharnhorst with Bales, *Lost Life*, p. 127.

39. Davis, *Corporations*, Vol. 2, pp. 270, 273. As Davis builds a case that "The purchaser of stock considers that he is acquiring an interest in an enterprise, not so much that he is assuming common relations with the numerous stockholders," he seems to paraphrase Marx on the fetishism of commodities. Relations among persons are masked as exchanges among things.

40. Walter Benn Michaels, "Corporate Fiction: Norris, Royce, and Arthur Machen," p. 194; in Sacvan Bercovitch, ed., *Reconstructing American Literary History* (Cambridge, Mass.: Harvard University Press, 1986); and p. 203, quoting George F. Canfield.

41. See, for example, the Supreme Court case of *Santa Clara County v. Southern Pacific Railroad Co.*, 118 U.S. (1886) 557.

42. Davis, *Corporations*, Vol. 2, p. 271.

43. On this image of the corporation, see Michaels, "Corporate Fiction;" in the second passage quoted on p. 199, he is writing of Royce's *The Feud at Oakfield Creek*.

44. John P. Davis, *Corporations*, Vol. 2, p. 252, writing in 1897.

45. Alfred D. Chandler, Jr., *The Visible Hand* (Cambridge, Mass.: Harvard University Press, 1977), pp. 203-4.

46. T. S. Arthur, *Advice to Young Men*, p. 237.

47. Horace Mann, *A Few Thoughts for a Young Man*, p. 78.

48. Alcott, *Young Man's Guide*, pp. 151, 135; T. S. Arthur, *Advice to Young Men*, p. 239.

49. Alcott, *Young Man's Guide*, pp. 109-14; see also T. S. Arthur, *Advice to Young Men*, pp. 237-42; Hawes, *Lectures to Young Men*, pp. 77-79. The quote is Arthur, p. 240.

50. Alger may have borrowed the incident from a Boston area newspaper or periodical. The scenario is almost identical to one mentioned by Thayer in *Success and Its Achievers* (p. 220, 1896 ed.), where a lady walks into a Boston dry goods store and fails to make a cloth purchase. The unprincipled merchant asks his young salesman why he did not represent the cloth as the Middlesex cloth she had wanted; the honest young man said he would not tell falsehoods to keep his place. "'Young man,' said the merchant, 'if you are so particular, and can't bend a little to circumstances, you will never do for me.'" The young man "left the store, and that God who requires as strict honesty in the warehouse as in the church, led him forth to prosperity. He became a leading merchant in a western city, while his dishonest employer became a bankrupt, and died in poverty."

51. Alger, *A Rolling Stone*, p. 217; see pp. 226, 236.

52. I am indebted to Michaels, "Corporate Fiction," for a juxtaposition of the human and the inhuman, natural and artificial in the emergence of the corporation in fiction and in law.

53. Alger in the *Golden Argosy*, 10 March 1883, quoted in Scharnhorst, *Horatio Alger, Jr.*, pp. 117-18. Scharnhorst claims Alger used Stewart as a fictional character.

54. Alger, *Dan, the Newsboy* (New York: A. L. Burt, 1893), p. 62.

55. Alger, *Frank Hunter's Peril*, p. 31.

56. Alger, *A Rolling Stone*, p. 257.

57. Alger, *A Rolling Stone*, p. 265.

58. Alger, *Dean Dunham*, p. 230. He asserts, in a letter to Edwin R. A. Seligman on 13 March 1877, that the climate in California is stimulating to the point that he can accomplish 50 percent more work per week than in New York. "Businessmen tell me the same thing." CU.

59. Alger, *Dean Dunham*, p. 244.

60. Hawes, *Lectures to Young Men*, p. 70: "When the love of money becomes in any man, a dominant principle of action, there is an end of all hope of his ever attaining the true excellence of an intelligent and moral being."

61. Thayer, *Success and Its Achievers*, 1896 edition, p. 214. Carnegie remarks to the students of a commercial college in Pittsburgh quoted by Thayer.

62. Horace Mann, *A Few Thoughts for a Young Man*, p. 66.

CHAPTER 7

1. Mention of an article by Gladstone he wished to read and of the impending death of Bismarck appear in Alger's letters to Blake, HL.

2. Scharnhorst and Bales, *Horatio Alger, Jr.: An Annotated Bibliography*, p. 16; Alger to Seligman 9 November 1876; CU. Cousin William Rounseville Alger was author and minister in Manhattan; Alger engaged a pew in his church.

3. Alger to Blake, September 9, 1896 and November 10, 1896; HL.

4. See also Scharnhorst and Bales, *Horatio Alger, Jr.: An Annotated Bibliography*, p. 14.

5. Although the author was a temperance man, he seemed to see abstention as a private obligation rather than an object for political decision making.

6. Horace Mann, *A Few Thoughts For A Young Man*, p. 61.

7. Alger, *Phil, the Fiddler*, p. 153, quote p. 154.

8. Alger, *Luck and Pluck*, pp. 18, 22.

9. Scharnhorst, *Horatio Alger, Jr.*, pp. 83-84, quoting *Ben, the Luggage Boy, Frank and Fearless, Bob Burton*, and *In Search of Treasure*.

10. Horace Greeley, "Why I Am A Whig: Reply to an Inquiring Friend." New York, 1852, p. 1.

11. Cooper, *The American Democrat* (Cooperstown, New York: H. & E. Phinney, 1838), p. 135; second quote, p. 140.

12. Horace Mann, *A Few Thoughts For A Young Man*, pp. 13, 57.

13. T. S. Arthur, *Advice to Young Men*, p. 153.

14. Alexis de Tocqueville, *Democracy in America*, translated by George Lawrence (Garden City, N.Y.: Anchor Books, 1969), Vol. I, Part 2, Chapter 5, p. 197.

15. Adams, *The Education of Henry Adams*, pp. 158-9; 150.

16. Alger, "Athens," pp. 66-67, writing of Aristophanes; HUA.

17. W. R. Alger, *Forrest*, Vol. 2, p. 601.

18. Cooper "A Letter to His Countrymen" (New York: John Wiley, 1834), pp. 49-50, quoting Noah Webster (1833).

19. Alger to General Russell A. Alger, 10 November, 1898, UM. Scharnhorst with Bales, *Lost Life*, pp. 17-18.

20. Emerson, journal entry of 1845, quoted in Daniel Walker Howe, *The Political Culture of the American Whigs* (Chicago: University of Chicago Press, 1979), p. 13. Emerson sometimes lampooned their didacticism and paternalism.

21. Edward Everett in the U.S. Senate, quoted in Howe, *Political Culture of the American Whigs*, p. 181; p. 21.

22. Chilton Williamson, *American Suffrage from Property to Democracy, 1760-1860* (Princeton, N.J.: Princeton University Press, 1960),p. 287.

23. Horace Greeley, "Why I Am A Whig," 1852, p. 13.

24. Howe, *Political Culture of the American Whigs*, p. 33, borrowing from E. P. Thompson's description of English "disciplinarians."

25. Greeley, "Why I Am A Whig," p. 13.

26. Williamson, *American Suffrage*, p. 292, citing the *Correspondence of James Fenimore Cooper*.

27. Hartz, *Liberal Tradition in America*, pp. 111-12. On the Whig support of extension of the franchise, see Williamson, *American Suffrage*, pp. 281-82, citing the *American Quarterly Review* (1836) and Charles F. Adams (1841).

28. Williamson, *American Suffrage*, pp. 267, 270-71. Even the Massachusetts Democrats remained opposed to dropping taxpaying qualifications in local and school elections. On small town opposition, see pp. 243-44, where Williamson speaks of Rhode Island in particular.

29. On the bipartisan support for suffrage reform in some other states, especially where an exclusively taxpaying qualification remained, see Williamson, *American Suffrage*, pp. 238-41, 262, 265; see pp. 268-69 on the assault waged on the size of the Massachusetts poll tax by Democrats in the early 1840s. On sunset laws, Williamson, p. 273. Democrats challenged these in 1851-53.

30. Williamson, *American Suffrage*, pp. 273-75. Part of the rationale for the open ballot was to try to get voters to vote a straight ticket.

31. See Edward Everett, "The Education of the Poor," Remarks at the examination and exhibition of the Everett School, 20th July 1863, in *Orations and Speeches on Various Occasions*, Vol. 4. Williamson, *American Suffrage*, p. 292, citing the *Correspondence of James Fenimore Cooper*.

32. Howe, *Political Culture of the American Whigs*, p. 27.

33. James Fenimore Cooper, *The American Democrat* (1838), p. 92.

34. Alger to J. Fenimore Cooper, Esq. dated September 12, 1850 from Cambridge, Mass.; YU.

35. Zuckert, *Natural Right and the American Imagination*, pp. 39; 59-60; 29.

36. Cooper, *The American Democrat* (New York: Alfred A. Knopf, 1931), p. 71.

37. Williamson, *American Suffrage*, p. 248.

38. William L. Clements Library, UM.

39. Richard Hofstadter, *The American Political Tradition* (New York: Vintage, 1973), pp. 218-19, quoting Woodrow Wilson and Henry Adams.

40. Scharnhorst and Bales, *Horatio Alger, Jr.: An Annotated Bibliography*, p. 14.

41. Alger to Irving Blake, November 7, 1897 from Natick; HL.

42. Gustavus Myers, *The History of Tammany Hall* (New York: Dover Publications, 1971), 2d ed., p. 305; pp. 282-83.

43. Hofstadter, *American Political Tradition*, pp. 218-19; pp. 221-22 on Arthur, Boss Quay, and Harrison.

44. Alger, *Rupert's Ambition*, p. 154.

45. Scharnhorst and Bales, *Horatio Alger, Jr.: An Annotated Bibliography*, p. 14. The observation concerning Micky Maguire as a political hack is theirs.

46. From Thayer, *Success and Its Achievers*, 1896 edition, p. 402. Scharnhorst first recognized this point.

47. See Scharnhorst and Bales, *Horatio Alger, Jr.: An Annotated Bibliography*, p. 16.

48. Alger, Jr. to General Russell A. Alger, May 2, 1888; UM.

49. Hofstadter, *American Political Tradition*, p. 226; Josephson, *The Politicos* (New York: Harcourt, Brace, 1966), quote p. 366.

50. Scharnhorst with Bales, *Lost Life*, p. 127.

51. H. Wayne Morgan, *From Hayes to McKinley* (Syracuse, N.Y.: Syracuse University Press, 1969), p. 200.

52. Hofstadter, *American Political Tradition*, p. 229, and quoting Wilson, p. 235.

53. Josephson, *The Politicos*, p. 389.

54. Quoted in Joseph Dorfman, *The Economic Mind in American Civilization*, Vol. 3 (New York: Viking, 1959), p. 118, from *The Nation*, August 23, 1888.

55. Josephson, *The Politicos*, p. 354.

56. William C. Whitney to Cleveland in 1892, quoted in Hofstadter, *American Political Tradition*, p. 234; Gould quoted p. 235.

57. Republican Senator Allison remarked that it was merciful Cleveland had won over Harrison in 1892, because "no Republican President could have secured repeal of the Sherman Silver Purchase Act." Hofstadter, *American Political Tradition*, p. 235. On Cleveland as a hard-money man, see also Michaels, *The Gold Standard*, p. 162.

58. Hofstadter, *American Political Tradition*, p. 222.

59. C. C. Buel, "Our Fellow-Citizen of the White House: The Official Cares of a President of the United States," *Century*, Vol. 53 (March, 1897): 664.

60. Alger to Russell A. Alger, November 10, 1898, recounting an event some fifteen years earlier; UM.

61. Alger to Irving Blake, March 25, 1897; HL.

62. Alger to Irving Blake, November 10, 1896, HL. Quoted in Chapter 8 below.

63. Horatio Alger, Jr. Papers; UVa.

64. Alger to Irving Blake, July 10, 1896; HL.

65. Quote is from Thayer, *Success and Its Achievers* (1896), p. 303.

66. Alger to Mr. Elderkin, August 2, 1884; YU.

67. Alger to Messrs Porter and Coates, August 19, 1884. Horatio Alger, Jr. Papers; UVa.

68. Morgan, *From Hayes to McKinley*, p. 246.

69. See Fisher, "Appearing and Disappearing in Public," pp. 181, 186-88. Alger collaborated, however, with his relative on the lengthy biography of celebrated actor Edwin Forrest.

70. Michaels, "Corporate Fiction," p. 201, discussing Royce.

71. Fisher, "Appearing and Disappearing in Public," p. 188, writing about James, Twain, and Howells.

72. Alger, *Dean Dunham*, p. 183. First serialized in 1888.

73. Alger, *Dean Dunham*, pp. 260-61.

74. Adams, *The Education of Henry Adams*, p. 150.

75. *American Review*, 1852, quoted in Howe, *Political Culture of the American Whigs*, p. 181. See also Howe, pp. 21, 29, 32.

76. Joseph Dorfman, *The Economic Mind in American Civilizaton, 1606-1865*, Vol. 2 (New York: Viking, 1956), p. 633.

77. Cooper, "A Letter to His Countrymen," p. 89.

78. Henry May, *End of American Innocence*, p. 18, quoting Roosevelt, "Realizable Ideals," 1912. These phrases, spoken over a dozen years after Alger's death, reflected a world with which Alger would have remained comfortable.

79. In 1896, after the McKinley election, Alger wrote to Blake: "I see Roosevelt is looking for a position in Washington. He will be a loss to New York"; December 3, 1896, HL.

80. Henry May, *End of American Innocence*, pp. 22, 28.

81. See Hartz, *Liberal Tradition in America*, Chapter 9 on the progressives' attempt to reverse the irreversible. Also May, *End of American Innocence*, p. 22; and Richard Hofstadter, *The Progressive Historians*.

82. Henry May, *End of American Innocence*, pp. 24-25.

83. May, *End of American Innocence*, p. 51.

84. See Louis Hartz, *The Liberal Tradition in America*.

85. May, *End of American Innocence*, p. 20.

86. Michael Wines, "Bush's Campaign Tries Madison Ave.," *New York Times*, Wednesday, May 27, 1992, A 18. Daniel Goleman, "For Presidential Candidates, Optimism Appears A Winner, *New York Times*, May 8, 1988, A 1, 18.

87. By this measure, in Eastern Europe, the power of the United States is exhibited, post hoc, in its historically steadfast rhetoric of opposition to Communism.

CHAPTER 8

1. Alger, *Dean Dunham*, p. 117.

2. Scharnhorst correctly points out that a few Alger characters *remark* that the wicked get away with it (e.g., *Horatio Alger, Jr.*, p. 134). This idea is generally not what Alger chooses to demonstrate. According to Malcolm Cowley, "poverty [is] the hell to which villains are assigned by Alger's Yankee theology." In "Horatio Alger: Failure," p. 64.

3. T. S. Arthur, *Advice to Young Men*, p. 8.

4. Joel Hawes, *Lectures to Young Men*, pp. 108-9.

5. Thayer, *Success and Its Achievers*, first quote p. 266 (1891 edition); second quote pp. 229-30 (1896 edition).

6. Hawes, *Lectures to Young Men*, pp. 111-12. Italics in original.

7. Horace Mann, *A Few Thoughts for a Young Man*, pp. 78-79.

8. Hawes, *Lectures to Young Men*, p. 84.

9. Thayer, *Success and Its Achievers* (1896), p. 432.

10. Howe, *Unitarian Conscience*, pp. 64, 67.

11. Francis Bowen quoted in Howe, *Unitarian Conscience*, pp. 67, 64.

12. Howe, *Unitarian Conscience*, p. 40.

13. Horace Mann, *A Few Thoughts For A Young Man*, pp. 13, 57.

14. Alger, *Rupert's Ambition*, p. 143. Scharnhorst and Bales think this theme only comes late in Alger's career; I do not.

15. Alger to Irving Blake, writing upon the completion of *Walter Sherwood's Probation*, January 1, 1898; HL.

16. Garfield quoted, without citation, by Thayer, *Success and Its Achievers* (1896), p. 184.

17. Alger, *Luck and Pluck*, Preface, v.

18. Victor W. Turner, *The Ritual Process: Structure and Anti-structure* (Chicago: Aldine, 1969), pp. 106-7; see also Halttunen, *Confidence Men and Painted Women*, p. 30.

19. Joel Hawes, *Lectures to Young Men*, pp. 93; 70.

20. Alger, *Ragged Dick* (Boston: Loring, 1868), pp. 283-84.

21. See also Malcolm Cowley, "Horatio Alger: Failure," 64-65. "Virtue has been rewarded, vice punished, and the whole operation has been pecuniary. In its preoccupation with exact sums in dollars, and in that alone, the Alger fable resembles the typical American success story as enacted in fiction or in life."

22. If the persons receiving the assistance or service are, too poor to offer more than their thanks, the provider is often rewarded by someone else.

23. Alger, *Mark, the Match Boy* (New York: Collier, 1962), pp. 222-23. Zuckerman has pointed out that the excessive price boys will pay for a room indicates how an ample home is the alternative to the "real independence and loneliness of the large city." "The Nursery Tales of Horatio Alger," 208-9.

24. Alger, *Making His Way* (New York: A. L. Burt, n.d., p. 268).

25. See, T. S. Arthur, *Advice to Young Men*, Chapters 6 and 7. Even Captain Frederick Whittaker's dime novel, *John Armstrong, Mechanic* (Beadle's Dime Library 378, January 20, 1886), bears the message that self-improvement pays off in secular terms.

26. Alger, *Ragged Dick*, p. 125. This printer-turned-inventor, a latter day Franklin, is unusual; see Chapter 6.

27. Alger, *Dean Dunham*, p. 158.

28. Tebbel, *From Rags to Riches*, p. 14.

29. Irvin G. Wyllie, *The Self-Made Man in America* (New York: The Free Press, 1954), p. 60.

30. Rodgers, *The Work Ethic*, p. 140; see also Zuckerman, "The Nursery Tales of Horatio Alger."

31. Zuckerman, "The Nursery Tales of Horatio Alger," 203.

32. Howe, *Unitarian Conscience*, p. 46 on the position of Scottish clergyman, philosopher, and ethical sentimentalist Francis Hutcheson; quote is Howe, p. 42.

33. Fadiman, "Party of One," 9.

34. Thayer, *Success and Its Achievers* (1896), p. 339: "Duty is something that must be done without regard to discomfort, sacrifice, or death; and it must be done in secret, as well as in public." Second quote, p. 419.

35. Thayer, *Success and Its Achievers* (1896), pp. 426-27.

36. Michaels, *The Gold Standard*, p. 232.

37. Charles Hartshorne and Paul Weiss, eds., *Collected Papers of Charles Sanders Peirce, Scientific Metaphysics*, Vol. 6 (Cambridge, Mass.: Harvard University Press, 1935), Ch. 5, "The Law of Mind," sections 148-57, pp. 108-13.

38. Alger, *Ragged Dick*, pp. 292-93.

39. Zuckerman, "The Nursery Tales of Horatio Alger," 205.

40. Alger, *Andy Gordon* (originally published as *Forging Ahead*), p. 193.

41. Alcott, *Young Man's Guide*, p. 160. See also Hawes, *Lectures to Young Men*, p. 86: "Sudden wealth, especially when obtained by dishonest means, rarely fails of bringing with it sudden ruin. Those who acquire it, are of course beggared in their morals, and are often, very soon, beggared in property."

42. Scharnhorst, *Horatio Alger, Jr.*, p. 135, points out that heroes become the wealthiest in the period following 1889 when Alger resorted to robber baron sensationalism to attempt to prop up sagging popularity.

43. *Tony, the Hero* had already been adopted by a young gentleman whom he saved from robbery or worse and had his heritage as icing and justice. Dodger, in *Adrift in New York* (New York: Street & Smith, 1904), had begun to remedy the defects in his education, had taken a responsible and well-paying job in San Francisco, and had reaped a reward for saving someone from robbery before he returned to New York to discover his real heritage. Kit Watson had prospered and risen in respectability through his career as *The Young Acrobat* (New York: Hurst, n.d.) before he inherited money from his deceased father's mining investment and was restored to the rest of the estate. There is a bit of Twain's *Prince and the Pauper* in all of this: One must learn important lessons before resuming one's proper position.

44. See Alcott, *Young Man's Guide*, pp. 171-76.

45. See, e.g., Joshua Drummond in *Strong and Steady* (New York: Hurst, n.d.).

46. It may be acceptable for mothers to be timid and to be security conscious. Mrs. Rushton in *Brave and Bold* represents an extreme case of this female tendency. She anticipates bad fortune and is apt to look on the dark side of things (pp. 47, 59, 137). She can not understand that her son would sacrifice his job for pride—even the honest pride in refusing to apologize for something he did not do. *Helen Ford's* father has a few of these characteristics. He lacks practical ability and a head for business; he cannot be concerned with earning a living, but rather dreams of airplanes. He works hard, but at an impractical endeavor. Luckily he has an inherited fortune waiting for him.

47. Alger, *Rough and Ready*, pp. 226-27.

48. Michaels, *The Gold Standard*, p. 225.

49. Henry Ward Beecher, *Lectures to Young Men*, 2d ed. (Boston: John P. Jewett; Salem, Mass.: D. Brainerd Brooks; New York: M. H. Newman & Co., 1851), pp. 74-75.

50. See *Tom Turner's Legacy*; Henry Martin in *Sam's Chance* (Philadelphia: John C. Winston, n.d.; copyright A. K. Loring, 1876).

51. William Greider, *Secrets of the Temple* (New York: Simon and Schuster, 1987), p. 257.

52. Marvin Meyers, *The Jacksonian Persuasion* (Stanford, Calif.: Stanford University Press, 1957), pp. 17, 19.

53. Jackson quoted in Greider, *Secrets of the Temple*, p. 258. Greider (p. 255) found the Jacksonians internally inconsistent. They "described themselves as conscientious hard-money men who supported the rigid discipline of the gold standard, yet they opposed the newly powerful national Bank because it restrained the expansion of credit and, thus, thwarted robust economic expansion."

54. Greider, *Secrets of the Temple*, pp. 256-57.

55. Meyers, *Jacksonian Persuasion*, all quotes p. 19.

56. Greider, *Secrets of the Temple*, pp. 256-57. For Jackson on debt, see Meyers, *Jacksonian Persuasion*, pp. 19-20.

57. Greider, *Secrets of the Temple*, pp. 258-59, quoting Bray Hammond, historian of the Federal Reserve.

58. Beecher, *Lectures to Young Men* (1851), pp. 50-51; second quote, pp. 68-69.

59. Bray Hammond quoted in Meyers, *Jacksonian Persuasion*, pp. 80-81; Greider, *Secrets of the Temple*, p. 259.

60. Meyers, *Jacksonian Persuasion*, p. 84.

61. Greider, *Secrets of the Temple*, pp. 249-51. He argues that many of these

very elites—the capitalists and their sympathizers—were probably mistaken about the relationship between stable prices and their economic interests. The process of capital accumulation may have actually produced periodic cycles of changing money values. If this was true, there was a deep paradox: "price stability was everyone's supposed goal and yet the economic system could not live with it."

62. David A. Wells, *The Silver Question: The Dollar of the Fathers Versus The Dollar of the Sons* (New York: G. P. Putnam's Sons, 1877), pp. 37, 15 respectively. See also William H. Harvey, *Coin's Financial School* (1895), edited by Richard Hofstadter (Cambridge, Mass.: Belknap Press of Harvard University Press, 1963).

63. Michaels, *The Gold Standard*, pp. 150, 159.

64. Alger to Irving Blake, September 9, 1896; HL. In the campaign of 1896, Bryan was also the standard-bearer of the People's Party, an insurgent party spawned in 1892 by the Farmers Alliance. See Greider, *Secrets of the Temple*, and Lawrence Goodwyn, *Democratic Promise: The Populist Movement in America* (New York: Oxford University Press, 1976).

65. Alger to Irving Blake, October 26, 1896; HL.

66. Michaels, *The Gold Standard*, pp. 144-47; p. 161, quoting Frank Norris, *McTeague*, ed. Donald Pizer (New York, 1977), p. 114.

67. Michaels, *The Gold Standard*, p. 151. He displays and discusses the Nast cartoon.

68. Greider, *Secrets of the Temple*, p. 246.

69. Greider, *Secrets of the Temple*, p. 247.

70. Milton Friedman and Anna Jacobson Schwartz, *A Monetary History of the United States* (Princeton, N.J.: Princeton University Press, 1963), pp. 30-31.

71. Greider, *Secrets of the Temple*, pp. 244-45; 247-48. Wheat dropped from $2.06 per bushel just after the war to 60 cents by the 1890s; in the Dakotas, the price dropped as low as 35 cents. Corn dropped from 66 cents to as low as 10 cents thirty years later. On railroad rates, see Goodwin, *Democratic Promise*, pp. 114-15.

72. Greider, *Secrets of the Temple*, pp. 250-51.

73. Goodwin, *Democratic Promise*, pp. 117-20; Greider, *Secrets of the Temple*, pp. 250-51.

74. Greider, *Secrets of the Temple*, pp. 244-45.

75. Friedman and Schwartz, *A Monetary History of the United States*, pp. 137-40, 686; Greider, *Secrets of the Temple*, p. 265.

76. See Greider, *Secrets of the Temple*, p. 264.

77. Greider, *Secrets of the Temple*, p. 252.

78. Alger, *Andy Gordon* (originally, *Forging Ahead*), pp. 25, 43, 280.

79. Alger to Irving Blake, September 9, 1896; HL.

80. Alger to Blake, November 10, 1896; HL. His postscript to Blake is of receiving a letter from a Georgia boy who says he is glad McKinley won; the boy adds that most of the people there are disappointed.

81. Greider, *Secrets of the Temple*, p. 247. History did not oblige for more than a few years at a time.

82. Friedman and Schwartz, *Monetary History of the United States*, pp. 91, 137.

83. Michaels, *The Gold Standard*, p. 139, quoting Ottomar Haupt (1898)..

84. Thayer, *Success and Its Achievers*, pp. 284-85.

85. Alger, *Store Boy*, p. 126. Young Rockefeller also studied the example of Amos Lawrence. See Allan Nevins, *John D. Rockefeller: The Heroic Age of American Enterprise* (New York: Charles Scribner's Sons, 1941), Vol. 1.

86. Thayer, *Success and Its Achievers*, 1896 edition, p. 274.

87. Alger, *Tom Temple's Career* (New York: A. L. Burt, 1888), p. 15.

88. See Uncle Brinton Pendergast in *Tom Turner's Legacy*, along with *Brave and Bold*, *Tony, the Hero*, *Andy Gordon* (*Forging Ahead*). See Scharnhorst on self-interest and charity, *Horatio Alger, Jr.*, p. 128.

89. Alger, *Bound to Rise*, pp. 25, 17.

90. Alger, *Rough and Ready*, pp. 48-49.

91. Cooper, *The Pathfinder*, p. 401.

92. Thayer, *Success and Its Achievers* (1896), p. 281.

93. Horace Mann, *A Few Thoughts for a Young Man*, pp. 64-65.

94. I am indebted, in this section on the relationship between misers, money, gold, and representation, to Michaels, *The Gold Standard*, especially Chapters 4 and 5.

95. Michaels, *The Gold Standard*, pp. 38, 35.

96. On counterfeit silver, see Alger, *Store Boy*, p. 11.

97. See Michaels, *The Gold Standard*, pp. 63-64.

98. Alcott, *Young Man's Guide*, pp. 100-1.

99. T. S. Arthur, *Advice to Young Men*, p. 34.

100. Benjamin Franklin, *Autobiography* (New York: New American Library, 1961), p. 195.

101. Beecher, *Lectures to Young Men* (1851), p. 76.

102. Michaels, *The Gold Standard*, pp. 65-66.

103. Greider, *Secrets of the Temple*, pp. 261-62.

104. Alcott, *Young Man's Guide*, p. 161; pp. 158-59.

105. Michaels, *The Gold Standard*, both quotes p. 144.

106. Beecher, *Seven Lectures* (1851), p. 76.

107. See, for example, Lydia Maria Child, *Letters from New York* (New York: Charles S. Francis and Company; Boston: James Munroe and Company, 1843).

108. Alger, *Ragged Dick*, p. 36.

109. Michaels, *The Gold Standard*, pp. 224-30, discussing Wharton's *The House of Mirth*.

110. Alger, *Store Boy*, pp. 279-80.

111. Scharnhorst with Bales, *Lost Life*, p. 128; Matthew Josephson, *The Robber Barons* (New York: Harcourt, Brace and World, 1962), p. 198.

112. Alger, *Luke Walton*, pp. 132-34. The speaker is Thomas Butler (aka Browning) of Milwaukee.

113. Scharnhorst with Bales, *Lost Life*, pp. 128-29.

114. Scharnhorst with Bales, *Lost Life*, pp. 127-28, draws the connection and narrates the story from *Number 91*. The revelation was of railroads granting special rate concessions, or "midnight tariffs," to oil companies such as Standard Oil.

115. Alger, *Number 91; or, The Adventures of a New York Telegraph Boy*, by Arthur Lee Putnam (New York: John W. Lovell Company, original; Des Plaines, Il.: Gilbert K. Westgard II, 1977 reprint), pp. 173, 192.

116. Allan Nevins, *John D. Rockefeller*, Vol. 1, p. 68. But who was the real gambler? "Most of the men who had rushed into the petroleum field were plungers, and an atmosphere of gambling hung over all the drilling there. But refining had attracted men of substance and conservatism." Rockefeller was among the latter. Nevins, p. 185.

117. The financier does not figure heavily by name as a character in Alger; the capitalist or the money lender appears to be performing the same trickery. See Michaels, *The Gold Standard*, pp. 63-69; quote is p. 67.

118. See Michaels, *The Gold Standard*, p. 64 for a discussion of speculation. He quotes Horace White's 1909 definition of speculation.

119. Halttunen, *Confidence Men and Painted Women*, pp. 17-18, quoting Henry Ward Beecher.

120. See Michaels's discussion of Howells, *Rise of Silas Lapham* and Dreiser, *Sister Carrie* pp. 41-42 in *The Gold Standard*. Quote, p. 51, discussing Howells.

121. Alger, *The Young Boatman* (Philadelphia: The Penn Publishing Company, 1899 [original, 1892]), p. 367.

122. Halttunen, *Confidence Men and Painted Women*, p. 20.

123. Alger, "Athens," 60-61; HUA.

124. On the capitalist's attempt to get control over nature's instability and on business cycles, see Michaels, *The Gold Standard*, pp. 70-83.

125. Thomas, "Utopia for an Urban Age," p. 138.

126. James A. Henretta, "Families and Farms: *Mentalité* in Pre-industrial America," *William and Mary Quarterly* 35 (January, 1978): 16, 19.

127. Thomas, "Utopia for an Urban Age," pp. 135-38; 154; quote, p. 136

128. Thomas, "Utopia for an Urban Age," p. 144. 136.

129. Bellamy (1875), quoted in Thomas, "Utopia for an Urban Age," p. 144.

CHAPTER 9

1. Alger, *Nothing to Do: A Tilt At Our Best Society* (Boston: James French & Co., 1857), pp. 5-6. Published anonymously; Alger later owned authorship. Second quote, p. 35; Alger parodies Southern theory of dual creation of the races.

2. Horace Mann, *A Few Thoughts For A Young Man*, pp. 48-49.

3. Alger, *Nothing to Do*, p. 41; pp. 44-45. John Smith, in the first quoted passage from the same work, also gets his just due. His daughter elopes with a very worthy clerk in his business establishment.

4. Scharnhorst, *Horatio Alger, Jr.*, p. 132: "Alger shared with Veblen a fear that the rich would 'get richer and the poor poorer.'"

5. W. R. Alger (or Horatio Alger, Jr.), *Forrest*, Vol. 2, p. 669.

6. Hawes, *Lectures to Young Men*, p. 97. The first edition appeared in 1828.

7. Thayer, *Success and Its Achievers* (1896), p. 266.

8. In *Tom Turner's Legacy*, Clarence Kent, son of the squire, keeps his uncle's lost wallet and half its contents, frames the hero for the theft of the remainder.

9. Alger, *Dean Dunham*, p. 61.

10. Alger, *Dean Dunham*, pp. 19-20.

11. A good example of genuine and phony gentlemanliness is found in *Herbert Carter's Legacy*. Scharnhorst argues that Alger seems to fear the cultural effects of rapid social mobility and new wealth, as stewards of wealth were being replaced by robber barons (*Horatio Alger, Jr.*, pp. 91, 125-26, 129-30). This view is not quite

sufficient, since inherited wealth is a serious danger and Alger proudly repeats that most businessmen and statesmen began life as poor boys. Real gentlemen—new or old—are enmeshed in a system of reciprocal duties and obligations; they understand and value community. What Alger *fears* is the erosion of this ethic as money becomes god.

12. Alger, *Store Boy*, p. 84.

13. The reader generally knows where the squire got his money, but may not know where some wealthy benefactors got theirs. It is often stated or presumed to be inherited; if the benefactor's, one is sometimes told they have acquired it in finance or trade. Quote is Alger, *Dean Dunham*, p. 205.

14. Borrowed from Benjamin Franklin's *Autobiography*, where, after establishing himself in Philadelphia, young Ben visits his Boston home wearing a genteel suit and deliberately displaying his gold watch.

15. Wren Winter tells a former employer he has done rather well as he draws out a five-dollar bill and hands it to a black shipboard acquaintance. Then he brings home a purse and a wallet for his aunt and uncle, both filled with money and sends a neighbor boy (whose mother underestimated Wren) a ten-dollar bill as a birthday present. Alger, *A Rolling Stone*, pp. 285, 291-93.

16. T. S. Arthur, *Advice to Young Men*, p. 27.

17. Alger to Russell A. Alger, November 10, 1898; UM.

18. See, for instance, Alger to Russell A. Alger, May 2, 1888, UM. Alger to Irving Blake, January 1, 1898 from Natick; HL.

19. Alger to Russell A. Alger, July 4, 1888; and on May 2, 1888; UM. Last Will and Testament, February 15, 1898; copy in HUA.

20. Alger to Irving Blake, November 23, 1896; November 12, 1898 and November 15, 1898, both from Natick; HL. Blake may well have made the request in a letter just prior to November 12. Alger was delaying in anticipation of some royalty money.

21. Alger to Russell A. Alger, May 2, 1888 and November 10, 1898; UM.

22. This formulation is used in reference to the American businessman in Calcutta who pays for Captain Rushton's care and board when he is incapacitated in *Brave and Bold*.

23. Everett, Lecture delivered July 20, 1863, *Orations and Speeches on Various Occasions*.

24. Lydia Maria Child, *Letters from New York*, 14 (February 17, 1842), p. 82.

25. David Harvey, *Consciousness and the Urban Experience* (Baltimore: Johns Hopkins, 1975), p. 14 for a comparable point about Dickens.

26. Alger, *A Rolling Stone*, p. 276; see also p. 282.

27. Zuckerman, "The Nursery Tales of Horatio Alger," 206.

28. Zuckerman, "The Nursery Tales of Horatio Alger," 209 (quote); 207.

29. See Chapter 11 for the struggle over the "manly" and over gender identity in Gilded Age discourse.

30. Anne Norton, *Alternative Americas*, pp. 45-46, quoting, respectively, Foner's *Factory Girls* and *The Voice of Industry* (1845, 1846).

31. Alger, *Store Boy*, p. 124.

32. Alger, *Ragged Dick*, p. 189.

33. Alger, *Shifting for Himself* (Philadelphia: Porter and Coates; copyright A. K. Loring, 1876), p. 147.

34. Veblen, *The Theory of the Leisure Class* (New York: New American Library, 1899, 1953), pp. 71-72.

35. Alger, *Shifting for Himself*, pp. 148-49.

36. Alger, *Shifting for Himself*, p. 149.

37. William Weber, *Music and the Middle Class* (New York: Holmes & Meier, 1975), p. 17, quoting *Conoisseur* (1846).

38. Alger, *Shifting for Himself*, p. 138.

39. John F. Kasson, *Rudeness and Civility* (New York: Hill and Wang, 1990), pp. 67; 214.

40. Henry F. May, *End of American Innocence*, p. 41, quoting Harvard President Charles W. Eliot in "Democracy and Manners," *Century* 83 (1911-12).

41. Kasson, *Rudeness and Civility*, p. 67.

42. See Halttunen, *Confidence Men and Painted Women*, p. 96. However, T. S. Arthur counsels boys to read one or more, to acquaint themselves with the laws observed in polite society (*Advice to Young Men*, p. 86).

43. T. S. Arthur, *Advice to Young Men*, p. 87.

44. T. S. Arthur, *Advice to Young Men*, p. 87, quoting the closing paragraph of an etiquette book for youth.

45. W. R. Alger, *Forrest*, Vol. 2, p. 666.

46. Fisher, "Appearing and Disappearing in Public," p. 174; also pp. 170-72.

47. Fisher, "Appearing and Disappearing in Public," pp. 178, 173 and passim. Alger's letters to Blake (HL) speak further of his admiration for Roosevelt.

48. See Denning, *Mechanic Accents*, p. 208.

49. Alger to Irving Blake from Natick, Massachusetts, April 28, 1896; HL.

50. Alger to Irving Blake, January 14, 1897 from Natick; HL.

51. Alger to Irving Blake, February 27, 1897 from Natick. This letter also mentions the new edition of the game "Authors"; the reference to repeating the first lecture can be found in the letter of January 14, 1897; HL.

52. W. R. Alger, *Forrest*, Vol. 2, p. 640.

53. W. R. Alger (possibly Horatio Alger, Jr.) *Forrest*, Vol. 2, pp. 668-69.

54. W. R. Alger (possibly Horatio Alger, Jr.) *Forrest*, Vol. 2, pp. 668-69.

55. W. R. Alger, *Forrest*, Vol. 2, p. 670.

56. Tocqueville, *Democracy in America*, Vol. I, Part 2, Ch. 5, p. 221.

57. W. R. Alger (or Horatio Alger, Jr.), *Forrest*, Vol. 2, pp. 669-70.

58. W. R. Alger, *Forrest*, Vol. 2, p. 670.

59. W. R. Alger, *Forrest*, Vol. 2, p. 670.

CHAPTER 10

1. Letter dated March 3, 1877 from the Grand Hotel, San Francisco; UVa.

2. David Paul Nord, "Working-Class Readers: Family, Community, and Reading in Late Nineteenth-Century America," *Communication Research* 13 (April, 1986): 156-81.

3. I am grateful to James Green, Library Company of Philadelphia, for pointing out some of the most egregious problems in this secondary literature. For an example of more current scholarship, see Michael Hackenberg, ed., *Getting the Books Out* (Washington: Center for the Book, Library of Congress, 1987).

4. Extant publishers' magazine subscription and book order records; estate inventories and probate records, such as have been examined by Robert Darnton; library charging lists, checked against city directories were all left untouched.

5. Scholars emphasizing Alger's cultural influence have tended to presume enormous circulation. Claims that Alger "is probably the most popular author America has ever had, and one of the most popular the world has ever known" are much overblown. For examples, see Scharnhorst, *Horatio Alger, Jr.*, 1980 and Chapter 1 above.

6. Biographical sketch supplied by Alger and enclosed with letter to George A. Bacon, Esq., Jan. 26, 1874; UVa.

7. Scharnhorst with Bales, *Lost Life*, pp. 90-91. This would be about 1869, possibly after Norcross's card game days.

8. Scharnhorst with Bales, *Lost Life*, pp. 75-76. The inspirational lecture was by John B. Gough. Publication history from Benett, *Horatio Alger, Jr.*

9. This and all subsequent references to Norcross are from the Grenville Howland Norcross Diaries, 1860-76. Unpublished manuscripts from the Children as Diarists collection, AAS.

10. Optic's magazine ran *Ragged Dick* in 1867, *Fame and Fortune* in 1868, *Rough and Ready* in 1869, *Rufus and Rose* in 1870, *Paul the Peddler* in 1871, and *Slow and Sure* in 1872. The run for each story was January-December.

11. He had also written *Nothing to Do* (anonymously), *Hugo, the Deformed*, and *Timothy Crump's Ward*.

12. The quote is Alger. Letter to Duyckinck, 28 January 1866, from Brewster, Mass; NYPLd.

13. "Tangled Threads," *Student and Schoolmate* 21 (March, 1868): 140; (May, 1868): 234.

14. "Tangled Threads," *Student and Schoolmate* 22 (August, 1868): 376.

15. Madeleine B. Stern in Stern, ed., *Publishers for Mass Entertainment in Nineteenth Century America* (Boston: G. K. Hall & Co., 1980), pp. 191, 193. Stern claims Loring published 36 Alger titles, and Bob Bennett, *Horatio Alger, Jr.*, pp. 148-49, finds 37.

16. "At Our Desk," *Student and Schoolmate* 27 (June, 1871): 292. See also "Tangled Threads," in *Student and Schoolmate* 21 (May, 1868): 282. See below on discounting practice.

17. John T. Winterich, *Three Lantern Slides* (Urbana, Il.: University of Illinois Press, 1949), p. 20. DeWolfe-Fiske and Company of Boston, publisher of Alger's biographies, also "sold new books to individuals and to libraries and acted as a wholesaler for small-town booksellers." Lehmann-Haupt et al., *The Book in America*, p. 243; p. 247 for a Chicago example. Bennett, *Horatio Alger, Jr.: A Comprehensive Bibliography*, p. 144.

18. Lehmann-Haupt et al., *The Book in America*, p. 195.

19. See Soltow and Stevens, *The Rise of Literacy and the Common School in the United States*.

20. Lehmann-Haupt et al., *The Book in America*, pp. 197-99 and 321. They place the number of etiquette/advice manuals in each period at 170. There was also growing interest in volumes on fine arts late in the century, perhaps stimulated by the Philadelphia Exposition's exhibit of American painting.

21. Lehmann-Haupt et al., *The Book in America*, p. 198.

22. Ronald Zboray, "Antebellum Reading and the Ironies of Technological Innovation," *American Quarterly* 40 (March, 1988): 66.

23. Frank Luther Mott, *Golden Multitudes, The Story of Best Sellers in the United States* (New York: Macmillan, 1947), pp. 158-59; 303; 307-13. By this definition, to be a best seller required a sale of 375,000 copies for 1870-79; 500,000 copies for 1880-89; and 625,000 copies for 1890-99. Runner-ups, pp. 315-22. With evidence that Alger's greatest volume of sales occurred in the two decades after his death, there were still no "best sellers" in the lot according to Mott's data. Whereas Mott draws heavily on the fake Alger biography by Herbert Mayes, he does not use Mayes's grossly inflated estimates for publication figures.

24. See Mott, *Golden Multitudes*, pp. 309-22.

25. Alger, to Russell A. Alger, letter of May 2, 1888, UM. See also Scharnhorst and Bales, *Horatio Alger, Jr.: An Annotated Bibliography*, p. 17.

26. Obituary, HUA. Mott, *Golden Multitudes*, pp. 158-59 quotes the 1910 figure, which he is inclined to accept as reasonable.

27. The phenomenon of subscription bookselling probably peaked in the 1880s. Michael Hackenberg in Hackenberg, ed., *Getting the Books Out*, p. 45.

28. Henry Nash Smith, *Democracy and the Novel*, p. 106.

29. Alger noted his inclusion there in a January 28, 1898 letter to Blake; HL.

30. C. N. Caspar, *Caspar's Directory of the American Book, News and Stationery Trade* (Milwaukee: Riverside Printing Company, 1889; copyright C. N. Caspar), listing approximately 450 subscription publishing houses, turns up five publishers of Alger's clothbound works; his paperback publishers were not included (pp. 1047-49). Among these, Hurst & Company of New York carried sixty-seven Alger titles. The Hurst firm, active in the 1870s and 1880s, leased their plates to the United States Book Company in 1890, and resumed publishing after that unique company failed shortly after (Raymond Howard Shove, *Cheap Book Production In The United States, 1870 To 1891*. Urbana, Il.: University of Illinois Library, 1937, pp. 70-71). See also Michael Hackenberg, "The Subscription Publishing Network in Nineteenth-Century America," in Hackenberg, ed., *Getting the Books Out*, p. 46. Alger's hard cover and paper cover publishers are listed in Bennett, *Horatio Alger, Jr.: A Comprehensive Bibliography*, pp. 139-71.

31. Smith, *Democracy and the Novel*, p. 106; also collections of drummer's samples, AAS.

32. Publishers' Broadsides/Prospectuses Collection, AAS. Stowe's *Lives and Deeds of our Self-Made Men* was published by Worthington, Dustin & Co., Hartford Conn. and Queen City Publishing Company, Cincinnati, and M. A. Parker & Co., Chicago, Il. in 1872.

33. Howells (1893), quoted in Justin Kaplan, *Mr. Clemens and Mark Twain* (New York: Simon and Schuster, 1966), p. 62.

34. Denning, *Mechanic Accents*, p. 208.

35. Smith, *Democracy and the Novel*, p. 106.

36. Publishers' Broadsides /Prospectuses collection; AAS. Salesman's dummy for *Mark Twain's Sketches, New and Old*. A sheet from N. D. Thompson & Co. of St. Louis and New York entitled "Confidential Terms to Agents for Professional Thieves and the Detectives by Allan Pinkerton" tells agents their profit for each $2.75 copy will be $1.10 and for each $3.25 leather copy, $1.30.

37. On this occasion, *Publisher's Weekly* collected data on book pricing for popular titles. Titles were put on the list by ballot, presumably by those receiving the trade publication. The roster of pre-1876 popular titles showed several $2 titles and one or two at $2.50. Winterich, *Three Lantern Slides*, pp. 14-15. On antebellum book pricing, Zboray, "Antebellum Reading," 74.

38. Winterich, *Three Lantern Slides*, p. 15, quoting the *Boston Globe*.

39. Winterich, *Three Lantern Slides*, pp. 17-18.

40. *Publisher's Weekly* deplored underselling, but ran advertisements by book sellers advertising rock bottom prices. Winterich, *Three Lantern Slides*, p. 20.

41. Anna Lou Ashby on Porter & Coates in Stern, ed., *Publishers for Mass Entertainment*, pp. 247-48. Many of these Alger titles appeared in 1882.

42. The Alger plates would be passed along again; at the end of the century, the list was taken over by the rising house, John C. Winston and Company of Philadelphia, Chicago, and Toronto. It was classified as a subscription firm and carried fifty-nine Alger titles (Lehmann-Haupt et al., *The Book in America*, p. 232). The text quote is Mott, *Golden Multitudes*, p. 158. The price drop may well have reflected the fact that no royalties need be paid.

43. The most prominent in the field was the Beadle dime and half-dime library.

44. Shove, *Cheap Book Production In The United States*, p. 141; ix on the use of the term. Clothbound, paperbound, and books without a separate cover of any sort at all are included, although dime novels were generally not included in the designation.

45. Bennett, *Horatio Alger, Jr.: A Comprehensive Bibliography*, p. 162.

46. *The Nation*, October 6, 1877.

47. According to the *American Bookseller* (1886) Ogilvie's output ranged "from works of worldwide reputation to stories that are never heard of in fashionable society." Quoted in Shove, *Cheap Book Production*, p. 95.

48. Paul earns around eight dollars per week, though on lucky weeks, he earns as much as eleven—more than he could get in a store or office, we are told. Alger, *Train Boy* (Leyden, Mass.: Aeonian Press, Inc., 1975; originally copyrighted 1883 by Street & Smith), pp. 9, 12, 92.

49. See Chapter 11, where this is also said of Alger novels.

50. Lehmann-Haupt et al., *The Book in America*, p. 143.

51. Bennett, *Horatio Alger, Jr.*, for serialization histories. *Frank's Campaign* was not serialized. Some stories were published anonymously or under pseudonyms. "Hugo, the Deformed," from 1857, was the one story not carried in the *New York Weekly Sun*.

52. Scharnhorst with Bales, *Lost Life*, p. 39.

53. Poe's 1846 article on Richard Adams Locke, quoted Terence Whalen, "Edgar Allan Poe and the Horrid Laws of Political Economy," *American Quarterly* 44 (September, 1992): 391.

54. Quentin Reynolds, *The Fiction Factory* (New York: Random House, 1955; copyright Street & Smith Publications, Inc.), p. 37. "Marie Bertrand, or the Felon's Daughter" is one of the few Alger stories never to appear in book form. See Bennett, *Horatio Alger, Jr.* for the *New York Weekly* serial stories and subsequent publication histories.

55. The number of copies in 1890 was about 4.5 billion. Nord, "Working-Class Readers," 161.

56. Lehmann-Haupt et al., *The Book in America*, p. 154.

57. Smith, *Democracy and the Novel*, pp. 104-5, citing Frank L. Mott's *History of American Magazines*.

58. Scharnhorst with Bales, *Lost Life*, p. 132.

59. Quentin Reynolds, *Fiction Factory*, p. 78.

60. Quote is Shove, *Cheap Book Production*, p. 145; the citation is omitted but appears to be *Publisher's Weekly* (1890). Lehmann-Haupt et al., *The Book in America*, p. 237, relying upon Mott's *Golden Multitudes*. The Street & Smith inventory comes from Bob Bennett, *Horatio Alger, Jr.*, pp. 164-69.

61. Quentin Reynolds, *Fiction Factory*, pp. 37, 83. Stratemeyer edited *Good News* for Street & Smith, which apparently occasioned the meeting with Alger around 1890 (Gardner, *Horatio Alger*, p. 283; pp. 364-65 on the unfinished works).

62. The largest group of paperback titles—104—was issued largely between the end of 1915 and 1919, although several additional titles were added in the fall of 1926. Other paperback series were issued from 1900-1906, 1903-4, and 1906-11. Bennett, *Horatio Alger, Jr., passim.*

63. Quentin Reynolds, *The Fiction Factory*, p. 79 on the origins of Medal Library; *Publishers' Trade List Annual*, 1900. The Alger titles listed were *Erie Train Boy, From Farm Boy to Senator, Dean Dunham, Young Acrobat; Adventures of a New York Telegraph Boy* and *Tom Tracy* were attributed to Arthur Lee Putnam, one of Alger's pen names.

64. Shove, *Cheap Book Production*, p. 142. The classification of publishers

known mainly for cheap books is Shove's; the list of publishers derives from Shove and from Bennett's comprehensive bibliography in *Horatio Alger, Jr.* The three titles were published from 1886 to 1900.

65. Shove, *Cheap Book Production*, p. 143.

66. Bennett, *Horatio Alger, Jr.*, pp. 156, 169-70; Gardner, *Horatio Alger*, p. 392.

67. Lehmann-Haupt et al., *The Book in America*, p. 226; Bennett, *Horatio Alger, Jr.*, pp. 141, 144. Carleton's successor, George W. Dillingham, published one of Alger's adult novels.

68. Stern, in *Publishers for Mass Entertainment*. See also Shove, *Cheap Book Production*; Bennett, *Horatio Alger, Jr.*

69. Chicago was later joined by Cincinnati, Akron, Cleveland, and other cities in Alger reprint publishing. The Donnelly Lakeside Library, which began publishing in 1875, may have also been among the early contenders. Bob Bennett, *Horatio Alger, Jr.*, p. 163 and passim.

70. Scharnhorst, *Horatio Alger, Jr.*, p. 141.

71. Lehmann-Haupt et al., *The Book in America*, pp. 242, 246.

72. Scharnhorst, *Horatio Alger, Jr.*, pp. 27-28, quoting *The Nation* for 14 December 1865, 757.

73. See Soltow and Stevens, *The Rise of Literacy and the Common School in the United States*, Chapter 5, for a rich study of changes in illiteracy 1840-70.

74. Zboray, "Antebellum Reading," 78.

75. Preface to Alger, *Fame and Fortune* (Philadelphia: John C. Winston; copyright Horatio Alger, Jr., 1896), viii.

76. "At Our Desk," *Student and Schoolmate* 24 (November, 1869): 530.

77. Alger, *Ben, the Luggage Boy* (Philadelphia: Henry T. Coates; copyright A. K. Loring, 1870), p. 39.

78. W. H. Bishop, "Story-Paper Literature," *Atlantic Monthly* 44 (September, 1879): 384.

79. Bishop, "Story-Paper Literature," both quotes, 384.

80 Michael Schudson, *Discovering the News* (New York: Basic Books, 1978). See also Denning, *Mechanic Accents*, Chapter 2. Story papers pure and simple were already in evidence by the 1840s.

81 Nord, "Working-Class Readers," 160. This appears to be the first use of such data to study reading behavior.

82 Nord, "Working-Class Readers," 162. This spending was greater than any other discretionary expenditures catalogued in the survey, and represents a figure comparable to 1929-68 data for media expenditures as a percentage of consumer

spending. Regional differences (p. 164) are partly attributable to differentials in literacy between regions and the fact that Southerners were less well integrated into reading distribution networks; income differentials do not explain regional differences.

83. Nord, "Working-Class Readers," 175, 177, 174 respectively for quotes.

84. Nord, "Working-Class Readers," 178; 175-76. These groups were Southerners and French Canadians. Nord examined four categories of expenditures touching the life-style of the family in the community, treating expenditure for family amusements, church, and charity as traditional expenditures; insurance and organizational expenditure were treated as linked to formal, contractual community.

85. On adult reading of juveniles, see Soltow and Stevens, *Rise of Literacy*.

86. *Student and Schoolmate* 16 (October, 1865): 127. "At Our Desk," *Student and Schoolmate* 29 (January, 1872): 51.

87. Written from South Natick, Mass.; letter in HL. Loring was apparently not happy with sales of *Timothy Crump's Ward*, which had been offered in both cloth and paper covers (Scharnhorst with Bales, *Lost Life*, p. 75).

88. Lehmann-Haupt et al., *The Book in America*, p. 217 (quote); Charleston and Richmond, literary production and distribution centers in the prewar South, lost influence, and Cincinnati became the region's principal link to the book trade. See also Zboray, "Antebellum Reading," 79.

89. Alger to Irving Blake, November 23, 1896; HL.

90. Alger to Edwin R. A. Seligman, dated May 7 [1877]; CU.

91. Alger to Edwin R. A. Seligman, February 21, n.y. from Palace Hotel in San Francisco; CU.

92. William C. Todd, "Free Reading Rooms," *Public Libraries in the United States of America: Their History, Condition, and Management. Special Report*. Department of the Interior, Bureau of Education. (Washington, D.C.: Government Printing Office, 1876), pp. 460, 462.

93. The Revere, Massachusetts Public Library, near the site of Alger's birthplace and housing a small Alger collection, is a Carnegie Library.

94. U.S. Department of the Interior, Bureau of Education, *Public Libraries in the United States of America* (Washington, D.C.: Government Printing Office, 1876), p. 404 [henceforth, *Public Libraries*]. See Soltow and Stevens, *Rise of Literacy* for the member costs at social libraries.

95. Todd, "Free Reading Rooms," p. 462 in *Public Libraries*.

96. Alger quoted in Scharnhorst with Bales, *Lost Life*, p. 90, from *Golden Argosy* (October 17, 1885).

97. Harvey, "Alger's New York," 3. His estimation of Alger's widespread popularity and sales antedates the Mayes hoax biography.

98. Dee Garrison, "Cultural Custodians of the Gilded Age: The Public Librarian and Horatio Alger," *Journal of Library History* 6 (October, 1971): 335, footnote 18. Inscriptions and book plates of copies of Alger books provide evidence they were located here. Sunday Schools may possibly have given these books as gifts as they divested themselves.

99. *Public Libraries*, p. 820. This table includes subscription as well as free libraries.

100. The percentage rises then declines during this period, for which an account is given: "A comparison of this table with those showing the classifications of the reading at the branches indicates the beneficial effects of the notes in the Lower Hall Class-list for History, Biography, and Travel, which has reduced materially the percentage of fiction used, while it is maintaining its old predominance, and in some cases, increases in the branches." *Public Libraries*, p. 821.

101. F. B. Perkins, of the Boston Public Library, in "How to Make Town Libraries Successful," p. 422 in *Public Libraries*.

102. James Mascarene Hubbard, "Fiction and Public Libraries," *International Review* 10 (February, 1881): 170.

103. Hubbard, "Fiction and Public Libraries," 170, again having recourse to the appendices to the annual reports of the Boston Public Library.

104. Perkins, "How to Make Town Libraries Successful," *Public Libraries*, p. 420.

105. Hubbard, "Fiction and Public Libraries," 171. His estimate includes those volumes lost or used up in service and is based on the 1880 report.

106. Hubbard, "Fiction in Public Libraries," 168; 174-75.

107. Davidson, "Towards a History of Books and Readers," 11.

108. Zboray, "Antebellum Reading," 79.

109. Smith, *Democracy and the Novel*, p. 104.

110. Scharnhorst with Bales, *Lost Life*, p. 132.

111. Denning, *Mechanic Accents*, pp. 203 and 235-36 (drawing on secondary sources) for a good, brief discussion of his reception over time by the "genteel culture" and by a mass audience.

112. Radway, *Reading the Romance*, p. 11.

113. Janice Radway, "Reading Is Not Eating: Mass-Produced Literature and the Theoretical, Methodological, and Political Consequences of a Metaphor," *Book Research Quarterly* (Fall, 1986): 7-29; second quote, Radway, *Reading the Romance*, p. 6

114. Scharnhorst with Bales, *Lost Life,* pp. 94-95, 106; citing Sandberg's *Prairie-Town Boy* and the *Fitzgerald/Hemingway Annual* (1978). Scharnhorst and Bales, *Horatio Alger, Jr.: An Annotated Bibliography,* p. 34.

CHAPTER 11

1. Joseph P. Loeb Collection, HL. This reminiscence is of Alger's second trip to California in 1890. He appears to be in more reduced circumstances than on his first trip.

2. Douglas, *Femininization of American Culture,* pp. 7, 283.

3. Douglas, *Feminization of American Culture,* p. 9; Washington Irving quoted in Douglas, p. 283.

4. *New York Times,* October 6, 1877.

5. Michaels, *The Gold Standard,* pp. 236-41; Introduction; pp. 10-13. Many authors of the period used noms de plume; three were mentioned to Duyckinck by Alger, with their given names. Though Alger was close to William T. Adams, he referred to him in letters as "Optic." The creation and the creator have been blurred. Alger published early works *anonymously* and employed pen names for travel correspondence from Europe and on occasions when two or more serials were running in a single magazine at once.

6. Quote is Michaels, *The Gold Standard,* p. 13, writing of Gilman's "The Yellow Wallpaper."

7. Manuscript collection, AAS. On William Lee, of the publishing firm of Lee & Shepard, Boston, see Winterich, *Three Lantern Slides,* pp. 5-6.

8. Alice D. Schreyer, "Copyright and Books in Nineteenth-Century America," p. 124 in Hackenberg, ed., *Getting the Books Out.*

9. 'The straitened circumstances of his (father's) home.' Horace refers to the smallness of his father's estate, especially in *Satires* 1, 6, 71, but he does not use the words Alger does. These particular words derive from the satires of *Juvenal* (3, 165): poverty stands in the way of virtue. Alger has perhaps used Juvenal's language to describe accurately what Horace said in a more poetic turn of phrase; the alternative is that Alger confuses the two satirists. Thanks to Chris Callanan for Latin assistance. Alger, Jr. to Mr. Stedman, November 29, 1875, YU.

10. Stern, *Publishers for Mass Entertainment,* p. 193.

11. Winterich, *Three Lantern Slides,* pp. 16-17. second quote, p. 17.

12. Alger to Russell A. Alger, May 2, 1888; UM.

13. This was the standard practice when a publishing firm's assets or stereotype plates were purchased. See Schreyer, "Copyright and Books," p. 124. On the price

paid by Porter & Coates at the Loring bankruptcy sale, see Scharnhorst with Bales, *Lost Life*, p. 120.

14. Schreyer, "Copyright and Books," p. 129.

15. See Lehmann-Haupt et al., *The Book in America*, pp. 203-4 for the protectionist tariff on foreign books, which remained until 1913. Reputable American publishers who paid for the advance sheets of works of English authors could not protect themselves from pirating shortly after U.S. publication.

16. Lehmann-Haupt et al., *The Book in America*, pp. 208, 209-10, 215.

17. For example, letters to Edwin R. A. Seligman 15 July 1878 and 5 September 1879. On the latter date: "I hope the book-trade may be better this coming year than in the last two." CU.

18. Alger to Mr. Elderkin, August 2, 1884, YU. The Garfield biography, *From Canal Boy to President*, was published by John R. Anderson & Company in 1881, as the first volume of the Boyhood and Manhood Series of Illustrious Americans. Garfield died September 19, 1881; Alger's story was completed by October 8, and "the publisher had the first printing off the presses prior to November 3d, the date on which it was deposited for copyright." Publication information from Gardner, *Horatio Alger*, pp. 416-17.

19. Alger to Messrs. Porter and Coates, August 19, 1884; UVa.

20. Stern, *Publishers for Mass Entertainment*, p. 195, drawing upon Gardner's biography. The Loring suggestion story is recounted in quite a few sources.

21. See Michaels, *The Gold Standard*, on writing as speculation.

22. See, for instance, the outset of *Paul Prescott's Charge* (New York: Hurst, n.d.) and *Jed, the Poorhouse Boy* (in *Struggling Upward and Other Works*. New York: Crown, 1945). Alger's chief biographer believes that "Alger apparently hoped to imitate Dickens's success in writing popular novels with a social purpose, though on the juvenile level." (Scharnhorst, *Horatio Alger, Jr.*, p. 72.)

23. Courts of the time did not consider an author's *ideas* or *inventions* to be protected by copyright, but only the combination of words. Ideas and imagination are common property. Alger's borrowings, however shameless, were considered perfectly acceptable at law. The court dismissed an 1853 suit brought by Harriet Beecher Stowe against a German translation of *Uncle Tom's Cabin*, arguing:

> Uncle Tom and Topsy are as much *publici juris*, as Don Quixote and Sancho Panza. All her conceptions and inventions may be used and abused by imitators, playrights and poetasters . . . Her absolute dominion and property in the creations of her genius and imagination have been voluntarily relinquished; and all that now remains is the copyright of her book, the exclusive right to print, reprint and vend it . . .

See Schreyer, "Copyright and Books," pp. 127-28.

24. Scharnhorst, *Horatio Alger, Jr.*, p. 73 notes the recasting of *The Prince and the Pauper* in the former and *Huckleberry Finn* in the latter Alger work.

25. Alger, "Advice From Horatio Alger, Jr.," 16.

26. Hubbard, "Fiction and Public Libraries," 169.

27. Hubbard, "Fiction and Public Libraries," 172.

28. Hubbard, "Fiction and Public Libraries," 172.

29. Alger, *Ben Bruce*, pp. 283-84. Snodgrass also tried to get Ben to write for his paper, although Ben had no literary background or aspirations—another indication that story paper authorship was not a highly skilled profession.

30. Denning, *Mechanic Accents*, p. 55 and passim; p. 23.

31. Gardner (*Horatio Alger*) terms some of them "fakes". The arrangement with Stratemeyer appears to have been worked out with Alger, whose late correspondence to Blake makes mention of Stratemeyer and his fortunes. When *Nelson the Newsboy* appears in 1901, it is by Horatio Alger, Jr./Completed by Arthur M. Winfield (a Stratemeyer pseudonym). "Winfield's" preface notes:

> In its original form Mr. Alger intended this story of New York life for a semi-juvenile drama. But it was not used in that shape, and when the gifted author of so many interesting stories for young people had laid aside his pen forever, this manuscript, with others, was placed in the hands of the present writer, to be made over into such a volume as might have met with the author's approval. The other books having proved successful, my one wish is that this may follow in their footsteps.

(pp. iii-iv, *Nelson the Newsboy*, The Mershon Company, 1901; HO).

32. Quoted in Douglas, *Feminization of AmericanCulture*, p. 77.

33. Alger to Irving Blake, February 2, 1897, also November 15, 1898; HL. He seemed ever ready to strike up new correspondence, offering to write General Russell Alger's son if provided the address; UM.

34. Joseph F. Dean letters dated August, 1862 through May, 1863. Rare Books and Manuscripts, Boston Public Library. These letters, written to his mother, were sometimes directed in care of Horatio Alger in Cambridge. Dean indicates receipt of Alger's letters (one included a piece of wood from the whipping post in Plymouth) and asks his mother to let Horatio see his letters to her.

35. Alger to Blake of January 28, 1898 and March 21, 1898; HL.

36. Including Charles K. Bishop, also of the *New York Weekly*. See letter to Irving Blake of November 7, 1897, HL.

37. Henry James, *Autobiography*, edited by Frederick W. Dupee (New York: Criterion Books, 1956), p. 401, "Notes of a Son and Brother." Henry James, Senior's letter of 1870 reports that "Horatio Alger is writing a Life of Edwin Forrest, and I am afraid will give him a Bowery appreciation." Alger has, according to the senior James, become a great reader and considerable understander of his productions. The insanity presumably refers to the Brewster matter. See also Scharnhorst, *Horatio Alger, Jr.*, p. 37.

38. Written upon the death of Blake's father, the letter comments upon the resemblance between Alger's father and Blake's own. Alger to Blake, December 14, 1897; HL.

39. Alger to William Conant Church, April 23, 1866, and letter of transmission of April 20, 1866; NYPLc.

40. Alger to Henry Wadsworth Longfellow, December 16, 1875; HO.

41. Alger to Stedman, January 9, 1888. Miscellaneous Papers of Horatio Alger, Jr., Manuscripts and Archives Division, NYPL.

42. Alger to Stedman, November 29, 1875; YU. Robert Lowell was author of poems such as "For the Union Dead."

43. Alger to Stedman, November 29, 1875, YU.

44. "I am aware that I am trespassing upon the scanty leisure of one who bears the double burden of a business and intellectual life, but your kindly reception of a small volume of my own . . . ten years since, encourages me to hope that you will examine the verses of my young friend, & favor me with a word respecting them." Alger likens Cardozo to "that remarkable woman" Emma Lazarus. Alger to Stedman, January 9, 1888, NYPL. He continues to be sloppy about dates: the transmission was thirteen years since.

45. Alger to Russell A. Alger, May 2, 1888, and again on November 10, 1898; UM. See also Scharnhorst and Bales, *Horatio Alger Jr.: An Annotated Bibliography*, p. 17.

46. Douglas, *Feminization of American Culture*, p. 7.

47. Alger to Church, April 20, 1866; NYPLc.

48. Boys occasionally carry the *Sun*. Newsboys cry out instead the names of the *Telegram, Mail, Commercial, Express, Evening Post, Times, Tribune,* and *Herald*, at prices of two to four cents. Alger, *Tom Tracy*, pp. 1, 9, 25; *Shifting for Himself*, pp. 267, 270. See also *Nelson the Newsboy*.

49. Bishop, "Story-Paper Literature," 387. Italics in original.

50. Denning calls Twain "the classic American writer closest to the dime novel in practice, influence, and audience"; *Mechanic Accents*, p 208.

51. Samuel Clemens to Andrew Lang, London. Charles Neider, ed., *The*

Selected Letters of Mark Twain (New York: Harper and Row, 1982), pp. 183, 202.

52. In 1896, Alger reminisces that he "heard Mark Twain give three lectures many years ago. They were peculiar lectures but interesting." He continued to read Twain's work, mentioning specifically *Innocents Abroad* and a piece in the November, 1897 issue of *McClure's.* Alger to Blake, April 28, 1896 and November 7, 1897; HL.

53. Samuel Clemens to Jane Clemens and family, June 1, 1867. Neider, ed., *Selected Letters of Mark Twain,* p. 55.

54. Scharnhorst with Bales, *Lost Life,* p. 77.

55. Scharnhorst with Bales, *Lost Life,* p. 77, citing *Golden Argosy,* 17 October 1885: 364.

56. Alger to Irving Blake, including January 14, 1897; HL.

57. In 1885, the Boston press censured that perennially controversial *Adventures of Huckleberry Finn,* and the Free Library of Concord banned the work from its shelves, claiming that it was "no better in tone than the dime novels which flood the blood-and-thunder reading population." Scharnhorst with Bales, *Lost Life,* p. 118, quoting Arthur L. Vogelback.

58. Stern, *Publishers for Mass Entertainment,* p. 192, quoting an 1864 letter from Loring to one of his authors, Louisa May Alcott. Italicized words are underlined in Stern's quotation.

59. Stern, *Publishers for Mass Entertainment,* p. 192.

60. On the split between story and information functions of newspapers, see Schudson, *Discovering the News.*

61. Alger quoted this part of the review to Edwin R. A. Seligman in a letter of 3 January 1878; CU. He is "ready to believe, as Loring tells me, that there is no higher critical authority in England than the Academy." The novelette had been issued anonymously.

62. See Scharnhorst with Bales, *Lost Life,* and Denning, *Mechanic Accents,* p. 203.

63. Nina Baym, *Novels, Readers, and Reviewers: Responses to Fiction in Antebellum America* (Ithaca, N.Y.: Cornell University Press, 1984), p. 83. See also pp. 82, 94-95.

64. Baym, *Novels, Readers, and Reviewers,* p. 85.

65. Baym, *Novels, Readers, and Reviewers,* pp. 90, 93-94.

66. Baym, *Novels, Readers, and Reviewers,* p. 91, quoting *Literary World;* p. 95; and p. 93, quoting *Putnam's,* November, 1853.

67. John Seelye noted the importance of physiognomy as a guide to character in Alger in his introduction to *The Young Miner* (San Francisco: The Book Club of California, 1965), xi. So has Scharnhorst in *Horatio Alger, Jr.*

68. Baym, *Novels, Readers, and Reviewers*, on Charlotte Bronte's novels, p. 94. See also p. 89.

69. Norman N. Holland, "Hobbling with Horatio, or the Uses of Literature," *Hudson Review* (Winter 1959-60): 552-53. Among these symbols are money and a watch. His Freudian reading of Alger is based on Mayes's hoax biography and stands discredited.

70. See Baym, *Novels, Readers, and Reviewers*, pp. 98-99.

71. Anne Norton, *Alternative Americas*, p. 48, quoting the *Workman's Gazette* (November 4, 1830). See generally Norton, Chapter 2.

72. Veblen, *The Theory of the Leisure Class*, pp. 23, 28, 41.

73. Captain Fredrick Whittaker, *John Armstrong, Mechanic.*

74. See Norton, *Alternative Americas*, p. 62 on passion, temperance, and civilization in the Whig-Puritan heritage.

75. Douglas, *Feminization of American Culture*, p. 4.

76. Quoted in Douglas, *Feminization of American Culture*, p. 17.

77. Baym, *Novels, Readers, and Reviewers*, p. 95, quoting *Harper's.*

78. *Publisher's Weekly*, 23-30 November, 1889: 80.

79. "Christmas Bookshelf," *Publisher's Weekly*, 22-29 November, 1890: 77-78.

80. Baym, *Novels, Readers, and Reviewers*, p. 91.

81. *The Nation*, December 30, 1869: 587.

82. *The Nation*, December 30, 1869: 587.

83. *Risen from the Ranks* is "the first story of Mr. Horatio Alger's we remember to have read." Quoted in *The Nation*, December 3, 1874.

84. *The New York Times*, October 6, 1877.

85. *St. Nicholas*, one of the more "highbrow" boys' magazines, begun by Scribner, published an Alger story in one of their first issues. However, they stopped noticing Alger not many years later.

86. Olivia Smith, *The Politics of Language* (Oxford: Oxford University Press, 1984), p. 64.

87. Douglas, *Feminization of Culture*, p. 48.

88. Garry Wills, *Reagan's America* (New York: Penguin, 1988), especially the notorious incident in which he informed the Israeli ambassador that he had seen the concentration camps after the war, when in fact he had made a movie on a set in Hollywood in which this was the case.

CHAPTER 12

1. Alger, "Athens," p. 62; HUA.

2. Alger, "Athens," pp. 63-64.

3. William Rounseville Alger, *Life of Edwin Forrest* [*Forrest*] Vol. 2, p. 414, quoting *The New York Mirror*, 1846.

4. W. R. Alger, *Forrest*, Vol. 2, p. 688 for this and the subsequent quote.

5. W. R. Alger, *Forrest*, Vol. 2, p. 690. It surely helped Forrest with the minister and ex-minister that he had a pew in and frequently attended the New York church of "the brilliant Unitarian divine," Reverend Orville Dewey (Vol. 1, p. 339).

6. W. R. Alger (or Horatio Alger, Jr.), *Forrest*, Vol. 2, pp. 691, 694.

7. David Grimsted, *Melodrama Unveiled* (Chicago: University of Chicago, 1968), p. 75.

8. Kasson, *Rudeness and Civility*, pp. 225-27.

9. Kasson, *Rudeness and Civility*, pp. 221-23; the story is recounted on p. 223.

10. Kasson, *Rudeness and Civility*, p. 221.

11. Kasson, *Rudeness and Civility*, p. 222. See W. R. Alger, *Forrest*.

12. W. R. Alger, *Life of Edwin Forrest*, Vol. 1, pp. 129-30; Vol. 2, p. 416.

13. John Kasson, *Rudeness and Civility*, p. 251, drawing upon Lawrence Levine's *Highbrow / Lowbrow* (Cambridge, Mass.: Harvard University Press, 1988) for the Forrest story. He draws upon Irving Howe's *World of Our Fathers* for a late-century incident. Famed actor Jacob Adler provoked similar response to *The Jewish King Lear* at the Yiddish theater of the Lower East Side. A man rushed down the aisle, shouting to Lear: "To hell with your stingy daughter, Yankl! She has a stone, not a heart. Spit on her, Yankl, and come home with me . . ." Alger builds a comparable incident into *Rupert's Ambition*.

14. W. R. Alger, *Forrest*, Vol. 1, p. 17.

15. W. R. Alger, though surely here, Horatio Alger, Jr., *Forrest*, Vol. 1, pp. 66-67.

16. W. R. Alger, *Forrest*, Vol. 2, p. 665; Vol. 1, pp. 390-91, 400.

17. W. R. Alger, *Forrest*, Vol. 1, pp. 389, 390. However, popular author Charles Dickens was Macready's closest friend (Grimstead, *Melodrama Unveiled*, p. 68).

18. W. R. Alger, *Forrest*, Vol. 1, p. 391.

19. Grimsted, *Melodrama Unveiled*, p. 60.

20. W. R. Alger, *Forrest*, Vol. 1, pp. 409-12; Kasson, *Rudeness and Civility*, pp. 222-23; Grimsted, *Melodrama Unveiled*, pp. 69-71.

21. Grimsted, *Melodrama Unveiled*, pp. 71-72, quoting Rees, *Life of Forrest*, p. 332.

22. London newspaper reviews quoted in W. R. Alger, *Forrest*, Vol. 1, pp. 392-93.

23. Quoted in W. R. Alger, *Forrest*, Vol. 1, p. 396. When Forrest played *Metamora* in London, the Lord Chamberlain censored some of the Indian's more violent speeches, and changed his talk about wanting to drink his enemies' blood to a desire to shed blood, which pertains to the quote here (Grimsted, *Melodrama Unveiled*, p. 218, fn 50).

24. W. R. Alger, *Forrest*, Vol. 2, pp. 644; 644-645.

25. W. R. Alger, *Forrest*, Vol. 1, pp. 396-97.

26. W. R. Alger, *Forrest*, Vol. 1, pp. 396-97, and p. 400, quoting the *Democratic Review*, "Mr. Forrest's Second Reception in England."

27. W. R. Alger, *Forrest*, Vol. 1, p. 400; Vol. 2, p. 664.

28. *Democratic Review*, quoted in W. R. Alger, *Forrest*, Vol. 1, pp. 400, 401; Vol. 2, p. 643.

29. Grimsted, *Melodrama Unveiled*, pp. 167-69 on the Bird-Forrest association.

30. W. R. Alger, *Forrest*, Vol. 1, p. 429.

31. Recounted in Kasson, *Rudeness and Civility*, p. 228; W. R. Alger, *Forrest*, Vol. 1, p. 430; Grimsted, *Melodrama Unveiled*, p. 71 and passim.

32. W. R. Alger, *Forrest*, Vol. 1, p. 431.

33. Bishop, "Story-Paper Literature," 390-91.

34. Denning, *Mechanic Accents*, p. 24-25.

35. See Alcott, *The Young Man's Guide*, pp. 176-78.

36. Pierre Bourdieu, *Distinction*, p. 7.

37. Kasson, *Rudeness and Civility*, p. 251.

38. Harold M. Harvey, "Alger's New York," 4.

39. Kasson, *Rudeness and Civility*, see pp. 248-49.

40. Harold M. Harvey, "Alger's New York," 4.

41. Grimsted, *Melodrama Unveiled*, p. 59.

42. Alger, *Dean Dunham*, p. 117. The depiction of the action in the melodrama is rare; Alger usually avoids showing us what is on stage at such establishments.

43. Gustave Flaubert, *Madame Bovary*. Edited with a substantially new translation by Paul De Man (New York: W. W. Norton, 1965), p. 163.

44. W. R. Alger, *Forrest*, Vol. 2, p. 696, speaking of what he called the old,

genuine melodrama in opera; Vol. 2, pp. 641-43.

45. New York General Root, quoted in Hartz, *Liberal Tradition in America*, p. 108. The quote, more properly, is "We are all of the same estate--all commoners . . .," and was delivered in response to Chancellor Kent's arguments against inclusion of the unpropertied in the franchise.

46. Vida D. Scudder 1903, quoted in Arthur Mann, *Yankee Reformers*, p. 1.

47. Henry May, *End of American Innocence*, p. 30.

48. May, *End of American Innocence*, p. 44, quoting Wilbur F. Gordy.

49. On taste as a class marker, see Bourdieu, *Distinction*, p. 2 and passim.

50. May, *End of American Innocence*, p. 39.

51. Alger to Irving Blake, November 12, 1898 from Natick; HL.

52. Tocqueville, *Democracy in America*, Vol. 1, p. 410.

53. *Letters and Reminiscences of Alexis de Tocqueville*, (London, 1861), Vol. 2, p. 276, quoted in Williamson, *American Suffrage*, p. 278.

54. *Phil, the Fiddler* and *Only an Irish Boy* (Chicago: M. A. Donohue, n.d.; original, 1894) are among the few exceptions.

55. Alger's antisemitism--despite the stories he published in *Young Israel* and the time he spent tutoring in the homes of wealthy Jews in New York--is noted by Gary Scharnhorst in *Horatio Alger, Jr.*, p. 87. Scharnhorst reads the evidence on Alger's treatment of ethnics more charitably than I do, but admits his increased ethnic stereotyping by the 1880s.

56. Basil Bernstein, *Class, Codes and Control*, (London: Routledge & Kegan Paul, 1971), Vol. l, pp. 47-48. See also Chapter 3, "Language and Social Class."

57. Alger, *Only an Irish Boy*, pp. 143, 11, 259-63.

58. Alger, "Are My Boys Real?," 29.

59. Robert Golding, *Idiolects in Dickens* (New York: St. Martin's Press, 1985), p. 3, quoting Angus Wilson; also p. 213.

60. Smith, *Democracy and the Novel*, pp. 118-19.

61. May, *End of American Innocence*, p. 40.

62. Beecher, *Lectures to Young Men*, Lecture VII, p. 148 (1890 edition).

63. Mercer, "A Poverty of Desire," p. 89, writing of English class struggles.

64. Mercer, "A Poverty of Desire," p. 89.

65. Alger, *Shifting for Himself*, pp. 138-39.

66. Harold M. Harvey, "Alger's New York," 4; Alger, *Ben, the Luggage Boy*.

67. Simon Frith, "The Pleasures of the Hearth: The Making of BBC Light Entertainment," in *Formations of Pleasure* (London: Routledge & Kegan Paul, 1983), pp. 101-23; quote is p. 113. See also Weber, *Music and the Middle Class*, pp. 26, 30-33.

68. Alger, *Ben Bruce*, p. 91 and again on p. 141, when Ben tells a "real" playwright with a production at the Public Theater about "The Ragpicker's Curse." The playwright says "I suppose it is hardly in the style of Howells."

69. Scribe "adapted his productions to the changing circumstances of the times . . . He did not attempt the perilous task of leading public taste. It has been his highest ambition to follow it . . . His object was to make himself an agreeable companion for the lighter moments, but nothing more . . . His works are clever specimens of the present state of the drama, but they do not seek to rise above the present." Alger, "Eugène Scribe," *North American Review* 201 (October, 1863): 334.

70. Alger, *Ben Bruce*, all quotes pp. 282-83.

71. Joel Hawes, *Lectures to Young Men*, p. 144.

72. May, *End of American Innocence*, p. 43.

73. T. S. Arthur, *Advice to Young Men*, p. 76.

74. Scharnhorst, *Horatio Alger, Jr.*, p. 67.

75. This is a late novel, completed in part by Edward Stratemeyer; if a bit didactic, it retains the flavor.

76. Alger, *The Young Book Agent* (New York: Stitt Publishing Company, 1905), pp. 120-21; 231. This is a Stratemeyer completion.

77. Alger, "Are My Boys Real?," 29.

78. Alger to Russell A. Alger, May 2, 1888; William L. Clements Library, UM.

79. Alger, "Are My Boys Real?," both quotes 29.

80. Denning, *Mechanic Accents*, p. 24.

81. Denning, *Mechanic Accents*, p. 24, referring to William Wallace Cook, who cited the letter from Street and Smith in his 1912 *The Fiction Factory*.

82. W. H. Bishop, "Story-Paper Literature," both quotes 391.

83. Alger, "Are My Boys Real?," 29. Charles Reade (1814-84) was an English novelist, journalist and playwright, whose most famous novel was *The Cloister and the Hearth* (1861). He was also a committed reformer, and his works often exposed social abuses. Reade accumulated data and information in the preparation of his works and sometimes introduced real characters who had been in the public eye into his fiction. He was considered rather unimaginative, his characterization was seen as crude, his stage morality conventional, and his work action/incident-oriented. Much the same could be said of Alger.

84. On Peter Parley stories, see Ellen Wilson, "The Books We Got For Christmas," 27-28.

85. Alger, "Writing Stories for Boys," 37. As far as I have been able to determine, his examples of dime novel titles are generic and fictitious.

86. Bishop, "Story-Paper Literature," 383.

87. Alger, *Paul Prescott's Charge*, p. 196.

88. Alger, *The Young Outlaw* (New York: A. L. Burt, n.d.), pp. 15, 16.

89. Alger, *Julius, the Street Boy*, pp. 66-67.

90. Alger, *Dean Dunham*, both quotes p. 103.

91. Alger, *The Young Book Agent*, pp. 154-59.

92. Alger, *Ben Bruce*, p. 250. Ben is a boy from a farm in a small village fifty miles from Boston, within the circulation routes of the New York story papers.

93. N. D. Thompson & Co, Publisher of St. Louis and New York. Publishers' Broadsides/Prospectuses collection (loose file, Graphic Arts Department), AAS.

94. Hawes, *Lectures to Young Men*, p. 154. For somewhat less hysterical counsel on the preference of history and science to fiction, see Horace Mann, *A Few Thoughts for a Young Man*, pp. 51- 54.

95. Denning, *Mechanic Accents*, pp. 203, 171-72, 61, 83. Denning calls Alger a "ventriloquist," that is, he throws his own voice into the form of another as he transmits a reform message. He contrasts this stance with that of dime novels in which the author represents and speaks for his audience in a certain character, which he terms impersonation (p. 83). He sees Alger engaged in an ideological battle with his working class audience rather than articulating their voice.

96. Scharnhorst with Bales, *Lost Life*, p. 96.

97. Scharnhorst with Bales, *Lost Life*, p. 97. The quote is from an interview given by Alger in *Golden Argosy*, 17 October 1885: 364. Scharnhorst and Bales quote Alger from *Frank Leslie's Pleasant Hours*, NS 1 (March, 1896): 354-55 as saying that the novel "was largely instrumental in breaking up the tyrannical padrone system by which poor Italian boys were brought to this country and made to work long hours on starvation wages."

98. See Denning, *Mechanic Accents*, pp. 203 and 235-36.

99. In *Public Libraries*, pp. 410-11. The author then urges moderation in censorship. Italics mine.

100. William I. Fletcher, "Public Libraries in Manufacturing Communities," in *Public Libraries*, p. 403.

101. Denning, *Mechanic Accents*, p. 50, citing Couvares, *The Remaking of Pittsburgh* (1984); Denning, p. 208.

102. Hawes, *Lectures to Young Men*, p. 149. Italics in original.

103. Denning, *Mechanic Accents*, p. 54; and p. 51, quoting Comstock.

104. Dee Garrison, "Cultural Custodians of the Gilded Age," 327-36.

105. Garrison, "Cultural Custodians," 333, quoting Miss Hewins in the Second Annual Report on the Reading of the Young, American Library Association, 1883.

106. Garrison, "Cultural Custodians," 331. She cites the first case as the Fletcher Free Library in Burlington, Vermont (p. 332). See Esther Jane Carrier, *Fiction in Public Libraries*, p. 149.

107. William I. Fletcher, Assistant Librarian, Watkinson Library of Reference, "Public Libraries and the Young," p. 413 in *Public Libraries*. The argument that institutions ought not to undermine parental supervision sounds like modern sex education and abortion positions.

108. Garrison, "Cultural Custodians," 333, citing 1894 American Library Association and *Library Journal* documents.

109. J. P. Quincy, "Free Libraries," in *Public Libraries*, p. 393.

110. J. P. Quincy, "Free Libraries," in *Public Libraries*, p. 393.

111. J. P. Quincy, "Free Libraries," in *Public Libraries*, p. 393.

112. J. P. Quincy, "Free Libraries," in *Public Libraries*, p. 396.

113. Report of the examining committee of the Boston Public Library, 1875, quoted in Quincy, "Free Libraries," in *Public Libraries*, p. 395.

114. J. P. Quincy, "Free Libraries," in *Public Libraries*, p. 394.

115. Brookline, Massachusetts librarian M. A. Bean, 1879, quoted in Dee Garrison, "Cultural Custodians," 331.

116. Garrison, "Cultural Custodians," 332; Dee Garrison, *Apostles of Culture*, pp. 67-71.

117. Fletcher, "Public Libraries and the Young," pp. 416-17 in *Public Libraries*.

118. S. S. Green, 1879, quoted in Garrison, "Cultural Custodians," 332.

119. Garrison, "Cultural Custodians," 332 quoting first Charles Welch, "Children's Reading at Home," *Library Journal* 27 (April, 1902): 197; and subsequently Clara W. Hunt, "The Children's Library: A Moral Force," *Library Journal* 31 (August, 1906): 100.

120. Perkins, "How to make Town Libraries successful," in *Public Libraries*, p. 422.

121. Fletcher, "Public Libraries and the Young," in *Public Libraries*, p. 414. This formulation is reminiscent of implicit argument behind some integrationists'

positions in the 1950s: Mere contact with white learning environments would be beneficial to minorities.

122. Fletcher, "Public Libraries in Manufacturing Communities," in *Public Libraries*, pp. 410-11.

123. William A. Kite, librarian, in the report of the Friends' Free Library in Germantown, Pa for 1874, quoted by J. P. Quincy, "Free Libraries," in *Public Libraries*, p. 394.

124. William Kite, 1874 report of the Germantown, Pa. Friends' Free Library, quoted in J. P. Quincy, *Public Libraries*, p. 394. The Germantown library lists 7,084 volumes and a yearly circulation of 18,400.

125. Garrison, "Cultural Custodians," both quotes 330.

126. Harold M. Harvey, "Alger's New York," 3.

127. Garrison, "Cultural Custodians," 333, citing 1894 American Library Association and *Library Journal* documents.

128. Garrison, "Cultural Custodians," 333, citing S. N. Behrman's preface to *Strive and Succeed; Julius; or The Street Boy Out West [and] The Store Boy; or, The Fortunes of Ben Barclay*, p. vii.

129. Garrison, "Cultural Custodians," 333, quoting W. M. Stephenson, 1897.

130. Garrison, "Cultural Custodians," 333.

131. Harold M. Harvey, "Alger's New York," 3.

132. Fadiman, "Party of One," 9.

133. Plato, *The Republic*, Book I, 327c. Translated by G. M. A. Grube (Indianapolis, Ind.: Hackett, 1974).

134. See, for instance, Robert Wiebe, *The Segmented Society* (New York: Oxford University Press, 1975).

CHAPTER 13

1. Roland Barthes, *The Pleasure of the Text*. Translated by Richard Miller. (New York: Hill and Wang, 1975), pp. 27-28.

2. E. P. Thompson, *The Making of the English Working Class* (New York: Vintage, 1963), p. 295.

3. Thompson, *Making of the English Working Class*, pp. 57, 139, 177, 831-32.

4. See Hartz, *The Liberal Tradition in America*, p. 206, where "the new Whiggery was able to attach to the Horatio Alger cosmos the grand and glorious label of 'Americanism'."

5. Hartz, *The Liberal Tradition in America,* especially pp. 62-63, 203-5.

6. Clifford Geertz, "Ideology as a Cultural System," pp. 193-233 in *The Interpretation of Cultures* (New York: Basic Books, 1973). Geertz seems to lack a theory of ideological change; it is exogenous.

7. Louis Althusser and Étienne Balibar, *Reading Capital* (London: New Left Books, 1970); see also the work of Adam Przeworski.

8. Claude Levi-Strauss, Chapter 11, "Structural Study of Myth," in *Structural Anthropology* (New York: Basic Books, 1963).

9. Jameson, "Ideology, Narrative Analysis, and Popular Culture," 549, 555.

10. Roland Barthes, *The Pleasure of the Text,* p. 16. "*Text* means *Tissue;* but whereas hitherto we have always taken this tissue as a product, a ready-made veil, behind which lies, more or less hidden, meaning (truth), we are now emphasizing, in the tissue, the generative idea that the text is made, is worked out in a perpetual interweaving; lost in this tissue--this texture--the subject unmakes himself, like a spider dissolving in the constructive secretions of its web" (p. 64).

11. Michaels, *The Gold Standard,* p. 19.

12. Charles D. Elder and Roger W. Cobb, *The Political Uses of Symbols* (New York: Longman, 1983), p. 35.

13. See Lance Bennett, *The Governing Crisis* (New York: St. Martin's, 1992).

14. For Kenneth Burke, this is not peculiar to discourse in the United States, since religious systems can be deduced (in form and content) from the vey structure of language as a symbol system *The Rhetoric of Religion* (Berkeley, Calif.: University of California Press, 1970).

15. See Sacvan Bercovitch, *The American Jeremiad* (Madison, Wis.: University of Wisconsin Press, 1978) and *The Puritan Origins of the American Self* (New Haven, Conn.: Yale University Press, 1975); Wilson Carey McWilliams, *The Idea of Fraternity in America* (Berkeley, Calif.: University of California Press, 1973); and Robert Bellah, *The Broken Covenant* (New York: Harper & Row, 1976).

16. This moralism could be seen in reactions to the New Deal. The Nixon-Wallace backlash was also something other than "Lockeanism gone under-ground" (Hartz) or the "irrational moods of mass Lockeanism" (Rogin). Wills, too, sees a thread running from this sense of moralism to the notion of the morality of the market, a notion betrayed by Nixon in Garry Wills, *Nixon Agonistes* (New York: New American Library, 1970).

17. Michael Kammen, *People of Paradox* (New York: Vintage, 1972).

18. Bercovitch, *Puritan Origins of the American Self,* p. 81 and passim. See also *The American Jeremiad.*

19. Religion in America and Americanism as religion have been held to help explain a peculiar resistance to socialist ideas. For a good discussion of these themes, see John H. M. Laslett and Seymour Martin Lipset, eds., *Failure of a Dream?* (Garden City: New York: Anchor/Doubleday, 1974), especially contributions by Leon Samson, Mark Karson, and Philip Foner.

20. Belief in collective striving—"we can" as well as "I can" (Kammen, *People of Paradox*, pp. 115-16) is both conducive to a positive role for the state and to acceptance of hegemonic logic: Rather than playing zero-sum games, we play a game where we think everyone can win.

21. For Bercovitch, there is a linkage between Emerson and Thoreau's reinterpretation of the search for the perfect community (for Thoreau, individual self-reliance is the economic model of the only true American) and Horatio Alger, who extolled conformity as an act of supreme individualism (*Puritan Origins*, p. 185). The American evidence on clerical exhortations to economic activity, self-help and the secular search for salvation has been marshalled by I. G. Wyllie in *The Self-Made Man in America*. I have greatly profited from conversation with J. David Greenstone on the individualist-collectivist (or communal) duality in American thought. The idea that there are losers produced (in fact, the whole concept of structure) is dissonant and unintelligible when the rhetoric of individual and collective success are conflated.

22. Communism, unlike almost all other possible beliefs, posed a simultaneous threat to *both* sacred and secular missions. For, it is judged "godless" and "atheistic" at the same time that it challenges private appropriation of property—or rather, property in the means of production.

23. Henry Ward Beecher, *Norwood* (New York: Charles Scribner & Company, 1868), p. 452. He is discoursing on Thanksgiving as a fast day.

24. Howe, *The Unitarian Conscience*, p. 6.

References

ABBREVIATIONS

AAS   American Antiquarian Society, Worcester, Massachusetts. Children as Diarists Collection; Publishers' Broadsides/Prospectuses Collection.

A-H   Andover-Harvard Theological Seminary Library, Cambridge, Massachusetts, contains correspondence between the Brewster Unitarian Church and Reverend Charles Lowe, Secretary of the American Unitarian Association, and other documents pertaining to Alger's ministry.

CU   Joseph Seligman Collection, Rare Books and Manuscripts, Columbia University. Alger's letters to Joseph and Edwin R. A. Seligman.

HL   Huntington Library, San Marino, California. Alger's letters to Irving Blake, other miscellaneous Alger letters (chiefly in HM 32600-32688), and Joseph P. Loeb Collection.

HO   Houghton Library, Harvard University.

HUA   Harvard University Archives, containing Alger's three student essays, files from the Class of 1852, library charging lists, faculty records, and Alger documents.

MI   William L. Clements Library, University of Michigan.

NYPL   Manuscripts and Archives Division, New York Public Library; Miscellaneous Papers of Horatio Alger, Jr.

NYPLc   William Conant Church Papers, Manuscripts and Archives Division, New York Public Library.

NYPLd   Duyckinck Family Papers, Manuscripts and Archives Division, New York Public Library.

UVa   Horatio Alger, Jr. Papers (#6938), Manuscripts Department, Special
       Collections, Clifton Waller Barrett Library, University of Virginia.

YU   Beinecke Rare Book and Manuscript Library, Yale University.

Titles Abbreviated

Athens Athenaicus (Horatio Alger, Jr.), "Athens in the Time of Socrates,"
       Bowdoin Prize Essay, Harvard University, 1851.

Forrest William Rounseville Alger, *Life of Edwin Forrest*, a work in which his
       cousin, Horatio Alger, Jr. assisted.

WSB   Horatio Alger, Jr., "Writing Stories for Boys," *The Writer* 9 (March,
       1896).

PRIMARY SOURCES: ALGER'S
PUBLISHED AND UNPUBLISHED MATERIALS

Books

Bibliographic reference is to edition used and cited. Original publication in
book form, followed by original serialization in boldface, (where applicable), in
brackets. Original publication dates come from Bob Bennett, *Horatio Alger, Jr.:
A Comprehensive Bibliography*.

Abraham Lincoln, The Backwoods Boy. New York: John R. Anderson & Henry S.
    Allen, 1883.
Adrift in the City. Philadelphia: The John C. Winston Co., n.d.; copyright Porter
    & Coates, 1895 [**1887**].
Adrift in New York. New York: Street & Smith, 1904 [**1889**].
Andy Gordon. New York: A. L. Burt, n.d. Originally published as *Forging Ahead*
    [1903; **1881**].
Andy Grant's Pluck. New York: A. L. Burt, n.d. [1902; **1885**].
Ben Bruce. New York: A. L. Burt, 1901; (original copyright Frank A. Munsey
    1892). [**1892–93**].
Ben, the Luggage Boy. Philadelphia: Henry T. Coates & Co., copyright A. K.
    Loring, 1870.
Bernard Brook's Adventures. New York: A. L. Burt, 1903 [**1893**].

Bob Burton. New York: Hurst & Company, n.d. [1888; **1886**].

Bound to Rise. Chicago: M. A. Donohue & Company, n.d. [1873; **1873**].

Brave and Bold. New York: A. L. Burt, n.d. [1874; **1872**].

Charlie Codman's Cruise. Boston: A. K. Loring, 1866. [**1859**].

Chester Rand. Chicago: M. A. Donohue, n.d. [1903; **1892**].

A Cousin's Conspiracy. New York: Hurst & Company, n.d. Reprint title of *The Young Bank Messenger* [1898; **1896**].

Dan, the Newsboy. New York: A. L. Burt, 1893. Reprint title of *Dan, the Detective* [1884; **1880**].

Dean Dunham. Leyden, Mass.: Aeonian Press, 1975; copyright Ralph D. Gardner [1891; **1888**].

A Debt of Honor. New York: A. L. Burt, 1900 [**1891**].

The Disagreeable Woman with *A Fancy of Hers.* New York: Van Nostrand Reinhold, 1981; copyright Ralph D. Gardner. *A Fancy of Hers* is the reprint title of *The New Schoolma'am* [*Disagreeable Woman*, 1895; *New Schoolma'am*, 1877].

Driven from Home. Chicago: M. A. Donohue & Co., n.d. Reprint title of *The Odds Against Him* [1890; **1889**].

The Errand Boy. New York: A. L. Burt, 1888 [**1883**].

Facing the World. Philadelphia: John C. Winston, n.d.; copyright Porter & Coates, 1898 [1893; **1885**].

Fame and Fortune. Philadelphia: Porter & Coates, n.d.; copyright A. K. Loring, 1868 [**1868**].

Five Hundred Dollars; or Jacob Marlowe's Secret. New York: A. L. Burt, n.d. [1890; **1889**].

Frank's Campaign. New York: Hurst & Company, n.d. [**1864**].

Frank Fowler: The Cash Boy. New York: A. L. Burt, 1887 [**1875**].

Frank Hunter's Peril. Philadelphia: Henry T. Coates & Co., 1896 [**1886**].

From Canal Boy to President. New York: Street & Smith, 1901; copyright John R. Anderson & Co., 1881.

From Farm Boy to Senator. New York: Street & Smith, 1882 [**1882**, Ogilvie].

From Farm to Fortune (Stratemeyer completion). New York: Grosset & Dunlap, n.d.; copyright Stitt, 1905.

Grand'ther Baldwin's Thanksgiving with Other Ballads and Poems. Des Plaines, Il.: Gilbert K. Westgard II, 1978; a reprint of Boston: A. K. Loring, 1875.

Hector's Inheritance. New York: A. L. Burt, n.d. [1885; **1883**].

Helen Ford. Boston: A. K. Loring, 1866 [**1860**].

Herbert Carter's Legacy. New York: New York Book Co., 1908 [1875; **1875**].

In A New World. New York: Media Books, 1972 [1893; **1885-6**].

Jack's Ward. New York: A. L. Burt, n.d. [1875; **1866**].

"Jed, the Poorhouse Boy", in *Struggling Upward and Other Works.* New York: Crown, 1945 [1899; **1892**].

Joe's Luck. New York: A. L. Burt, 1887 [**1878**].

Julius, the Street Boy. New York: Hurst & Company, n.d. [**1874**].

Luck and Pluck. Boston: Loring, Publisher, 1869 [**1869**].

Luke Walton. Philadelphia: John C. Winston; n.d.; copyright Porter & Coates, 1889 [**1887-8**].

Mabel Parker. Hamden, Conn.: Archon Books, 1986. With a preface by Gary Scharnhorst [who dates its completion as 1878].

Making His Mark. Des Plaines, Il.: Gilbert K. Westgard II, 1979; reprint of edition published by The Penn Publishing Company, 1901 [**1897**].

Making His Way. New York: A. L. Burt, n.d. Reprint title of *The World Before Him.* [1902; **1880**].

Mark Mason's Victory. New York: A. L. Burt, 1899 [**1892**].

Mark, the Match Boy, in *Ragged Dick and Mark, the Match Boy.* New York: Collier Books, 1962 [1869].

A New York Boy. New York: Street & Smith, 1891 [1890; **1888**].

Nelson, the Newsboy. The Mershon Company, 1901 (Stratemeyer completion).

Nothing to Do: A Tilt At Our Best Society. Boston: James French & Co., 1857. Published anonymously.

Number 91; or, The Adventures of a New York Telegraph Boy, by Arthur Lee Putnam. Des Plaines, Il.: Gilbert K. Westgard II, 1977; reprinted from New York: John C. Lovell, n.d. [1887; **1886**].

Only an Irish Boy. Chicago: M. A. Donohue & Co., n.d. [1894; **1874**].

Paul, the Peddler. New York: Hurst & Company, 1903 [1871; **1871**].

Paul Prescott's Charge. New York: Hurst & Company, n.d. [1865; **1859**].

Phil, the Fiddler. Chicago: M. A. Donohue, n.d. [**1872**].

Ragged Dick. Boston: Loring, Publisher, 1868 [**1867**] .

Ralph Raymond's Heir. New York: Hurst & Company, n.d. [1869; **1869**].

Risen from the Ranks. New York: Hurst & Company, n.d. [1874; **1874**].

A Rolling Stone [Wren Winter's Triumph]. Leyden, Mass.: Aeonian Press, Inc., 1975 [1902; **1894**].

Rough and Ready. Philadelphia: Porter & Coates, n.d. [1869; **1869**].

Rufus and Rose. Philadelphia: Porter & Coates, n.d. [1870; **1870**].

Rupert's Ambition. Philadelphia: John C. Winston, n.d.; copyright Henry T. Coates, 1899. [**1893-4**].

Sam's Chance. Philadelphia: John C. Winston, n.d.; copyright A. K. Loring, 1876.

Shifting for Himself. Philadelphia: Porter & Coates; copyright A. K. Loring, 1876 [**1876**].

Sink or Swim. Chicago: M. A. Donohue & Co., n.d. [1870; **1870**].

The Store Boy. Philadelphia: John C. Winston, n.d.; copyright Porter & Coates, 1887 [**1883-4**].

Strive and Succeed. Boston: A. K. Loring, 1872. (also New York: New York Book Company, 1909) [**1872**].

Strong and Steady. New York: Hurst & Company, n.d. [1871; **1871**].

Tattered Tom. Philadelphia: Henry T. Coates & Co., n.d., copyright Horatio Alger, Jr., 1899. [1871; **1871**].

Timothy Crump's Ward. Des Plaines, Il.: Gilbert K. Westgard II, 1977; reprint of A. K. Loring, 1866.

Tom, the Bootblack. New York: A. L. Burt, n.d. Reprint title of *The Western Boy* [1878; **1873**].

Tom Temple's Career. New York: A. L. Burt, 1888 [**1879**].

Tom Thatcher's Fortune. New York: A. L. Burt, 1888 [**1882**].

Tom Tracy. (Arthur Lee Putnam, pseud.). New York: John W. Lovell Company, 1889 [1888; **1886-7**].

Tom Turner's Legacy. New York: Hurst & Company, copyright 1902 A. L. Burt [**1890**].

Tony, the Hero. New York: A. L. Burt, 1890 [1880; **1876**].

The Train Boy. Leyden, Mass.: Aeonian Press, Inc., 1975; originally copyrighted 1883 by Street & Smith [**1882-3**].

Wait and Win. Des Plaines, Il.: Gilbert K. Westgard II, 1979; reprinted from A. L. Burt edition of 1908 [**1884**].

Walter Sherwood's Probation. New York: A. L. Burt, n.d. [1897; **1890-1**].

The Young Acrobat. New York: Hurst & Company, n.d. [1888; **1887**].

The Young Bank Messenger. Philadelphia: John C. Winston Company, n.d.; copyright 1898 Henry T. Coates. [**1896**].

The Young Boatman. Philadelphia: The Penn Publishing Company, 1899 [1892; **1884**].

The Young Book Agent. New York: Stitt Publishing Company, 1905 (Stratemeyer completion.).

The Young Circus Rider. Philadelphia: Henry T. Coates, 1883 [**1882**].

The Young Explorer. Philadelphia: Henry T. Coates, n.d.; copyright A. K. Loring, 1880.

The Young Miner; Or, Tom Nelson in California. Philadelphia: Henry T. Coates, n.d.; copyright A. K. Loring, 1879.

The Young Miner; Or, Tom Nelson in California, with Introduction and Bibliographical Note by John Seelye. San Francisco: The Book Club of California, 1965.

The Young Outlaw. New York: A. L. Burt, n.d. [**1875**].

The Young Salesman. Rahway, N.J.: The Mershon Company, n.d. [1896; **1894-95**].

Articles, Serialized Stories, and Unpublished Manuscripts

"Advice From Horatio Alger, Jr.," *The Writer* 6 (January, 1892): 16.

"Are My Boys Real?," *The Ladies' Home Journal* 7 (November, 1890): 29.

"Athens in the Time Of Socrates," ("Athenaicus," pseud.), Bowdoin Prize Essay, Harvard College, 1851. Unpublished manuscript, Harvard University Archives.

"Ben Bruce," (Arthur Lee Putnam, pseud.) in Frank Munsey, ed., *The Argosy* 15 (December 10, 1892)–installment of serial story.

"Cicero's Return From Banishment," English Oration Prize Essay, Harvard College, graduation, 1852.

"Eugène Scribe," *North American Review* 201 (October, 1863): 325-38.

"Marie Bertrand, or, the Felon's Daughter," *New York Weekly* 19 (January 7-February 4, 1864).

"The State of Athens before the Legislation of Solon." (Zeta, pseud.). A Greek Version. *Grote's History of Greece*, Vol. III, Chap. XI. Bowdoin Prize Essay, Harvard College, 1851. Manuscript, Harvard University Archives.

"Writing Stories for Boys," *The Writer* 9 (March, 1896): 36-37.

Manuscript letters housed in the Huntington Library, Columbia University Library, Beinecke Library, New York Public Library, University of Virginia Library, University of Michigan Library, American Antiquarian Society, Boston Public Library, Andover Harvard Theological Seminary Library, Houghton Library of Harvard University, Harvard University Archives.

Letter to Mr. Lee, of Lee and Shepard, November 15, 1872. Manuscripts of the American Antiquarian Society.

Bales, Jack, and Gary Scharnhorst, "Alger's European Tour 1860-61: A Sheaf of Travel Essays," *Newsboy* 19 (April, 1981): 7-26.

"Horatio Alger, Jr. and the *Sun* Travel Essays" from the Collections of Jack Bales and Gary Scharnhorst, *Newsboy* 20 (December, 1981): 11-14.

Library Charging Lists for Horatio Alger, Jr. Harvard University Archives.

OTHER PRIMARY SOURCES

Abbott, Jacob. *Rollo At School*. New York: Thomas Y. Crowell & Co., 1855.

Adams, Henry. *Democracy*. New York: New American Library, 1961. (Originally published anonymously in 1880.)

Adams, Henry. *The Education of Henry Adams*. New York: Modern Library, 1931.

Adams, William T. (Oliver Optic), ed. *Student and Schoolmate*. Boston: Joseph H. Allen, 1855(?)-72.

Alcorn, Edgar G. "Are the Characters of Juvenile Literature Real?," *The Writer* 6 (August, 1893): 153-57.

Alcott, William A. *The Young Man's Guide*, 16th ed. Boston: T. R. Marvin, 1844.

Alger, William Rounseville, *Life of Edwin Forrest, the American Tragedian*. 2 vols. New York: Benjamin Bloom, Inc., 1972; reprint of the 1877 edition. (In collaboration with Horatio Alger, Jr.)

Arthur, T. S. *Advice to Young Men on their Duties and Conduct in Life*. Philadelphia: John E. Potter and Company, 1847.

Arthur, T. S. *Ten Nights in a Bar-Room and What I Saw There*. New York: A. L. Burt, n.d.

Beecher, Henry Ward. *Lectures to Young Men, on Various   Important Subjects*, 2d ed. Boston: John P. Jewett; Salem: D. Brainerd Brooks; New York: M. H. Newman & Co., 1851. (Also New York: John B. Alden Publisher, 1890).

Beecher, Henry Ward. *Norwood; Or, Village Life in New England.* New York: Charles Scribner & Company, 1868.

Bellamy, Edward. "America the Only Land of Freedom," editorial in the *Springfield Union* [Massachusetts], July 8, 1876.

Bishop, W. H. "Story-Paper Literature," *Atlantic Monthly* 44 (September, 1879): 383-93.

Brace, Charles Loring. *The Dangerous Classes of New York and Twenty Years' Work Among Them.* New York: Wynkoop & Hallenbeck, Publishers, 1872; NASW Classic Series, n.d.

Buel, C. C. "Our Fellow-Citizen of the White House," *The Century Magazine* 53 (March, 1897): 645-64.

Buntline, Ned (E. Z. C. Judson). *Tombstone Dick, The Train Pilot/ Or, The Traitor's Trail/A Story of the Arizonian Wilds.* Beadle's Dime Library 361, September 23, 1885.

Carnegie, Andrew. *Autobiography of Andrew Carnegie.* Boston: Houghton Mifflin Company, 1924; copyright 1920.

Carnegie, Andrew. *Triumphant Democracy.* New York: Johnson Reprint Corporation, 1971; original Charles Scribner's Sons, 1886.

Carnegie, Andrew. "Wealth," *North American Review* 148 (June, 1889): 653–664.

Caspar, C. N. *Caspar's Directory of the American Book, News and Stationery Trade.* Milwaukee: Riverside Printing Company, 1889; copyright C. N. Caspar.

Child, Lydia Maria. *Letters From New-York.* New York: Charles S. Francis and Company; Boston: James Munroe and Company, 1843.

Cicero. *The Treatises of M. T. Cicero.* Translated chiefly by the editor, C. D. Yonge. London: Henry G. Bohn, 1853.

A Complete List of Booksellers, Stationers, and News Dealers in the United States and the Canadas. New York: John H. Dingman, with Charles Scribner & Co., 1867 (copyright 1866).

Conwell, Russell. "Acres of Diamonds," (1861). Excerpted in *Free Government in the Making*, 3rd ed., edited by Alpheus T. Mason. New York: Oxford University Press, 1965.

Cooper, James Fenimore. *The American Democrat.* Cooperstown, N.Y.: H. & E. Phinney, 1838. (Also, where especially noted: New York: Alfred A. Knopf, 1931.)

Cooper, James Fenimore. "A Letter to His Countrymen." New York: John Wiley, 1834.

Cooper, James Fenimore. *The Pathfinder.* New York: Modern Library, 1952.

Davis, John P. *Corporations: A Study of the Origin and Development of Great Business Combinations and of their Relation to the Authority of the State.* New York: Capricorn Books, 1961; reprint of the 1904 edition with new introduction by Abram Chayes. Originally written 1897.

Dean, Joseph F. Manuscript letters, August, 1862 to May, 1863. Boston Public Library, Rare Books and Manuscripts.

Dickens, Charles. *Oliver Twist*. New York: Dutton/Everyman's Library, 1907.

Dreiser, Theodore. *Sister Carrie*. New York: Modern Library, 1917.

Edes, Grace Williamson. *Annals of the Harvard Class of 1852*. Cambridge: Privately Printed, 1922. HUA.

Engels, Friedrich. *The Condition of the Working-Class in England*. Moscow: Progress Publishers, 1973.

Everett, Edward. *Orations and Speeches on Various Occasions*. In 4 Vols. Boston: Little, Brown, and Company, 1868.

Farley's Reference-Directory of the Booksellers, Stationers and Printers in the United States. Comprising Booksellers, Stationers, Printers, Publishers, Paper Dealers, Bookbinders, Paper-Box Manufactures and News Dealers. The Purchasing Agents of Stationery for the Railroads in the United States and Canada, and the Names of the Buyers of Wholesale Houses. Philadelphia: A. C. Farley & Co., 1885.

Flaubert, Gustave. *Madame Bovary*. Edited with a substantially new translation by Paul De Man. New York: W. W. Norton, 1965.

Franklin, Benjamin. *Autobiography*. New York: New American Library, 1961.

Garland, Hamlin. *A Son of the Middle Border*. New York: Macmillan, 1924.

George, Henry. *Progress and Poverty*. New York: Robert Schalkenbach Foundation, 1955.

Greeley, Horace. "Why I Am A Whig: Reply to an Inquiring Friend." New York: Published at the Tribune Office, 1852.

Hart, William. *The Travelling Book-Agent's Guide and Instructor*. Boston: D. C. Colesworthy, Publisher, 1865.

Harvey, William H. *Coin's Financial School*. Edited by Richard Hofstadter. Cambridge, Mass.: Belknap Press, Harvard University Press, 1963 (original 1895).

Hawes, Joel. *Lectures to Young Men*, 7th ed. Hartford, Conn.: Cooke and Co., 1834.

Howells, William Dean. "Editor's Study," *Harper's New Monthly Magazine* 81 (July, 1890): 314-18.

Howells, William Dean. *The Rise of Silas Lapham*. Boston and New York: Houghton Mifflin and Company, 1884.

Hubbard, James Mascarene. "Fiction and Public Libraries," *International Review* 10 (February, 1881): 168-78.

Hubbard, James Mascarene. *The Public Library and the School-Children. An Appeal to the Parents, Clergymen, and Teachers of Boston*. Boston: Privately published, October 21, 1881.

Hughes, Thomas. *The Manliness of Christ*. Boston and New York: Houghton Mifflin Company, n.d. [lectures dated 1879].

James, Henry. *Autobiography*. Edited by Fredrick W. Dupee, New York: Criterion Books, 1956.

Juvenal. *Satires. Juvenal and Persius.* Translated by G. G. Ramsay; Loeb
    Classical Library. Cambridge, Mass.: Harvard University Press, 1979.
Machiavelli, Niccolò. *The Prince and Discourses,* with an introduction by Max
    Lerner. New York: Modern Library, 1950.
Mann, Horace. *A Few Thoughts For A Young Man.* Boston: Tichnor,
    Reed, and Fields, 1850.
Marden, Orison Swett. *The Secret of Achievement.* New York: Thomas Y.
    Crowell & Co., 1898.
Norcross, Grenville Howland. Diaries, 1860-1876. Unpublished manuscripts
    from the Children as Diarists Collection of the American Antiquarian
    Society.
Optic, Oliver (William T. Adams). *Bear and Forbear.* Boston: Lee and Shepard;
    New York: Charles T. Dillingham, 1869.
Optic, Oliver (William T. Adams). *Little By Little.* New York: A. L. Burt, n.d.
Optic, Oliver (William T. Adams). *Through By Daylight.* Boston: Lee and
    Shepard; New York: Lee, Shepard and Dillingham, 1873.
Optic, Oliver (William T. Adams). *Try Again.* New York: New York Book
    Company, 1911.
Optic, Oliver (William T. Adams). *The Yankee Middy.* Boston: Lothrop, Lee
    and Shepard Co., 1893.
Peirce, Charles Sanders. *Collected Papers of Charles Sanders Peirce,* Vol. 6,
    Scientific Metaphysics, edited by Charles Hartshorne and Paul Weiss.
    Cambridge, Mass.: Harvard University Press, 1937.
Pinkerton, Allan. *Strikers, Communists, Tramps and Detectives.* New York: G. W.
    Carleton & Company, 1878.
Plato, *The Republic.* Translated by G. M. A. Grube. Indianapolis: Hackett
    Publishing Company, 1974.
*Private Instructions: Strictly Confidential. The Henry Bill Publishing Co's Private
    Instructions To Their Agents For Selling their Subscription Books.* Norwich,
    Conn.: The Henry Bill Publishing Co., 1874.
*Public Libraries in the United States of America: Their History, Condition, and
    Management. Special Report.* Department of the Interior, Bureau of
    Education. Washington, D.C.: Government Printing Office, 1876.
Publishers' Broadsides and Prospectuses. Collection of the Graphic Arts
    Department, American Antiquarian Society.
The Publishers' Trade List Annual, 1890. New York: Office of the Publishers'
    Weekly, August, 1890. Also 1895 and 1900 annuals. 1882 Annual
    published New York: F. Leypoldt.
Rousseau, Jean Jacques. *The Social Contract and Discourses.* Translated by G. D.
    H. Cole. London: Everyman, 1973.
Smiles, Samuel. *Self-Help.* London: Sphere, 1968.
Stowe, Harriet Beecher. *My Wife and I: Or, Harry Henderson's History.* New-
    York: J. B. Ford and Company, 1871.
Thayer, William Makepeace. *Success and Its Achievers.* Boston: A. M. Thayer,
    Publishers, 1891; also Boston: James H. Earle, 1896 (c. 1893).

Tocqueville, Alexis de. *Democracy in America.* Translated by George Lawrence. Garden City, N.Y.: Anchor Books, 1969.

Twain, Mark. "The Story of the Good Little Boy and the Story of the Bad Little Boy," (1867). In *Sketches New and Old,* Vol. 19 in *Mark Twain's Works.* New York: Harper and Brothers Publishers, 1904.

Twain, Mark. *The Prince and the Pauper.* New York: Penguin, 1983.

The Uniform Trade List Annual, 1875, 1876. New York: Office of the Publishers' Weekly.

Veblen, Thorstein. *The Theory of the Leisure Class.* New York: New American Library, 1899, 1953.

Voltaire. *Candide.* Translated and edited by Robert M. Adams. New York: W. W. Norton, 1966.

Weber, Max. *The Protestant Ethic and the Spirit of Capitalism.* Translated by Talcott Parsons. New York: Charles Scribner's Sons, 1958.

Wells, David A. *Robinson Crusoe's Money; or, the Remarkable Financial Fortunes and Misfortunes of a Remote Island Community.* New York: Peter Smith, 1931 reprint of 1876 edition. Illustrations by Thomas Nast.

Wells, David A. *The Silver Question: The Dollar of the Fathers Versus The Dollar of the Sons.* New York: G. P. Putnam's Sons, 1877.

Whittaker, Captain Frederick. *John Armstrong, Mechanic, Or, From the Bottom to the Top of the Ladder/ A Story of How a Man Can Rise in America.* Beadle's Dime Library 378, January 20, 1886.

Whittaker, Captain Frederick. *Nemo, King of the Tramps; Or, The Romany Girl's Vengeance./ A Story of the Great Railroad Riots.* Beadle's Dime Library 132, May 4, 1881.

Wood's Illustrated Hand-Book to New York and Environs. New York: G. W. Carleton, 1873.

Wyckoff, Walter. *A Day with a Tramp and Other Essays.* New York: Charles Scribner's Sons, 1901.

Wyckoff, Walter. *The Workers, An Experiment in Reality: The East.* New York: Charles Scribner's Sons, 1899.

Wyckoff, Walter. *The Workers, An Experiment in Reality: The West.* New York: Charles Scribner's Sons, 1904.

ADDITIONAL SOURCES

Althusser, Louis, and Étienne Balibar. *Reading Capital.* London: New Left Books, 1970.

Auerbach, Erich. *Mimesis.* Princeton, N.J.: Princeton University Press, 1953.

Bailyn, Bernard. *The Intellectual Origins of the American Revolution.* Cambridge, Mass.: Harvard University Press, 1967.

Barth, Gunther. *City People: The Rise of Midern City Culture in Nineteenth-Century America.* New York: Oxford University Press, 1980.

Barthes, Roland. *The Pleasure of the Text*. Translated by Richard Miller. New York: Hill and Wang, 1975.

Baym, Nina. "A Boy's Book for Adults," *New York Review of Books*, July 20, 1986: 10.

Baym, Nina. *Novels, Readers, and Reviewers: Responses to Fiction in Antebellum America*. Ithaca. N.Y.: Cornell University Press, 1984.

Bellah, Robert. *The Broken Covenant: American Civil Religion in Time of Trial*. New York: Harper & Row, 1976.

Bennett, Bob. *Horatio Alger, Jr.: A Comprehensive Bibliography*. Mt. Pleasant, Mich.: Flying Eagle Publishing Co., 1980.

Bennett, Lance. *The Governing Crisis*. New York: St. Martin's, 1992.

Bercovitch, Sacvan. *The American Jeremiad*. Madison, Wis.: University of Wisconsin Press, 1978.

Bercovitch, Sacvan. *The Puritan Origins of the American Self*. New Haven, Conn.: Yale University Press, 1975.

Bernstein, Basil. *Class, Codes and Control*. Vol. 1: *Theoretical Studies towards a Sociology of Language*. London: Routledge & Kegan Paul, 1971.

Bourdieu, Pierre. *Distinction: A Social Critique of the Judgment of Taste*. Cambridge, Mass.: Harvard University Press, 1984.

Boyer, Paul. *Urban Masses and Moral Order in America, 1820-1920*. Cambridge, Mass.: Harvard University Press, 1978.

Burke, Kenneth. *The Rhetoric of Religion*. Berkeley, Calif.: University of California Press, 1970.

Carrier, Esther Jane. *Fiction in Public Libraries 1876-1900*. New York: The Scarecrow Press, 1965.

Carter, Paul A. *The Spiritual Crisis of the Gilded Age*. DeKalb, Il.: Northern Illinois University Press, 1971.

Cawelti, John. *Adventure, Mystery, and Romance: Formula Stories As Art and Popular Culture*. Chicago: University of Chicago Press, 1976.

Cawelti, John. *Apostles of the Self-Made Man*. Chicago: University of Chicago Press, 1965.

Chandler, Alfred D., Jr. *The Visible Hand: The Managerial Revolution in American Business*. Cambridge, Mass.: Harvard University Press, 1977.

Chinoy, Eli. *Automobile Workers and the American Dream*. Garden City, N.Y.: Doubleday, 1955.

Cowley, Malcolm. "Horatio Alger: Failure," *Horizon* 12 (Summer, 1970): 62-65.

Crouse, Russel. Introduction to Alger's *Struggling Upward and Other Works*. New York: Crown Publishers, 1945.

Darnton, Robert. *The Great Cat Massacre*. New York: Basic Books, 1984.

Davidson, Cathy N. "Towards a History of Books and Readers," *American Quarterly* 40 (March, 1988): 7-17.

Davies, Tony. "Transports of Pleasure: Fiction and its Audiences in the Later Nineteenth Century." In *Formations of Pleasure*, pp. 46-58. London: Routledge & Kegan Paul, 1983.

Denning, Michael. *Mechanic Accents: Dime Novels and Working-Class Culture in America*. New York: Verso, 1987.

Dorfman, Joseph. *The Economic Mind in American Civilization*. New York: Viking, Vols. 1-2 (1606-1865), 1956; Vol. 3 (1865-1918), 1959.

Douglas, Ann. *The Feminization of American Culture*. New York: Avon Books, 1977.

Edwards, Richard C. *Contested Terrain*. Lexington, Mass.: Lexington Books, 1979.

Elder, Charles D., and Roger W. Cobb. *The Political Uses of Symbols*. New York: Longman, 1983.

Fadiman, Clifton. "Party of One," *Holiday* 21 (February, 1957): 6-14, 118.

Fink, Rychard. Introduction to *Ragged Dick and Mark, the Match Boy*. New York: Collier Books, 1962.

Fish, Stanley. *Is There A Text In This Class?: The Authority of Interpretive Communities*. Cambridge, Mass.: Harvard University Press, 1980.

Fisher, Philip. "Appearing and Disappearing in Public: Social Space in Late-Nineteenth-Century Literature and Culture." *In Reconstructing American Literary History*, edited by Sacvan Bercovitch, pp. 155-88. Cambridge, Mass.: Harvard University Press, 1986.

Friedman, Milton, and Anna Jacobson Schwartz. *A Monetary History of the United States*. Princeton, N.J.: Princeton University Press, 1963.

Frith, Simon. "The Pleasures of the Hearth: the Making of BBC Light Entertainment." In *Formations of Pleasure*, pp. 101-23. London: Routledge & Kegan Paul, 1983.

Gardner, Ralph D. *Horatio Alger, or the American Hero Era*. New York: Arco Publishing Company, Inc., 1978.

Garrison, Dee. *Apostles of Culture: The Public Librarian and American Society, 1876-1920*. New York: Free Press, 1979.

Garrison, Dee. "Cultural Custodians of the Gilded Age: The Public Librarian and Horatio Alger," *Journal of Library History* (October, 1971): 327-36.

Geertz, Clifford. "Ideology as a Cultural System," pp. 193-33 in *The Interpretation of Cultures*. New York: Basic Books, 1973.

Golding, Robert. *Idiolects in Dickens*. New York: St. Martin's Press, 1985.

Goleman, Daniel, "For Presidential Candidates, Optimism Appears a Winner," *New York Times*, May 8, 1888, A1, 18.

Goodwyn, Lawrence. *Democratic Promise: The Populist Movement in America*. New York: Oxford University Press, 1976.

Gordon, David M., Richard C. Edwards, and Michael Reich. *Segmented Work, Divided Workers*. New York: Cambridge University Press, 1982.

Greider, William. "Democratic Money." In *Secrets of the Temple: How the Federal Reserve Runs the Country*. New York: Simon & Schuster, 1987.

Grimsted, David. *Melodrama Unveiled: American Theater and Culture 1800-1850*. Chicago: University of Chicago Press, 1968.

Gruber, Frank. *Horatio Alger, Jr.* West Los Angeles, Calif.: Grover Jones Press, 1961.

Gusfield, Joseph R. *Symbolic Crusade: Status Politics and the American Temperance Movement*. Urbana, Il.: University of Illinois Press, 1963.

Gutman, Herbert. *Work, Culture and Society in Industrializing America*. New York: Vintage Books, 1976.

Hackenberg, Michael. "The Subscription Publishing Network in Nineteenth-Century America." In *Getting the Books Out: Papers of the Chicago Conference on the Book in 19th-Century America*, edited by Michael Hackenberg, pp. 45-75. Washington, D.C.: Center for the Book, Library of Congress, 1987.

Halttunen, Karen. *Confidence Men and Painted Women: A Study of Middle-class Culture in America, 1830-1870*. New Haven, Conn.: Yale University Press, 1982.

Hareven, Tamara K. *Family Time & Industrial Time: The relationship between the family and work in a New England industrial community*. New York: Cambridge University Press, 1982.

Hartz, Louis. *The Liberal Tradition in America*. New York: Harcourt, Brace & World, Inc., 1955.

Harvey, David. *Consciousness and the Urban Experience*. Baltimore: Johns Hopkins University Press, 1985.

Harvey, Harold M. "Alger's New York: A Story For Old Boys," *New York Tribune*, January 28, 1917, Section 5, 3-4.

Henretta, James A. "Families and Farms: *Mentalité* in Pre-Industrial America," *William and Mary Quarterly* 35 (January, 1978): 3-32.

Hicks, John D. *The Populist Revolt: A History of the Farmers' Alliance and the People's Party*. Minneapolis, Minn.: University of Minnesota Press, 1931.

Hirschman, Albert O. *The Passions and the Interests: Political Arguments for Capitalism before Its Triumph*. Princeton, N.J.: Princeton University Press, 1977.

Hobsbawm, E. J. *Bandits*. London: Weidenfeld and Nicolson, 1969.

Hofstadter, Richard. *The Age of Reform*. New York: Vintage Books, 1955.

Hofstadter, Richard. *The American Political Tradition and the Men Who Made It*. New York: Vintage, 1973; copyright Alfred Knopf, Inc.

Holland, Norman N. "Hobbling with Horatio, or the Uses of Literature," *Hudson Review* (Winter 1959-60): 549-57.

Howe, Daniel Walker. *The Political Culture of the American Whigs*. Chicago: University of Chicago Press, 1979.

Howe, Daniel Walker. *The Unitarian Conscience*. Cambridge, Mass.: Harvard University Press, 1970.

Hoyt, Edwin P. *Horatio's Boys*. New York: Stein and Day, 1974.

Huber, Richard. *The American Idea of Success*. New York: McGraw Hill, 1971

Jameson, Fredric. "Ideology, Narrative Analysis, and Popular Culture," *Theory and Society* 4 (1977): 543-59.

Johnson, Paul E. *A Shopkeeper's Millenium*. New York: Hill and Wang, 1978.

Josephson, Matthew. *The Politicos*. New York: Harcourt, Brace, 1966.

Josephson, Matthew. *The Robber Barons.* New York: Harcourt, Brace & World, 1962.

Kammen, Michael. *People of Paradox.* New York: Vintage, 1972.

Kaplan, Justin. *Mr. Clemens and Mark Twain: A Biography.* New York: Simon and Schuster, 1966.

Kasson, John F. *Civilizing the Machine: Technology and Republican Values in America, 1776-1900.* New York: Penguin Books, 1976.

Kasson, John F. *Rudeness & Civility: Manners in Nineteenth Century Urban America.* New York: Hill and Wang, 1990.

Katznelson, Ira. *City Trenches: Urban Politics and the Patterning of Class in the United States.* New York: Pantheon, 1981.

Kett, Joseph. *Rites of Passage: Adolescence in America, 1790 to the Present.* New York: Basic Books, 1977.

Kirkland, Edward C. *Industry Comes of Age: Business, Labor, and Public Policy 1860-1897.* New York: Holt, Rinehart and Winston, 1961.

Kolodny, Annette. "The Integrity of Memory: Creating a New Literary History of the United States," *American Literature* 57 (May, 1985): 291-307.

Lane, Robert. *Political Ideology.* New York: Free Press, 1962.

Laslett, John H. M., and Seymour Martin Lipset, eds. *Failure of a Dream?: Essays in the History of American Socialism.* Garden City, N.Y.: Anchor / Doubleday, 1974.

Lehmann-Haupt, Hellmut, with Lawrence C. Wroth and Rollo G. Silver. *The Book in America,* 2d ed. New York: R. R. Bowker Company, 1951.

Levine, Lawrence. *Highbrow/Lowbrow: The Emergence of Cultural Hierarchy in America.* Cambridge, Mass.: Harvard University Press, 1988.

Levi-Strauss, Claude. *Structural Anthropology.* New York: Basic Books, 1963.

Mann, Arthur. *Yankee Reformers in the Urban Age.* Cambridge, Mass.: Harvard University Press, 1954.

Marx, Leo. *The Machine in the Garden: Technology and the Pastoral Ideal in America.* New York: Oxford University Press, 1964.

May, Henry F. *The End of American Innocence.* New York: Alfred A. Knopf, 1959.

May, Henry F. *Protestant Churches and Industrial America.* New York: Harper & Row, 1949; introduction 1967.

Mayes, Herbert R. *Alger: A Biography Without a Hero.* Des Plaines, Il.: Gilbert K. Westgard II, 1978; originally published 1928.

McWilliams, Wilson Carey. *The Idea of Fraternity in America.* Berkeley, Calif.: University of California Press, 1973.

Mercer, Colin. "A Poverty of Desire: Pleasure and Popular Politics." In *Formations of Pleasure,* pp. 84-100. London: Routledge and Kegan Paul, 1983.

Meyers, Marvin, *The Jacksonian Persuasion.* Stanford, Calif.: Stanford University Press, 1957.

Michaels, Walter Benn. "Corporate Fiction: Norris, Royce, and Arthur Machen." In *Reconstructing American Literary History,* edited by Sacvan

Bercovitch, pp. 189-219. Cambridge, Mass.: Harvard University Press, 1986.

Michaels, Walter Benn. *The Gold Standard and the Logic of Naturalism.* Berkeley, Calif.: University of California Press, 1988.

Miller, Perry. *The Life of the Mind in America: From the Revolution to the Civil War*, Books 1-3. New York: Harcourt, Brace & World, 1965.

Monkkonen, Erik H., ed. *Walking to Work: Tramps in America, 1790-1935.* Lincoln, Nebr.: University of Nebraska Press, 1984.

Moon, Michael. "'The Gentle Boy from the Dangerous Classes': Pederasty, Domesticity, and Capitalism in Horatio Alger," *Representations* 19 (Summer, 1987): 87-110.

Morgan, H. Wayne. *From Hayes to McKinley: National Party Politics, 1877-1896.* Syracuse, N.Y.: Syracuse University Press, 1969.

Morrison, Samuel Eliot, and Henry Steele Commager. *The Growth of the American Republic*, Vol. 2. New York: Oxford University Press, 1938.

Mott, Frank Luther. *Golden Multitudes: The Story of Best Sellers in the United States.* New York: Macmillan, 1947.

Mott, Frank Luther. *A History of American Magazines.* Vols. 2-4. Cambridge, Mass.: Harvard University Press, 1938 (Volumes 2 and 3); Belknap Press of Harvard University, 1957 (Volume 4).

Myers, Gustavus. *The History of Tammany Hall*, 2d ed. New York: Dover Publications, Inc., 1971.

Nackenoff, Carol. "Economic Dualism and What it Means to American Labor Force Participants," *Journal of Politics* 45 (February, 1983): 110-42.

Nackenoff, Carol. "Of Factories and Failures: Exploring the Invisible Factory Gates of Horatio Alger, Jr.," *Journal of Popular Culture* 25, #4 (Spring, 1992): 63-80.

Neider, Charles, ed. *The Selected Letters of Mark Twain.* New York: Harper & Row, 1982.

Nevins, Allan. *John D. Rockefeller: The Heroic Age of American Enterprise*, Vol. 1. New York: Charles Scribner's Sons, 1941.

Nord, David Paul. "Working-Class Readers: Family, Community, and Reading in Late Nineteenth-Century America," *Communication Research* 13 (April, 1986): 156-81.

Norton, Anne. *Alternative Americas.* Chicago: University of Chicago Press, 1986.

O'Malley, Michael. *Keeping Watch: A History of American Time.* New York: Viking, 1990.

Palmer, Bruce. "The Disappearance of Community and Responsibility in the Literature Of The American Dream of Success: Cotton Mather To Robert Ringer, With Some Stops In Between," *Knowledge and Society* 6 (1986): 153-207. Edited by Henrika Kuklick and Elizabeth Long. Greenwich, Conn: JAI Press.

Pessen, Edward. *The Log Cabin Myth: The Social Backgrounds of the Presidents.* New Haven, Conn.: Yale University Press, 1984.

Pocock, J. G. A. *The Machiavellian Moment: Florentine Political Thought and the Atlantic Republican Tradition.* Princeton. N.J.: Princeton University Press, 1975.

Propp, Vladimir, *The Morphology of the Folktale.* Edited with an Introduction by Svatava Pirkova-Jakobson. Translated by Laurence Scott. Bloomington, Ind.: Indiana University Research Center in Anthropology, Folklore, and Linguistics, 1958.

Radway, Janice. "Reading Is Not Eating: Mass-Produced Literature and the Theoretical, Methodological, and Political Consequences of a Metaphor," *Book Research Quarterly* (Fall, 1986): 7-29.

Radway, Janice. *Reading the Romance.* Chapel Hill, N.C.: University of North Carolina Press, 1984.

Railton, Stephen. *Authorship and Audience.* Princeton, N.J.: Princeton University Press, 1991.

Reynolds, David S. *Faith in Fiction: The Emergence of Religious Literature in America.* Cambridge, Mass.: Harvard University Press, 1981.

Reynolds, Quentin James. *The Fiction Factory; or From Pulp Row to Quality Street; The Story of 100 Years of Publishing at Street & Smith.* New York: Random House, 1955 (copyright Street & Smith Publications, Inc.).

Ringenbach, Paul T. *Tramps and Reformers 1873-1916: The Discovery of Unemployment in New York.* Westport, Conn.: Greenwood Press, 1973.

Rodgers, Daniel T. *The Work Ethic in Industrial America 1850-1920.* Chicago: University of Chicago Press, 1978.

Rogin, Michael Paul. *Fathers and Children: Andrew Jackson and the Subjugation of the American Indian.* New York: Vintage, 1975.

Rogin, Michael Paul. *The Intellectuals and McCarthy: The Radical Specter.* Cambridge, Mass.: M.I.T. Press, 1967.

Scharnhorst, Gary. *Horatio Alger, Jr.* Boston: Twayne Publishers, 1980.

Scharnhorst, Gary, and Jack Bales. *Horatio Alger, Jr.: An Annotated Bibliography of Comment and Criticism.* Metuchen, N.J.: Scarecrow Press, Inc., 1981.

Scharnhorst, Gary, with Jack Bales. *The Lost Life of Horatio Alger, Jr.* Bloomington, Ind.: Indiana University Press, 1985.

Schreyer, Alice D. "Copyright and Books in Nineteenth-Century America." In *Getting the Books Out*, pp. 121-36. Washington, D.C.: Center for the Book, Library of Congress, 1987.

Schudson, Michael. *Discovering the News.* New York: Basic Books, 1978.

Shove, Raymond Howard. *Cheap Book Production In The United States, 1870 To 1891.* Urbana, Il.: University of Illinois Library, 1937.

Slotkin, Richard. *The Fatal Environment: The Myth of the Frontier in the Age of Industrialization, 1800-1890.* Middletown, Conn.: Wesleyan University Press, 1985.

Smith, Henry Nash. *Democracy and the Novel: Popular Resistance to Classic American Writers.* New York: Oxford University Press, 1978.

Smith, Olivia. *The Politics of Language: 1791-1819.* Oxford: Oxford University Press, 1984.

Soltow, Lee, and Edward Stevens. *The Rise of Literacy and the Common School in the United States: A Socioeconomic Analysis to 1870.* Chicago: University of Chicago Press, 1981.

Stern, Madeleine B., ed. *Publishers for Mass Entertainment in Nineteenth Century America.* Boston: G. K. Hall & Co., 1980.

Susman, Warren I. *Culture as History.* New York: Pantheon Books, 1984.

Tebbel, John. *From Rags to Riches.* New York: The Macmillan Company, 1963.

Thernstrom, Stephan. *Poverty and Progress: Social Mobility in a Nineteenth Century City.* Cambridge, Mass.: Harvard University Press, 1964.

Thomas, John L. "Utopia for an Urban Age: Henry George, Henry Demarest Lloyd, Edward Bellamy." In *Perspectives in American History*, Vol. 4, edited by Donald Fleming and Bernard Bailyn, pp. 135-63. Cambridge, Mass: Charles Warren Center for Studies in American History, Harvard University.

Thompson, E. P. *The Making of the English Working Class.* New York: Vintage, 1966.

Tompkins, Jane. *Sensational Designs: The Cultural Work of American Fiction, 1790-1860.* New York: Oxford University Press, 1985.

Trachtenberg, Alan. *The Incorporation of America: Culture & Society in the Gilded Age.* New York: Hill and Wang, 1982.

Turner, Victor W. *The Ritual Process: Structure and Anti-Structure.* Chicago: Aldine Publishing Company, 1969.

United States Department of Commerce, Bureau of the Census. *Historical Statistics of the United States, Colonial Times to 1970*, Series P1-12; Series D152-66; D182-232; D728-34; and D735-38. Bicentennial Edition: Series C 89-119. Washington, D.C.: Government Printing Office.

United States Department of Commerce, Bureau of the Census. *Statistical Abstract of the United States*, 1985 (105th edition), Table 123. Washington, D.C.: Government Printing Office.

United States Department of Commerce, Bureau of the Census. *Twelfth Census of the United States Taken in the Year 1900*, Statistical Atlas, Plate 93.

Weber, William. *Music and the Middle Class: The Social Structure of Concert Life in London, Paris and Vienna.* New York: Holmes & Meier, 1975.

Weiss, Richard. *The Myth of American Success.* New York: Basic Books, 1969.

Whalen, Terence. "Edgar Allan Poe and the Horrid Laws of Political Economy," *American Quarterly* 44 (September, 1992): 381-417.

Wiebe, Robert. *The Segmented Society.* New York: Oxford University Press, 1975.

Williamson, Chilton. *American Suffrage from Property to Democracy, 1760-1860.* Princeton, N.J.: Princeton University Press, 1960.

Wills, Garry. *Nixon Agonistes.* New York: New American Library, 1970.

Wills, Garry. *Reagan's America.* New York: Penguin, 1988.

Wilson, Ellen. "The Books We Got for Christmas," *American Heritage* 8 (December, 1956): 26-37, 120-24.

Wilson, R. Jackson. *In Quest of Community.* New York: Wiley, 1968.

Wines, Michael. "Bush's Campaign Tries Madison Ave.," *New York Times* (May 27, 1992), A18.

Winterich, John T. *Three Lantern Slides: Books, the Book Trade, and Some Related Phenomena in America: 1876, 1901 and 1926.* Urbana, Il.: University of Illinois Press, 1949.

Wohl, R. Richard. "The 'Country Boy' Myth and Its Place in American Urban Culture: The Nineteenth Century Contribution." In *Perspectives in American History*, Vol. 3, edited by Moses Rischin, pp. 77-156. Cambridge, Mass.: Charles Warren Center for Studies in American History, Harvard University, 1969.

Wohl, R. Richard. "The 'Rags to Riches Story': An Episode of Secular Idealism." In *Class, Status, and Power*, 2d ed., edited by Reinhard Bendix and Seymour Martin Lipset, pp. 501-06. New York: The Free Press, 1966.

Wood, Gordon S. *The Creation of the American Republic, 1776-1787.* New York: W. W. Norton & Company, 1969 (copyright University of North Carolina Press, 1969).

Wright, Will. *Sixguns and Society: A Structural Study of the Western.* Berkeley, Calif.: University of California Press, 1975.

Wyllie, Irvin G. *The Self-Made Man in America: The Myth of Rags to Riches.* New York: The Free Press, 1954.

Wyman, Mark. *Hard Rock Epic: Western Miners and the Industrial Revolution, 1860-1910.* Berkeley, Calif.: University of California Press, 1979.

Zboray, Ronald J. "Antebellum Reading and the Ironies of Technological Innovation," *American Quarterly* 40 (March, 1988): 65-82.

Zuckerman, Michael. "The Nursery Tales of Horatio Alger," *American Quarterly* 24 (May, 1972): 191-209.

Zuckert, Catherine H. *Natural Right and the American Imagination: Political Philosophy in Novel Form.* Savage, Md.: Rowman & Littlefield, 1990.

Name Index

Subject Index

A

Accidents, 169
  personal contact between economic unequals, 139-40
  sacred and secular meanings, 139, 141
  separating men and machines, 140
Advice manuals, 33, 38, 46, 49, 105, 233
  Alger on, 24, 167
  on business practices, 105
  on choice of occupations, 45, 89
  etiquette, 173-74
  on fiction reading, 243, 250
  on strangers, 38, 41
Alger, Horatio Jr.
  as author in marketplace, 207-8, 211, 214-15
  biographies, 111, 144, 148, 210
  compared to
    Dickens, 175, 187, 238
    Dreiser, 82
    Reade, 245
    Twain, 3, 175
  on dime novels, 24-47, 235
  on distinguishing fact and fiction, 224
  on factory work, 78, 82, 85
  faith in democracy, 259-60, 263. *See also* Democracy
  fictional republic of, 271
  as a gold Republican, 146
  on Greek tragedy, 27
  influence of Boston Unitarians, 23, 163
  influence of classics on, 12-13, 15-16, 25, 27, 29-31, 37, 116, 159
  influence of Scottish common-sense philosophy, x, 9, 16-17, 27
  and James Fenimore Cooper, 119–20

as a leveller, 162, 165, 174, 179-80
Mayes hoax biography of, 6
on melodrama, 233, 235
optimism of, 23, 49–51, 94, 97, 119-20, 179, 259, 269-71
pedagogy, 27, 29
poetry, 21-23, 183–84, 214-15
portrayal of capitalists, 89, 106, 108, 146, 151, 153, 159-60
pulpit in Brewster, 17-18, 20, 22
response by critics, 202, 216, 219, 225
  characterization, 219
  literary realism, 219, 223
on sensational fiction, 48, 113, 245
serial publication, 201
success formula, 135
as a symbol of American political creed, 3-4
travels
  Europe, 17, 94, 98, 207
  U. S., 100, 181, 199, 206-7
as a Whig, 117, 144, 222
Alger formulas, durability of, x, 5, 10, 264, 266-69, 271
Alger publishers, 190-91, 193-94, 198
  A. K. Loring, 186, 189, 198, 202, 210, 220
  Porter & Coates, 125, 190, 198, 210-11
  Street & Smith, 192-93, 198, 245
Alger stories
  action-adventure axis, 218-19, 221, 223, 257
  as allegories of the Republic, 11, 34
  benefactors in, 131, 139, 167
  boundaries of fact and fiction, 248
  guidebooks dealing with change, 56
  incorporating tensions of Gilded Age, 5, 7, 261–62, 266-68
  merging moral and material rewards 138

357